David Collins is a war baby and many traits remain.
A strong aptitude towards engineering led his career development to an early election into the institutes of Mechanical and Production Engineers. Various management positions steered him into 'Export Sales and Marketing' and a jet set style existence. Tired of this he decided on a new venture and emigrated to Portugal where he now lives, happily retired, in the Algarve.

THE ALGARVE ASPARAGUS MAN
PLUS ONE

This is dedicated to Aileen, alias 'Plus One' for her continuing support, hard labours, constructive ideas and total faith in our venture without which the book could not have been written.
Also to all my family and friends who frequently visited bringing with them many essential goodies not readily available at the time. Whilst resident they were never backward in coming forward to muck in and assist with the many numerous chores that always required urgent attention.

David Collins

THE ALGARVE ASPARAGUS MAN
PLUS ONE

AUSTIN MACAULEY
PUBLISHERS LTD.

A CIP catalogue record for this title is available from the British Library.

ISBN 978 184963 378 9

www.austinmacauley.com

First Published (2013)
Austin Macauley Publishers Ltd.
25 Canada Square
Canary Wharf
London
E14 5LB

Printed and Bound in Great Britain

Acknowledgments

There are too many people to thank individually but special mention must be made of our original neighbours and friends in the village. All gazed quizzically at our initial efforts and voiced strongly their disapproval at the techniques we employed. Eventually they all realised that, despite everything, we were succeeding and wholeheartedly supported us through every twist and turn.
All the people, places and events in this book are real but to protect some individuals I have taken the liberty of changing their names.

Chapter One

Two dabs of the right foot, a quarter turn clockwise of the right hand and the old fart box burst into life. Its two-litre engine as reliable as ever, purred smoothly and effortlessly on the automatic choke.

The Ford Cortina Ghia Estate, with metallic silver paint and black covered vinyl roof, registration number TCY 615 S was about to set off on its second visit to Portugal. The first time it had toured with the previous owners, and now it would transport us, Aileen (AC) and David Collins as we headed for the Western Algarve in the south of the country.

It continued to piss down with rain as the car was coupled to a caravan with a lot of assistance from Don, a friend. We were parked in the driveway of his home where we had stayed overnight, just outside the town of Alcester in Warwickshire.

At eleven o'clock in the morning on the tenth of October nineteen eighty-seven, I gradually inched through the gates onto the roadway and felt a mixture of anxiety and trepidation. As I had never towed a vehicle of any kind before and with a very long journey ahead of us, this came as no surprise.

The exact location of our destination was a three-hectare plot of agricultural land, on which there was a very old ruin, a well and concrete poles that supported an electrical distribution cable. It was in an area named Hortinha and was situated along a dirt track on the outskirts of the village of Bensafrim eight kilometres inland from the seaside city of Lagos.

We had signed a contract and purchased the land two years earlier but it had still not been registered in our names. A lawyer had been engaged to legally file the contract in an effort to protect our interests. Over this period however, the goalposts had continually moved further and further apart, sods law as usual applied so it was always against us. All of our attempts to qualify for the differing requirements had been frustrated by a variety of reasons beyond our control. At the back of our minds we remained most uncomfortable at the thought that the vendors could and would consider the option of a resale.

Sat on our butts in England would never resolve the situation so we had made the decision to sort out the problems on the spot.

Chapter Two

AC and I were employed by an international Contracting Company, a subsidiary of a major British engineering firm. In early nineteen eighty-three it announced that it would no longer continue to trade. The staff complement were highly motivated, exceptionally well qualified, but in my opinion suffered from a shortage of hairy-arsed practical engineers.

As a sales engineer it meant that I would be one of the first on the chopping block and then out of the door; redundant. AC, in the legal department, would remain employed for the period it took the company to complete its contractual obligations but eventually she faced redundancy.

On my last day at work the 31st March, it was Maundy Thursday, and it was the first day of our new lives together. We spent that evening in a pub that offered bed and breakfast in Flyford Flavell, near the city of Worcester. On our late arrival we were informed that an evening meal was not available but as there was the smell of stale cooked cabbage in the air, we were not terribly disappointed. Sat by ourselves in the small gloomy bar it soon became obvious that there were no other guests. After a couple of drinks and some nibbles, which included a packet of porky scratchings, it took a lot of effort to climb the creaky stairs to a rather amazing heavily furnished bedroom, complete with a four-poster bed. The room was extremely cold and lacked any form of central heating. Overnight there had been a sharp frost and when the curtains were drawn back early in the morning the spring lambs seemed quite subdued and there was not a frolic from any of them.

After a substantial English breakfast, spoiled by the stewed coffee, we sped down the M5 Motorway to Exeter to spend the Easter weekend on campus with my ex-secretary, Susie "Q", a very close friend, who was reading for a law degree at the university. It was time to relax and begin the slow process that would enable us to unwind. The many traumas that we had experienced over the past few months, marriage break-ups and redundancy announcements had been a gruelling time and had taken a stiff toll on both of us.

Other students had remained in the dormitories but as I was the only male there it fell to me to carve the turkey for the Easter Sunday lunch. There was only one car on the car park and it was AC's company one. A French girl asked if we could take her to the ferry terminal at Weymouth on the Bank Holiday Monday. We agreed, as it would also give us the opportunity to have another break. It turned out to be a disaster, as she took so long fannying around to put her face on, packing and getting her things together that we left later than planned. Even though I ignored all the speed limit signs, for most of the journey, the final boarding time was missed by several minutes and we all had to return to Exeter.

With the brief holiday over it was time to return to the Midlands. AC went to meet her parents, Lucie and Les, affectionately referred to as AC's Pees. She would then granny sit as they were taking a few days away from it all and I travelled on to stay with friends, Don and Sandra, in Birmingham. This major problem had arisen, as we had not been able to sort out any suitable accommodation before we had got together. Despite the inspection of many flats in the Southern parts and outskirts of

Birmingham none were up to our acceptable standards. To tell the truth most were in a down right disgusting condition, barely habitable.

It was far from a perfect start to our new relationship, a few moments were grabbed together and then we were off on our separate ways but thankfully it was not for long. On one of our frequent pub crawls where we sampled different brands of porky scratchings and soon became connoisseurs on the flavours and crispiness or otherwise of them, notice of a vacant holiday flat in the village of Inkberrow, of *"The Archers"* fame came to our attention. We quickly made arrangements to view and although it was tiny with a very strange room orientation, it was spotlessly clean and tidy. We decided there and then that it would suit us for the immediate future to form our base from which stock could be taken and our short and medium term situations be reviewed. So with just a small suitcase apiece we moved in.

AC was employed for the moment, so the immediate cause for concern was for my prospects. Rather than dash around like a headless chicken and scour the employment sections of every National newspaper and then tailor my Curriculum Vitae to make it compatible with the subtle differences of the positions offered, I had the germ of an idea at the back of my mind.

It was simplicity itself with more than an outside chance of success. Discussions were held with my former employer when I requested access to and ownership of all my files, connected with an organisation's project that I had been pursuing in the Middle East. I explained that I intended to get together with another contractor to prepare and submit a tender for it. After much consideration the Company agreed to my proposals as long as they were not compromised in any way. That was at least a positive start in the right direction.

The easy part completed, I now had to find a contractor. The hard part of the sell would be how to convince them that the prospects of success were so astronomically high that they take on board all of the costs of a tender preparation and other associated expenses, including my out of pocket ones. The key to it all was that I had in my file a telex which I had received in the past from the same organisation and this indicated in typical Arab fashion when one knew how to read between the lines, although not in direct words, that any future serious tender proposition would be favourably received.

There was a need for urgency but where could I begin? With only limited funds available and the tender closing date only three months away, time and money were at a premium.

Late one evening AC hurtled into the flat highly excited, a friend of mine from Khartoum had rung the office earlier on in the day and had wished to speak to me. He was sad to learn of my present circumstances. She knew him from her recent visit there with me some months ago and considered him to be an extremely likeable person. His tribal scars intrigued her, more so the highly unlikely tales he told her of how he had obtained them.

He had explained to her that he was in London on a visit to see a civil Engineering Company. They were in the process of considering whether or not to submit a tender for a contract. From his description of the scope and location she knew that it was the same one that I had already been involved with and had now taken the decision to actively pursue it on my own.

I could not believe it, "Manna from Heaven". He had given AC his hotel telephone number and I rang, from the local pub, and arranged to meet him in their offices the next morning. It was then one hell of a mad scramble, in the evening, for me to prepare a proposal for the company's assessment. We had barely enough time for a cup of coffee before AC drove me to Birmingham International to catch the early train the next morning. At Euston station I nervously tucked into a full house breakfast while photocopies were taken of all my detailed views and recommendations.

My proposals were presented to two company executives and my friend and were thought to be very constructive. The emphasis was on an angle and approach that they had not even seriously considered. All in all they were thought to be worthy of a more detailed examination after which they would make a report to their Chief Executive. I would be contacted after this meeting and the indications appeared to be favourable.

Whilst I awaited that decision I got in touch with a European equipment manufacturer, a very reputable company with whom I had had lots of close successful dealings with in the past and spoke with their sales director. They were also aware of the project but could not go it alone. I proposed a joint venture with the company that I had recently had talks with, broad parameters of this potential arrangement were suggested to them and they promised to get back to me within two days.

There was nothing else that I could do other than sit on my backside, chew my fingernails and wait. I did not like hanging around like this when I was in the U.K. It was different in the Middle East countries as there I could happily sit for hours on end twiddling my thumbs until I was called into a meeting.

The day before I had an appointment with the Chief Executive, the equipment supplier telephoned and gave a very positive "yes" to the proposed joint venture, a decision that was vital if further progress was to be made. It also gave me another bullet in my arsenal that could be used with great effect in the forthcoming discussions.

I travelled to London the next day and spent most of that evening in my hotel room where I honed up my presentation. Sleep did not come at all easy but a nice cold shower left me somewhat refreshed. There was no way that I could face any form of breakfast and settled for a couple of cups of coffee and a few cigarettes in a small café just around the corner from the offices. I felt really stressed and more than a little nervous and hoped that it did not show. They allowed me free reign to present in full my ideas and recommendations and the need to submit a tender as a joint venture bid to "The Client", with whom I was very well acquainted and had held several negotiations with in the past, albeit unsuccessfully. On the last occasion a telex was received from them which apologised for not awarding the contract to my previous employer, and that they would welcome favourably our response to their future tender invitations. This was tabled and after a few minutes I was asked to leave the room and left the Chief Executive with the two people with whom I had had the initial discussions. After what seemed an eternity to me, it was less than ten minutes, I was recalled and given the green light to proceed. There were handshakes all round and the only outstanding matter that remained to be completed was the simple preparation of the tender documents.

I then telephoned the equipment supplier and requested that a senior executive should travel to London the next day to draw up and sign a "Heads of Agreement" protocol. This was duly executed and a time scale drawn up for the tender preparation.

There was however one more important hurdle to overcome. "The Clients" tender enquiry documents had been purchased in the name of my former company. It was now essential to obtain their agreement that they would accept our tender with the joint venture being represented by myself. A flying visit was made to their head office where I outlined my proposals and handed over both companies' references with full supporting financial information. Would the saga never end were my thoughts at the time? Intense discussions followed and a decision was eventually reached that a tender would be accepted for consideration. This was a radical move on their part as should a contract award stage ever materialise, there would be a "Third Party" signatory to it.

At long last, the final peg had slotted into place, my relief and excitement knew no bounds and this was equally shared by AC who through all of my toing and froing had gainfully plodded on at the office. A colleague of hers, Karen, had suggested that she could possibly qualify, under her present situation for a local Council flat. She obtained an application form, filled it in and submitted it with tongue in cheek. An invitation for an interview soon followed where she found that for the first time in her life, the little ticks in all of the boxes fitted the requirements exactly.

One week later we moved into a one bedroomed flat, above two garages, one went with the flat, at Winyates East near Redditch. It was a fantastic improvement on what we had just vacated and her offices were only a five-minute drive away.

Two days a week spent in London and part of a day at the local Labour Exchange left little time to actively seek full-time employment so that process was shoved onto the back burner. In any event I did not want to get tied down for the foreseeable future. Even extended holidays had to take second fiddle

We did however become members of the Redditch Allotment Association and rented two plots. One of these bordered a natural running stream, which made life a little easier when the crops were watered. It certainly saved us having to hump countless buckets from a standpipe about a hundred metres away, which was necessary on the other plot. Work there gave us the opportunity to satisfy our latent desires for agricultural activities. AC had wished to attend Pershore Horticultural College after she had left school but failed to obtain "O" level biology. As a chalk and cheese difference she read Law at Birmingham University and eventually became fully qualified. I was perhaps subconsciously endeavouring to prove a point. My father, a market gardener after the Second World War, managed to get himself into serious financial difficulties. It was a major problem so much so that he had to sell off all of his lands, at Hinton-on-the-Green near Evesham and off the Badsey Lane, where we lived, less than a mile from the village. How could anyone have foreseen that some thirty years later AC's Pees would live on the outskirts of Badsey, almost next door to my father's house and land? I was only ten years old at the time and with my seven-year-old brother had to work in the early hours of the winter mornings wearing fingerless gloves to pick hard frozen Brussels sprouts into nets, which were then sold in the local and Birmingham markets. The tips of my fingers have remained intensely sensitive to this day.

At that age I was completely oblivious to the fact that there were problems, which forced him into the situation. All of the agricultural machinery and lastly the family home had to be disposed of and we moved as he took up employment as an assistant to an immigrant who had designed and developed some of the first garden cloches. He never ever came to terms with it and there was no form of counselling in those days.

It was many years later that I came to appreciate his difficulties. One was very poor financial management; he owned and had paid for out of capital, highly expensive farming machinery. Tractors by Fordson Major, Caterpillar and Ferguson manufactured together with all of the associated implements. They were totally under utilised as he could not afford to employ any labour, full- or even part-time and therefore they gave zero return. What was even worse was that they devalued with age. With thick wooden blocks attached to the brake, clutch and accelerator pedals I had to drive the Fordson Major tractor, a real brute of a thing. His other problems, common to all who worked on the land, were crop surpluses when market prices were so low that it was better to leave them in the ground, and at the other extreme a series of crop failures. They were difficult times in the "Vale of Evesham" during the late nineteen forties.

So why did I still have a latent desire to return to the land at this stage of my life? It could have been that when we lived in the house in Badsey Lane I tended a very small flowerbed and each year entered a local riverboat owner's garden competition. On every occasion I was awarded a prize, some years later I discovered every child who entered was given one. At the age of thirteen we moved again, this time to Worcester. In the back garden I watched my father plant a row of several one-year-old asparagus crowns, funny looking things they were, a little circular clump with about a dozen six inch long fleshy roots. One still survives and throws up fern each year. When he had finished he told me that an acre of asparagus would provide a very good living and could support a family over the year. Why he did not grow it when he had all that land available remains a mystery to me this day.

With these childhood memories relatively fresh in my mind there were no desires whatsoever of becoming a farmer or to have anything to do with agriculture. When I left the Worcester Royal Grammar School with the magnificent tally of three "O" levels, Maths, Geography and Art at the tender age of fifteen I entered into a five-year indentured apprenticeship with a local engineering company with the ambition of becoming a draughtsman. My inner dream was to be a bridge designer but that would have meant having to commute or move to Bristol. Unfortunately for me neither of these options had been possible.

Several years later after day release studies and attendance at evening classes, often four nights a week, and further studying I obtained a Higher National Certificate in Mechanical Engineering with endorsements in Industrial Administration. Over this period I was promoted regularly and moved quickly up the ranks to a position of Project Manager and so applied and was admitted, one of the youngest ever, as a Member of the Institution of Mechanical Engineers, a Chartered Engineer. A few years later membership of The Institution of Production Engineers followed.

All too quickly the tender deadline date approached. One suitcase filled with documentation was collected in London and I travelled on to submit our offer to "The Client" on the final date. All we could do now was await the outcome of our intense efforts over the past few months.

In October the London office telephoned to say that had received a telex from "The Client". The contents were read out to me, which was basically an invitation to attend their offices for discussions. I literally trembled with excitement as I had already experienced this scenario and knew what was about to happen. On the two previous occasions I had frustratingly failed to secure the contract. A meeting was arranged for the next day and the equipment supplier's representative would also attend. I took great care to spell out to them in detail the sequence of events that was about to occur, and also recommended that a full team, led by myself, should be taken to the meetings. This should comprise a senior executive, technical and financial experts and a lawyer; preferably one with a Middle Eastern background. There many pooh-poohs at my final remark that if we could avoid any major cock-ups we should be able to negotiate ourselves into a contract. Never, at the first round of talks, was everyone else's firm conviction.

We landed at the new airport in the countries capital city and after checking into our hotel I visited "The Client" to arrange a timescale for the initial discussions, which I was informed, would begin the next day.

There followed two exhausting long hour days of talks on technical clarifications together with the commercial and contractual conditions. The price for the civil works for the project had been based on a "Bill of Quantities". Some items in this had been substantially increased so recalculations were necessary.

Late that evening we had to evacuate the hotel as a safety procedure. A fire had occurred in one of the bedrooms. After an hour we were allowed to re-enter and all of us felt starved, probably as a result of all the nervous tension and strain. Unfortunately, maybe due to the fire, there was a power cut and the kitchen was not fully operational so only a limited choice of evening meals was available.

I knew after my second mouthful of a double beef burger with chips and salad, that I was in for a spot of bother. So it turned out to be as, before midnight, I was in absolute agony with excruciating pains that ripped through my upper torso. It was like a red-hot poker that was twisted into the bottom left hand side of my rib cage and right through to my stomach. It was not the only time that I had suffered this experience which I thought to be just serious bouts of indigestion. The first was a few years ago when I was entertaining an Algerian delegation in the U.K.

The pain remained for the longest sleepless night that I could remember. I could certainly pick my moments, what a time to be taken ill especially as it had not occurred for well over twelve months. I had not fully recovered in the morning so was unable to attend the further negotiations with the team. These were postponed due my absence.

The next day I was on my feet but still felt a little sore although fit enough to join in at what I hoped would be the final session. Many of the outstanding points were resolved, but progress was painfully slow and no complete agreement was reached on the unit prices in "The Bill" at which I felt a brief moment of despair. Eventually we were told to return at eight o'clock. I sensed, and told the team, that the crunch time had arrived and that a decision would be made then, but still no one would believe me.

That evening a long drawn out haggle concentrated on the price, some increases, a few decreases and potential discounts were floated across the table and a "ball park" figure was arrived at. The only positive side was that the "The Bill" unit prices had been finalised. Arabic coffee and tea was served after which "The Client's" Director General entered the room. Further talks ended when our final price was handed over to him.

After a lengthy silence he beckoned me over to his side and held out his hand, which I grasped and shook eagerly, it was the "Handshake" and confirmed that the price was acceptable and the contract was ours. The team was fairly gob smacked at the speed of the events and elated at the decision, but no one could have felt more satisfied and pleased than me, at long last I had cracked it.

The contract value was 7.27 million American dollars and I named it the Boeing contract. I had a natural habit, good or bad, to nickname people or things so this was named after the Boeing 727 rear engine jet on which I had flown many times.

After all the tension and excitement we then spent the next five days in negotiations on the contractual and commercial conditions. The teams lawyer proved his weight in gold, without him we may well have been there still. We were sworn to secrecy until the letter of intent was received and the official contract signatory ceremony would be held on the twenty-first of December. In the intervening period all of the documentation would have to be processed and finalised. This would have been impossible but for the introduction of new technology, the Fax Machine.

The ceremony date presented us with a problem; Murphy's Law could throw up last minute hiccups so to pre-arrange return flights would be inadvisable. If necessary, our Christmas would have to be spent abroad. It turned out that everything went as smoothly as clockwork although we all finished up with writers' cramp after so many copies of the contract, and all of its pages were initialled. We were ready to depart on the evening of the twenty-second but all flights to Europe were fully booked due to the mass exodus of homeward bound foreign nationals.

The Chief Executive however, had had the foresight to reserve on standby a private jet, which was flown in and enabled us to fly out, very late at night to Orly airport. We then taxied to Charles de Gaulle and were soon able to fly on to Heathrow. I had flown on Boeing 747 aircraft more times than I had had hot dinners and had always boarded through the access pods. I had also seen them take off and land from a distance and had not fully appreciated just how large they were. On the take off runway in the small executive jet we were given preferential clearance over one, which was right behind us, and I finally realised how massive they were. Halfway through the flight, between lashings of gourmet food and unlimited glasses of champagne, I made a radio telephone call to AC from thirty-five thousand feet to tell her the exciting news.

Christmas and the New Year period was a quiet occasion spent on cloud nine, not really being able to believe that it had all happened. I continuously pinched myself to see if I was awake or in the middle of a crazy dream. My final obligation to the successful contractors was to agree and finalise with "The Client" the wordings of the necessary banking and financial documents.

Despite all of the activities over the last nine months, time had been taken to squeeze in a couple of job applications and two interviews were attended, luckily both were in London. Several approaches had been made from headhunters and had been politely declined. Two offers of employment were considered and I eventually accepted a position as an export Sales and Marketing manager with a prominent Engineering manufacturer in the West Midlands. It suited me down to the ground as the journey to the office was an absolute doddle to drive through uncrowded and very pretty countryside and a new housing location was unnecessary.

The decision to take up this appointment was to prove a poor one and led to a hazardous incident. I still get the shudders when I recall the time of tense but amicable negotiations with the Ministry of the Interior. They were all held with the General. My sales executive and I had on a Thursday requested from head office a telex concerning very sensitive pricing information, relative to the discussions at that stage, to be sent to our hotel.

The next meeting had been fixed for Saturday after the Friday weekend and by then we had not received anything so we had no alternative but to adopt stalling tactics. We entered the General's office and quickly sensed as we passed through the guarded door that all was not well. The General, flanked by two Colonels on either side were seated at the large oval table, with the customary picture of the President of the country, resplendent in military uniform, who glared down from the wall behind them. I secretly used to refer to him as Stanley, another fine mess you've got me into Stanley, a la Laurel and Hardy. Their expressions were to say the least, extremely grim, something had gone badly wrong.

Normally the General would open up the discussions but he did not say a word. Before I could commence my spiel he held up a piece of paper and very slowly passed it over the table to me with a wry smile on his face. What an absolute screw up! Our financial department, back in the UK had sent the telex that had been requested by us directly to him. What a load of tosspots. We had been landed right into the fertiliser, with a capital F.

The Ministry controlled the Secret Police and the General knew that we were in the final negotiating stages with the Ministry of Defence. The Immigration and Residents department were also under their domain and I knew that they had opened up a file on me. An entry visa was normally valid for only fifteen days and an application had to be made to them for any extension with no guarantee that one would be granted. Many times previously, on business with my former employer, these had been obtained without any problems but I did notice after the first one that a number, in Arabic, had been written on the inside leaf of my passport. At all visits since then, after it was handed over and the inevitable queue joined, the wait was only ended when this number was called out for the process to begin. The only advantage there seemed to be was when they wanted to get rid of me as this number certainly speeded up the issue of an exit visa.

I was very glad that on this visit I had entered with a different passport and had not had to apply for an extension. In theory therefore I was not yet in the computers records so when I was ready to leave the country it would only involve the usual airport interrogation before I could enter the departure lounge.

We had been placed in a difficult and extremely delicate position and it was with a heavy gulp and knees that quivered when I asked for a thirty-minute adjournment, which was thankfully granted. Time was desperately needed to study the contents of the telex, to catch our breaths, wipe the sweat from our brows and quickly rethink our strategy. On our return, for the first time no Arabic tea or coffee was offered. Negotiations continued but in a tense and nervous, for us, atmosphere. Two further meetings were held before the contract was signed and at each one it was painfully clear that the earlier, and any future amicability, had been lost forever.

There were many other stupid cock-ups but none as scary as that. A major millstone around my neck was that the company had decided to appoint an ex-government employee as an agent in one of my territories. He had no commercial acumen, would sell at any price to obtain his commission and lacked even a miniscule degree of negotiating skills. He really was the most incompetent person to have at ones side, a complete and utter wanker.

On a lighter note and lots were needed, especially in a competitive environment where potential clients were only prepared to pay for a Mini car but expected a

Roller. This was the daily difficulty that we all had to face and it was quite nerve racking and a very slow process to achieve even a modicum of success.

Some years earlier, at a particularly boozy session on one business trip in a Baghdad hotel, someone had suggested that a competition should be held to find and hire the worst of the decrepit bunch of taxis that operated there. By the early nineteen eighties no one had laid a claim to the prize. On my last visit to the city, which was one of my favourites of all the Middle East countries I had travelled to, I succeeded and won hands down.

It was a Friday and the weekly day off so a visit to the "Brit Club" for the traditional lunchtime curry was a must. It was only a fifteen to twenty minute walk away from my hotel; time to work up a good appetite and thirst.

As I carefully negotiated my way down the steep steps from the hotel to the pavement level, the sight of an old taxi, which indicated that it was available for hire, caught the corner of my eye. It did not need a second look to know that this one would scoop the first prize; surely nothing could have been in a worse condition. Other participants had been driven in cars which should have long ago have been sent to the knackers yard but I was confident that this was the one that would outshine them all.

Never had I seen such a spectacle like it on four wheels. It would have disgraced a sadly neglected and run down English scrap yard and I had visited a fair few over the years for spare parts for my old bangers.

The intended walk never came into the equation as I signalled frantically to the driver to stop. He slowly pulled over and came to a halt about eight metres past me. Poor brakes or a lack of them I surmised but was not unduly perturbed, as it was a relatively short journey.

To confirm my initial gut feelings I carried out a quick circumnavigation of the vehicle and became even more impressed with its state of dilapidation. The front had been in a collision and the bonnet had been pushed up, so the top of the radiator and its cap was fully exposed. A slight whisper of steam could be seen as it wafted from the cap that had been temporarily fixed in position with some form of masking tape and several strands of copper wire, probably salvaged from some old electric cables. There was a front bumper but nothing at the back.

I then scrambled into a single back seat; the other one was missing, and signalled to go forwards as, unlike many of the drivers, he spoke no English. After many grinding attempts to engage first gear we eventually got off to a very bumpy start. No other gear changes were made, not even into second. It was first gear all the way so I assumed that he was fully aware of his car's capabilities or lack of them. As we reached one huge roundabout I thought that it would have been quicker to have walked but speed was not of the essence, I was in pole position to win the competition.

As we cruised along, hardly the right definition, I decided to take stock of the vehicle or what was left of it. There was no passenger seat or door in the front and no windscreen. It was the original open-air saloon, no glass at all. It was also a daytime only one as I had noticed that there was only one front headlight and no rear lights were to be seen. The boot lid was missing and the only instrument on the dashboard was a speedometer, the needle stuck on zero.

Suddenly he switched off the ignition with the car still in gear so it shuddered to a halt on a pedestrian crossing. I heard mumbled curses as he got out, walked to the front and used his calloused hands to tear off the radiator cap with all its trimmings.

For his next trick he jumped onto the front bumper, raised his gallabieh, and with his percy in hand peed into it. I could not believe my eyes but was sure that he had carried out this emergency procedure many times before as he wore no underpants and his aim was uncannily accurate. He was not in the front row when genitals were handed out but his bladder must have been the size of an elephants as I could have sworn that a full flow of urine was maintained for what seemed to be well over a minute. The only way that I could have waited behind him at a gentleman's loo's one holer would have been with firmly platted legs. All of the oncoming traffic witnessed this performance and hooted their horns and cheered enthusiastically. As cool as a cucumber, oblivious to the noise he got down onto the road, replaced the radiator cap as best he could and calmly got back into the car. The engine was restarted and we again lurched forward. Eventually we arrived at the club without any further excitement but by then the radiator made noises similar to that of a pressure valve that was knackered and I was sure that the engine had seized up.

I indicated that he should stay put, it was doubtful that the car could continue anyway, and dashed inside to find six friends who luckily were all still in the competition, there were originally ten of us. They were dragged outside for an inspection and all immediately agreed, one or two somewhat reluctantly, that it would be virtually impossible for any of them to find and be driven in anything that even approached the state of this one.

The driver pointed to the radiator and I twigged that he wanted water. I returned inside and brought back a full watering can the contents of which were all poured in and the engine appeared to give a huge sigh of relief. He indicated more water so the can was refilled and he proceeded to pour it down his gullet in one continuous swallow. The can was less than half full when he was sated, no wonder he could pee for such a long time.

By this time my stomach thought that my throat had been cut, I was starving. There was a standard fare for the journey so I shook the driver by the hand and handed the dinars over. He then placed one arm over my shoulder and with a toothy grin held the other one out for one more. Under normal circumstances I would have politely told him to get stuffed but as I had thoroughly enjoyed the trip, especially the crude impromptu cabaret act and had won the prize, was happy to give him two.

My prize was collected on the spot, a free curry lunch washed down with more than a few bottles of Farina and Sheherezad, in the customary dumpy bottles. They were the locally brewed strong beers but I managed to remain sufficiently sober to walk back to the hotel as I had had enough of taxis for one day.

It was in one of the many cab rides taken in the competition that I suddenly became aware of the true definition of a "Split Second", maybe not the Oxford dictionary one. The more I considered it the more obvious it became. It was in fact the time taken for the traffic lights to change to green and the Baghdadi taxi drivers to honk their horns in impatience three times.

In the previous years we had not taken a holiday but intended to make up for it now and had booked a three week one to commence at the end of May to the Algarve in Southern Portugal. It would be AC's first visit there, I had enjoyed one before with my now ex-wife and two daughters and had been lucky enough to have had the opportunity to spend many periods in Lisbon on business. Then weekend journeys by train down to Faro and a taxi to the West was an experience not to be missed.

We arrived to what has now become an extremely familiar sight, a brilliantly clear blue Algarvean sky with warm sunshine. After the hired Mini car was collected it was a relatively simple matter to set off to a complex near the small village of Pera and we passed through the only set of traffic lights between Faro airport and the extreme Westerly town of Sagres.

Our first week was thoroughly enjoyable and we ate and drank in the many surrounding towns and villages and explored the numerous nearby beach bars. Inland there were large quantities of huge stones and boulders scattered all over the fields, some of which had been placed into mounds and had been piled up to make space for fig orchards, olive groves and vineyards. The land did not seem to favour arable farming at all.

The final two weeks were to be spent in another complex in the seaside village of Praia da Luz. The Mini car was collected after which a taxi drove us there. Unlike the complex at Pera this one was almost full and hummed with life. We carried on as before and found that there was a more impressive selection of bars and restaurants, all within easy walking distance from our apartment. When we had booked the holiday the tour operator had emphasised that a car would not be essential for a stay in this village. After dinner on our first night we relaxed over a nightcap in the bar next to the reception entrance. There we were disturbed by the noisy arrival of a crowd of newcomers. They had flown in from Manchester and we nicknamed them the "Manchester Mob". Three of the party with whom we immediately bonded with actually hailed from Fullwood on the outskirts of Preston.

One of our favourite restaurants overlooked the sea. Leased or owned, no one ever discovered which, was run by an English butcher from Bournemouth, it served meals to die for. We had eaten there several times and had loved it on every occasion. There was a fixed price menu at one thousand escudos, a little under four pounds sterling, which seemed very expensive to us at the time. Invariably we started with the smoked mussels followed by grilled plaice with ample fresh vegetables for our main course. The plaice was enormous and was at least two and a half centimetres thick either side of the bone and cooked to perfection. There was a different selection of puddings each time and the price included half a bottle of house wine each, with coffee and a complimentary liqueur to finish.

Unfortunately it all had to come to an end and we were taxied back to Faro airport exceedingly hung over as we had experienced, the day before, our first totally alcofrolic three hour sardine luncheon which was followed by a liquid pissy-arsed farewell party in the evening. Throughout these continuous celebrations we promised ourselves that we would return, sooner rather than later.

As the year wore on my employment situation became increasingly less tolerable and after I had attended an overseas International Trade Fair I made up my mind to tender my resignation.

At that moment torrents of memories flooded up from deep down in my subconscious mind, almost half drowned, but still alive and indelibly printed there. They resurfaced for the umpteenth time to recall both the happy times and the times of utter frustration that I had experienced during my International Sales career. The hard slog and grind that involved endless hours spent in airport lounges and thence in the air, some to semi-exotic destinations, others to what could only be described as the assholes of the Empire. The wasted hours and days spent waiting, always on the fifth floor of the office building with the lifts forever out of order; to meet with technical committees some of whose members had a ready made excuse not to be present. Unforgettable, not really, why I ever agreed to accept an appointment in these regions I do not know? Perhaps it was because it involved a move into the unknown? It was certainly different, definitely so.

Some situations that amused me at the time flashed by, but were a little reckless on reflection. They did help to relieve the many periods of utter boredom. A classic case was to play the fool on my numerous visits to Syria. When one landed at Damascus airport it was necessary to fill in an entry form in support of the visa in your passport. These were never handed out on the plane but had to be obtained and completed in the arrivals hall before you could clear the immigration officials. There was always a mad scramble to get hold of one, fill it in and then present it with your passport. On my second visit I picked up a handful for future use and hoped that the format would not be changed so I could use one on my next entry. I was lucky, as it didn't. Questions and details were requested such as Mothers and Fathers name, I wrote "Mum" and "Dad". Every time one left the country an exit form had to be completed. In the reason why you were departing section, my written response was always "Pissed off". Never ever was one of these answers queried.

Before you were allowed into the departure lounge you had to present to an emigration officer your completed exit card, with the official stamp that you had just purchased stuck in your passport on the same page as the original visa issued in London and the one collected on entry. On one occasion the issuing clerk failed to tear the complete stamp off the full sheet cleanly, a few perforations were missing in the top right hand corner. When I handed my papers over the officer gravely shook his head and pointed to the stamp as he handed them back and refused to allow me to proceed. With a shrug of my shoulders I turned and beckoned to the clerk to come over. With his right hand forefinger firmly stuck into his right nostril and left hand vigorously scratching his bollocks he indicated a total lack of interest in my predicament. After he firmly shook his head and turned his back on us I realised that he was a lost cause so I then opened the passport, took a pen out of my pocket, and artistically filled in with blue ink the missing parts of the perforations and handed it back. Immediately the official rubber stamp was thumped onto an inkpad and the page ceremoniously imprinted in green and thrust back into my hand. At the same time the barrier was opened to allow me through.

On the flight path from Cairo to Damascus, in the winter, I had often seen snow on the Golan Heights and woke up one morning in the Sheraton Hotel there to see that there had been more than a good dusting of it over the city. After breakfast I organised a snowball fight between some of the waiters and porters in the car park. The taxi ride to the airport the next day, after a heavy overnight frost, was a real knicker gripper as it was obvious that it must have been the drivers first experience of such conditions. Before we had exited the city limits four minor shunts occurred and the arguments as to who was to blame raged. The last one got very heated and had almost come to blows so as a dent free taxi approached I waved it down. As it slowly skidded to a halt I quickly stuffed some dinar notes into the first driver's hand and with a sense of relief fell into its back seats, glad to be on my way.

There was one very fraught incident when I travelled to Damascus for a meeting with The Arab League Boycott Committee. I had to take some documents that contained very sensitive information and unfortunately a last minute change of plan made it necessary to fly via Libya. It was just my luck to be shepherded in the arrivals hall at Tripoli airport to a customs line where a junior was being trained. He was thorough, extremely thorough, in the examination of my suitcase and hand luggage contents. I had sealed all the files of paperwork but he tore one open and flipped through the pages and stopped at probably the only one where any reference was made to Israeli companies. His training officer lurched forward and bellowed loudly. Within seconds five armed guards surrounded me, grabbed all my baggage and frog marched me out of the hall, which left my two travelling companions rooted to the spot with mouths wide agape in total shock.

I did not feel at all scared but the cold muzzle end of an AK-47 against the bottom lobe of my right ear put a chill down my spine. A four hour long session followed when I was interrogated and in this period, amongst many other things accused of being Jewish as my name was David. It went on and on and bullying tactics were adopted but all the time it went round and round in ever decreasing circles, they got nowhere and neither did I. Under the circumstances I thought that I kept remarkably calm and my request for some water was surprisingly granted. I repeatedly suggested that they contacted The League's local branch office or better still the Head office in Damascus.

Except for a period of about twenty minutes when I was left alone, probably to sweat a little, there were always at least two inquisitors present, most often more. At the end they said that they would confiscate and destroy all the files and I argued that this action would not be in The League's best interest. It would be better to confiscate them only and that they could then be collected by me, as the courier for onward delivery to Syria. After many long-winded telephone calls this was agreed to. I insisted on a receipt, which they provided, as was an armed escort when I was driven to my hotel in the early hours of the morning.

My companions were surprised to see me at breakfast and I gave them a rather vague explanation, as they had no idea as to why I was to travel on and not return with them. The really constructive meetings that followed more than made up for the previous evening's hassle. I returned to the airport the next day and they were left to tidy up a few loose ends.

The new airport at Tripoli was not large by International standards but to find one's way around the maze of exterior terminal buildings with all the signs in Arabic and forced to listen to the constant verbal diarrhoea over the tannoy from Colonel Gaddafi was a test of patience. I entered one large store and handed the receipt in to the reception desk clerk. He slowly shook his head but beckoned me to follow him to another store. It was just as well: I would never have found it on my own and would have needed a guide to get out. This one was larger and another clerk took the receipt and shuffled off and did not return for twenty minutes. To my dismay he was empty handed and it was difficult to understand his explanation. The gist of it was that the parcel, as he referred to it, had been delivered outside the normal operating hours and was not logged into the computer system. He made two telephone calls and within minute's three men, two armed officers, guards and another storeman appeared. The two stayed close to me whilst the storemen disappeared into the long rows of storage racking. Fifteen minutes later all the files were safely in my grasp after I had checked them over and signed for them.

My estimate on how long this procedure would have taken meant that it was necessary to leave the hotel some five hours prior to the flight departure time. Tons of time so I had thought. So pre-occupied in obtaining the files I had not bothered to check my watch. Now with mission accomplished, much to my relief and amazement, I did and found that the flight departed in less than thirty minutes. I decided that it was not the end of the world and would therefore catch the same flight the next day. After handshakes all round I turned to leave the store to return to the hotel. I had sufficient credit cards to purchase another ticket at the airline's offices just around the corner from it.

This move apparently presented a serious problem to the Authorities. As I had been in the country without the documents this was not a problem, but with them it was a totally different situation, they would have to ensure that I was sent on my way. An armoured vehicle skidded around the corner and came to a halt less than a metre away from us. I was then shoved in unceremoniously with all my baggage and seated between the two armed personnel. A fantastic high-speed ride followed and all four tyres screeched and squealed continuously. Reminiscent of a *Keystone Cops* chase we crashed straight through a closed gate in the outer perimeter fencing. The vehicle accelerated again and we drove directly to the plane I had to board. It's turbines were rotating as a baggage handler took the suitcases, one of the guards handed me a boarding card and at the top of the steps a pretty stewardess directed me to a first class seat that had been reserved in my name. I had been upgraded and it was the first and only time in my life that I had caught a flight, with the exception of private ones, without the need to queue in line at the check in desks.

It is a simple stark fact that if any authority wishes to be shot of you, then you are sure to be given the first class star treatment when you are booted out.

Of all the airports I have travelled through Tripoli does not figure in my top ten. It was visited many times after this little incident but never en route to Damascus where my business dealings were successfully completed after eighteen months of continuous backwards and forwards visitations.

Once, as I left Cairo airport, my taxi was halted at the main exit gates. A policeman thrust a clipboard complete with a blunt pencil through the open window and indicated that I should sign my name on a dotted line. Already on it were four undecipherable signatures so I scribbled "Christopher Columbus" and handed it back. After a cursory scrutiny, with a wave of his hand he indicated to the driver to move on. I had never experienced that procedure before and assumed that it was some new regulation that related to foreign visitors or more likely a random spot check. Some time later it came to my notice that a British citizen had been murdered and his body left just off the roadside on the main drag into Cairo from the airport only a few weeks before.

In Algiers one moment of extreme embarrassment was experienced in negotiations that were conducted totally in French with the aid of a female interpreter. It was for a consultancy service contract to examine and make recommendations on machine installations at the companies many production units and we had almost reached a successful conclusion. There was, as usual, a small problem on the contract price and we had appeared to have reached an impasse. The interpreter, although professionally qualified, struggled to explain the nuance of the situation. The Head of the Client's delegation did not agree with the way in which we had priced the local content of our obligations. He chuntered on and on but was unable to get down to the real nitty-gritty and had got his knickers into a proper twist. Our price was quoted in Sterling and it was obvious that he was not a happy bunny about it. I muttered under my breath, bloody pillock and had momentarily forgotten that he had an excellent command of the English language. He snapped at the interpreter who then turned to me and asked what is a Pillock? My immediate response was to tell her that it was a colloquialism for a fine upstanding Scottish gentleman. She looked a little blank, shrugged her shoulders and translated it as far as I could ascertain. This brought smiles all round and eased a situation that had got progressively tenser. To try and maintain a calm situation and to resolve the local issue I requested a recess until the next day.

Over a few beers with the interpreter that evening, I asked if it was the normal practice, under this type of contract, for the Client to be responsible for the provision and payment of accommodation, transport expenses and meals for all the Consultants and Engineers who would visit their various factories. She considered that it was. I then decided to prepare a new set of proposals for submission and discussion at the next meeting. At no time did she ask me about the word pillock. I believed that she was far too polite to even contemplate such a thing.

That evening I modified the contract details with respect to our local expenditure liabilities and split the price into two distinct figures, one in Sterling and the other in Algerian Dinars. These had been recalculated and resulted in an increase to our potential overall profit margin. I had only offered a token reduction to the Sterling element that had been included to cover some of the in country costs that we would be no longer liable for and had added a more than generous local currency requirement amount.

At the meeting the Client's delegation was extremely pleased with the dual priced presentation and all points were soon agreed. After the handshake and when all of the Contract documents had been signed, the Head came over to me and with a nod and a wink told me that he much preferred my definition of a pillock to the one that he had found in his English dictionary

The contract was not the type that I would have normally bothered to even consider pursuing but I was keen to get close to the client. They were a State organisation and had intentions to build a large forging production facility in the expansion of their overall industrial programme. They had commenced the preparation of their invitation to tender documents so it presented an ideal opportunity for our specialists to work alongside some of their more senior personnel.

I also arranged for a delegation, headed by the pillock, to visit companies in England within our engineering group who had extensive expertise and led the field in the production of forged components. The co-ordination of the factory visits; entertainment and social aspects would be my responsibility.

I had always had a gut like a goat and been glad and happy to leave plates with only the pattern on them, a war baby perhaps. Three course meals were a must with starters such as French onion or asparagus soup followed by a six hundred and seventy-five gramme "T-bone" steak and an old-fashioned nursery pudding presented no problems. There was a hotel in Pershore which took pride in its "He Man Mixed Grill" item on the menu. I had ordered this on many occasions when the knife and fork settings were moved out to accommodate the huge oval plate on which was heaped lamb and pork chops, a four hundred and fifty gramme sirloin steak, liver, bacon, sausages and kidneys, two fried eggs, mushrooms, tomatoes and fried onion rings. A more than adequate portion of chunky chips and a side salad was served on a separate plate. The look on the waitress's face when she lowered the plate to the table, with both hands, said it all. Finish that lot off if you can. I did every time but there was always a drawback, as before you could eat it all some of the food had become only lukewarm. After this the meal would be rounded off with a substantial pudding, spotted dick or blackberry and apple tart or sometimes a knickerbocker glory, and then a coffee and liqueur.

In downtown Seattle there was a restaurant that specialised in a whole boiled Alaskan lobster and the chef's offer was that if you could eat it all then he would throw in another one free of charge. Both he and I agreed that I could take it up some other time.

One day on the Algerian's visit we attended a heavy industrial display at The National Exhibition Centre near Birmingham and a more than substantial lunch was taken to set us up for the afternoon session. In the evening I entertained them to a gastronomic pig out at a restaurant in Worcester, the King Charles in Friar Street. There they had a reputation for serving more than generous portions and certainly lived up to it that night. It was an excellent meal with good service and I dropped the visitors off at their hotel and promised to collect them in the morning.

Not long afterwards I felt distinctly uncomfortable and soon began to suffer with extreme pains between my ribs and back, which increased with intensity by the minute. It was obvious that I had overdone it on the food intake and thought that if I could throw up the pain would diminish, I could not and it didn't. The only minor respite came when I sat on a bean bag with my back against a central heating radiator and a really hot water bottle was held firmly into my upper stomach area. The agony continued for most of the night and by morning I felt totally washed out and still not without some degree of pain. My wife had to telephone the office to explain my predicament and get them to make alternative arrangements to collect the visitors and that I would attempt to catch up with them later in the day, which I was eventually able to do.

That was the first time anything like that had ever happened, it must have been a bad case of indigestion. If I took it a little easier on the food front in the future it would probably never occur again.

There were many more humorous moments and not one trip failed to produce something unexpected. I had now reached the stage of my career when I was able to make the ultimate decision that all of this was not important to me any longer. It was painfully obvious that I did not get any kicks out of this style of business operation. I certainly did not bond with my current employer and was light years ahead of them in terms of negotiating skills and overseas contract dealings. The so called joys of the "International Jet Set" way of life had become really old hat and had at last forced me into a gradual "Feel good Decline" with a rather crappy family lifestyle. Any further involvement in Engineering and an overseas scenario were for me a thing of the past.

Chapter Three

We had promised ourselves another holiday to Praia da Luz for four weeks and this was arranged, again to commence in late May. This time a Mini car was rented for the whole period, as was an apartment in the centre of the village. We ate at many different restaurants as well as those frequented before and all of the Western Algarve was extensively travelled.

I did manage to fit in the second nine holes of golf at Palmeres just to the East of Lagos with three other players, all of whom were at the complex we had stayed at before. It was my first experience of golf in the Algarve and not a really enjoyable one. It took over three and half hours to complete by which time I was mentally knackered. I have forgotten how many times I had to call, two, three and four balls through as my companions were the most awful hackers and were completely oblivious of the very basic rules of golf etiquette. They continued to play on and failed to notice, or ignored the queues on the fairways and tees that built up behind us.

We explored the many surrounding villages with their principal cafes and bars and invariably stopped for refreshments on a daily basis. In one of the villages we nicknamed the café "Miserables" bar as the proprietor always looked as if he had found a penny and lost a pound.

The tranquillity and natural beauty of the inland areas impressed us tremendously, as did the apparent quality of life the locals appeared to enjoy. It was a whole wide world away from the rat race that had started to develop in England. Over our late night glasses of port – very moreish – we joked about the purchase of a holiday home, or even two and live in one and rent out the other. Ideas then developed into the purchase of a plot of land and then to build a large split villa to live in as our permanent residence and let out the other half.

In a more sober moment the thoughts of what could be done in this situation was considered more seriously but we still ended up with not much of a clue. Both of us were convinced however that one way or another something would be possible. In another long brain storming session the conclusion was reached that we should revisit later on in the year and meanwhile give it further detailed consideration back at the flat. There we could seriously investigate the prospects of such a venture.

Come the November, we were there again with the hire car, another Mini, and in a rented villa in Lagos, not on a holiday but with the intention to develop our latent ideas. Lots of discussions were held with the three estate agents in town and with the people who lived there and who we had met on our previous trips.

We had always used the same bank to cash our traveller's cheques or we had paid with our credit cards, there were no "holes in the wall" then and enquiries were made to see if a "Tourist bank account" could be opened. After numerous forms were filled in and signed, a princely sum of twenty pounds, about five thousand escudos was deposited. Two days later we collected our cheques and somewhat sarcastically were told that they looked forward to more substantial deposits.

Eventually we came to the decision that the area between Espiche, a small village to the West of Lagos, and Sages in the far West was a little too wild and woolly for our needs, it also appeared quite barren and what vegetation was there had suffered from the effects of the cold Atlantic winds. So over a beer, we very scientifically stuck a pin in our map with the point in the centre of Lagos and a circle was drawn on it of about twelve kilometres radius.

It seemed to us that we then covered hundreds of kilometres, either on our own or with various estate agents to look at derelict farmhouses and landlocked plots with access only through neighbouring farmyards. One plot with only a very small cottage had the arable portion of the land at the bottom of a very steep incline of at least forty-five degrees. "Thrombosis Hill" we termed it and did not consider that it was a serious proposition. Lots of total ruins and a disused rabbit farm were inspected and no progress was made. Visits continued and we came across an old farmhouse that was for sale, it was occupied by an Englishman and his French wife. He wished to return to the U.K. to take up a position as a teacher. Many other oddly shaped parcels of land were looked at and notes made. When we sifted through these, all failed to really impress.

On the way to this inhabited farm we both noticed, at the same time, a plot of land that had recently been ploughed. It was along a dirt track in the Hortinha area near the village of Bensafrim, the home of "Miserables" bar. It had been a long hard day and an *exhaustipating* slog. Even for November it had been hot and sticky and we were tired with numb bums, as we had constantly rattled along rough tracks, which had severely tested the Mini's suspension, and over countless fields. As we passed it again on the way back to Lagos we mutually agreed that it looked flat and uninteresting but noticed that it possessed a well, a ruin and had concrete electricity distribution poles on it.

After a long hot soak in the tub with a very welcome aperitif to wash the dust down we had a powwow and attempted to analyse the results obtained so far. The basic ground rules that we had been given were never to purchase anything without easy access to water and electricity and that a ruin would grant automatic approval for a new construction project such as a villa. We had seen nothing that had appealed to us at all. Only the land at Hortinha seemed to qualify on these fundamental requirements so it was decided to go and have another look.

We arose rather lethargically, probably as a result of too many glasses of port and after our acts were eventually got together brought some food and drink and decided to have an AC/DC style picnic when we visited the land. As we sat on the ground at the back of the ruin, the picnic had as usual been a complete success: we began to get more than a little bit excited. The ruin, a very thick stone walled structure, was approximately thirteen metres long and ten wide. It had been constructed on an elevated piece of land, probably man made, and faced in a South Easterly direction. The frontage overlooked a fig orchard and the rear elevation was about fifty metres from the track. One section – they could hardly be classified as rooms – of thirty square metres had roofing tiles and appeared waterproof. With a vivid sense of imagination it could be considered habitable, as long as one was prepared to rough it in the initial stages, in any event it was a good storage area. Next to this was an unroofed section that still contained the concrete feeding troughs where the livestock had been fed and housed. The third section, behind the other two, again unroofed gave us no clue as to its use.

Behind all of this was an excavated area not unlike a large pond, which we deduced would become a substantial reservoir with all the winter rainfalls. From the dried up heavily indented oxen hoof marks we were sure that this must have been the case.

Before our picnic we had walked all over the land and looked closely at the fig, olive and pomegranate trees and had concluded that it was naturally divisible into three main portions. The first was the fig orchard below the ruin and to the left of the plot when viewed from the track. The second the central piece above and below the well, which had good sandy/loamy soil ideal for arable farming and the third, was a cork, oak and eucalyptus wood. This portion was on the other side of a natural gully and watercourse that ran down through the land and formed the plot's right hand side. Alongside the gully were several thickets of bamboo, ideal for home grown runner bean sticks I thought at the back of my mind.

This gully had an ox-bow shaped bend in it about two thirds of the way down from the track. In its centre were a few young olive trees and the whole area was covered with deep green lush grass. Another picnic spot was AC's immediate reaction and I fully agreed.

Local resident ex-pats had told us that the bark of the cork oak trees was cut peeled and skinned from the trunk and main branches every ten years. This was then processed to produce corks for wine bottles, the top quality for the champagne industry, and many other uses. They did over emphasise that one should not expect to make an even small fortune from this operation, unless one had a few hundred hectares of them. Eucalyptus poles were used in the building industry and for garden gazebos or shipped off to the nearest pulp mill for paper production but we did not have enough to make any of these a viable proposition.

There was water in the well, which from chisel marks in one of the blocks at the well head indicated that it had been sunk in seventeen seventy-four, around two hundred years ago. In the past water was lifted from it by donkey power. The poor animal blinkered and with a nosebag filled with oats draped over its head, walked around the top, on this one in an anti-clockwise direction, continuously. It was harnessed to a stout pole the other end of which was attached to a vertical shaft. The rotation of this shaft drove a bevel gear and through this mechanism a large wheel was turned. Fitted to this was an endless chain with buckets fixed to it. As the wheel turned the buckets, filled with water, would be raised up to the well head and then tipped at the top. This water was then directed into a sluice and from there into the flume and cistern. We had seen many wells in the locality that still operated in this manner but the equipment on this one had long since been dismantled.

Its location was in a dip just below the level of the track and with its above ground concrete cistern storage tank and a flume connection was ideally situated for the installation of a gravity irrigation system to supply the whole of the central arable area.

A tunnel had been excavated to a depth of about three metres where a hole had been cut in the well wall. At the bottom there was a pump and motor, petrol driven, and two black plastic pipes were connected to it, one fed into the water and the other down the land into what appeared to be an orange grove. Half way down along the length of this one was a small leak, which was surrounded by a mass of green weeds. The land was therefore definitely fertile and there were no large stones or boulders to be cleared away.

The overall shape of the plot was almost as a segment of a circle and the frontage along the track was paced out to be approximately two hundred and twenty metres. If we eventually constructed a villa any next-door neighbours would not be too close for comfort.

More or less central in this frontage close to the track, were two magnificent Ent like cork oak trees and at the base of one of them, on the ground and partially hidden was a rather battered estate agents sign. There were another two trees at the bottom of the land, which had a gradual slope down to them away from the track and again this favoured gravity irrigation.

It definitely had all the *pissibolities* for a market gardening operation should we wish, for some unknown reason, to change tack in our lifestyle. This was backed up after a close inspection of the surrounding district where we found ample evidence of active arable farming. Almost two full rolls of film were taken of various shots at different positions around the perimeter. A sketch plan was made and the direction and locations of the photographs marked on it. At the end of our picnic we had convinced ourselves that we should make an offer and see what happened.

After a quick drink in "Miserables" bar we took a two-hour stroll around the village and found it to be extremely interesting during this detailed survey. When we had driven through it on the E.N.120 – the main road from Lagos to Lisbon – there was not a lot to be seen, only a row of houses on either side. As we now made our way through the many little back streets we found that it was much larger than we had thought and lots of facilities were discovered. One, which we considered would be useful, was the local Council office. We then returned back to the villa to plan our next move over a few nibbles and bevies.

In the past I had surfed the Souks – markets – in all of the Middle Eastern countries that were frequently visited and meandered around them many times over a period of days evenings or even weeks, sometimes I made an offer for an article that had caught my eye. It was at the most fifty per cent of the asking price, which normally had to be coerced from the stallholder who had meanwhile had the opportunity to suss out the naivety of his client, in this case yours truly. You are a hard bargainer "Sir" was the immediate response. A very serious haggle then commenced until an agreement was concluded or I threw up my arms to the skies and walked away. I always considered that the deal had been lost whenever I purchased an article. With it clutched or firmly grasped in both hands I knew deep down that the stallholder had won on the transaction and had made some, or even a substantial profit, otherwise it would not have been so ceremoniously handed over.

The next day we called into the estate agents and presented our offer. From the state of the for sale sign it must have been on their books for some time so we pitched this at fifteen per cent below the asking price. This was immediately rejected and as we had nothing more to say left the office a little frustrated. I was somewhat miffed and wondered what to do next as my souk tactics had not achieved the desired result. Over a cup of coffee and some toast our situation was assessed. The offer had not been made on a take it or leave it basis, or even a final one so we had not got ourselves stuck into a corner. The door was still open which left us with some room to negotiate at a later date should we wish to do so.

We continued to carry out a more detailed survey of the surrounds. Many foreigners, predominantly English, Dutch and Germans resided in the locality, which we referred to as the greater Lagos area and suburbs. It was extremely popular with tourists of various nationalities as it offered many clean and unspoilt beaches and more than ample villa complexes and apartment accommodation.

The shelves in the tiny vegetable shops we discovered in the back streets throughout the town – the largest one was smaller than the average corner shop in England – were examined and we quickly realised that there was a complete lack of the common seasonal vegetables readily available in Northern Europe. Parsnips, swede, spring onions, cherry tomatoes, coloured lettuce and peppers were typical examples.

In the Lagos open air Saturday market, near the bus station, we noticed what looked like asparagus. It actually was with extremely small spears similar to the sprue, a very thin inferior asparagus from the first cut taken in England. The tips were wide open and not fully shut and firm as they should have been. The seller told us that it was Espargos Bravo; wild asparagus. Some fern had been seen on the land at our picnic but it had not occurred to us what it could have been. Some people there, who had purchased bundles in the past, told us that it tasted very yucky and bitter when eaten, even after it had been cooked in the traditional way, steamed or boiled in water with a sprig of fresh mint.

We were fully aware that asparagus was native to the Mediterranean region and had now discovered that it grew on our potentially owned plot of land here in the Algarve. On that basis then it must surely be possible to cultivate it from crowns, or seeds, produced from genetic breeding. To farm a market garden that produced some or all of these vegetables must have more than an outside chance of becoming a winner, it was certainly food for thought.

It did not take us long to convince ourselves, obviously on a high, that the answer was a distinctly probable yes and if so did we raise our offer by ten per cent? My gut view was that it would be a complete waste of everyone's time; the price was fixed and not negotiable. At our next visit to the agent we offered the asking price. There was an immediate handshake, smiles all around and a general air of satisfaction. They enquired if we were going to build on the land and told us that they owned a construction company and knew a good architect. We informed them that it was our intention and as and when everything was ready they would be invited to submit a quotation. Don't try and patch up the old ruin, flatten it and start from scratch they advised. They rang the architect and arranged a meeting for us where we discussed our potential requirements and notes made of his scale of fees.

The next stage was to draw up the Promissory Contract for us to purchase and the Vendors to sell. Should either party default after signatures had been added they would be liable to a fine, which would be proportional to the contract value.

Our working holiday had by now rapidly drawn to a close and a frenetic scramble developed to arrange for the agent to have a Power of Attorney to act on our behalf. The fact that they would represent both parties posed a slight risk to us. We had examined all the various other alternatives and had anticipated that this situation would arise but had still decided to proceed on this basis.

On the return flight we mused over the past events and tried to guess how things would develop thereon. There was no need to have had any worries, everything went as smoothly as silk with the Vendors, and all five of them once one was discharged from hospital, had added their signatures to the contract. The necessary monies were transferred but the exchange rate had moved against us and it cost a lot more than we had budgeted for. As usual the Vendors received their payments after the agent had pocketed his commission.

In early nineteen eighty-five we had paid for a plot of land out in the sticks in the Western Algarve in Southern Portugal. The country was not at that time a member of the EEC. This situation was greeted with sighs of relief and also a huge degree of nervousness. We had finally got to this position so should we hang on to it purely as an investment or pursue the possibilities of actually emigrating and then make a permanent home there.

Meanwhile life continued in the flat and on the allotments. AC finally served out her redundancy period and left the company exactly two years to the day after me. It had been an extremely difficult and emotional time with staff gradually whittled down as contractual commitments were concluded. She did however have the opportunity of legal work as a part time lawyer at the companies' head office. I was in a totally negative mood with regard to alternative employment and was prepared to sit it out until the land was registered in our names and then make a decision.

As the time passed by it was considered that another visit was necessary to try to chivvy things along. When I called in on the agents they told me that a slight problem had arisen. A new law had been recently introduced that prevented foreigners from purchasing agricultural land with an area in excess of five thousand square metres unless they had resided in the country for over a year. Our registration paperwork was stuck in the system and would now be rejected.

Deep in our hearts we had already decided, ninety-nine point nine per cent, to emigrate, it was agreed on my early return, that an application for a Resident's Visa should be submitted. Once it was granted we could go and live there for the twelve-month period and then everything would be hunky dory. It was all left a bit loose as we had no idea what we could do while we waited and we could not afford to treat it as an extended holiday.

Before I had left, to protect our interests, the services of a local lawyer who was very highly recommended were engaged. He would register the Promissory Contract to prevent the Vendors from being able to put the land up for resale. His "up front" retainer payment was quite substantial and boded ill for when it came to the final settlement. However if he turned out to sufficiently proficient to resolve our predicament, then we would have to pay up whatever the amount, and keep a brave smile on our faces.

I also met with the architect and handed over all my "back of an empty fag packet engineering sketches", which had been prepared in the flat over the past few months. AC had problems in the visualisation of the building areas so I had to pace out distances in the lounge to enable her to form some ideas on the sizes of the rooms that we wanted in our new house. It would be possible from these for him to formulate its design. Then he could prepare all the necessary detailed drawings, which would allow any competent builder to construct a villa to the specifications that met our requirements.

Our room sizes and their layout had been carefully decided over many weeks and we were not prepared to let anyone produce what we termed "an architect's wet dream". We had seen many that had been built in England and even more in the Lagos suburbs. Estate agents glibly referred to them as spacious, roomy and well proportioned. In reality they contained too many square metres of unusable and wasted space that needed to be kept cleaned and occasionally decorated. We considered that they did not add anything to aid the function of the villa and more often than not reduced its efficiency.

At the airport I literally bumped into the owner of the complex where our first holiday was taken in Praia da Luz. Over a period of time on our visits an acquaintanceship had gradually developed. She was vaguely aware of our intentions to purchase some land and come and live in Portugal and had shown us one of her plots which she was prepared to rent out to us to farm. During this brief chat she strongly recommended that before we decided to reside here permanently, we should try an "over-winter stay" first, away from the tourist regions.

The applications for our Residents Visas with all of the supporting documentation was submitted to the Portuguese Consulate General in London at the end of November nineteen eighty-five and receipt was acknowledged on the second of December when we were notified that the process would take no more than six months.

To kill time whilst these were in the system another holiday was spent in the Algarve. A car was hired, yet another Mini car and we booked into a small guesthouse, again in the centre of Lagos. Discussions followed with the agent and our lawyer when we were informed of another major setback. This time it was really bad news as it now required a five year residence period not one to purchase the land. Why neither of them had written to inform us of this new situation was never explained satisfactorily. We could not believe it and were more than a little pissed off with the whole debacle. Even with a Visa there was no way that we could hang around, sat on our arses for all that time. Without ownership of the land we were therefore absolutely powerless to build or farm on it. Any investment, substantial or not, could prove very risky as the goalposts could be moved yet again in the wrong direction.

The Mini car was not used every day and once remained parked in a side road off the Avenida, in Lagos, for four days. When we came to use it we found a parking ticket copy had been placed under one of the windscreen wiper blades. It could have been ignored as we would soon be on our way home but as we had only just applied for Residence here we could not afford the risk, however slight, that a minor criminal act could be recorded against us as we could be traced through the car hire company.

I knew that the police station was nearby, around the next corner, so we made our way to it with ticket in hand. There was only one Sergeant on duty there sat at a large desk covered in paperwork held down by five half-filled ashtrays. On the wall behind him was a picture of the Benfica football team. I knew that it was an old one as Eusabio was one of the players. I handed over the ticket and at the same time pointed at it and muttered Manchester United. His eyes lit up and a huge smile spread across his face and after about fifteen minutes of knowledgeable football banter he picked up the ticket and withdrew a file from a drawer in the desk. He thumbed through a large amount of papers and eventually found the original one and tore them both up and despatched them into a waste paper basket. He then shook my hand enthusiastically and waved us out through the door. I really did appreciate his attitude, even more his style.

At one session, a general chat really in the agent's office, a Portuguese borehole-drilling specialist was introduced to us. He was aware of our problems but agreed to visit our plot the next day to test for water availability. On his arrival he pulled out of his pocket what looked like an endless metal coil about one centimetre in diameter and thirty in length, with a sphere attached at each end. On a spot about thirty metres north of the ruin he placed one sphere in his right hand and the other in his left. The coil was then pointed at the ground and with forearms outstretched he walked slowly forward and suddenly the coil quivered into a horizontal position. Here is agua, water, he told us. We were totally gob-smacked, as we had never witnessed anything like this in our lives before.

Then after he had moved over to the two Ent like cork oak trees he proceeded to repeat the process. Again the coil moved into a horizontal position and we both shook our heads in total disbelief. He then offered the coil to AC who very nervously followed his instructions and found to her amazement that it happened with her. I was still very sceptical but to my surprise I obtained the same result despite my instinctive reaction to fight against the upward force. He told us that there was a much stronger signal at that position and a good supply of water was available. If he eventually drilled and found no water then we would not be liable for any of the costs of the drilling operation. This gave us a considerable degree of reassurance and confidence in his capabilities and competence.

Our ideas on what could be done, when or even if we emigrated after the latest bad news, to generate some income had gradually developed into a three way financial plan. The first part was to construct a large villa divided into two independent living quarters and the information given to the architect was for this type of design. We would live in one and receive rental income from the other. As a fall back situation, should the capital investment be beyond our means then we could design a much smaller one arranged so that accommodation on a bed and breakfast basis could be offered.

The second was to farm the arable section of the land as a market garden and sell its produce locally and of course to feed ourselves. AC had suggested that as there was more than sufficient land we should keep some chickens, pigs, goats and sheep. I was not that fully into the *"Good Life"* and wanted no involvement with livestock whatsoever.

Thirdly, that any left over and spare capital could be invested and give a very healthy return at the then current high interest rates.

In this hiatus period as we waited for visas, a set of *Lingua* tapes and books were purchased so that, in theory, our holiday Portuguese could be extended and hopefully a more fluent command of the language achieved. Neither of us could be classified as linguists, I had even been denied the opportunity to fail in French at "O" level. My mock exam results were so pathetic that I was not even allowed to sit the exam. To make matters even worse it had taken me five attempts to achieve a pass level standard in English. Despite a thorough search of the shelves in all the bookshops and libraries in our district there was not a sign of any dictionaries, English-Portuguese, most other European languages but not Portuguese. There was no reference at all to the country; it was as if it did not exist.

AC continued with her part-time duties as a commercial lawyer and also provided assistance to the Company Secretary of a large Civil Engineering firm based in Birmingham. She was offered the Company Secretaries position with a company in Ilkley; but with very little or even no prospects for me in that part of the country, declined. Meanwhile my time was spent most weekdays with Don and Sandra as we worked on the renovation of their recently purchased old house. I also tended the allotments, painted and decorated for Lucie and Les and carried out all of the peripheral construction works at their new home near Broadway. There was never a great deal of time to get bored.

The periods of time spent on the allotments kept us sane, they were thoroughly enjoyable and helped us to relax. It also enabled us to put to the back of our minds the problems overseas. We frequented a pub in the nearby village of Studley, it became our favourite watering hole and on most Sunday mornings we would stagger into the bar with plastic sacks filled with freshly harvested surplus vegetables. All the compartments in our upright freezer in the garage were crammed full so we were quite happy to distribute what was left over to the landlord and our friends. They all thought that we were more than slightly demented.

I had a unique opportunity to provide us with a cock pheasant for lunch but it was not to be. One morning as we neared the spring on the allotment with implements in hand, a huge cock pheasant could be clearly seen as it grubbed up our new potatoes. It saw us and immediately started to run away. I dropped the spade and with the garden fork in my right hand gave chase but it was a lot faster than me. I had only one chance to down it so in desperation hurled the fork like a javelin, but unfortunately missed by a mile, it was such a shame. The bird was so heavy that it must have covered at least ten metres before it could get both of its feet off the ground.

On a Sunday morning when I leant over to push a stick in to support the peas I felt my back go, the pain was savage and immediate. AC didn't believe me, but it had and I asked her to collect all the tools together as I struggled to get back to and into the car's passenger seat. She drove us home where an even bigger struggle followed to get up the stairs in the flat. I finally succeeded as I reversed up on my bottom. It was the second time that it had gone; the first was many years earlier when as I wheel barrowed some three foot by two foot concrete paving slabs it tilted. I should have let go but tried to steady it, a really foolish instinctive action. I was not at all pleased at the thought of more contortions on an Osteopath's bed cum table.

Although I considered that my dietary habits did not involve massive blowouts or even over indulgencies my stomach problem had become more frequent and certainly more painful. I therefore saw my doctor who recommended that I see a specialist consultant and take a series of tests to ascertain the problem. He suggested that it could well be gallstones. The tests were carried out but no positive results were obtained.

AC's ex sister-in-law, Mary, with whom she had maintained a very close contact was a nurse and was married to a "guts and bowels" surgeon, Peter. When she explained the problem to him he was in no doubt that it was gallstones and invited us down for a long weekend. There I could have a private scan at the local hospital in Dorchester. This confirmed in less than a minute that that was the problem, I could see them myself, and a fat free diet was immediately advised. He would be pleased to carry out the operation and told me to apply to my doctor for a cross border referral as in his opinion I would have to wait a lot longer if it was performed in Redditch.

Upon our return I booked an appointment with my doctor and explained the situation. He thought that I would probably have to wait at least six and more likely nine months to have the operation locally and that I was extremely lucky to have been given the opportunity to have it carried out elsewhere.

In less than eight weeks I received a letter from the Dorset Health Authority with a date for the operation, which was only one week away. AC again spoke to Mary who was very pleased and suggested that we spend a couple of days with them before the big day and for as long as it took afterwards to convalesce.

I was under the knife first thing on a Wednesday morning and on Thursday managed to manoeuvre the drip support structure into the toilets for the usual and a quick cigarette. On Friday I asked AC to bring in a few *tinnies* of beer with her when she came to visit. She mentioned this to Peter who came in especially in the late afternoon, gave me a thorough check up, discharged me immediately and then drove me to his home to be cared for in good hands. Saturday lunchtime I wore a long white dressing gown and easily downed a pint of bitter in the local pub, I could have easily managed another one but was not allowed to have one. I hung heavy curtains up in the lounge on Sunday and felt no discomfort at all. There was only a brief period of convalescence and as soon as the stitches were removed I was fit enough to be driven back to the flat.

Our local pub had a very wide range of clientele and a large core of regulars, we included. It was a free house with three bars, the long one, the central Snug area and one that led to the two pool tables and statutory dartboard. Pub grub was also available and it was owned and run by the landlord and his wife with whom a friendship quickly developed.

A range of draught beers was on tap, which made it a popular venue for all ages. We had toyed, only toyed, with the notion of a move to the West Country to take ownership of a pub with a restaurant. It was an idea that had been placed at the back of our minds and had really been overtaken by other events. One day the landlord mentioned that they desperately needed a short break, but it would mean that the pub would have to be closed as they were not tied to a brewery and could not call up a relief. I glanced at AC and we both said with one accord, "why don't you leave it with us?" It could remain open in our capable hands. The only bar experience I ever had had been when I was in digs in a pub near Basingstoke, and that was only on darts nights. After several serious discussions and brief lessons on how to flush the beer pipes and tap the new barrels, I had made copious notes on scrap paper, we all agreed that it was a goer and as it would be their first holiday in four years, they should take a fortnight away.

We took over on a Friday, after the lunchtime session and did not really have a clue as to what was in store and had certainly not realised what we had let ourselves in for. All too soon it was time to open up for the evening start to the weekend. Every bar was chock-a-block full and the place heaved all night; it had never seemed that busy when we were there as clients. AC and I with the three regular barmaids did not have any time to stand still, we were so rushed, forever having to pull the beer engines and push up the optics until our arms almost dropped off. It was not until I shouted last orders, raise your glasses, shift your bloody arses and bug off home that I was able to pull myself a pint.

The cash takings for the evening were checked out in the lounge upstairs after all the doors had been locked and double bolted. They tallied to a little over one thousand pounds, no wonder we had not been able to take any time out. We were still on such a high buzz that although it was by now way past one o'clock in the morning it was difficult to settle to sleep.

As we tried to drift away, I thought to myself what stupid idiot had volunteered to take on board this routine and anguish for a fortnight. That morning completely tied us up as we dealt with all the empties and then bottled up the shelves and were barely sorted out when it was time to open up for the Saturday lunchtime session. It was as usual very busy and we closed at two o'clock and then girded our loins for the five thirty start. It hit us much harder then as we grimly realised that we were on this treadmill until the owners returned.

The liquid side of things was only one part of the business as there was the pub grub preparation. This was mostly carried out when there were a few spare moments available but more often than not normally became a complete and utter scramble just before lunch with little or no time to clear away the chaos in the kitchen. There were lots to be done on every single day. To clean and flush the beer pipes seemed to take me forever as every different ale had to be treated separately, and I had not fully appreciated how many brews there were and I always had problems with the draught Guinness.

The barrels had to be tapped and left to settle and the draymen dealt with. They always managed to turn up early in the mornings with both of us half asleep. Not only that but there was also the daily shop for fresh vegetables and groceries and the visits to the bank to deposit the previous day's cash income. It was necessary to ensure that each of the three tills was charged with a float and that an emergency one was to hand.

There was a large old fashioned Juke Box up in one of the empty bedrooms and this was wired to two speakers and a selection console in the long bar. The Christmas before my two daughters had given me a present, it was a forty-five rpm vinyl record of a tune that I was very partial to. The singer was Marianne Faithfull and the song on the "A" side was *"The Ballad of Lucy Jordan"*. I found the melody quite haunting and the words somewhat nostalgic. It concerned a thirty-seven-year-old girl bemoaning the fact that she would never drive through Paris in an open topped sports car and AC had loved the city on all of her previous visits. The number one selection in the console did not appear to be that popular so I substituted it in the Juke Box for mine. I could then select it as and when I wanted to.

The first time that I managed to take a breath of fresh air, on the car park, was on the Tuesday morning after we had taken over. We battled on and became more and more exhausted as we counted off the days to when the owners would return. I have forgotten the total amount of monies handled, it was quite considerable, but at the end there was only a little over one pound out on the overall balance.

We received many compliments, all hard-earned, for our sterling performances, the chilli-con-carne was a better one and some hard core drinkers even, on more than one occasion, raved about the fact that the beers had never been so sparkly and clear. Several clients complained, half-heartedly, that one of the five record selections made was not the one that they had chosen. I apologised but told them there was not a lot that could be done about it but remembered to recover my record before our stint was completed.

It had been a totally knackering two weeks, we had never worked such long hours before, a real non-stop merry-go-round with no opportunity to get off. The landlord and his wife believed that we had done them a favour, not so, they had done us one. From that final day, not at any time has our involvement in a booze and food related environment on a full time basis, ever been considered or even been discussed.

I had played with the idea over many months but it was still a difficult decision to make. Having had no link with Engineering since I had terminated my employment and certainly had no intention to do so in the future, I resigned my membership of both Institutions in the May of nineteen eighty-seven.

Many visits had been made to the Portuguese Consulate General over the past year but there was still no sign, when or if, our visas would be issued. In desperation and at our lawyer's suggestion we wrote to the Ambassador and explained the situation.

Our patience finally snapped, sick and fed up as we bumbled along and waited for things to happen, we made up our minds, said "sod it" let's go and get things sorted out. So we booked a ferry for the eleventh of October from Plymouth to Santander in Northern Spain. Then we would travel on to the Algarve and our un-owned plot of land. We believed that if we were on site, at least we could kick things along. There must be a way or means to get around our problem and we certainly wouldn't find it if we stayed in the flat.

AC's Pees, Lucie and Les had a caravan that could be utilised and parked on the land, which meant that we would not have to doss down in the ruin. This space could then be utilised as a storage room. It would also be very economical and save us a considerable amount of expenditure on local accommodation, which would have been our largest weekly cash outlay. He also knew of a good sturdy second hand car, an ideal vehicle to tow the caravan, which was for sale in a nearby garage.

It was organised chaos from the time that the decision to go was made to when we drove onto the ferry. I proposed marriage to AC, which to my relief, she accepted. A quiet wedding was decided upon with just family and very close friends, and then to hold a large bash in the evening for our other numerous friends and acquaintances.

The arrangements were made at the Bromsgrove Registry office as Redditch did not have one, for Friday the twenty-fifth of September as all the Saturdays in the month had already been booked. Droitwich Golf and Country clubhouse would be the venue for the lunchtime reception. After arrangements had been made there and a headcount carried out, it was realised that there were two people short on numbers. Stupid idiots that we were, we had overlooked ourselves.

A pub in Alcester was a central location for the evening bash and the town also boasted had a couple of hotels, some of our friends could therefore book accommodation and not have to bother about the journey home afterwards. Don and Sandra offered to put up Peter with Mary and the family for the night, but Peter could only attend the wedding and reception as he was on emergency call at the Dorchester hospital in the evening. An extension to the licensing hours would have to be applied for and the landlord would lay on a buffet and arrange for the provision of live music.

Would you ever believe it, between the arrangement of the wedding and the wedding day, our Portuguese visa authorisations spewed out of the system and were dropped through the front door letterbox, it had taken an astonishing nineteen months to filter through. I still have on file a copy of our original application. The fact that the Post Office lost one of our important letters to the Consulate General may well have had a considerable influence on the delays. So, another trip to Brompton Road was necessary to have our passports rubber-stamped. On this occasion it was a fruitful visit and we left the Consulate feeling chuffed to death. A classic case of Murphy's Law, having made the decision to travel without a visa, we were each now in possession of one after such a long wait.

Extensive lists and an approximate time scale were eagerly prepared for everything. All had to fit in with the two fixed dates, the wedding and the ferry departure. Items associated with the wedding, such as rings, dress, suit, invitations and flowers etc. should not have presented any problems and be quickly crossed of the list. All were organised with consummate ease, except the rings. They were chosen in what we thought was plenty of time, three weeks prior to the day. Despite almost constant harassment at the jewellers they were unable to be collected until the day before.

The old fart box, new to us, was given a general overall service and found to require a replacement front wheel bearing and two top steering column bushes. These were fitted under the guarantee from the garage. As a precaution four new tyres were purchased together with a new rear section of exhaust and silencer. Whilst this was being carried out I crawled all over the caravan, checked out the electrics and greased everything in sight.

A portable generator would be essential to continually top up the caravan's and occasionally the cars batteries. One was ordered, delivered and tested on the day before we vacated the flat.

AC had pointed out on numerous occasions that when I read the newspapers my hands had gradually extended further and further away from my body. I disagreed in a somewhat vain manner but quickly arranged for an eye test anyway. The result was that I became the not so proud owner of my first pair of spectacles.

Time as always passed by very quickly. I enjoyed my stag night at the Studley pub, AC passed on a hen party. A council official called to inspect the flat to check that it was in the same condition as when we took possession and he left completely satisfied. We thought that they had been very efficient, as the Town Hall had only been given notice three days earlier.

Everything went like clockwork on the wedding day, even the weather was perfect. It was a very emotional experience for both of us in the Registry Office especially during the actual ceremony, Don was my witness and AC's ex sister-in-law hers with all our family and friends huddled together behind us. The Golf Club reception was a complete success, beautiful surroundings and an excellent meal with plenty of champers. Even so one or two of us, myself included, managed to down a couple of pints of Bank's Bitter. To cap it all, the evening bash was a marvellous rave up and went with a real swing, an absolute sell out. Family, friends of many years standing and many ex-colleagues from our previous employment, were present, as were most of my golfing chums.

The ex-colleagues presented us with a huge Fortnum and Mason picnic hamper. This was to serve us proudly over the forthcoming weeks. We received lots of other presents, but unlike the usual bed linen and other household effects, more practical gifts were presented, items to assist us in setting up our new life, lump hammers, a bow saw and hundreds of D.I.Y. articles.

As the noise level increased it suddenly hit us that we would be on our way in less than two weeks time, a really "phew and cor blimey" moment.

A taxi had been booked to collect us and arrived on time. We therefore avoided the hassle of staying on much later as the party was going from strength to strength and invitations were being thrown out to come home with us for a nightcap. All were declined and with a borrowed fiver to cover the cost, fell into its back seats. We did however partake of a swift nightcap in the lounge before both of us crashed out not long after midnight, totally knackered after a truly wonderful brim full day that we would always remember, a real *lalapalooza* one.

That morning saw us in one of the hotels in Alcester to share breakfast with AC's Pees and some of her friends, who were with her at university, all of whom had spent what was left of the night there. We then called round to Don and Sandra's for a last chat with Mary and the family who we sadly waved goodbye to as they set off back to Dorset.

As quickly as things were crossed off our lists others were added, so it appeared that little or no progress had been made. Our very old banger had to be sold. We called it *Poxey-Yoxy*. It was a clapped out red coloured old Vauxhall Talbot, so nicknamed as the registration number was YOX 268T, which continuously suffered from punctures in one of the front tyres. On one weekend visit to the surgeons home we had one on the journey down there, another whilst we were there, and a third on the M5 during the drive home. To change an offside wheel on a motorway's hard shoulder is not to be recommended. This problem disappeared after the spare wheel was substituted permanently. It sold more easily and at a better price than we had expected.

Once unable to remove the front wheel to replace a punctured tyre, outside the garage door, I suffered the indignity of having to call out a nearby tyre service company. They knew me well as they had repaired so many of our punctures in the past. The smirk on the man's face as he arrived to remove the wheel and fit the spare is burnt in my memory. Sometime later, after he had had to use a one metre length of tubing to extend the wheel nut brace before he could remove them, I felt somewhat vindicated and his expression at that moment confirmed this.

All of our allotment tools and accumulated clutter in the garage had to be disposed of. This was achieved when we attended the many local car boot sales, which were thoroughly enjoyed, the old fart box estate proved to be invaluable on these occasions.

Then there was all of, a complete exaggeration, our second/third hand furniture and white goods to get rid of, sell if possible, dump at the local rubbish depot or give away. The upright freezer sold very easily despite the fact that the handle came off in the hand of the prospective purchaser. I convinced her that it was not a big problem, just a dab of super glue and it would be better than new and that I could deliver it the next day. The small fridge and the twin-tub washing machine didn't budge so they were left in the flat together all the odds and sods of carpeting we had laid. The remaining pieces disappeared slowly but surely, mostly at really knocked down prices.

Now it was time to turn our minds to the nitty-gritty aspects and arrange to pack all of our personal possessions and the items we wished to retain. Eventually they would be imported into Portugal. Well used tea chests that were *donkies* old, were provided by our friends Don and Sandra and filled, capped and lidded. Afterwards we painted on each of them a unique identity mark. It was then necessary to make a list of the contents. This had to be fully detailed and specific, and had to include the names of all books, LP records and music tapes etc. to assist in the future importation process. AC's piano would continue to remain in a special warehouse, available for collection as and when called for.

All the tea chests were slowly but surely transported and loaded into Don's garage. When the final one was positioned the stored packed volume of our total possessions didn't seem to amount to very much at all. How lucky we were to have access to this free storage facility. Don and Sandra despite everything that we have burdened on them over the years remain our closest friends to this day.

It would have been unforgivable not to have given our personal farewells to other very close friends and relatives across the country, so we braced ourselves to undertake the visits to accomplish this obligation. The first was a trip to Liverpool to catch with my number two daughter Michelle, Shelle Belle or Shelle for short, who was studying for a Master of Science degree in Pharmacy. The opportunity to inspect her new flat was taken and we thought that it was not too bad as student flats went. She was a little down in the dumps, but after a couple of Pils over a free supper she cheered up considerably, even more so when I gave her a cheque for her pocket money.

We continued on to Fullwood near Preston, arrangements had been made to stay with a member of the original "Manchester Mob". It so happened that there was a rave up in the evening and I borrowed her late husband's dress suit, which fitted perfectly, and bow tie. We all piled off to the Rotarians Ladies Evening held at a very upmarket hotel for what turned out to be another night never to be forgotten. A truly magnificent meal followed by an *exaustipating* bop to a five-piece band who belted the music out until one o'clock in the morning.

My mother telephoned on our return to tell us that my father had been admitted to Ronkswood hospital in Worcester and was on an insulin drip; he had developed diabetes. We could well have done without news of that nature. When we visited him he was as cantankerous as ever, did not appear to be in any difficulties and wanted to discharge himself and go home. Afterwards we called in on my mother, who only lived two kilometres away, she offered us the usual cuppa tea with plenty of biscuits that could be dunked, and a good long natter quickly ensued.

The owners of the pub in Studley laid on a special farewell party for us and suggested an overnight stay so that we could let our hair down. They put on a splendid buffet and the place was full to overflowing. AC retired to bed at around two o'clock. To this day I cannot remember when I did but was probably the last. It seemed to be a never ending eating and boozing binge but surprisingly our weights remained stable, probably as a result of all the nervous energy that we expended on a daily basis.

Our next journey was Southbound to Dorset and we called in at Bristol to see my number one daughter Sharon, Shazzy Babes or Shaz for short, who was a practicing Psychologist at a nearby hospital. Then it was down to stay in Dorset with Peter, Mary and family. Again there was more wining, from the bottles laid down in his cellar, and dining. Their eldest son had just returned from a holiday in Greece and was due to commence his first term at Warwick University. We offered him a lift as we lived not a million miles away. After the usual tearful goodbyes he managed to squeeze in between all his baggage as the boot was completely full. The two of us in the front were quite comfortable but he in the back, being over six feet tall was not. On the way back it had been arranged to call into a small hamlet just South of Bristol for him to see his grandfather. AC's ex father-in-law and then directly to Warwick to register him into the new hall of residence which was amazing, he had his own bathroom.

A few days later, as we travelled to the pub in Studley for the ultimate quite night out, a white Ford Granada, that was trying to overtake on a blind bend and was on our side of the road crashed into us. I desperately tried to swerve out of the way but to no avail. The driver quickly reversed, turned around and proceeded to do a runner, which left us and the other car drivers, who had been unscathed in the incident, quite dazed and shell shocked. I had made a mental note of his registration number, which AC scribbled down on a piece of paper which she happened to have in her handbag. Full details of two witnesses were also jotted down even though we considered that the likelihood of any prosecution was highly improbable and we would not be able to attend the court proceedings anyway.

We drove on slowly, as the damage had not been inspected and reached the local garage only half a mile away and immediately telephoned the police. Their patrol car arrived within five minutes and they took my statement. I suggested to them that it was a company car, this was soon confirmed, and that the driver had had a few drinks too many and was over the limit. They were extremely sympathetic but would not be able to follow this up until the next morning, by then it would be too late to prove whether he had had a few bevies too many or not.

AC was very badly shaken up by the incident so our stay in the pub was short lived and a general damper all round had been cast over the whole evening. Just before we left to go home a cake laden with lighted sparklers was produced which AC managed to hack into bite-sized pieces despite the fact that her hands shook visibly. A quick survey of the damage indicated that there appeared to no serious problems with the steering or the suspension but the modified front-end side panels and bonnet looked in a very sorry state.

First thing in the morning I telephoned my golfing partner in our regular Saturday four ball. He owned a garage near Bromsgrove and was a time served mechanic and vehicle bodywork specialist, as a Jaguar car enthusiast he owned several. He suggested that I drove over straight away for him to make an inspection. Up on the ramp he quickly confirmed that there was no damage to any mechanical parts but his list of body repair requirements grew rapidly. There was a Ford agent nearby so replacement parts did not present a problem. He knew that we were due to catch the ferry in three days time so he was prepared to give the work top priority and eventually worked long hours into the night. His main concern was that the metallic paint would not have time to dry out properly, I didn't give a toss as to whether the new panels and bonnet were painted or not. As a good friend he loaned us a car, unfortunately for us, not one of his Jaguars.

We continued on from Bromsgrove to Worcester to pay a final visit to my father who was still in hospital but stabilised. Despite his protestations they would not discharge him until the day we caught the ferry. As such he was not amused and was very tetchy so after a very brief chat we said our goodbyes.

My friend, as good as his word, delivered the old fart box back to the flat, it looked better than new even though the metallic paint was still a little bit soft. He then collected the loan car and a cheque for over six hundred pounds, which hurt us more than a little.

On that evening a table had been reserved for a final farewell meal with Lucie and Les at a local pub with highly rated and recommended restaurant facility. Over yet another really superb meal the conversation was somewhat subdued and the atmosphere more than a little tense. Tearful farewells were made and we very, very wearily returned home.

The flat, which had proved to be a boon, was tidied up on our final day there and the all the last knocking things packed away. The double bed, our final stick of furniture, was dismantled and after a struggle we managed to load it and the mattress onto Don's borrowed Mini pick-up. We had promised it to them for one of their spare bedrooms.

After the flat keys had been deposited with a cheque for the final payment with the local Council, arrangements were made for our bank to transfer funds to our tourist account in Portugal and we collected the pre-ordered pesetas. We already had escudos that had not been spent on our last holiday. Back at the flat we met up with Don and the totally overloaded fart box and the Mini pick-up in a similar condition travelled in convoy fashion to his house near Alcester.

AC then stashed, stowed and battened down as much as she possibly could into the caravan whilst I fitted the necessary extension wing mirrors to the car. That was it, at long last we were ready for the off!!!!!

Long soaks in the bath for both of us, accompanied by stiff gin and tonics with nibbles which of course included porky scratchings was followed by a lovely evening meal. Champagne cocktails, Lasagne and salads followed by various cheeses and the inevitable dreaded bottle of port. During all this Don hurtled around between the lounge and the conservatory like a Whirling Dervish. He was certainly livelier than the drugged up ones AC and I had seen in Omdurman, on the opposite side of the river Nile to Khartoum just a few years ago. He taped Moody Blues albums for us on his brand new toys. After he had re-assembled our bed we crashed into it for the last time, thoroughly dazed and exhausted, too tired even to anticipate the events of the next few days.

At our very recent wedding, how the time has flashed by since, in my speech I had referred to us as two dreamers, who had a long path to follow and that those dreams would be made to come true. By now, some progress in the right direction had already been made, even if it was, yet again for me anyway, into the unknown.

Chapter Four

I quickly realised as the car climbed up through the gears that there was more than enough power under the bonnet to pull all of us to our destination. After about four hundred metres we approached a tee junction onto the old Alcester to Stratford-upon-Avon road. When the brakes were applied there was a tremendous thud in our backs. "Oh no", we thought, "Had a car behind run into us?" Unable to see anything in the extended wing mirrors I yanked on the hand brake, heaved open the door and jumped out to find that there was nothing in sight. Somewhat puzzled we drove on only to find that when I applied the brakes again the same thud occurred.

We were not seasoned caravaners by any means and it took me some time to realise that the *thingumajig* in the towing bar, which automatically applied the caravan's brakes when we slowed down, didn't function. There was nowt that we could do about it now, to travel on the motorway would not present us with many problems, however, the thoughts of the thumps and bruises we were likely to suffer on the roads in Spain and especially in Portugal, made me flinch.

The drive to Gordano service station was a wet one but went without a hitch although we found that when we travelled at over eighty kilometres an hour problems were produced by the heavy goods vehicles that hurtled past. There was no stabilising gismo fitted to the caravan so we were badly affected by the yawing effect produced by their slipstreams.

We had arranged to meet up with Shazzy Babes who had our green card and insurance documents. As we arrived somewhat earlier than anticipated there was ample time for a coffee and a slow drag on a fag. She was soon going off to a Kibbutz, but now had second thoughts about it. After a quick snack and a bevy, another sad farewell, we then drove on to Plymouth as the weather slowly improved. There were no problems finding the Riverside caravan park. No one was at the reception so we just parked in one of the many available spaces, unhitched and plugged into a mains electricity socket. Our stomachs thought that our throats had been cut so it was necessary to drive into the town to find somewhere to eat. After having window gazed at the menus in various establishments and compared their prices, we opted out of a decision making process and eventually settled on a cheap and cheerful fish and chips supper with added salt and vinegar. These were eaten with some relish, sat on a nearby pedestrian precinct bench, out of greaseproof bags wrapped in the pages of last weeks *Daily Mail*.

Shazzy Babes had spent lots of time in Plymouth when doing her Master of Science degree in Psychology and had recommended several popular bars. As we sipped a couple of drinks in one of them we found that most of the clientele were youngsters so for us two poor knackered old *roos* we found it a better policy to bugger off and spend our first night in the caravan. The oversized bed was very comfortable and we crashed out at nine thirty and slept like the dead until seven o'clock the next morning. It was the best night's deep and contented sleep that we had experienced in ages. We had covered three hundred and twenty kilometres and I had driven for five and a half hours.

Next morning we both took a very quick cat lick in the ablution block, it was so cold. The caravan was hooked up after many puffs and pants and able assistance from another caravaner, who obviously had far more years of experience than me, and we left the park around eight fifteen. The route to the ferry terminal was well signposted and we arrived there in less than fifteen minutes, had boarded, and were in our cabin in another thirty.

The cabin was quite cosy and we were glad that we did not have to share, as that would have been a little too cosy. The ferryboat was explored from top to bottom and from stern to prow and to our dismay we found that there were no banking facilities on board. We were therefore unable to top up our cash and foreign currency reserves.

The crossing of the English Channel went very smoothly with the weather warm and pleasant and the sea as calm as a millpond. We made a deliberate effort to be on the deck when the coastline of England disappeared over the horizon. Both of us felt a sense of relief, as much as anything, that we had actually made it this far. We sat and read the *Sunday Times* over a drink and nibbled the Fortnum and Mason's nuts and then retired to have an afternoon *ziz*. It lasted a whole two hours, what bliss.

The spread out map was studied for the umpteenth time since we had booked the ferry. It had been decided that it would be easier to keep to the main roads rather than take a scenic route. At one stage we had considered a slow journey across the Iberian peninsular to do "The Tourist bit", but now having been delayed for so long, we couldn't get to our destination quickly enough. The plan was to only spend one night in Spain, two in Portugal and from then on in the caravan parked on the land.

In the evening grilled gammon steaks with chips was polished off for supper after which AC retired to bed as she felt quite grotty. I had a few beers before I made my way to the cabin. She woke up in the middle of the night as the ferry was being tossed about all over the place. I was dead to the world but was shaken awake and both of us were alarmed as we could hear creaks and groan like sounds everywhere. In a bit of a *tizwas* she insisted that we go up to the deck so a few clothes were thrown on and we climbed up above to find lots of other people milling around in their dressing gowns, and that access to the outer deck was prohibited due to the bad weather conditions. After a quick glance through the windows had shown that the waves were not twenty metres high she became a little calmer although we both felt uneasy when the boat seemed to remain stationary as it hit every seventh wave with a tremendous shudder. We returned to the cabin where she went back to bed, fully clothed just in case, and woke up at six-thirty completely knackered.

Almost flat out of sterling currency I paid for our breakfasts, during which a conversation sprang up with an English couple who were emigrating to Southern Spain, with my plastic credit card and obtained some additional cash reserves in the process.

The ferry docked at Santander an hour later than scheduled due to the overnight storms, and berthed at ten-thirty. It was almost noon before we reached dry land, customs clearance was a formality, just a wave of our passports and we drove straight through and then intended to head on towards Burgos. We had serious difficulties finding our way out of the town. After twenty minutes I recognised, for the third time most of the buildings, as we had gone around in circles. At one point we took the wrong turning and this was realised after we had travelled about five hundred metres. There we successfully completed, only just, a fifteen point turn in the road and created a major traffic jam in which every car driver hooted their horns continually. With cheeky grins on our faces we waved them all goodbye and proceeded along quite a reasonable stretch of road to start off with but from the study of the map we knew that a steep hilly section would soon be encountered.

How steep hadn't been really appreciated, we went up and up and up and the road was very windy. At one stage I could see a heavy goods vehicle that laboured up the hill about one kilometre in front of us some way from the summit. From this my brain quickly calculated that even at our slowest speed, it travelling even more slowly due to the lower gear ratios, we would catch up just before the top was reached. This would mean the likelihood of a stop, as it would be impossible, or extremely dangerous to overtake. From where we were it looked to me that when we reached that point the incline could be in the order of one in two: extremely steep.

If that situation arose we would have two serious problems. One was that the caravan's brakes didn't work so we had to hold only on the fart boxes brakes, with the possibility that we would slide back into the vehicles that tailed back behind us. The other, of a certain clutch burn out as we attempted a hill climb restart. I didn't relish either so we continued with fingers and AC's legs crossed. Slowly but surely we gradually caught up with it even though our speed, in first gear, was below four kilometres an hour with the temperature gauge well into the red sector.

Almost at the summit on a blind bend to the right, the heavy goods vehicle flashed it's right indicator light and the driver with his arm out of the window waved to indicate that it was safe to overtake. An immediate decision had to be made. With nerves of steel, in a muck sweat really, perched a little higher in my seat, a brown pants job, I jammed the accelerator pedal to the floorboard as hard as I could and gave the engine full throttle. It screamed like a banshee as we pulled out and oh so slowly crawled past completely on the wrong side of the road. The rev counter was totally ignored as my eyes were fixed firmly at the road in front with a hope and a prayer that I would not see anything heading towards us on their right side of the road.

Nothing but nothing could describe my emotions as I drove around that bend and it seemed to take forever. Thankfully the driver in his elevated cab position had been able to see that the road in front was in fact clear. The incident left us badly shaken especially so soon after the previous evenings scare on the ferry. The map showed another hill, even higher than the one that we had just negotiated a few kilometres further on. It actually turned out to have a much more gradual incline and was almost a straight climb to the top. There was not a problem but even so the apprehension of it was pretty desperate.

We pulled into the next garage to fill up with petrol and the hill incident had obviously addled my brain as I drove out on the wrong side of the road and neither of us noticed until after we had travelled for way over two kilometres.

Burgos was navigated without incident and the road to Valladolid was excellent, almost up to motorway standards. We had planned to overnight at a caravan park at Tordesillae but found on arrival that it was closed. Shit, we hadn't bargained for this. It meant that the journey would have to continue south for another eighty-five kilometres to Salamanca in the fast approaching dusk.

Our driving had for obvious reasons, been intended to be in daylight. This leg of it was not to be. On this section we saw a most amazing traffic jam, that headed north. For no particular reason there was a stationary tailback of at least ten kilometres. Contrary to popular belief, we had not passed a single lay-by where one could rest or park since we had left Santander.

Upon arrival at the large city of Salamanca we found the world and his wife on walkabout, a typical Spanish tradition at that time of the early evening but an unfamiliar performance to us. Eventually a campsite was found and after the caravan was parked there was no way that I could get the electrics to work. Stuff it I thought, it could be left until the morning. We then staggered over to the hotel café for a meal and a couple of cool beers.

As I stood in the toilet with my percy pointed at the cracked white tiles I came over all queer. My legs swayed one way and my body the other and only just managed to reel back to our table where I was grateful to sit down. AC also experienced the same problem, it was most peculiar. Over our meal we concluded that it must be similar to seasickness without the vomit. We had been at sea for twenty-five hours, buffeted by the storms for almost twelve of them, and for the past seven been rocked and thumped as we towed the caravan. In this second phase of the overland journey we had covered four hundred kilometres in a little over six and a half hours.

The next day was grey and distinctly cool. After we had taken a lovely hot shower in the ablution block I tackled the electrical problem. It turned out that the battery connections were loose and this was easily corrected. It was a relief to find out that it was not a more serious problem.

We left the park at ten-thirty and had not paid as there was no one around to collect any money. The next stop was to refill with petrol but it seemed that I drove for a long time before we reached a service station. The sun gradually broke through the weak cloud layer and we entered Portugal at Vila Formosa, where there were no signs of a boarder point or any customs officials. The scenery changed dramatically over the next few kilometres. It became very hilly and rocky and we both had yet another nervous breakdown, in view of our recent past experiences, but were pleased to find that the climbs were in no way as severe as those encountered the day before. Ahead was a fantastic new road bridge, viaduct, over a steeply sided gorge to the East of Guarda but to our chagrin it was not yet opened. So we had to make a hairy descent to the bottom of the gorge, and an even more hairy ascent on the other side of a dry riverbed to climb out, onto a road which was little better and certainly no wider than a very roughly surfaced track.

We stopped for lunch, which was ordered in our best Portuguese, and despite our accents was completely understood as exactly what we had asked for was presented to us at the table. The owner was definitely perplexed, as we were obviously foreigners. Over coffees the next stage was discussed and we assumed that as the bridge had not been opened then the new road would also be closed. We would have to continue along the old one, which we found to be bloody bumpy and very patchy in places.

Onwards to the city of Castelo Branco, which began with a drive of about nineteen kilometres down hill with a sheer drop on our side of the road that appeared to be a thousand metres deep. It was really scary as the caravan bounced around continuously due to the poor road conditions. We by-passed Covilha which was just as well as this was perched seven hundred metres up on the side of a mountain. We re-filled with petrol in Fundao and then started a long slog uphill before the gradual descent into Soalheira. This stretch of road was the worst we had driven on so far. What gave us most cause for concern was that as well as being uneven and rough the verges had crumbled away and in some parts had completely disappeared. There was no margin for error as on either side was an avenue of very mature eucalyptus trees with massive trunks.

On the outskirts of the city an old wagon tooted at us. The driver pointed quite excitedly at the caravan so we had to stop and see what all the fuss was about and found that the small door to the battery compartment had swung wide open. The battery had fallen out and dangled from the two cables and it must have been like this for some time as the connections had almost parted. We had been very fortunate that he had noticed the problem. I then gave him a Thumbs up sign to acknowledge our eagle-eyed Good Samaritan and after the battery was replaced, ensured that the door was securely locked, drove on. There was no bypass and we got completely lost in the city centre, as AC had failed to realise that the N18 road to Lisbon was also the road to Portalegre, our next port of call. We screeched at each other that it wasn't "My fault", but this was no help at all as it did not sort out the situation. After I managed to change direction which needed more intricate manoeuvres, we were on our way again, along the by now all too familiar narrow bumpy roads with necks, shoulders and bums that ached from the constant buffeting. Once we had to stop at a level crossing to allow the daily freight train to Lisboa to plod on its weary way.

Portalegre was a fantastic town, built along a valley and into a hillside. We followed the signs to a caravan park, I did not believe it possible that anyone would consider constructing one carved into the side of a small mountain at an elevation of one thousand metres. It was a slow crawl up the hill in first gear, shades of that hill in Spain, I said to AC, "this must be a joke", we will reach the moon soon but eventually we came to a partially hidden sign "Caravan parking" on the right hand side of the road.

The entrance was steeper than the hill we had just climbed so a three-point turn procedure and other manipulations were necessary to get us in. We booked in at the reception and found a spot to park. It wasn't a particularly large site, more suited to tents, car trailers and campervans. I threw several wobblers as I unhitched and jacked up the caravan in the wrong sequence whilst AC sussed out and examined the sanitary arrangements. When the bad language had ceased and the air had finally cleared it was decided, with extreme hunger pangs, to drive back down to the nearest restaurant. On the way we admired the magnificent views over the valley on our right hand side. We promised ourselves to look more closely on foot in the morning. On our return to the caravan quite replete and almost relaxed we re-plotted our next route. We changed it slightly and decided to cover the distance to Sines on the West coast in one day, as it appeared to be a reasonable driving distance. After today's slog we had covered another three hundred and fifty kilometres but had taken seven hours.

We awoke to a cold and misty morning but enjoyed a leisurely breakfast and a cat lick wash. It was far too cold for a shower. I had to bodge the wing mirrors again as they had given continuous trouble all the way from Alcester. The problem was that the metallic paint had not fully dried out when they were first fitted. There was no point to attempt to admire the vista. You could hardly see your hands in front of your face never mind trying to gaze out over the valley.

The site was exited with great difficulty on an almost ninety degree steering lock and I nearly bottomed the caravan towing bar as we edged onto the hillside road. This was descended at a crawl in first gear due to the lack of the caravan brakes and the thick fog, which proceeded to get even denser as we entered the town.

"Turn left here," said AC. Left I queried? "Yes left," she said again and I ignored her and turned right, to have followed her instructions would have put us on a road back into Spain. She readily admits that she must have been in the back row, fast asleep, when navigational instincts were handed out.

Initially the road was much as before and the sun struggled to break through. At Estremos a lovely walled town, again on the top of a hill, we had to stop for more petrol. The next section of road was brilliant and was the best we had driven on since we had entered Portugal, there was even a two hundred metre stretch of dual carriageway and unlike Spain there were actually lay-bys. We could not benefit, as damn our luck, it was impossible to pick up any decent speed due to the extremely strong cross wind. It came as no surprise when we got totally lost again in the next town, Montemor-o-Novo. With many hand gestures and muttered incomprehensible Portuguese I spoke to one of the locals and asked where we could find the road to Faro. He pointed towards a narrow track and nodded his head furiously. We had little option but to follow this instruction and hope for the best.

Not only was it narrow but also unclassified as it was not shown on the map. After we had passed through a ford, with quite a deep fast flow of water in it, I murmured to AC that the likelihood of us ending up stuck in a farmyard was highly probable. We actually drove through one before we knew it, ducks, geese and chickens were scattered in all directions and we only just missed two huge black pigs. There was no choice other than to travel in a forward direction, as no amount of skilful manoeuvring would enable us to about turn. It was straight on or nothing.

Our luck held out and eventually we came upon a tee junction, where this track cum road, to our relief, joined the N2 Southbound out of the town to Faro.

It must have been due to the continuous nervous energy that we expended because we were always either peckish or felt starved. Breakfast had not been that substantial so we drove on to Alcacovas and were disappointed not to find a restaurant, or anything else for that matter, along the way. We continued and stopped at the first hostelry we came to in Torrao. The lunchtime dish of the day was a very rich goat stew and large portions were polished off in no time at all, together with lots of thick chunks of homemade bread, placed on side plates, which we used to mop up the lovely gunge. We also quaffed a couple of glasses of the locally produced red wine it was a really pleasant and hearty meal.

As we climbed back into the car we both felt fully sated for the first time in days. The next stop was intended to be Sines but after I had driven only a couple of kilometres it was necessary to make a forced stop as my bowels felt a little queasy. I had to dive rapidly into some roadside bushes and was abruptly taken short and extremely thankful that AC had packed the bog rolls.

At Ferreira do Alentejo we turned west towards Canhestros and Santiago do Cacem and I just about managed to squeeze past some major road works on a wing and a prayer. We then came across a large flock of unattended sheep, which charged towards us so I had to make an emergency stop. It was in the middle of the only decent patch of grazing land so we were surrounded and could not drive on for some twenty minutes, even an angry toot on the horn failed to disturb them.

The campsite at Sines was found very easily and we booked in and parked like well practised veterans. We then enjoyed a most welcome cup of coffee and chewed through a few fags. I then visited a small bar nearby for a few beers and to take the opportunity to obtain some small change so that we could take a hot shower in the communal ablution block. It cost twenty escudos, about nine pence, and after a general clean up both of us felt surprisingly low. AC actually had a touch of homesickness.

There was only one cure and that was a good slug of moonshine, a very high percentage alcoholic drink, distilled illegally, that I had brought back from Mo I Rana, a small town just below the Arctic Circle on the West coast of Norway when I was employed there I the mid-seventies. Originally there were three bottles, this one was the last. Thank goodness that our Leonard Cohen tapes had been left in one of the tea chests.

Along this arduous slog we had covered two hundred and eighty kilometres in five and a half hours and had effectively zigzagged across the whole of the country, from the Eastern frontier with Spain to the Atlantic West coast. As a result we had travelled one hundred and fifty kilometres south, what a hell of a trek!

Our past few days experience on the Portuguese roads coupled to a caravan had certainly left their marks. The overnight ferry shake up almost palled into insignificance. After another hot shower and then breakfast, we were as ready as we possibly could be for the final leg of the journey.

We called in at the reception kiosk to find that the little man was nowhere to be found. I couldn't be bothered to *fartarse* around so I climbed over the counter to rummage through an assortment of drawers and desks. It took about five minutes to find and pocket my passport and the amount of the site fee, more or less, was left on top of his diary. We then drove away in very drizzly weather with eager anticipation.

The road conditions worsened and we were unable to refuel in Cerca as the pumps were empty. There was no choice but flog on to the next petrol station, wherever that would be, and hoped that there was another one. Another spectacular bumpy and windy narrow road led us into Odeceixe over a grand viaduct. We had not seen hide nor hair of a branch of our bank and were pretty short of the readies so were only able to afford one thousand five hundred escudos, about six pounds, worth of petrol that was put in the tank by means of a hand pump, at the only garage there. This left us with only two hundred escudos, ninety pence, for any emergencies and we were still about forty kilometres short of our goal. The weather became even wetter and greyer as we approached Aljezur around more bends and over and down more hills. All the way we were continuously stuck behind heavily laden lorries, buses and even donkeys and carts with few or no places where we could safely consider an overtaking manoeuvre.

At long last we entered the outskirts of the village of Bensafrim and turned right onto the track, slowly drove along it and came to a halt under the two ent like cork oak trees. Two weary shattered and totally knackered travellers, with exceedingly sore arses and bruised backs had finally made it. That day's slog only covered one hundred kilometres and it had taken us two and a half hours.

The overall road journey from Redditch to Bensafrim, had in time behind the wheel, occupied twenty-seven hours, was a distance of one thousand five hundred kilometres at the break neck average speed of around fifty five kilometres an hour and had consumed one hundred pounds worth of fuel. There had been five night stop-overs including one at sea.

It was and will forever be the longest, hardest and biggest ball's aching slog one could ever envisage, never to be experienced again. We could not have chosen a more difficult route even if we had tried. You do not have to take my word for it all you have to do is just study closely any road map, at that time, of Spain and Portugal. How often we have rued that afternoon on the ferry when the decision was made. We should have travelled directly South through Spain to Sevilla and then headed due west to the Algarve. It would have been a much wiser option and a far, far easier journey.

After our limbs had been agonisingly stretched, tuna rolls were prepared for lunch, the tins of tuna having been purchased in England as part of our emergency provisions. A brief survey of the site was conducted and we found that it was very much the same as when we had last visited it. With the caravan unhitched it was possible to beetle off to Lagos. It was a new experience to drive the old fart box without it, no more tugs, thumps and a much smoother acceleration, what a difference. We did not know ourselves.

It came as a shock to find that the bank was closed and only then did this pair of intrepid jet-set international travellers realise that our watches were set one hour ahead of local time and had been ever since we had altered them as the ferry docked at Santander. We had a beer as we waited for it to open. When I presented a cheque for a cash withdrawal there was some degree of consternation and the manager was called over. Since the cheque had been issued, the bank had introduced a computerised system and none of my cheque numbers had been programmed into it. All of them were now noted to enable me to use them as and when and the cash handed over. I did take the opportunity to order some more, just in case!

It was necessary to shop for some provisions and I also brought a small padlock and hasp to enable us to secure the door to the waterproof part of the ruin.

Back at El Rancho it was time to make yet another decision, did we move the caravan to its permanent spot or leave it for later. A do we, or don't we situation? A suitable entry point was found to tow it closer to the ruin, also a good level area to park it reasonably adjacent. It was possible to drive in forwards or to reverse it in. There was a space between one side of the ruin and the track, which if it was towed in front ways would allow me to turn almost a full circle. Then it would be possible to unhitch and manually reverse it into the final position. We decided to go for broke and I drove very slowly onto the land and the first part of the operation was completed successfully. However as AC frantically waved her arms to give me signals she fell into a pot hole that neither of us had noticed and slightly ricked her ankle.

After the caravan was unhitched I pulled and AC, in a lot of pain, pushed and it was almost in position when I stumbled and fell, she, with her head down did not notice and almost managed to run me over, a real comic cuts exercise. Finally the task was completed and the front and rear jacks lowered onto the support blocks, that we had brought with us, to secure and stabilise it.

We had just started to sort out the contents of the car, when as if by magic, two of our neighbours descended on us, Alfonso 1 and 2 we named them. They had first been seen when we had had our picnic but other than the cursory *bom dia*, good morning, had never struck up any other conversation with either of them. After much *natterment* and advice on light, water and the location of the car we were not any the wiser and had not finished the sorting out exercise.

Alfonso 2 then brought his wife and introduced us to her. They actually lived in the village and farmed the neighbouring piece of land below another narrow track at the bottom of ours. Alfonso 1 was a bachelor and lived in a small tin clad shack on his land. We opened the caravan door and showed them that we had light and running hot water, at which they nodded sagely and with handshakes all round they pootled off and left us to contemplate over a fag what they had chuntered on about.

Now left in peace, we managed to clear quite a lot out of the car into the ruin. Having fixed the hasp for the padlock it could now be secured. Our stomachs craved nourishment so it was time to pop into the village for supper in the one and only restaurant.

Both of us ordered soup of the day and hake fillets with chips and a salad. This was washed down with a bottle of the house wine, all very good value for money. Sat at the next table was an English man who told us that he had lived in the locality for sixteen years. He was very much a bit of a gloom and doom merchant and put a damp squid on our aspirations. In his opinion it was all going down hill, to the dogs, there were too many changes that had taken place too rapidly. There was no way that he would consider starting a venture such as ours at this time. There were six Portuguese sat in one corner and he told us that they were telephone engineers from Lisbon, linesmen, and that he had had to wait seven years for his to be installed. It was not the first night's conversation or subject matter that we had expected.

After supper we called in at "Miserables" bar for a nightcap, brandy for me and a port for AC. Before we drove home, it was referred to as home already, we sussed out where the nearest community water taps were situated. From these we would be able to fill our two twenty-five litre plastic water containers to supply the caravan.

The car was left under the two cork oak trees, which would be its permanent parking location, and we staggered to our beds by torchlight and gladly crashed out for the first night on our land. It was a Thursday, the fifteenth of October nine eighty-seven.

Chapter Five

The rains lashed down but we managed to sleep like the proverbial logs and thankfully found when the caravan door was opened in the morning that we had not been washed away. It was still raining and by the look of the land had done so all through the night, what a start. This was our introduction to, and experience of, "The Real" Algarve rain, which we found to be quite awesome. Extreme weather like this had not been mentioned in the many holiday and villa rental brochures that we had studied intently when we formulated our income strategy and we readily appreciated why.

We had our first visitors far too early in the morning for me, it was only seven o'clock. They were two "Little" owls obviously agitated by our presence, which screeched, bowed and curtsied on the roof of the ruin only a few metres away.

Our first drink of the day had always been instant coffee with milk and no sugar for me, between puffs on at least one cigarette. Over this a list was prepared. The priority was to establish the base camp as quickly as possible. Both of us felt rather peckish so I went into the village to collect some water and some paposecos, small bread rolls, and failed on the latter as the Mini Mercado, store, had not yet opened. So I returned to the caravan and after a quick strip wash we unloaded all of the rest of the gear from the car and it was then time to pootle into Lagos for another coffee with a sticky cake and a shopping fix for general items and provisions.

Inside one of the numerous hardware stores, it could easily have been considered Aladdin's cave, everything was piled up sky high in rows that contained what appeared to be all one could require. Our main purchases included an *enchada*, a Portuguese hoe, a spade that looked more like a shovel, a broom and various other odds and sods including plastic pipes for the drains and new electric cables for the generator. I also required four crocodile clips to connect these from it to the battery, two red and two black. Only black were available which meant that great care would have to be taken to identify the positive and negative terminals when they were connected up to charge the battery from the twelve volt Direct Current side of the generator. A discount was requested and ten per cent given, as well as two cigarette lighters and a three metre steel tape measure.

As we piled it all into the car we realised that most were replacements for those items that had been sold off at all the car boot sales back in England. I went back into the store for a further mooch and ended up buying a pair of black – would have preferred green – Wellingtons together a few more basic requirements whilst AC meandered up the road to stock up on food supplies.

The next stop was to the downtown Lagos post office where we attempted to rent a Posta Restante facility with them. This was stymied as there was a twelve-month waiting list which was not being extended.

After lunch I changed into my scruffs and was just about ready to start proper work when who should turn up but Alfonso's 1 and 2. They immediately started to jabber on about electricity and water, specifically water from the well, which had been drawn off under some agreement with the previous owners for the past four years. The penny suddenly clicked; the black plastic pipe that ran down the land was Alfonso 2's. With a shrug of my shoulders I indicated that it was not a problem for us, it could remain and he could continue to have water. With more handshakes all round they beetled off and both looked very pleased.

The number one storage depot was unlocked and all the rubbish and clutter cleared out to make a bonfire on the concrete floor of the open-air back portion of the ruin. Our recent purchases and all of the things that had been transported in the car and caravan were neatly arranged in it as well as the dreaded "porta-potty" from the caravan. This was sited in one of the corners and was in full view when one entered through the door.

It was then necessary to fully commission the caravan. The generator was connected up to the battery and its motor started at the second pull on the rope. It was left to run for a period of three hours to give the battery a much needed charge. The external plastic pipes from the water containers were linked to the water pump and the gas cylinder piping attached to the cooker, fridge and heater. With fingers and legs crossed all switches were activated and would you believe it, everything was fully functional. AC in the meantime had sorted out and arranged all the internal storage cupboards and shelving. So our, hopefully, temporary home, was now habitable. All that remained was to link and bury all the outside plastic piping from the shower unit and sink to a drainage soak away.

During the latter part of our journey on our radio – a present from Don and Sandra – the world service news mentioned that strong hurricane winds had swept through Southern England. That would explain why on the occasions when we had attempted to make a telephone call to respective parents no connection was possible. We were in luck when we tried at the local Council office and were able to give them news of our safe arrival. My father had been discharged from hospital and was on a special diet, but from my mother's comments he continued to ignore it.

Some years earlier the electrical pylon engineers had left behind a spoil heap of gravel. This was a bonus as I was able to spread it all around the caravan and make an extremely useful hard standing pathway.

At the end of all these exercises I was the proud owner of several small, but very painful, Portuguese hand blisters. However that was a small price to pay, as our base was now one hundred per cent complete. My golfing partner used to say that I had hands like those of a small tart especially as I could not hold my clubs using an interlocking grip and that I would never be a good golfer. Needless to say, he had hands like large plates of meat.

The truth of the matter proved him so wrong. I started playing golf at the tender age of thirty at Tolladine Golf Club in Worcester and achieved my first hole in one on the par-three third. It was only my fifth game and I took an eight iron to an elevated green and became the proud owner of a one-holer tie. I was the runner up in the final of one of the club's major competitions I was six down after seven holes but only one down at the eighteenth, which was halved.

I joined Droitwich Golf Club in the early seventies, where I met up with my partner who was already a member, and soon got down to a single figure handicap. Our fourball played almost every Saturday morning with a tee off time at eight o'clock. In one round, after an overnight flight from Toronto, I scored my second hole in one. It was another par three with an elevated green so I never saw the ball drop into the hole on either occasion. A King one-holer tie was soon in my possession.

One year I won the captain's prize and in another the Raven Bowl, the latter after a play-off. This competition was for the previous twelve months medal winners and runners up. So my name is on the Honours board in the clubhouse alongside my partner who won that same competition twice. In another I won the prize for "closest to the hole", it was on the eighteenth and I was only two centimetres away from my third hole in one. In many games I won the money for the longest drive, not that I was the biggest hitter, but the most accurate as my ball almost always finished up on the fairway.

Before the weekend was over I had chiselled off the plaster/cement rendering on the East facing ruin wall: The *Vendese*, – for sale sign – that had been painted on this wall in bold black letters and was clearly visible to all and sundry who passed by along the track. Hopefully removing it would mean that any other potential buyers would be completely unaware that the land was technically still for sale.

I had also taken the opportunity to plumb the water level in the well using a ball of string and a weight. I measured the level to be five metres below the top of the wellhead and this was as near as dam it is to swearing, one and a half metres above ground level.

On examination of our list of things to be done we concluded that every item could be classed as top priority, indeed they all were, but a logical order was soon established. Number one was to obtain our residence permits: The entrance visa allowed us ninety days in which to submit an application, secondly contact the lawyer and thirdly meet up with the architect. Then everything else could be progressed on an as and when basis.

It was necessary to visit the British Consulate in Portimao to have AC's name changed to Collins in her passport and after paying the standard fee, collect the Registration Certificate, Afterwards on to the Residence offices to fill in the numerous standard forms and provide photocopies of passports, marriage and birth certificates. One of the questions on the application form was "Means of Living". For AC the answer was easy, dependant on husband but for me quite difficult. Unemployed with no work permit and no future employment prospects I had to think of something that would be readily accepted. Based on my Middle East experience where one had to fill in all of the sections on a form, I wrote just one word "Income". "No way, there is no way that would be accepted," said AC. I argued with her that it was adequate and basically true. Maybe not fully spelt out but it was an answer. Everything was signed and yet more lolly handed over and it was intimated that the permits would be available for collection in six to eight weeks time.

The rains absolutely teemed down on our return to Lagos to call in on the estate agent. It was a bit of a shock to find that they had sold the agency and their wine shop but had retained the restaurant. The new owner's son and his girlfriend were now in charge of the business. Our situation was outlined to them. "Join the club", they said and pointed out that there were many less expensive but still competent lawyers available and two names were recommended.

Eventually after we had failed on the telephone, we made a visit to the lawyer's office and to our surprise found him there, and not as was usual, in court. An appointment was made to see him in one week's time.

Before the hatches were battened down for the evening I took the opportunity to cut some stakes from the cork oak wood, these could be used to peg out the villa perimeter when time permitted. During this exercise the bow saw and first aid box were christened in five minutes flat; only a cut finger thank goodness.

The evening supper was courtesy of Alfonso 2 who had provided free-range eggs, cabbage, beans, onions, peppers, chillies, tangerines and enough garlic to last us for *yonks*. AC's lash up was swilled down with several glasses of red plonk bought in the village in a five-litre carafe at the princely price of thirty pence a litre.

It rained and rained with terrific thunderstorms all night and still slashed down the next morning. Despite this, the caravan remained secure on its mountings.

A heavy session of paperwork meant a trip to the village to post some letters at the local Council office. After a mega shop in the nearby store a visit to "miserables" was made for a coffee and a stickies and to our surprise he actually smiled.

Just after lunch a little old lady called in as we sat on the caravan steps with a cup of tea and a cigarette. She was quite agitated and it took us some time to realise that she was concerned about some straw stored in the ruin. It was hers and by an agreement with the original owners was allowed to keep it there. I was not to burn it! Obviously she had seen the smoke from my bonfire. To get to the gist of what she was trying to tell us our dictionary was produced. A really big booboo; it went down like a rat sandwich, how were we to know that she could neither read nor write?

Since our arrival there had been many problems in our understanding of the language and it was not difficult to comprehend why. In our self-taught lessons in England we had listened to tapes voicing a Lisbon, or Coimbra accent, the equivalent of BBC English. Here, our eardrums were being blasted by a strong countrified and coarse Algarvian one.

With all the rain the dry gully that divided the land had become a raging torrent that roared under the track through a concrete culvert. It smashed onto the stonewalling that had had to be constructed when the track was first converted from a rough path used mainly by goats and sheep several years earlier. Lots of flood water had washed down onto the land at the lowest section of the track and had caused considerable damage and some form of protection would have to be built in the future to prevent it happening again. The pond area behind the ruin was filled to overflowing and most of the agricultural land had become more than a little squidgy

There was an extremely large bramble bush that grew all over this stonewalling which I decided should be cleared away. I fought to hack my way into the centre to get at the main root system when my back went and this put paid to any further physical activities. "*Oh horlicks*" I thought what price that we could find a qualified osteopath locally? There was one in Lagos but we had difficulty in finding his office, There I sat, with great difficulty, at the top of the stairs on the second floor outside the door for over two hours and had almost seized up when a lady arrived and told us that the gentleman was in Lisbon for a week. I was in despair as there was no way that I could wait that long as the periods of immobility had become longer. There was a sports club nearby so we tried there without success but the owner recommended one in Carveiro about thirty-five kilometres east, the other side of Portimao. He rang and arranged an appointment for the next day and wrote down some directions.

The journey seemed to take forever although it was not that far away. AC drove and I sat on a cushion with my back propped up by another. It took us over one and a half hours to locate and enter the consulting rooms and it poured down with rain all the way. There were heavy traffic jams in Portimao followed by a long meandering diversion and at least a half hour search in Carveiro and surrounds, as the directions were not very clear at all, in fact most confusing.

It took, over a month before I was given the all clear, four gruelling sessions of being heavily pummelled and with my back contorted into various positions. Sometimes as I limped out of the treatment room I felt worse than when I had entered. It took just over an hour, in pouring rain, on each trip to get there. At the final session it was suggested, as he wrote out his invoices, that I should be able to claim the costs on our medical insurance.

The time for our appointment with the lawyer soon came around. He told us that one way to get over the problem was to form a company and that it should purchase the land. Would the authorities accept an "AC.DC.Enterprises" Lda, I thought? However yet another law had recently been passed and he was of the opinion that it would be possible to obtain the land once we had our residence permits. He would investigate further. Why had he not already done so we asked ourselves? We should have asked him. It was agreed to arrange the next meeting once they were in our possession.

On more mundane matters, AC's first attempt to empty the "porta-potty" was not as horrendous as expected, after it had taken me a couple of hours to bail out the hole that I had dug out three days previously.

It continued to rain on and off most days but with beautiful weather in between. Once, the generator had to be used protected by my golfing umbrella. What weird foreigners the locals who passed by must have thought. One of them travelled by at least twice daily on his red tractor and waved to us on every occasion. He stopped and came over one day. We called him Alfonso 3, and he chatted away ten to the dozen always with wild gesticulations. Over the course of many visits it transpired that he wanted to plough our land, but firstly he insisted that it would be necessary to spray with a chemical weed killer as it was infested with couch grass, or scutch, a troublesome weed due to its creeping rootstocks. Not an ideal time I thought in view of the weather conditions that prevailed and a rather heavy handed and drastic approach. It was not intended to farm totally organically, but even so, his suggestion did not appeal at all. It was left up in the air for review.

Another regular we called Ben Hur as he drove his donkey and cart at breakneck speed like a charioteer. He held the reins firmly in his left hand and with the whip in his right, which he waved madly at us, and always flashed a lopsided toothy grin in our direction. Once we had to drive the car swiftly off the track as he hurtled towards us not fully in control. All in all life was great, we had everything we needed, ate like pigs and drank like fish and could very easily have become recluses on our patch of God's earth. What more could one wish for? It certainly beat jet setting any day of the week!

One day in the Co-operative store we saw "Miserables" in there. He had not realised that we lived in Bensafrim but knew where the land was and the previous owners. He suggested that a membership card would prove advantageous as it granted discounts, and that he would be happy to sponsor my application to obtain one. His attitude was quite friendly, maybe because he wasn't stuck behind his bar. Perhaps we should re-christen him as M. We were dismayed to find that Alfonso 3 was hanging around on our return but before he could get into full flow it started to rain, real Algarve rain, so we were saved again.

AC had some good news to tell me that evening. Our weekly outgoings, extraordinary items excepted, were ridiculously low. They were much less than had been anticipated. That was a relief and in a rather buoyant mood, after supper, it was heads down for the almost nightly teach yourself Portuguese lessons. It was not really that difficult, just our inability to get it to stick in the grey matter.

In an effort to keep all the balls in the air we arranged to meet the architect, when a hefty cheque was handed over after receipt of all the drawings with the exception of the structural design, he had also forgotten the swimming pool plans and promised to deliver them in two weeks time.

The structural design included the steel reinforcement details for all the building columns, the ground beams in the foundations and all the interlocking roof beams. I had a sneaky suspicion that although he called himself an architect and could produce elaborate building layouts, he was not a qualified civil engineer and therefore had to subcontract this to someone else to prepare the designs. In the end this proved to be the case but as long as he was able to provide sufficient detailed information to submit to the Lagos Council, and obtain the planning approval and a license to build it was of no concern to us.

Having kick started the processes and put into motion the priority items on our list we could now turn our minds to things agricultural. Packets of seeds had already been bought and these should allow us to produce some early vegetables.

The opportunity was taken on one shopping trip to Lagos to explore and browse around the back streets and a fairly large bookshop was discovered. AC immediately thought great, a book fix, one of her pleasures, however it came as no surprise to find that most of the books were in Portuguese or Spanish with a small number in French. More by luck than judgement when the numerous shelves were examined two tomes were discovered. One volume was an illustrated dictionary, English-Portuguese and the other Portuguese-English. The first edition was in nineteen fifty-seven and these two were the forty first updated ones. It was a good find and although they were expensive by our standards they have been proven to be a sound investment. Feeling very chuffed with this all the other shelves were perused with eager anticipation.

In the Agricultural/Horticultural section a comprehensive manual written by an Italian author, was found. It had been repositioned incorrectly and was not easily visible. As I thumbed through it, even with our limited command of the Portuguese language, it was easy to see that it would fit our bill admirably, there were even nineteen pages devoted to the planting and production of asparagus, a positive gardening Bible. I had been on a bit of a downer over the last few weeks and my list of works to be done, written on a tatty bit of foolscap seemed never ending. AC surprised me when she rummaged along one shelve and handed over a small note-book. On its front and back cover there were lots of small coloured circles with a much larger yellow one in the centre. Each one contained two eyes and a mouth, which had a huge smiling grin. It was immediately referred to as DC's "Smiley" note book and all my outstanding jobs were eagerly written in.

The dictionaries would enable us to translate any word we would require from the manual as and when necessary, that was theory anyway! The amount of hours that were spent in the evenings just to complete a very small relevant section, even when we took it in turns, put us under an enormous strain and proved to be a lot more difficult than we ever could have imagined.

Our self-inflicted learning curve was about to begin with a vengeance. It started with the translation of the names of all the vegetables and fruit trees and then the awareness of their respective planting seasons. This latter information had been based on the then current practice in the central and Southern regions of Italy. It was therefore necessary to discreetly pick, as and when, Alfonso 1 and 2's brains in our almost daily conversations to find out if the local practices coincided or differed. In the majority of cases they tied in exactly much to our relief.

Both had, on different occasions, mentioned that all of the olive trees adjacent to the gully that ran down the land had been sadly neglected and needed some drastic pruning. One said cut all the branches down to the main trunk, the other indicated that one or two should be left. I had counted forty-three, some very mature with a girth at the base I could not get my arms around. With only a large axe and bow saw, certainly no chainsaw, I could foresee a lot of sweat and toil basically for nothing. I did not intend to go into the olive production business, maybe a small collection for our own olive oil requirements.

A soil testing kit had been brought with us and samples were taken at two locations to ascertain the levels of nitrogen, phosphate and potash. At the same time the pH value of the soil was checked. This would analyse the measure of acidity or alkalinity, a value of seven being neutral, higher would indicate alkalinity, lower acidity. Problems arose when we tried to use the syringe, I could not operate it at first, it seemed to stick. At the second attempt I sprayed AC from head to toe. Many samples were to have been tested but with the difficulties experienced it was decided to settle on just the initial two. It was obvious that we were not the stuff from which chemists and lab-boffins were made.

The results obtained did however show low to medium levels of Nitrogen, high Phosphate and high to medium levels of Potash with a pH of seven. This was very good news almost ideally suited to asparagus, which does not like excessively alkaline soils but thrives in Phosphate and Potash abundant ones.

It was time to start the preparation of our first vegetable plot. An area was selected close to the well and towards the gulley and in size was about equal to the two allotments we had tended in England. The broad beans would be sowed first so a section was dug over and cleared of weeds. After three days work we had not come across one single earthworm only long, orange with black stripes, centipedes were uncovered which quickly wriggled away. They were soon caught and chopped into small pieces with the spade. When the whole area was completed we still had not found any worms and this came as quite a surprise and we couldn't understand why. The required area for the asparagus seedbeds would have to be calculated and prepared as it was intended to sow them in the early spring, probably during March and April.

Years before we had both watched and enjoyed the television series *"The Good Life"*. To a certain extent we were playing the role of the agricultural half of its cast here, but much to AC's disappointment without the livestock. Many times we had talked about the role of Margo whose moods were more than often aggravated by Tom, who was able to change her happy and tranquil state of well being into one of aloofness and disdain to fellow human beings, with consummate ease. We referred to this situation as having a Margo day. AC had one when I found traces of vermin in the store, a chewed up screwdriver handle. Small ones were barely tolerable, large ones, no way!

Alfonso 1 called in to say that he knew a man who would cut down the olive trees and remove the wood free of charge, alternatively just cut them down and charge us. He also knew of a borehole man and would write to him. A long time ago he had drilled for a living and the old broken down rig was still on his land. It must have been designed in the nineteenth century, a small wonder that one successful drilling would have taken upwards of eight weeks or even more. We thanked him for his interest and assistance and told him that the question of the olive trees would be considered.

If one was prepared to shell out money then it appeared that anything would be possible to be carried out quickly. However our venture was not being pursued with a bottomless pocket, far from it. Outgoings had been budgeted quite tightly and there was not a lot of spare cash to throw around. The decision to proceed with asparagus seeds and not plant one-year-old crowns, was based purely on economics, a difference of a few thousand pounds, although the logistics of the importation and then the transplantation of several thousand crowns into their permanent beds was sure to boggle the mind, and this aspect, tended us to favour the use of seeds.

The technical section on asparagus in the manual was finally translated so the seedbed requirements could be ascertained. Based upon my father's comments on one acre of asparagus, it was decided that this should be, although very ambitious, our ultimate target. To plant one acre would require around nine thousand five hundred crowns. From the seed catalogue we found that a two hundred gramme packet should contain ten thousand seeds.

Seedbeds would have to be prepared and access provided so that they could be watered and weeded easily. A one metre square bed, with seeds spaced at fifteen centimetres apart would contain more or less fifty. Therefore two hundred beds would be required. The overall area would be twenty metres by ten plus the necessary access allowances. Simple mathematics had always been my forte, nothing too technical that could cause even the slightest brain damage. All this was based on the assumption of a one hundred per cent germination rate, not a very realistic probability, but the thought of having to prepare even more seed beds to cater for an unknown failure factor, phased us totally. The easy answer was to order another packet of seeds and if necessary sow them the following year.

There was more than enough work to be carried out in quite a short space of time anyway. The task now was to prepare an area roughly the size of a doubles tennis court, plus more for the extra vegetables. It was quite daunting and I really got my knickers in a twist at the thought of it.

A man walked down to the caravan, we had nicknamed him the "Vaca" man, cowman. His land was on the side of the hill north of the track and we had seen him, with a single bladed hand plough, being pulled by a team that consisted of a lead horse coupled to two huge cows, more akin to oxen. He proposed that if he could graze all his beasties on our land then he would provide us with a cartload of manure, with another one in a month's time. In a fit of madness we agreed, but some time later had second thoughts. Without supervision and with no electric fencing, how could he keep control of the animals movements to avoid them trampling all over our carefully prepared vegetable areas, It really was a stupid idea so when he had unloaded the contents from the cart he was given a more than sufficient amount of cash and told that the deal was off. We had thankfully chickened out of a difficult situation. With a shrug of his shoulders he drove away. On the many times our paths crossed afterwards, the usual exchanges were not as cordial as they should have been.

We often walked into the village and nearly always, outside a relatively new but small villa, stood an elderly woman invariably in the throes of her, weekly or daily, cold-water wash. She never failed to wave and gave us a big smile. We named her Nora Batty in view of her headscarf and just below the knee brightly coloured pop-socks. Her husband walked back from the village every day except Sunday with a small sack of sardines or some other type of fish clutched in his hand and we called Happy Harry, as he never smiled or even looked in our direction. His eyes were always kept firmly in front as he completely ignored our cheerful greetings.

Alfonso 3 called in for the umpteenth time, on a smaller tractor, which he wanted to sell to us. Were we interested? Did I what to drive it? He then continued to rabbit on about the weeds that should be sprayed and then ploughed in. I was more than a little pissed off by this time and suggested very politely, not in words, but with dexterous arm movements, that he should bugger off which he eventually did, but still with a smile on his face.

It had been decided, very foolishly as things turned out, to convert the well cistern into a secluded garden space with a wrought iron entrance gate. There would be a circular table with chairs surrounded by garden pot plants and the whole area would be covered with light green plastic netting. This would support some form of climbing or creeping plant to grow over it. The wall of the cistern therefore had to be modified. Firstly an opening had to be made for the gateway. This was a hammer and chisel operation not having a pneumatic drill or Kango hammer. About half way through this quite physical exercise the man who had started to plough the lower fields on the other side of the track stopped his work and came down to talk to us. It was the village postman and was probably moonlighting during his holiday period. He had seen us before, in the downtown Lagos post office, when we had called in there soon after our arrival. Mail was not delivered this far out from the village, not yet anyway so he advised us that the simplest method of collecting our post was to open a Posta Restante address at the local Council office in the village. That possibility had not occurred to us two thickheads and we thanked him profusely as he returned to his work.

Some weeks earlier whilst in M's bar – where else – a stocky fellow shuffled over to our table and in somewhat unstructured English introduced himself. He was a retired stonemason and had taught himself to paint, an artist, another budding Picasso I mused. When asked how he had learnt our language he replied that this had also been self-taught, but many further lessons, preferably with Nationals, were needed together with practice to make faster progress. He was aware of who we were and where we lived, by this time everybody in the whole village, and surrounding districts, must have known. An offer from him to provide help, advice and assistance on the land was made and in return he would require guidance and conversations in English. I was far from convinced that this was a situation that we wanted to get involved in but as it was our intention to try to integrate into the local community, I agreed in principle to give it a try.

That weekend we visited to the annual gypsy fair on the outskirts of Lagos, which we had seen being set up a few days earlier. It was much larger than we had anticipated with loads of stalls that sold everything from clothes and shoes to cooking pots and wheelbarrows, harnesses and saddles, to music tapes, the price of which indicated that they had been pirated. There were lots of places where one could get food and drink. Most offered freshly grilled octopus tentacles, candy floss, waffles and doughnuts and many of them sold sweets.

The whole place vibrated with energy and everyone appeared to be having a whale of a time. The fairground was in full swing and long queues had formed for tickets to see the circus matinee. We had seen a few moth eaten lions with half eaten bones in their cages, a woman scantily clad, with a boa-constrictor wound round her neck and a poor scraggy little monkey on a heavy chain, so decided to give it a miss. Not great animal lovers the horses, cows, sheep and goats that milled around the bullring, were given the same treatment. By the late afternoon it had become more than a little chilly as a very cold wind had sprung up.

Just before we left we succumbed and sampled a hot, freshly baked bread roll with a chorico, sausage in it. The stall had four large bread ovens that were domed roofed kilns, a little Mosque like. These were constantly in operation and it was an experience to witness the process. They had already been fired and heaps of wood were thrown in onto the still burning ashes of the previous cooking cycle and when a really good blaze had started the oven door was closed, After several minutes the door would be opened, the coals and ashes raked to one side and each bread dough that contained a sausage was placed on and slid in off a long handled wooden shovel onto the hearth. It only took a few moments before the cooked roll was removed and immediately sold, a prepaid ticket system was employed, piping hot and really delicious with an ice-cold beer to wash it down. It was one hell of a struggle to fight our way back to the car as we headed against the flow of the hordes coming in.

Back in the caravan we changed into some warmer clothes and had a cup of hot steamy Oxo to warm up our cockles. It was then on to M's bar where our intentions were to sample the grilled prawns and the deep-fried tiny birds. We had no luck at all, only bread rolls. Both of us were not amused. M and his wife were at the fair. A beer and a glass of red wine was ordered whilst we collected our thoughts and sat at a table next to a couple from the village who had brought with them a large sack of small crabs. These were cooked in the kitchen and when placed on their table with the bread rolls, they offered us one each and although small we found them very tasty. It was obvious that we enjoyed them so much that they asked for another plate and proceeded to pile on lots of crabs before it was handed over to us. We were a little embarrassed and thanked them very much. As soon as their plates had been emptied they left and the husband was forever afterwards known as the "Crab man".

After another couple of drinks M and his wife returned and we had a long chat before the bill was paid and we went over the road to the local restaurant, as by this stage we were more than a little peckish. The time was around nine o'clock and the place almost deserted, earlier there had been no spare tables. Boring old farts that we were we ordered our usual selection and a bottle of the house wine and later had no problems in crashing into the pit knackered, exhausted and more than a little squiffy.

More heavy rain overnight prevented any outdoor work, what a shame voiced I, glad of the opportunity to take a well-earned rest. Rain still bucketed down as we went into the village to arrange our Posta Restante address at the Council offices. This was a simple procedure and there was no charge. As we left we bumped into Picasso who almost forcibly dragged us to his downstairs gallery, which had a studio on the first floor. He had produced some impressive works with quite a distinct and slightly amateurish style. Many finished and half finished paintings were scattered about. I asked him the cost of a commission to paint a picture of our land with the old ruin on it and he replied cautiously that it would depend upon the size.

Despite the rains work progressed quite well on the land preparation, the hoe was used as a spade and was swung down from above the head and dug into the soil, it was very good for shoulder and chest muscle development. AC had sown the broad beans, some garlic and coriander. At least for the present they did not require any further water. A start was also made on olive tree pruning and a grand total of eight had been completed. The thick branches were cut up for logs and the twigs and leaves burnt on quite a large bonfire. I had always enjoyed tending them and as usual afterwards a good shower was necessary as I ended up looking like a coalminer who had just exited the pit shaft cage.

On one occasion on the journey into Lagos we were stopped by the police who asked me for the car documents, passport and driving licence. Of course these had all been left in the caravan, as was the usual practice in England to leave everything in the house. There we were given three days to produce them at a local police station. In Portugal it was obligatory to carry a means of identity and car documents with you at all times. The senior officer politely told me that I must return home and bring them back for inspection, which I did. He then proceeded to give us a mild bollocking and made some sarcastic remark about our next journey. Leave the car at home and just travel with all the papers he suggested.

In the main fish market we bought some lovely thick white succulent chunky steaks, they looked like cod but obviously were not. I grilled them for our supper and this turned out to be a major disaster, the longer the time they spent under the grill the more rubbery and tougher they became. The flesh refused to come off the main central bone and they finished up inedible. We found out later that it was conger eel and should have been boiled in lightly salted water. The flesh would then have remained moist and could then have been removed very easily.

Towards the end of November there was a hard ground frost first thing in the morning. It came as quite a shock to us as we had never dreamt that this could occur so far South in Europe. Maybe it would be necessary to review our strategy on vegetable production. With regard to the asparagus we did not consider it to pose a major problem. Most of the fields in the vale of Evesham were subject to heavy frosts in the early spring without any serious damage caused to the eagerly awaited new crop.

Whilst I continued with the olive pruning Picasso turned up with his sketch-pad. He and AC came over and he immediately criticised me on my efforts to date, I was not doing it properly, they had been cut down too short he implied. I muttered under my breath to AC, yet another bloody olive tree expert and carried on regardless.

He was taken to the spot where it was thought that the view of the land and the ruin should be painted and left there to his own devices. One point had been emphasised repeatedly, it was that we required to see his final sketches before he put paint to paper. He had not had time to draw a line when it started to pour down once again so all of his belongings and he were shoved unceremoniously into the back of the car and driven to M's bar for an English/Portuguese lesson and discussion. After about fifteen minutes into this he called over and introduced a man who had some land for sale. He was deaf and dumb. That was the end for me, it was a real struggle to cope with and understand Portuguese, never mind the thought of a crash course in sign language. We quickly excused ourselves and left the bar at a rapid rate of knots.

Chapter Six

It was time to put some serious thought into where the permanent asparagus beds should be situated. So on a walkabout under our umbrellas it was half decided to plant at the bottom of the arable section. The seed beds would definitely be next door to the second vegetable plot adjacent to the broad beans, which had already started to pop through. There were disadvantages in situating the permanent beds in this location. A more extensive irrigation system would be required and lots more leg work would be involved in the transfer of the trugs filled with spears to the villa to be cut and bundled. A final decision was therefore put on hold.

A definite agreement on what type of asparagus would be grown had been made; it would be the ever reliable "Connover's Colossal" variety. Lots of seed merchants' catalogues had been closely studied and a supplier selected. With Portugal now being a member of the EEC there would be no complications with regard to the importation of the seeds. Although one two hundred gramme packet would suffice Don was requested to place an order for two

I awoke to my first birthday on the land after yet another tempestuous night and made the usual cups of coffee. It was supposed to be a bit of a rest day but it was soon time for a mammoth shopping expedition in Lagos kitted out with our Wellingtons and brollies. On the off chance we continued on to Portimao and found that we were in luck, we were able to collect our residence permits. On the downside we were issued with the standard "A" type, valid for only twelve months. We had anticipated being given the far more beneficial EEC ones. Nevertheless it was now possible to contact our lawyer and an appointment was made for that evening, wonders would never cease

The discussions lasted one and a half hours and left us none the wiser, in fact completely flummoxed. Our views on the formation of a company were outlined; basically anti! He agreed with this stance even though it was not a long complicated process. There were no real tax advantages and in his opinion was not a practical answer. There then followed a long tirade that the matter should be pursued through the courts in Strasbourg to obtain an EEC permit. Even when we pointed out that it would prove costly and time consuming he still insisted that this action was by far the best solution. By now I had started to become more than a little suspicious of his motives. He then changed tack and was amazed to learn that we had not started the building construction and dug out of one of his filing cabinets a copy of the contract that he had registered and said that it protected us fully. If we built, then entitlement to the land was automatic, provided that it had been paid for. This statement seemed to us to be in total contradiction to the current law and could not be true. If in fact it was, why he had not told us to proceed on that basis before, and ignore all of the other crap. It did not make any sense to us at all. This diatribe sounded pretty dodgy, so unable to make an immediate decision we told him that we would consider our position.

After that session, the birthday celebrations never really got off the ground and into second gear. Supper was eaten in a nearby deserted restaurant and afterwards we experienced the highlights of M's bar, which had much more activity going on. There we enjoyed a plateful of home made stickies and a few glasses of port with him and his wife. The day ended when two clapped out, mentally exhausted persons, collapsed onto the bed a little after midnight.

Over the early morning cup of coffee, the previous night's discussions with the lawyer were reviewed. Both of us were convinced that he was trying to manoeuvre us into the position where we would finance his attempts to make a reputation for himself. He wanted a platform from which he could launch a legal argument in the higher courts. Win or lose it would be at our expense but we were too worldly wise to fall for it. As far as we were concerned that was not a solution that warranted any further consideration.

The overall pros and cons were examined after which we decided to go for it, land ownership or not, and build. We would also chase up through the Embassy in Lisbon the issue of E.E.C. permits. Out of the blue the architect arrived and handed over all of the drawings. Later on in the day I studied them and was sure that from the details there was more than a sufficient amount of information to invite building quotations.

Our permits however allowed us to make an application for Identification cards and to transfer our tourist account with the bank into a residence one. The latter was an easy peasy operation, only one form to be completed and signed and a photocopy of the cards taken and that was that as the account number was modified. The rains still hissed down as we called into the Council offices to enquire about our ID cards. Two standard application forms were produced for signature and the permit details taken down and we were told that in two days time the paperwork would be ready for collection. That was difficult to believe!

The rain continued for the rest of the day followed by another stormy night. In the morning it was clear that a lot of damage had occurred. Part of Alfonso 1's retaining wall had collapsed and had been swept down on to our land together with many cubic metres of his soil. At one point, midway along it, the level of the wall was about two and a half metres higher than our land. A few thousand litres of floodwater had again washed down from the track onto the land by the well and had caused a real mess. Some of the vegetable plot soil had literally been carried to a position thirty metres away. Had the caravan not been parked in an elevated position it would have been a modern Noah's ark. There was water everywhere and we had to drive through deep floods to get into Lagos where the car stalled twice. Lots of trees had been blown over and the orange orchard, just before the left turn to Sargacel, was submerged in water up to a depth of two metres.

Almost annually, reports from around the world had warned of the increasing problems of soil erosion due to the changing weather conditions. On the approach into Lagos at the top of the hill beyond Portelas that morning it was scary to see that the river Bensafrim, deep brown in colour had discharged millions of litres of water born top soil into the marina and thence on into the sea. It had spread out over a distance of more than one kilometre and some of that was ours. This was a first hand experience of the forces of nature.

This weather was really abysmal, what would hit us next? M, through his brother who had worked in Australia for a long time and spoke some English, offered us the use of his Quinta until the weather calmed down, and took us to see it. On a conducted tour it was seen to be fairly rustic and basic, although all the necessary facilities were available and there was a bath; which had a running hot water supply. He had wine-making facilities there and the finished product was sampled and found to be very moreish. There were very few chemical additives and that appealed to me. We thanked him for his kind offer but had to decline. It was difficult to explain that the total comforts and compactness of the caravan were more than adequate and acceptable for us even during this period of foul weather.

How naïve we were to expect to collect our ID cards so soon. The girl handed over two letters, which stated that we resided in Bensafrim. These had to be presented to the Tribunal in Lagos. On our visit to them we were issued with a list of all the necessary documents that would need to be presented before our ID's could be issued. Yet more paperwork to be chased but it did not prove to be too difficult and all were soon lodged with them.

With a view to possible or essential utility requirements I called in at the Lagos water department and was told that the local authority would prepare a quotation once the building licence to construct the villa had been issued. Installation would normally take around four to six weeks but they warned me, after they had checked on their map the location relative to the nearest supply line that it would be extremely expensive. It was not possible to order a telephone in Lagos, they only carried out services. It must be ordered in Portimao or I could ring number fourteen. The latter was not a sensible choice in view of my limited linguistic abilities, so it was off to Portimao. After the forms were completed to order the telephone the receptionist said, "that she could not accept a Posta Restante address, even at the Council offices in Bensafrim". A no way forward situation but not to be phased, I asked if the forms could be left there anyway, "yes" she said, "that would not be a problem"

We called into three shops that sold water pumps, petrol and electric ones but I could not find anything that met with my requirements.

The olive tree pruning was finally completed and inroads continued to be made into the clearance and preparation of the asparagus seeds beds. Extremely good progress when the awful weather conditions and the constant backwards and forwards visits for the necessary documentation were taken into account.

Time had also been found to catch up with all of the outstanding important paperwork. Two letters had been sent to Lisbon in relation to our permits, three to the UK, two requested private health insurance quotations to give us an idea of a possible forward expenditure, and one from AC to the BBC for their world service programmes. Whilst we were posting these, a letter was received from Don that told us that the asparagus seeds had been ordered and that he would forward them as soon as he had received them.

The building plans were examined most evenings, with electrical and plumbing requirements added in full detail, some architectural points were also slightly modified to suit our specific needs.

AC pointed out that the fireplace in the lounge was in the wrong position. As designed any open fire or log burning stove would effectively heat up the external wall on the terrace and only a small part of the internal wall to our bedroom. I had to agree, she was absolutely right. I had not spotted that, a grave oversight. She indicated that the ideal location should be in the corner exactly opposite. Any radiant heat would warm up one portion of our bedroom wall and the corridor between the lounge and the kitchen, and would be much more effective. It did not take the architect too long to modify the drawings.

We seemed to be making remarkable progress with everything until sod's law kicked in. There was one poxy day when we met the Bank Manager to request that they apply for an import licence for the funds to construct the villa. He then asked us if we had the actually title to the land? It was very embarrassing, "Yes, well, ere um, not exactly," we said, and made a rather lame excuse before we quickly backpedalled out of his office. The next stop was back to the Tribunal only to be told that our addresses on the letter from the Council and our permits did not match. They would forward all the papers to Lisbon with our Bensafrim address on but it was essential for us to get the address in the permits changed. What a shambolic situation. In Portimao this was quickly corrected in less than five minutes. When I enquired about the five year residence permits they informed me that they were only available for people who had work permits but that the circumstances could change early next year, maybe. Bureaucracy being the same all over the world, we were always impressed with the polite attitude and friendliness of the Portuguese. Rules were rules and regulations had to be adhered to.

During one afternoon session in M's bar, when we gave Picasso another lesson, he enquired as to when we intended to start building construction as he was very friendly with a builder who lived in the next village, they went to school together and he offered to introduce us to him. Nothing ventured nothing gained was our attitude so it was loosely arranged for us to be in the bar at the same time the following afternoon. We only had to wait five minutes until the builder arrived and we tabled the principle plans. Over a beer he said that he would like the opportunity to prepare a quotation and indicated that the price would be very competitive as he was familiar with the land, lived less than four kilometres away and had two other potential contracts along our track. With the drawings under his arm he invited us to his Christmas celebratory supper with his builders in M's bar the next Friday at six o'clock. We happily accepted but thought that it was a very early start to an evening meal and not really in typical Portuguese style, we had found that they normally ate rather late, similar to the Spanish tradition.

It would be our first experience of a full social occasion with Portuguese company en masse so it would be necessary for us to have even more intensive language swot up sessions over the next few days.

Back in the caravan we listened to the rain that beat noisily onto the double skinned roof and it was powwow time again. What the hell did we do next? A familiar dilemma for us, chain-smoking throughout the session we decided to speak with the lawyer early in the New Year. Advice had been offered that indicated that if an agricultural project/proposal was prepared and submitted to the appropriate Institute in Lisbon and accepted, then approval would be granted to purchase the land, register it and then proceed. This possibility would be fully explored at our meeting with the lawyer.

The evening with the builder and his men was an experience not to have missed. It had started, to our surprise on time, dead on six o'clock, twenty of us stuffed into grilled prawns as a starter accompanied with loads of home made bread, freshly baked that afternoon, and BBQ'd sausages on the side. Next we scoffed into chicken in a lovely gungy stew of peas, carrots, broad beans and spuds. M's wife was quite concerned that we would not appreciate Portuguese cuisine so to allay her misgivings we eagerly accepted the huge second helping that was offered. Little did we know that a third course would also be presented and this consisted of special pieces of chicken together with selected cuts from the loin of the recently slaughtered home reared pig, both meats having been grilled to perfection. If that was not enough, there were five rich puddings; again all homemade, which had to be sampled. Beer and M's red wine was available in abundance as was whisky brandy and coffee. The booze loosened everyone's tongues so that the general chatter did not become too stilted. Even so it was very *exhaustipating* for us. At the end we were all on Christian name terms and it was a fantastic and unique experience.

I was more than a little tiddly and should have stayed off the brandy, M and his wife, who had prepared all the food, were totally knackered, the host his family and workers had had to varying degrees more than sufficient. A taxi called to collect one of the men to take him to the airport as he was on his way to France to spend the holiday with his daughter, so we nicknamed him Frenchy. It was with many thanks and cheerio's all round as AC was left to navigate us home around midnight, a six hour thrash.

The builder had mentioned during the festivities, I only vaguely recollected it, that he was building a villa just outside the village for his family and when it was completed he would sell the one he lived in, in Barao de Sao Joao. He wanted to show it to us so that we could see the standard of his workmanship and for the right price he would be prepared to sell.

It was an extremely sluggish start to the day for me but I eventually got my act together. AC was fit and energetic and neither of us had a headache although she told me that I deserved one. We met the builder in M's bar, where much to AC's amazement I declined a beer, and were taken to the site. The entrance was up a steep dirt track, which was in an atrocious condition. Most tracks were, as a result of the recent bad weather. Ours was often like a river in flood and had deep channels cut into it by the fast flowing waters. It did not give a very good first impression and the villa was far from finished. It was a single story structure built up to the roof beam level and would consist of more or less four bedrooms, a dining and living room, a large kitchen and utility room, and three bathrooms, two en suite, Next to it was a large store which could be used as a garage. At that moment it was full of the usual builder's rubble.

It was situated on the top of a hill and commanded a lovely position with excellent views over the river valley, the village and surrounding countryside. The down side came when he told us the for sale price. Although we liked its location and general layout it was way outside our budget. A hand written quote to construct our villa and to demolish the ruin was handed to me, the price for the pool would follow. That gave us the feeling of even more gloom and doom. It was a situation where one could easily have taken the soft option and cut ones throat. The price was far too expensive to consider seriously.

M had also opened up the previous evening and had told me that he had a plot of land along our track for sale. It was a quarter the size of ours and he wanted fifty per cent more than we had forked out. During our next head banging session it was calculated, based on these figures, that the value of our land had in theory appreciated in the order of six hundred per cent, absolute madness, and without rhyme nor reason. Again we mused about what to do! Even if prices had increased by only a fraction of this then one possibility was to sell, make a good profit and buy the builders villa. This certainly appeared to be our favourite solution, However we were in a catch twenty two situation. The possibility of there being any Portuguese buyers we considered to be extremely remote. Any foreigners who were interested and had the dosh would find themselves in the same situation that we were trying to extricate ourselves out of. The prospects of selling it were practically zilch and on this point we fell into bed mentally knackered once again.

Work continued on the asparagus beds and as soon as any spare vegetable plots were ready. AC dived in and promptly filled them, with cabbage, leek, lettuce and pea seeds. The broad beans were now almost thirty centimetres tall with an excellent germination rate and a good crop was anticipated.

I had intended to swipe a couple of golf balls down the land but got side tracked when Picasso arrived. He was quick to point out that our sowing methods were all wrong, much different to their system and would not be successful. With a little smug look on his face he then cleared off to start his sketches for the painting. I felt deflated after this unwelcome criticism and decided to leave the golf ball bashing for another day. Late that afternoon a telegram was collected and it contained brilliant news. Don and Sandra had booked to come out in the New Year.

A table had been reserved for our Christmas lunch at the restaurant owned by the estate agents who had sold us the land. It meant that I would have to wear a tie for the first time since our arrival, and that the car would have to be spruced up for appearances sake.

Lots of cards and parcels were collected daily from the Council office and the caravan decorated, I even managed to find a holly bush and some mistletoe up in the hills and this was tastefully arranged, unfortunately there was not enough room for even a small tree. M and his wife invited us to their Christmas Eve celebrations in the apartment over the café bar to be held after midnight mass. This was delayed as the priest turned up late and this meant that the celebrations had to be put on hold. It was a splendid feast sat at a table that groaned under the weight of all the food and drinks. During the meal all the family, with exception of number one son who was at some rave up with his friends, exchanged presents. Stuffed to the eyeballs we eventually left them still in celebratory mood, at about two thirty in the morning.

We woke, understandably, very late to a beautiful bright sunny day with a cloudless sky. It was also warm enough to sit outside for our corpse-reviving coffees and cigarettes. Bulldozer Joe, the son of the sweet old lady that lived on the opposite side of the track came over, and brought with him two bottles of his home made wine. AC had christened him this as he continually drove around on his machine when he visited his mother, often three times a day. The name stuck even though AC had made a feminine mistake as he actually drove a JCB, not a bulldozer. He explained that it was necessary to clean out the water from the borehole and the well after heavy rains. The suspended solids had to be pumped out and then allow natural filtration to clean the water. This basically confirmed what Picasso had rabbited on about the day before. His mother was a lovely person who had worked on our land some twenty years earlier. We had given her permission to collect the acorns from the cork oaks to feed her pigs but she always called in to ask again every time she wanted more. Dossed down in one of her outbuildings was an amicable fellow we nicknamed Bobbly hat, for obvious reasons, he was not very tall but quite a snappy dresser and always walked around with a very old nobbly stick for a support.

After he left there was a mad scramble to have a major manicure and a tart up ourselves up session before we left for Lagos. Halfway there I asked AC if she had brought her diary with her as in it was a list of telephone numbers. She fumbled in her purse and could not find it so there was a quick about turn around back to the caravan to collect it. We could not find a credit phone that was functional so we asked if we could use the telephone in the restaurant and made brief calls to our families in England.

The restaurant was full but the only people that we knew were the owners. The champagne cocktails flowed continuously before we were led to our tables. The couple who were supposed to share our table had, cancelled at the last minute, so we ate in solitary splendour with the service second to none. Lunch consisted of smoked salmon and avocado mousse, seafood crepes, slices off the breast of a roast turkey with all the trimmings; the parsnips had been brought in from England. We finished with traditional Christmas pudding, mince pies coffee, After Eight mints and liqueurs.

When everything was almost at an end, and we were enjoying a cigarette, the owners came over to join us. They were obviously very interested to find out how much progress had been made in our venture. I jokingly told them that we could supply the parsnips next year, he replied that would be fine but he did not want to be deprived of his quick U.K. fix before Christmas for other goodies. They invited us back to their villa for more drinkey poos and a continuation of the festivities. Three other couples joined us including the chef and his wife. It was all good fun. I won my first game of snooker with ease and potted on more than one occasion over four balls in succession, once seven. This was classed as almost professional so no one else would accept a challenge. Other silly games and party pieces followed but all too soon it was time to leave. At this point I briefly mentioned the agricultural project/proposal route that we proposed taking to get the land into our names. They responded with a positive yes, it was the best solution in our situation!! The thought immediately crossed our minds why hadn't the knacker nuts of a lawyer – reputably the best in Lagos – proposed this option.

After we had surfaced late the next day the conclusion was rapidly reached that a Portuguese Christmas eve celebrations followed by a typical English Christmas Day, was only for those people with a solid gastronomical stamina and no gall bladder problems.

Picasso was given yet another lesson with Alfonso 2 present so it was an opportunity to discuss the efficiency of sprinkler irrigation systems, "Not in the Algarve" they said, totally anti in principal but reluctantly agreed that some crops could benefit. Plastic greenhouses were however a definite hit as were tunnel type cloches, after I had explained what they were.

Some time later, AC and I managed to roll the well paddle wheel, which was on its side half way down the land, up to the well head, but it was far too heavy for us to manoeuvre it into the operating position.

A full bundle of post was collected on the last day of the year. A cheque from the medical insurance company to cover the osteopath's bill, the *London Calling* magazine from the BBC, and letters from Lisbon, one saying that EEC permits would be issued in nineteen eighty-eight and the other spelt out that the Faro office was where we should discuss the problem, in Portuguese.

It was New Year's Eve; how should we celebrate? We had never found it very interesting and a bit of a damp squid in England so it was difficult to whip up any enthusiasm here. There was nothing going on in Lagos, everybody who had got their act together had booked into private parties, the rest of the bars were closed. M's bar closed at eleven o'clock and the local football club was open to members and families only. We lay in bed and struggled to stay awake as we listened to the radio and crashed out like lights the second after Big Ben's twelve o'clock chimes had stopped. It was another scintillating start to a new year.

On the first of January nineteen eighty-eight we had been on site for only eleven weeks and had coped with the worst weather conditions, so our neighbours had told us, for over twenty years. Vegetables had grown well and the asparagus seed bed preparation was on the way to completion. Tons of wood, it seemed like it anyway, had been cut laid and covered in a nice neat pile, the rest, not suitable for logs had been burnt. The whole agricultural side of our venture had been a resounding success despite the atrocious weather, something to feel really chuffed about. There had been lots of ups and downs on the land ownership front but there was no change in our circumstances. The formation of a company still did not appeal although discussions with another lawyer were to be arranged. We had totally ignored our present lawyer's advice for what it was worth and were keen on the option to pursue the agricultural project/proposal or obtain a five-year permit. The latter would only be available when our existing ones were renewed in November and there would still be problems to overcome.

The car was given its annual once over, oil, water, and battery checked out, spark plugs cleaned and their gaps set, the same with the distributor, cleaned and a spare set of points fitted. The tyres had the correct pressure and I decided that the air filter, after I had knocked most of the dust out of it did not need to be replaced.

Then we were off into the village, M's bar of course, it throbbed with energy and the building seemed to heave with pulsed excitement and was almost chock a block full. M managed, with some difficulty to arrange for us to sit at a table with two Portuguese couples. There was much back slapping, double cheek kissing, handshakes and happy New Year shouted to all around before we actually managed to sit down at the table.

Within five minutes of our arrival, who should turn up but, Picasso. Uncanny, he must have had eyes in his ass and everywhere else, we were never given any peace. We agreed on the spot that there was no chance of him being given a lesson that day. Just before we left he insisted that we should follow him on a guided tour of the village starting at the club.

This was situated down by the river and was very impressive, with a large dance/function room complete with a stage on the first floor. There was a bar and sports rooms, pool and table tennis areas downstairs. Outside there was another stage and a large dance floor, with a bar and BBQ cooking facilities, all of which were used extensively during the summer months. Off the downstairs bar corridor was a door that was normally locked but which was opened for us to reveal Trophies, hundreds of cups, medals etc. for football athletics, chess, in fact for any sport you could imagine. I was given the opportunity to become a member, AC would automatically be included as family, which I gladly accepted and was immediately enrolled as member number 351. As such, amongst other benefits I had opened up the opportunity to celebrate the next New Years Eve party there.

Over on the other side of the riverbank positions were pointed out where some of the older villagers still did hand washing. There was also a new crèche and a football pitch together with a large building, which housed some communal baths, toilets and changing rooms. Beyond this were some prefabricated type houses which had been erected for those people who had had their homes destroyed during the earthquake some seventeen years or so ago. It was quite an eye opener and gave us a further insight into the layout of the village and certainly expanded on what we had seen on our initial exploration when we had made the decision to buy the land. As we parted company he told us that he was going to Tavira his birthplace in the

Eastern Algarve and would we care to join him. I was more than a little bit iffy as it would rest on me to do the chauffeuring bit, but it would be a good experience to see a lot more of the country and it was agreed to pick him up at eight o'clock opposite the restaurant, by the bus stop.

Our first visitors arrived for a one week visit. They were collected at Faro airport where we had the strangest of feelings. We had always been there before with suitcases ready to depart for our holiday, it was therefore quite weird to have to wait for people who had travelled to see us.

Their suitcases were wheeled out and on top of them was an English garden fork and spade. Apparently Don had had to do his real "bolshy bit" to get them booked in at Birmingham airport as the check in girl had not been very co-operative. He had argued that if they had been stuffed into a golf bag then no one would have been any the wiser, she had had no answer to this so they were checked through.

We had booked them into the hotel Lagos and when they had checked in we found that their room was very spacious and well appointed. The next port of call was to our estate for a general inspection, look around and then it was time for all the goodies that they had brought with them to be unpacked, it was like Christmas all over again. The first two items to be produced were the packets of asparagus seeds quickly followed by numerous other presents, two full rounds of mature stilton cheese included. Then a quick visit to M's bar was fitted in for introductions to be made and after a few bevies we moved on to the restaurant on the hill on the left of the main road as one drove into Lagos for supper, The girls had a fish course and the boys had suckling pig, all with home made chips. There was an organist who played quite loudly and a television camera crew so we enjoyed one or two quick dances but the ambience was really quite flat as it was a large room and less than a quarter full.

We dropped them off back at the hotel where they gave us the Sunday papers, what a treat! These were avidly read in bed until well after midnight, very late for us under normal circumstances and a few more were bound to follow.

The next day we caught up on all the news and visited the nearby beaches at Praia da luz and then on to Porto do Mos. Here we had an enjoyable and typical Portuguese lunch. Grilled sardines with a salad and boiled potatoes. Every time a plate of sardines was finished, as if by magic, another one appeared.

The evening meal was in Lagos after we had both enjoyed the luxury of a long dunk in a bath of steaming hot water, we had forgotten how wonderful it was. Before we left them at around eleven thirty they had mentioned that they would like a couple of days to themselves to mooch around and explore. This suited us down to the ground as the Tavira trip had been arranged to start on the Wednesday.

Picasso was picked up on time and the journey started with no apparent problems. He wanted to travel via Loule. My map was rather a fairly small scale one and not really of any use and his sense of direction was pretty vague, even worse than AC's so we got lost a couple of times, but not desperately so, en route. Breakfast was taken in a small café where he produced some cold fritters. Our next stop was at a factory that produced cork products, it was a one man and his dog set up in a clapped out old building with more than antiquated equipment. The majority of the production was made by hand and the quality was very good indeed, but the output was severely limited. Even so he did manufacture the size and style of cork stopper that M needed to bottle his home produced wine and a job lot were bought for him.

We travelled on eastwards where we visited a large modern cork production factory. It contained up to date, state of the art manufacturing equipment, all made in Italy. A conducted tour was quickly laid on and I thoroughly enjoyed the technical discussions with the chief engineer who, thankfully for me, spoke very good English. Despite my initial feelings about the trip I had began to warm up to the whole "jolly". It was distinctly noticeable the further east we travelled that all the olive and other trees were much better looked after than in our locality. They were laid out like proper orchards, neat and orderly.

One of Picasso's cousins lived a few kilometres before Tavira. He owned a small plot, which was intensively cultivated and used a trickle irrigation system. This comprised basically flat plastic tubes with small holes made in them that allowed the water to be fed directly to the individual plants. On the wall of his lounge was hung the first of the many paintings our friend had produced, it was a little Lowryish. Nearby was a local co-operative that produced olive oil, Medronho, and fig brandy and we were taken for a tour around. The olives, after a thorough wash, were pulped and this mass was placed on matting in several layers, which were then loaded onto a platen in a hydraulic press. The vertical pistons on this descended and squeezed the virgin olive oil, the first pressing, out into stainless steel tubes, which fed to the bottling room. Additional pressings produced a reduced quality of oil. The Medronho, a potent drink, similar to Norwegian moonshine, was distilled from the fruit, formed from the flowers of the previous year, of the strawberry tree, Arbutus Unedo. This evergreen tree with neatly serrated leathery foliage grew wild over many parts of the Algarve. Brandy was not being produced at that time. It was another tour of considerable interest, especially for me, and the samples tasted were very moreish as well.

Lunch was taken in the centre of Tavira, a very interesting town going back to Roman times. It contained many churches, two of which we visited. More cousins were introduced and all of us had a good walkabout around the old part and we witnessed an auction at the fish market. Picasso and none of his cousins could understand one word of the proceedings. We didn't have a cat in hells chance to follow the action although it was obvious who the successful bidders were. We finished up at the art exhibition where some of Picasso's works were on display and for sale at prices that I thought were quite reasonable.

I did not relish the long drive home in the dark so it was decided to leave just before four o'clock. The rain started as we left the town and poured down for the whole of the journey home.

The last few days of Don and Sandra's visit flashed by and included one memorable session in M's bar. They could not get their heads around the fact that when we took some stilton and digestive biscuits in with us a paper tablecloth was laid down on which small side plates and knives and forks were set out. All we had to pay for was the numerous glasses of port that we polished off. It was a very different from the attitude in most of the cafes in England where there was often a cover charge. There was no way that could happen in a bar here.

We drove them to the airport and finally saw them through passport control and again felt strangely uncomfortable as we had travelled there and not caught a flight.

One day sat on the porta-potty as one did, for a call of nature, I happened to look up and to my horror saw a snake, well over a metre in length, half coiled around a timber roof beam. Snakes were my pet hate and I had never considered the possibility of finding one here. But one certainly was, almost right above my head.

They made me nervous, loathsome things I thought and this one made me shudder. The feeling must have been inherited from my mother, but certainly not to the same degree as hers as she could not bear to see them even on the television. My problem at that time was that it was difficult to tolerate the idea of it being around and me not able to know exactly where it was. I raised myself slowly off the potty and managed to reach a small sickle that had been hung on the wall. With this in my right hand I took an almighty swipe at the snakes head, with both feet off the ground, and missed completely. It didn't move but it's tongue still flicked in and out. I tried to remain calm and braced myself for another attempt and managed to decapitate it quite cleanly although the rest of the body writhed for what seemed to be a long time afterwards. I could have murdered a very stiff brandy but there was none available. I quickly pointed out to AC that picnics in the gullie's ox-bow glade, or anywhere else, were off indefinitely.

Alfonso 1 had just turned up and indicated that it was not poisonous but added that some varieties up in the hills were dangerous. He indicated that it was good to eat after being dried out in the sun, but when it was offered to him he declined so it was quickly buried.

There seemed little point in meeting up with our lawyer until such time as the trip to Faro had been made and the outcome of those discussions known. We did however meet two other lawyers and an accountant and finished up as usual going around in circles, with little or no sense of direction achieved.

We continued to keep an eye on the pound to escudo exchange rate, which fluctuated over quite a wide range. A meeting with our bank manager was organised to discuss the possibility of us being able to purchase escudos forward, at a fixed exchange rate, which would eliminate any future financial risk to ourselves. Unfortunately this proved not to be an option available to us but it was worth a try. We did however obtain the address of the Institute in Lisbon to which an agricultural project/ proposal should be submitted.

A snotty letter was received from the lawyer that gave us a right bollocking as we had not agreed to his suggestion to go through the courts and also requested another steep interim payment. This attitude got right up my nose and it was one of the first nails in his coffin that finally led to the decision to dispense with his services that we had not been very pleased with from day one.

One day Picasso arrived clutching some garlic bulbs. The cloves were planted in a small plot and when the new green tips had burst through a large sack of ashes was spread over them. It was intended that the eventual crop be divided equally between us. He, as a font of wisdom, mentioned that the new Bensafrim football pitch would be officially opened the next Saturday so I promised to meet him there and join in the festivities. He also told us that he had finished the painting. We both felt more than a little exasperated at this news as no opportunity had been given to view any sketches, not even the final one, so had no idea whatsoever of the composition and what it would look like. It was a bit late in day to object now but I pointed out to AC that it was his risk, if we did not think it was worth the money then we would not buy it!

The football pitch opening ceremony was typically low-key but the festivities certainly weren't and went on for quite a while. AC met up with us afterwards and we went to his studio to see the picture and found much to our surprise that it did look rather grand. We could both visualise it mounted on one of the lounge walls. I asked him to paint a date on it to the left of his signature, the actual day of our arrival on the land and then the question of the amount of commission was raised. I was not at all upset when it turned out to be higher than had been previously indicated when the topic had been first mooted. It was obvious to me that it would be and I had mentally made an allowance to cater for this situation. His figure was a lot less than I had anticipated. He was happy for it to stay there until such time as we had a wall to hang it on.

On our visit to Faro to try to sort out the problems to obtain a five year permit, we were notified that when our existing ones were renewed in November, provided that we could produce evidence to them that a business had been established, it was an automatic procedure. Here we go again was our immediate reaction, another merry go round.

We decided on our return home to call in on a removal company in Lagoa to find out what documents were needed to enable us to import our belongings. A fully detailed list was handed over but it was a somewhat unreal and premature exercise in view of our situation at that stage.

The information gathered in Faro was posted to the lawyer and an early meeting requested. At this, after more verbal diarrhoea about the merits of the court process, he re-emphasised that it was the only sure solution. He was then asked for his opinion on the submission of an agricultural project/proposal for consideration by the Institution in Lisbon and was surprised that this route had come to our attention and gave a very neutral response. Not completely against, certainly not in favour and that it should not be considered too seriously. It was obvious that we were going around in ever decreasing circles as again no progress had been made. So we were left for the umpteenth time to review all the angles and contact him afterwards. The question of the interim payment was deliberately avoided.

After this meeting I had completely lost trust in his handling of the situation and considered that he was certainly not acting in a professional manner. We then decided that at an appropriate time we would get shut of him and kick him into touch.

I seriously considered that the project route should at least be examined further and AC fully agreed. A letter was sent to the Institute, which requested information on the details that they required and for the appropriate application forms. We both felt much better and secure after this step had been taken, much to our surprise.

The roof of the store in the ruin had deteriorated and was now far from waterproof as a result of the inclement weather that continued and seemed to go on forever. It was then decided to construct a new one and the ideal position would be adjacent to the cistern. What bloody pillocks we had been! A principal factor when it had been decided to buy the land and farm it was that the cistern had been constructed in the optimum location for a gravity irrigation system. In our stupidity we had started to convert it into a dry garden area. This had to be speedily corrected, as when the drier weather arrived and all the asparagus seeds had been sown, a water storage container for distribution would be vital. The gateway that had been laboriously hacked out would have to be rebuilt and this could be achieved quite easily if I ensured that the rear wall of the new garden shed was made integral with that particular section of the cistern wall.

The cistern had dimensions of five metres wide and long and one deep, a volume of twenty-five cubic metres which equated to twenty five thousand litres. On the inside of one of the walls there had been constructed three piers and these had been capped with hand chiselled slightly sloping slabs. These had been used in the past to scrub and beat clothing on them prior to their being hung out or placed on top to dry. I had calculated that at three quarters capacity there would be more than sufficient water to meet our requirements.

The design of the pressure distribution system, pump and pipe sizes still had to be finalised and it was very important to make sure that both were compatible. I had prepared some preliminary layouts and calculations whilst in the flat, back in Redditch, but it required some investigation and experiments here to see if they would be feasible.

The quantities of store/garden shed materials were estimated, sourced and ordered, delivery charges were included in the prices, This, was to be the first of the never ending construction projects that would be carried out over many years.

I pegged out the base area of the garden shed and it was then possible to start on the foundation excavations. During this period I saw out of the corner of one eye, a fairly tall man, who shuffled down towards me from the two cork oak trees. He sported a fairly natty trilby, had a fag, which hung onto or was stuck to his bottom lip and wore a really battered crombie that had seen better days. Not quite the apparition one would have expected to see anywhere, never mind along a dirt track in the middle of nowhere. As he got closer I could hear him wheeze with a slight hoarse cough obviously caused by his exertions. He probably had emphysema and I guessed to be well into his eighties. Only a metre away he stopped and I could clearly see deep-set eyes that twinkled and were full of mischief in a craggy face with a sallow complexion and a grin that stretched from ear to ear.

That old crombie of his must have contained more hidden pockets than a magician's frock coat. From one, he produced a grubby tangerine, five dexterous hand movements later I was in possession of half a dozen from nowhere. He sat on the ground, spat out his fag and immediately lit up another one and indicated with different hand movement and a nod that a drink would not come amiss. The scorn on his face when I handed him a glass of water made me flinch. In a deeply rasped voice, much harsher than Darth Vader's it was made clear, after many efforts, that he preferred red wine. It was lucky that some was available and when handed a full glass he proceeded to down the contents in one continuous swallow, the second glass followed in the same way.

This was to be the first of many regular visits, sometimes twice a week by whispering death as we nicknamed him. The same ritual was performed on every occasion and always for a cadged fag. I reluctantly complied with this request as they were certainly not doing him any favours. It was some time later on his visits that we realised that he was the husband of the lady who had been so concerned about her straw in the ruin.

All the materials for the new garden shed were delivered and offloaded by the two cork oak trees about twenty metres from the construction site. It took no time to cast the foundations and all the concrete was hand mixed, as we did not have a machine. The cistern wall was repaired at the second attempt, the shuttering had slipped badly on the first, and it had proved to be a disaster. I continued to progress quite rapidly laying the bricks until Alfonso 1 appeared with two people, borehole men.

Neither of them were the same person who had tested some time ago. They told us that there was good quality water in the cork oak and eucalyptus wood and walked us to an outcrop of sandstone there. I was far from impressed with this location as it was at least eighty metres from the cistern. Another drawback was that the delivery pipe from the borehole head and the electrical supply line would have to be supported at a height of about two metres with a span of nearly seven, over the gully. It would be expensive, unsightly and not really practical.

I suggested that they tested by the two cork oaks. Unknown to them that same location that had been tested before and with a torn off olive branch in his hand the same result was obtained, he indicated that there was good water there. Both AC and I tested as we had done previously again with the same results, a positively strong quivering action. As they and their rig were working locally they told us that it would be possible to drill in two days time. A rapidly written down quotation that gave pipe sizes and the cost per metre depth was handed over. I asked that if the drill was dry, would there be any charge?

The three of them drifted away and murmured amongst themselves, then returned and answered no. I felt sure that some amount of commission was included in their price for our neighbour, and more than a little hustled. It seemed that I had been manoeuvred into a similar situation to that of the ploy of the Irish gang's technique where they always had a load of tarmac left over and with the immortal words that, "we could do yer drive tomorrow surr", were always said in a rather threatening manner. I told them that I needed some time to consider their proposals and they left after saying that the drilling rig would be moved off the site, to another district later that week.

Alfonso 1 stayed behind and asked if he could use the stones and boulders that we had collected to rebuild his collapsed wall? We apologised as they were intended for use when we built our future rockeries but indicated that he could have whatever he could salvage from the two old disused pigsties.

On our next visit to Lagos our Identity cards were collected. Two wheelbarrows, his and hers, were ordered from the co-operative, too late in the day to help in the garden sheds construction as most of the materials had already been humped to the site by hand, from the unloading area. AC had been our number one and only labourer. This had slowed progress to a certain extent as had the fact that other essential items such as a ladder, scaffolding and planking were not available. Bricks that had been laid up to eye level and above were done so with difficulty as we stood on temporary blocks, and this necessitated having to continuously step up and down. We both became extremely tired with not a lot to show after a really full hard days work. But before long all of the walls had been completed up to roof level and the eucalyptus poles to support it cast into position, the openings for the door had also been formed.

During this phase of the construction I came up with the idea that the caravan could be parked nearby. It would have to be moved anyway when the excavations for the Quinta were made. This new location would be ideal, next door to the garden shed, close to the top of the well, the tunnel and cistern where the irrigation equipment and piping would be installed. It would also be much nearer to the asparagus seed beds and the other vegetable areas.

Someone had purchased the French girls old farmhouse on the other side of the track and Alfonso 1 had been retained as a part-time gardener to look after it in their absence. Included in the sale was a knackered old rotavator and a diesel-engined tractor. He asked me if I could look at them and see if I could get them to work. If I was successful then we would be able to share in their use. It seemed like a good idea to me as either would be invaluable in our efforts. So an agreement was struck up on the spot with a handshake. The next day, full of confidence, the rotavator was given a partial strip down and a full service with what materials I had to hand. The gearbox was filled with clean oil and the clutch and throttle cables cleaned and greased. Six hours later, completely dejected, I returned to the caravan and left the machine as dead as a Dodo, not a spark of life in it.

Whilst I collected my membership card from the co-operative I bought a spark plug, air filter and a couple of litres of petrol. The previous day, Alfonso 1 had provide me with a can of kerosene as that was what he had found in the shed next to the rotavator and had assumed that it was the correct fuel. I had not been convinced as the machine was of English manufacture where petrol engines were normally supplied and fitted as standard.

A second session of tinkering on the engine produced the desired results. The new spark plug and filter were fitted, the carburettor stripped down and thoroughly cleaned, especially the float valve and fuel jet. With a full tank of petrol it coughed sluggishly and reluctantly into life at only the third pull on the starter rope. After a few seconds I closed the choke and the engine ticked over quite healthily, much to my surprise as it had not operated for a considerable period. We now had a part share in a piece of agricultural machinery which could revolutionise our lives and would certainly reduce the constant backaches and toil in any type of plot preparation. Not being that familiar with glow plugs and diesel engines I didn't even bother to look at the tractor.

Chapter Seven

Between showers, some heavy, others just drizzly but still enough to soak everything including us, all the remaining asparagus seed beds were completed. Alfonso 1 was not using the rotavator so it was trundled down to our patch and over a strenuous two-day period the whole of the seed bed area, previously hand dug, was prepared into an extremely fine tilth. The next stage was to form all the individual squares with ridged sides to retain the water after irrigation, and the various access pathways. This took us a fortnight and was carried out using our English rake and the Portuguese hoe, the first item that we had bought here. We had had an early introduction to this multi-use hand held implement. Initially we found it very difficult to use but after the handling technique was mastered it had proved itself very adaptable and invaluable in all methods of the land preparation.

Whilst the beds were prepared lots of peculiar looking insects were unearthed. They were identified as ralos by Alfonso 2 who nodded his head very gravely. He told us that they were a serious pest that was almost impossible to eradicate. Our dictionary referred to them as mole-crickets. They looked ugly, like a squat wrinkled prawn, and were of the cricket family with strong forelegs just like a mole. One booklet referred to them as singing crickets but I could not see this connection. They were vigorous insects that burrowed just below the ground and were very rarely seen on the surface and certainly had never been seen on our two allotment plots in Redditch. The horticultural manual had one section devoted to "Enemies of the Garden" in which an article on the ralo featured prominently. They would destroy completely any transplanted vegetables as they cut through the stems above the root just below the soil surface and could devastate newly planted seeds, especially those sown in drills. This was really bad news for us, just as we were about to set out on our asparagus venture. Their underground pathways could be clearly seen on the surface as the soil became slightly ridged and they would be most active and destructive in their reproductive period between April and June. When the weather was hot and with damp conditions, such as after irrigation, they would be at their most rampant. Thankfully however we found out that they could be controlled, although not totally, and the damage minimised. Immediately before sowing or transplanting a granulated or powdered compound that contained Aldrin, a chlorinated hydrocarbon, which acted as a contact insecticide, would have to be spread all over and lightly raked in. We therefore bought a five-kilo sack and were thus as prepared as we could be.

Through various contacts two other building contractors had been invited to submit a quotation and these were eagerly awaited.

On my building front all that was left to complete the garden shed was to fit the roof battens, supports and tiles the window and last but not least the timber jambs and a framed ledged and braced door complete with a padlock. There were sufficient battens and tiles in good condition on one part of the existing roof of the ruin to complete the store. To save a few bob these were removed and re-fixed. The window glass was easily sourced and did not present a problem but I decided not to get it cut until the frame was made and fitted. However to obtain the necessary timbers proved to be quite a difficult exercise. The amounts I required were miniscule in comparison to all the other local construction activities and no one seemed particularly interested in my order. Many of the builder's merchants did not even stock my required specifications.

A wood yard was eventually discovered in a nearby village. After I had discussed my sketches with the Patrao, or boss man, it was agreed that I could collect the prepared materials the next day. It only took a couple of days to knock-up and fit the window frame and hang a rather posh rustic looking slatted door into its frame. The cement and sand mix rendering to the outside walls was carried out on an as and when time was available basis and finally completed. The standard was not up to the satisfaction of Alfonso 1 who was decidedly unimpressed. As it was my first attempt I considered it perfectly adequate for the purpose and thought that a blind man would be glad to see it. A note was made in my "Smiley" book to do the inside walls at some date in the future. It was a low priority exercise.

There were many very early mornings during this period when we lay wide awake, many fags were chewed and endless cups of coffee drank as our minds raced at the thought of the enormity of the tasks to be achieved. The problem was that we were attempting to progress everything at the same time and failing dismally. With spring and then summer soon to be on us and the asparagus seeds to be sown in the not too distant future, the installation of a reliable and regular supply of water for irrigation was essential. To obtain the land and an affordable building quotation together with planning permission was still on going. The list, and with it, the associated problems seemed insurmountable and all of this resulted in our going through many Bah-Humbug sessions.

One day we returned from M's bar after liquid refreshments where Picasso had just bent our ears with his latest suggestion that we should rebuild the ruin to save a lot of money, the concept did not really appeal to us not at this stage of the proceedings, the poor old fart boxes engine died. I quickly disengaged gear and we luckily managed to freewheel off the main road and came to a halt at the beginning of the track. A brief examination under the bonnet revealed nothing untoward, everything appeared normal, but the engine was completely lifeless. As it was getting dark I decided to have a closer look the next day. We both trudged dejectedly back to the caravan and bemoaned the fact that a car problem was the last thing we needed now, or at any time.

It took three hours of grazed knuckles and greasy hands with my very limited array of tools to discover that the toothed timing belt to the overhead camshaft had split in two and was wrapped around the water pumps drive pulley. I then had the problem to find a replacement. Visits by bus to Lagos, Odiaxere and Chinicato proved fruitless, no one had an exact replacement, some were found as a very close match such as one tooth too many or one too few none of them suitable. Our friend Susie "Q" with whom we had spent our first Easter on campus at Exeter University, was to visit us soon so I telephoned her, gave her all the technical details and asked if she would contact a local Ford agent. Hopefully if successful she could bring a new one out with her.

Alfonso 1 advised us to move the car as there was the distinct possibility that we might find that various parts had disappeared if it stayed where we had left it for too long a period.

We decided that it would be in our best interest to do what he had suggested so we wearily traipsed along the track and started to push it towards home. The slight inclined from the main road to the crest of the dip before the land was much greater than it looked. After only seventy metres we had convinced ourselves that we were pushing it up Mount Everest. Three young lads on motorcycles passed us by and didn't stop even though they could clearly see our struggles. Another thirty metres and we were both totally bolloxed with blood temperatures at boiling point and hearts that pounded louder than a big base drum and we could go no further. We then had a stroke of good luck. A local farmer realised our predicament as he passed us by on his tractor and stopped, threw down a length of strong rope and towed the car with us inside to its parking spot under the two cork oaks and refused to accept anything but our grateful thanks.

Now that we had to rely on public transport there was no possibility that we could buy any major bulky items and get them back to base. It was decided, with little choice, to continue to clear new areas for vegetables and chase up the outstanding building quotations. Amazingly the two potential contractors delivered their quotes during the next three days.

When we examined them our stress levels shot up through the roof. We had nowhere near enough funds to place a contract. We thought that stress had been left behind, back in England, but sadly it appeared not, especially at this stage of our adventure. It was not supposed to be an adventure as such, but a real life successful operational activity.

With our limited budget, building quotations had been requested for high quality standards as opposed to the super duper luxurious top of the market ones. On the broad assumption, that like with like was being compared; an analysis of the three quotes was made. It soon became very apparent that we could arrive at a price per square metre simply by the division of the total price by the fixed area of construction. So three prices were calculated and were discovered to be within plus or minus five per cent of each other. To take the mean of the three would give us a reasonably accurate figure to work with.

Our original idea of a dual purpose building, live in one half and rent out the other was financially well out of range. The fall back position was to design a house that could cater for guests that would pay on a bed and breakfast basis. As we now knew the construction costs per square metre and our maximum budget figure we could prepare a design that would fit in with these requirements. A cut and stick exercise allowed us to present to the architect the details of a new house layout with a request for him to draw up a revised set of building plans as quickly as possible and present them to the local authorities for planning permission. It was just as well that the first set of designs had not been submitted. We asked him for three sets as soon as they were completed so we could invite revised quotations.

Susie "Q" arrived and had caught the train from Faro to Lagos, then the bus to Bensafrim and a stroll along the track to our pad. Amongst many surprise presents that she had brought was a genuine Ford spare part for the fart box. I spent a few hours in a vain attempt to remove an obstinate nut to fit the new belt without success. After all this wasted effort it suddenly dawned on me that should I be able to reassemble the bits and pieces, there was no way that I could sort out the timing to ensure that the engine cylinders fired in the correct sequence. The fart box would have to be towed to the nearest garage. We were told that this operation could only be carried out by a registered towing operator and they were very few and far apart.

Under the circumstances our friends visit – she slept on the single bed in the caravan – went without any major incidents and a thoroughly enjoyable time was spent as we caught up on old times.

M paid us a quick visit, which was very kind of him, to tell me that my co-operative membership was ready for collection. I took the opportunity to explain the problems with the car and he promised to speak to the owner of the garage that serviced his vehicle. The next day, at mid morning, two mechanics arrived, and after half an hour of grunting and groaning under the bonnet drove off for lunch. I said to AC and Susie "Q", "that's the last we shall see of them," but they returned after an hour. They asked for the owner's manual, to check the cylinder firing order, and in less than forty-five minutes the engine purred away as good as new. How lucky we had been that no serious damage had occurred, such as a broken camshaft. I was extremely impressed as they had brought a stroboscope to check everything out and even more impressed when they presented the bill, it was less than the equivalent of twenty-five pounds.

We had wheels again so we could do the tourist bit with our visitor and have the opportunity to eat out which made a nice change from only socialising in the caravan. Over one meal she talked about her intentions to write a book and after most of them, many hours were spent head bashing, soul searching, gazing into ones navel and even an attempt to reach the seventh level. The heavy discussions sometimes up to three o'clock in the mornings were so intensively psychological, not really my cup of tea and AC struggled to get to grips with most of it. It had been years since we had talked so earnestly about the meaning of life, we just got on with it. She had been through a hard time over the past few years and life had been so unkind to her so she had our deepest sympathies. Her holiday would continue in southern France but she would return to England via Portugal and she asked if she could call back in on us before this last stage of her journey, the answer was an obvious yes. We both sadly admitted after she had left how nice it was to relax in our little rut, even if it was a boring one.

My co-operative membership card was collected, it was number 2548, I had previously prepared an extensive list of requirements for the permanent irrigation system. Top priority was a pump and there were a few there that took my interest. All my calculations had been labouriously converted from the U.K. system of units; inches and gallons, to the metric one; centimetres and litres. Well that turned out to be a complete and utter waste of valuable time, every pipe, valve and tap, in fact anything to do with water that was in stock was in inches!

Back in England manufacturers still had difficulties coming to terms with metrication and here in southern Europe where it was the norm, I could only buy items sized in the English unit of measurement. I had quickly adjusted to the way that articles such as nails, timber, plastic sheeting wire netting etc. were sold by weight but I found this pipe work situation a rather weird experience. Not only that but I had to carry out a quick mental conversion backwards to get to the numbers I had thought of in the first place. I had expected to find that the fittings had been imported from England but to my surprise found that they had been manufactured and imported from Spain and Italy. How wrong my assumption had been.

The extent of the irrigation design had been based on the future requirements of the permanent asparagus beds and a *guestimate* of the areas that would be needed for other vegetable production. To serve this, two, one and a half inch pipes would be laid on the ground, from the bottom of the cistern, where an isolating valve would be fitted to allow maintenance and repair work to be carried out even with the cistern full of water, one to the top of the land and the other down to a point some seventy metres below it. Connected to this at ninety degrees would be as many as were necessary three quarter inch pipe laterals each one with its own isolating valve. The whole pipe work system would be able to deliver water by gravity directly from the cistern and under pressure from the pump.

This would need to have one and a half suction and delivery connections, which would be placed down the well tunnel. There was one in stock with a three-quarter horsepower engine, which was more than adequate. It had a twin fuel tank, one section for kerosene for the initial ignition procedure. It then had to be switched over to the petrol supply section once the motor had started. Starting was by means of a rope "pull start" which did not fill me with too much enthusiasm. Normally at least several pulls were necessary before there was even a hint that the engine had fired. They were always bloody difficult to start but I had no option, it was the best that they had and I had not seen anything more suitable elsewhere.

I asked for a demonstration and that was when the one-man band performance began. The engineer pulled and pulled on the rope but there was not a flicker of life from the engine. Very ominous I thought as a small audience gathered around to watch the antics. Fuel got through to the carburettor and then flooded onto the floor. He then stripped it off and replaced it with another one that he had taken from a different pump motor after it had been dismantled and checked over very thoroughly.

In these circumstances, and I had witnessed similar incidents on many occasions in the middle east, the longer the pantomime continued, the larger the audience grew. Most casual passers-by were inquisitive by nature and were attracted to small groups who had gathered around any unusual scenes of commotion. Instinctively they felt that they had to investigate and find out what was going on. This exhibition was no exception and the spare floor space was soon filled to capacity. Some three hours later, the engineer achieved complete success with the engine on full throttle as the unit bounced around all over the floor. He was so elated that he continued to start and stop it until I indicated that it was not a good practice as there was no water in the pump and that it had been constantly run in a dry condition. The pump together with all the pipe fittings, valves, jubilee clips and a small camping gas blow torch were finally crammed into the estate which left just enough room for the two of us to clamber in as well. I presented my membership card at the cash desk and a handsome introductory discount was obtained.

For the next three days I was in my element. The two main pipelines were laid and I fitted an eight metre length of pipe to the suction side of the pump and at its bottom installed a suction lift foot valve. This simple little device meant that after it was filled with water, which I did, up to the back of the pump then if there were no leaks it would remain in a primed condition ready to supply water at the pull of the rope. With gritted teeth, it was my least favourite place to be, but if I wanted water it had to be done. I struggled down the well tunnel with the pump and piping. Alfonso 2 had removed all of his equipment a month before at my request so I had a clear run at my installation.

I had been down twice before and felt distinctly uneasy and very nervous, in fact quite claustrophobic which was unusual for me. It was narrow with no room to swing a cat around. The floor where the pump was to be placed was almost three metres below the ground surface level and was accessed down seven steps, that had been hewn out of the sandstone, onto a short level section, Then I had to step down two rungs of a four stepped timber ladder which had obviously been hand made and was quite rickety. A more than generous opening had been cut into the well sidewall through which the pipe was fed down into the water. On the highest part of the tunnel roof half a dozen swallows or house martins had made nests, which seemed to have been used regularly. A ventilation shaft had been formed through the roof to enable exhaust fumes from the pump motor to escape.

There could have been but luckily there weren't, all sorts of creepy crawlies and nasties down there. It made me shudder to think about it. Much to my surprise when I peered through the opening, with the sunlight that beamed down the well shafts open top onto water that was crystal clear I thought that I could see small fishes that swam around, I blinked and did a double take, but they were still there. On the very bottom two black plastic buckets were submerged and lay on their sides, probably dropped by Alfonso 2 when he had had his pump down there. I cleared up the dross off the floor by the pump, left by him after his clearout which included two empty oil cans, some filthy old rags and a clapped out old spark plug and with heart felt relief got my head safely above ground level again. It had not taken many minutes but it had seemed like an eternity to me.

Now that the pump was in position it was necessary to return to it to connect the delivery pipeline. It was a very simple operation and took less than five minutes and I did not suffer any traumas when I descended the tunnel for the second time in the space of only a few hours. This pipe was then connected directly to the top of the cistern wall to allow water to be pumped into it. Any of the stored water could then supply the two main gravity pipelines. I then made two connections from this delivery line, one to each of the main lines, and fitted a non-return valve in each one and this allowed them to be pressurised.

This design had one slight drawback, to build up pressure in any line a stop valve needed to be fitted to restrict the supply in the delivery line to the cistern. That was only a ten-minute exercise but I now had to consider the possibility that the pump could be started with all the various valves in the closed position. If so there would be a rapid pressure build up and some connections would burst. The fitting of a pressure relief valve set to operate at a pre-determined level would prevent this from happening. None were available so I opted for a far simpler and cheaper solution. The stop valve in the delivery line would be cracked slightly open on a permanent basis. If maximum pressure was required then as long as one valve in the system was open then this one could be closed.

A check up on the efficiency of the foot valve showed that had been no water losses so that it was an all systems go situation but before I charged down the tunnel to fuel up the pump motor I decided to go over all my design layouts that evening and walk around the installation in the morning.

Susie "Q" turned up in the late afternoon and as there was not a lot in the cupboard we had supper in the village. She had met up with some friends in France and the whole holiday appeared to have done her the world of good as she was far more relaxed and less intense than she was those few days earlier. Her stay would only be for two days so I was determined to commission the pump before she left. It was just as well that I checked my designs as I had forgotten one thing. If the suction lift foot valve somehow stayed in the open position then all of contents of the cistern would flow back down into the well so another non-return valve in this delivery pipe had to be fitted.

At long last, after a final check, everything was ready to be tested, it only took four pulls on the rope to get the motor started and in less than five seconds we had water, cool sparklingly clear water which gushed into the cistern. AC cheered, Susie

"Q" squeaked with delight, I felt very relieved and there were big hugs all round. A bottle of good red wine was opened and I sipped from a large glass and smoked a cigarette as I walked round and checked out the pipe work. Slurping another one I was able to report there were only a few minor leaks, nothing at all serious. For both of us this was a major achievement, a trip down the tunnel followed by one or maybe a few more pulls on a piece of rope and we has access to one of the world's natural abundant resources. The lifeblood on which all of our future planned crop production would depend.

With the duel fuel system, once the motor had been started on kerosene and then switched to petrol it was essential to continue running until all of the petrol had been consumed as this would avoid a difficult start up problem when it was next used. That was the theory anyway. If it wasn't then there would be petrol left in the carburettor and not the more easily ignitable kerosene. It was possible to control the amount of water pumped and the time of the operation by the amount of petrol in its section of the tank. It was a rough and ready guide and a yardstick, which could be used to our advantage as long as the pump was reliable.

The simplicity and beauty about the whole system of piping away from the cistern was that if necessary it could, if required, grow like "Topsy" and be extended as and when required. The main pipes were relatively flexible but all the fittings, unions, tees, and elbows were formed in rigid plastic. Connections were made by gently warning up the end of the pipe with a blowtorch, which made it supple and expandable, this allowed the fitting to be inserted into it and as the pipe cooled, shrank onto it. I adopted a belt and bracers attitude and also secured the assembled joints with Jubilee clips. Flexible expansion joints were built into the main pipelines but even then, when the weather became really hot as in mid-summer, the rigid connectors occasionally cracked. This always happened at the most inconvenient times and a quick repair job was necessary after the isolating valve by the cistern was closed.

After many abortive trips to his office we finally caught up with the architect. He surprised us and handed over the new plans ninety per cent completed. We took these away after we had agreed to meet him the next week to discuss and finalise all of the details. On a closer examination his new designs met our requirements in full although we did pick up on a few minor points. Our next meeting resolved everything and he agreed to make the small modifications necessary and to submit all the documentation for approval. His opinion was that the process would normally take four weeks but that we should anticipate at least six. A small amount of his fee was withheld and we asked him to exert whatever pressure he could to speed things up,

A letter was collected from Lucie, which asked if she and one of the "Manchester Mob" from Fullwood could visit us and catch up on progress and all of our news. They would be our third visitors in less than half a year, it felt really nice to be the flavour of the month. We were sure that accommodation would be available in the village and made a mental note to talk to M or his wife, as and when, to find out all the details.

It was now time to get down the nitty-gritty and serious side of our business plans; to plant the asparagus seeds. All of the beds had been prepared and there was lots of water in the cistern. Two sturdy bamboo canes were cut down to a bed sized length and holes drilled in each at fifteen centimetres centres. These when presented crosswise on each bed indicated the position where the dibber had to be pushed in to make a hole into which a seed was to be dropped.

We opened one of the two packets that Don and Sandra had brought out with them. Each had cost one pound and ninety-nine pence so if it went through the slats it would not have cost us an arm and a leg. The seed packet was numbered Lot No 6145 and had been sealed on the twelfth of December nineteen hundred and eighty seven by Asmer Seeds Limited.

Neither of us had ever seen an asparagus seed before and we were very surprised to find that they were about the size of a pin head, shiny and jet black. We hadn't quite known what to expect but they immediately became our little black pearls. When the article on asparagus in the Horticultural manual had been translated, the section on seed preparation strongly recommended that they be soaked in water for at least five to six days before they were sown. We had in the past soaked parsley seeds for twenty-four hours before sowing on the allotments and fully understood the principle. It would not have crossed our minds to carry out this treatment on asparagus seeds but full advantage of the information had to be taken.

We really didn't have a clue as to how many beds a day could be filled with seeds. At five a day it would take at least five weeks and we had to prepare each one with the anti-ralo granules. As the operation would be carried out with both of us on hands and knees with our arses pointed at the heavens, with the hope in our minds that if there was anyone up there, they would look down favourably on us, five beds a day was set as an optimistic target. To set out the bamboo canes presented no problems and we arranged to sow with AC at the top of the bed and me at the bottom. I would push in the dibber and then both of us would drop in the seeds

A simple operation was anticipated but to our dismay we found that it was far from easy. The seeds being wet were terribly difficult to pick up between finger and thumb, one at a time, and once this had been accomplished it was an even bigger *buggers muddle* to release them into the hole, they just stuck there and defied gravity as they glistened in the sunlight. So it was back to the drawing board to sort out a solution. Small tweezers were tried and were very good at picking individual seeds up but they then still refused to drop into the hole. An attempt was made with the use of a drinking straw, again excellent at picking up but even with hearty puff through it failed to dislodge them. As a last resort they were drained through a sieve and partially dried on copious amounts of kitchen roll. We achieved a commendable degree of success although on the last beds some dibbed holes finished up with more than one or even two extra seeds in them as we had gone too far past caring whether perfection was achieved or not.

There was a builder's merchant's depot at the start of the track. On a looksee we saw that they stocked almost everything that the co-operative in Lagos did. No discount was offered but it was nearby and handy for our small-scale requirements. The first thing we bought was fifty-kilo sack of a ready mixed granular compound fertiliser. There were many different concoctions to choose from and as the land had not been worked for years we selected a high percentage balanced one. It was roughly three times stronger than what we had used on the allotments. The bulk contained fifteen per cent Nitrogen, and the same percentage of soluble Phosphoric acid and Potash. There were also minute quantities of other trace elements. On the sack was stamped 15:15:15, a ratio of 1:1:1 and it was a general fertiliser generally considered suitable for outdoor crops. It was applied as a top dressing, sprinkled by hand onto the seed beds immediately after the seeds had been sown. It was not raked in as it would burn the seeds on contact.

The beds were watered by gravity and we had done this as each was completed to assist in the germination and to ensure that the applied fertiliser worked more quickly. The level of the water in the cistern dropped quite rapidly so the pump was started to top it up. The engine coughed into life at the first pull but after only half an hour conked out. That meant a repeat of hate job number one and I went down the tunnel with a touch of the *collywobbles*. There appeared to be nothing obviously wrong but I stripped down the carburettor, cleaned and primed it with kerosene ready for the next operation. As I climbed back up the tunnel I was not amused and had a sense of foreboding that there would be a lot more problems to come.

The manual also stated that the germination period would be in the order of four to five weeks. We carried out a daily inspection and sure enough before we had finished the sowing exercise little seedlings had started to appear. They looked to all intents and purposes like miniature fir trees. During one inspection the alface man from across the track, whispering deaths neighbour, arrived with his wheelbarrow filled to the brim with very rich pig manure, a prized gift. His nickname was on account that he had brought some weeks earlier a couple of dozen lettuce plants, "alface" for us to plant out.

Despite the anti-ralo treatment all of the beds showed ample evidence of their activities when they were examined every morning after the previous evenings irrigation. There were small ridges up and down and to the left and right, in fact all over, the pathways included. Whether or not the seeds had been decimated remained to be seen. The irrigation of the carefully prepared beds was totally screwed up has they had been distorted and had sunk in many places. We were devastated as we looked at the damage to think, that after all those long hours of painstaking labour, it could all have been for nothing. We were on a hiding to nothing as the land had lain fallow for many years and we were dealing with a colony of ralos who had reproduced every one of them without any form of pesticide control. As an orange orchard some twenty odd years or more ago such treatment to the soil would not have been necessary.

I had managed to find the time, during the mega seed sowing session, a most welcome relief, to sort out the best route that the car and caravan would have to take when it was moved down to the garden shed location. After many treks backwards and forwards it was finally sussed out. There were a few humps and hollows that would need to be levelled out, also the standing area by the shed and the well needed a lot of work done to it.

With two visitors soon to descend on us it was thought that a small covered terrace connected to the shed would prove a useful adjunct to the caravan. We had often thought about the purchase of an awning but that was as far as it ever got. It would be an ideal place to sit and relax over a few nibbles and quaff some stiff G & T's and the endless cups of tea and coffee, whilst the many anticipated long and heavy discussions, between the four of us about our immediate and long term intentions would be raised.

Before we knew it Easter had arrived. Bulldozer Joe's mother walked over and gave us a special seasonal loaf, homemade in her bread oven, it was still warm and when AC cut it into slices to have with our lunch she was most surprised, So was I, as when she was half way through a slice she felt the knife had found something hard and solid and therefore paused. I told her to carry on and when the slice was completed we found that she had cut through a hard boiled goose egg still in its shell. More slicing discovered another three eggs. The loaf was glazed with aniseed and it was absolutely delicious and its contents came as a complete surprise.

When we went into M's café he introduced us to all of the relatives who lived in Lisbon and who had come down for the weekend. He then, surprisingly invited us up to his Quinta for a picnic lunch on the Easter Monday. It was up in the hills about two kilometres out of the village. We arrived around one o'clock to find all of the family there together with some friends from Portimao who had lived in Australia for many years and spoke some English. That was a tremendous help for us. It was a typical Portuguese gastronomic pig out. BBQ'd bacalhau, dried salted codfish, salads, broad beans and sausages also rissoles for starters washed down with his homemade red wine. Many helpings later there were lashings of kid stew and potatoes, which were followed by almond tart, fruit, prawns and Easter cake. We left about five o'clock and drove M and his wife back to the café only to be invited in for another bean feast. A cold beer washed down yet more prawns and nibbles followed by a few more glasses of red wine. We didn't leave until way past nine o'clock and went straight to bed, fully clothed, stuffed and more than a little woozy. Early on during the feast the opportunity was taken to discuss accommodation in the village for our visitors. They could recommend at least three and would arrange for us to visit each one.

The pump continued to give me problems so the pipes were disconnected and I humped it back up the tunnel. Oh how I cursed and swore. It did not take me long to discover that there was water in the engine crankcase so it was obvious that a bearing or seal was knackered. The engineer at the co-operative said "that it would have to be sent up to Lisboa to be stripped down but I could borrow another one in the meantime". This one had a two stroke engine so it was necessary to buy yet another fuel container. We were now in possession of nearly as many of them as they had in stock. Its installation was a real comic cuts operation. I went down the tunnel and when all of the pipes had been connected the pump started up without any problems at all and once again we had water. After five minutes the engine spluttered to a stop. By this time I was totally convinced that the whole procedure to extract water from this well was jinxed. After the pump was humped back out of the tunnel and fiddled around with for over an hour there was still not a flicker of life. Suddenly out of the inside of the pump section, from where I did not see, popped out the plastic top of a packet of chocolate smarties. There was nothing else that I could do other than to return back down the tunnel and repeat the pipe connection exercise.

By this time it was almost impossible to do anything. I paddled around with water up to my knees and some very agitated swallows returned, Having young in their nests they screeched high pitched alarm calls as they flew ever closer above my head. A quick inspection of the joints was carried out before the fuel was switched on and the starting rope pulled. At the second tug the engine fired and AC bellowed down the tunnel that we had water. There were big sighs of relief from the two of us, especially me, as I managed to drag myself up on hands and knees to the surface and gulp in some fresh air.

The eucalyptus poles that I had ordered to support the terrace roof netting were delivered and soon placed into position, all of the ground works having been previously prepared. What was left of the gravel that had been deposited close to the car parking area was moved and spread around to form the terrace floor and to give us a generous hard standing pathway for the caravan. We had decided on a close mesh dark green plastic netting for the roof to give us some protection and shade. This was collected when we shopped in Portimao. It was a two-person exercise to lift it into position and fix with staples. When the works were completed the whole area looked quite homely and very snug and cosy. The only thing that was missing was the caravan.

Despite the damage created by the ralos all of the asparagus seed beds had seedlings that had pushed through. Under these extreme circumstances the germination rate was extremely good with only a few blank spaces, despite our earlier horrendous misgivings. We could not believe our luck but on the downside, as well as the seedlings there was the inevitable proliferation of weeds, which would have to be eradicated on an ongoing basis. Irrigation and weed removal would take up more than a fair proportion of our daytime hours. With respect to the weeds, we had spotted on our last visit to the co-operative a well-known brand of weed killer on one of the shelves. A note was made as we thought that it could prove to be a useful backstop. The other areas that had been prepared contained spring onions, potatoes, peppers and sweet corn with a few rows of parsnips as an experiment and all were growing well. The earlier broad beans and peas had been harvested and eaten. We could never have had fresher vegetables, collected and into the pots in less than five minutes, even more quickly than those from the allotments, which were at least a five minute drive away from the flat.

It was the fourteenth anniversary of the twenty fifth of April revolution in Portugal when we decided to move the caravan, AC battened down everything in sight whilst I hitched up the car. The move went like clockwork and in less than fifteen minutes the caravan had been towed and manoeuvred into its new location. We were amazed at how smoothly the operation had gone. AC then sorted out the inside things and after the car was driven out of the way I reconnected all of the various pipes and rigged up the generator to give the battery a much needed booster charge.

The success was celebrated with a most welcome cool beer. It should have been champers, and the usual fag. Whilst we sat on the newly completed terrace we both felt quite smug and contented and firmly believed that after all of the hassles experienced so far, there was a glimmer of light at the end of a very long tunnel. It seemed so natural to have the caravan next to our first building project.

Just before we fell into the sack I popped outside for a quick jimmy riddle, which gave less wear and tear on the porta-potty and almost bumped into a figure who shuffled in the pitch blackness towards the caravan. I didn't know who was more surprised, him or me, but he shot off at quite a pace clearing the gulley with two massive strides. He must have been very familiar with this top portion of the land because his escape route took him to the only place where a crossing was possible. Despite my appeals in pidgeon Portuguese for him to stop and talk, he carried on and crashed through the brush in the cork oak wood. About ten minutes later a figure strolled nonchalantly down the track. From the snatched glimpse I had just had of him, I was sure that this was the same fellow. I walked up and intended to make some form of conversation with him but without looking over his shoulder, as I got closer, he set off like a streak of lightening so I never had the opportunity to see his face.

We eventually fell into bed and felt somewhat *discombobulated*. What also concerned us was that he may well have snooped around the caravan in its original location and we were blissfully unaware of it, which was a little scary.

The caravan's new position must have created quite a stir in the local community as the visits of the alface man and whispering death became more frequent, always laden with small gifts. It also stirred up my imagination, as I opened the curtains that first morning I had a flash of inspiration and suggested to AC that it would be a good idea to build the house in this location, not in place of the ruin. She was more than a little gob smacked and said "that this would mean a total rethink especially as the plans had only just been submitted" but thought the suggestion was worthy of further consideration.

I didn't and couldn't believe it when the temporary pump played up yet again. The engine started every time but there was no water. After many trips up and down the tunnel I discovered that the suction lift foot valve was stuck in the open position so there was no water in the suction pipe, the pump was just trying to move air. A new valve was fitted and the problem was resolved so we then had water by the bucketful, hopefully forever I prayed.

On a quick trip into the village we went to see the available bed and breakfast accommodation and settled on the second one we inspected. The bedrooms and bathroom were small and basic but spotlessly clean and would be more than suitable for our visitors. A load of post was collected and included a letter that contained an application form from the Institution in Lisboa.

A study of all of the papers quickly revealed that most of the bumph actually referred to the decree that prevented us from the purchase and legal ownership of the land but indicated that it was possible to get around it. We were both absolutely furious, what had our smarty-pants lawyer been playing at? When we had suggested that we follow up this approach he was distinctly lukewarm about it.

Photocopies of several documents that he had retained would need to be submitted if an application was to be presented. A really snotty letter was posted which stated that our requirement of his services would cease immediately and that we would telephone to arrange for a meeting with him at the earliest opportunity. We required and were desperate to collect all of the papers relating to our case and to settle the account, which we considered to be a lot of wasted money thrown down the drain. He was not available for discussion when we called in, we knew that he was there but we only saw his secretary. It was probably just as well as I would have had great difficulty in not putting my hands around, and giving them a squeeze to, the *sprawnsy eyed wassacks* throat. That was my special and most derogatory term for the little shit. The final cheque was handed over for the services which, as I had suspected, were expensive and far from helpful at the end of the day. We left with a receipt and all of the original documents, most of which had been handed to him in the first place, so we had got sweet sod all of fanny Adams for our money, just a long drawn out load of agro.

Irrigation of all of the crops was now almost a daily routine and the new asparagus seed beds needed to be watered at least twice, in the early morning and the late evening. The weed removal was also a continuous process and we decided to buy a container of concentrated liquid weed killer, from the co-operative, before it was all sold out.

I was really keen to get to grips with the project proposal but with visitors soon to arrive it had to be put on hold.

The dreaded duo, Lucie and our Fullwood friend, as we called them, were collected from the airport in the late afternoon, taken to settle in their digs and after they had unpacked, we all went out for a meal in the village restaurant. It rained during supper and we suffered the inevitable power cut and ate surrounded by gas lamps. We took them round to the lodgings with the use of a torch as one was always kept in the car for such an emergency. They got to bed with great difficulty as it was an unfamiliar house and they had to use candles. It was not a very auspicious start to their holiday as it gave them a somewhat bleak impression.

We caught up with them the next morning when we spotted them as they wandered around a small back street in the village and both looked a little dazed. The digs were okay but there had been no breakfast and no hot water, so we went round to try to sort the problems out. The breakfast issue was due to a misunderstanding; we had thought that they would have it in M's café, which we had pointed out to them as we took them to the digs after supper. The lack of hot water was because they had not let it flow through the tap for a sufficient length of time. The systems installed here were very similar to the old "Ascot" gas heated ones in the U.K. hot water was not instant.

We had lunch on the new terrace and they were amazed at how much land we had though both of them thought the locality was a little remote. We then took the opportunity to do the tourist bit and ferried them around here there and almost everywhere. A picnic under the huge eucalyptus trees at Odelouca, was very enjoyable and they loved the tour of the old walled castle In Silves. Every evening a different restaurant was tried and we certainly didn't stint ourselves. Local beaches were visited as was Alvor and Praia da Rocha and two shopping expeditions were made to Portimao. There was only one difficulty, when asked what they wanted to do, one said, "I don't mind," and the other said, "I don't know" and these continuous responses made us very frustrated.

The digs situation did not work terribly well so the bill was paid and we booked them into a two bedroom apartment in the complex in Praia da Luz. It was the very same one that we had stayed at on our first holiday here and where we had met our Fullwood friend. It meant a lot more travelling for us but it was a very good move, there were a lot of English people around and plenty to do. Our friend was familiar with the whole area so they settled down very easily and became less agitated. All in all they had a lovely time, as did we, but the time passed oh so quickly and as they were shopaholics it was a struggle to get their suitcases to close. All too soon we were off on the road to Faro and the check in at the airport was the quickest on record. We were sorry to see them go and it was tears all round but we were relieved in a way as we could now get back to normal and crack on.

Chapter Eight

We made a more detailed investigation of the documents from the Institute, especially the instructions that were to be followed when a project proposal was to be submitted. Of particular interest was that it could be in the support of a business enterprise as a, "Sole Trader". This would be ideally suited to my requirements.

Vague references had been made about this route by various contacts over the months since our arrival, especially the estate agent. They all considered it to be the only way to gain title to the land. During these conversations the majority of them had recommended that the services of a Portuguese Agricultural Engineer would be beneficial. In my engineering career, before I transferred into one that had a sales orientation, I was employed as a project proposals engineer so I was able to convince AC that there was no one more qualified than myself to prepare this one, and as it was for us, the motivation was far greater by more than a few hundred per cent.

In the mid to late seventies I had prepared a massive proposal, which my employer had submitted; it was, "The Russian Timber Project" with a budgeted cost in excess of two hundred million pounds. It included heavy machinery for large scale logging operations, saw mills, plywood factories, chipboard making facilities and also a pulp and paper mill. Despite frequent visits to Moscow and the deep interior for negotiations, no contract was ever awarded. On my initial visit with the temperature down to minus thirty-six degrees I bought a fur hat with two flaps that could be pulled down over the ears in a dollar shop at a cost of only four. It proved to be essential on my daily exercise walks from the Rossia hotel across the Red Square past the tomb of Lenin, with its endless queues, to St Basil's Cathedral and back. These walks certainly worked up a thirst for my favourite tipple, in the hotels dollar bar; large vodkas with fresh orange juice and great care had to be taken after a few had been savoured later on in the evening, to be somewhat aloof when the ladies of the night magically appeared dressed in what little finery they had decided to wear. Some were quite brazen, obviously desperate to make a business arrangement, and one young and amply built very attractive girl had set her sights on me. She made it clear with subtly displayed leg movements that she wasn't wearing any knickers. Any thoughts or ideas on "foreplay" would certainly not be included in her fee. I had seen similar scenarios in most of the countries that I had visited and had decided never to fall into this tempting trap especially here and get involved in some potential blackmail or diplomatic incident. As the evening drew on she became quite agitated at my lack of response and even opened her legs wide apart and made very suggestive movements with her hips, all to no avail as far as I was concerned. When I left the bar, quite late in the evening, she looked over in my direction, shrugged her shoulders in despair and appeared to be extremely disappointed. She must have plied her trade in other bars as I never saw her again on any of my subsequent visits.

That long drawn out flash, with her legs wide apart, reminded me of the morning when I cheerfully had my virginity snaffled away. It was during my morning paper round delivery before going to school. A house in a very upmarket road was occupied by a vivacious dark haired divorcee in her late twenties and she always opened the door, to reveal a very attractive figure in skimpy nightdresses, before I could drop the papers and magazines through the letter box and made it obvious what she had in mind. It was very tempting so one day I started the deliveries early and left her road and house to the last. As she opened the door, with her papers in my hand, I nodded and was pulled in with some force and the door quickly slammed shut. What followed was awesomely frantic and savage, but also physically very exciting. She was insatiable and pleaded with me to call in on my afternoon round which I was quite happy to do and experience similar pleasures again. These frenetic sessions continued for over a month until one morning the newsagent told me that the papers had been cancelled as the lady had left and I never saw her again.

Once with an exit visa already stamped in my passport at Moscow airport I was prevented from entering the departure lounge and led to one side into a small room that appeared to be rather like a doctor's surgery. There, without so much as a word, I was subjected to a full – a really full – body search by a male nurse. It was a very embarrassing and painful experience.

One major success was the preparation and submission of a proposal to build and equip three multi thousand cubic metre cold stores, at a cost of twenty one million pounds, in Iraq. Not only did I prepare the proposal but also held the subsequent negotiations in Baghdad. I commuted there and travelled backwards and forwards some fifteen times over a seven-month period. The final discussions were, as always, on the price. All the technical details had been thrashed out and agreed with a team of engineers, the Technical Committee. I had yet to meet the President of the Organisation.

If any price reductions, discounts were to be made, then it would be just before the handshake with this person. The Committee were insistent that a reduction was essential; they had to be seen to have obtained their best possible deal. I decided to only give a nominal discount and keep some in reserve up my sleeve and told them that this was the final offer and that I could go no further. There was a lot of excited chatter between them but as the conversation was now in Arabic I couldn't understand a word. From the looks they gave me it seemed that their decision would not be a favourable one. Having told them that it was my final offer I had closed the back door. I had no way out. It was a terribly disappointment at this stage of the proceedings, so close to success. I stood up and closed my briefcase, walked over to their long table and shook each member firmly by the hand, with a forced smile on my face, then abruptly turned around and without another word opened the door and swiftly left the office with my shoulders erect. If I had had a tail it would have between my legs.

As was usual the engineer's department was situated on the fifth floor and again the lifts failed to operate. I dashed down the stairs desperate for a breath of fresh air and stormed across the car park. As I walked through the gates onto the main road one of the Committee members caught up with me, he shook my hand and said, "come back, please come back, the contract is yours". My legs almost collapsed under me at this turn of events as it dawned on me that we had won. Over the next few days the contract conditions were drawn up and the price only inserted after a handshake with the President, who accepted my absolute final discount.

With our project here in Portugal it was as if the clock had been turned back after all of those years. I was in proposal preparation mode once again, but this time it was for us! AC did most of the leg work and finally collected all of the photocopies that had to be submitted whilst I sat on my butt and drafted, and then finalised the necessary annexes for a, "Proposed Market Garden and Horticultural Project". There were four of them, the proposal, soil and seed test results, preliminary designs and sketches of a permanent sprinkler irrigation layout and a budget costing together with the short term feasibility study

As a sole trader the object would to import the necessary funds from the U.K. for the purchase of the land, construction of a farmhouse and the development of the enterprise, which would specialise in the production of good quality crops for sale in the Algarve. The second phase would be to try and open markets in Lisboa and the third would be to take advantage of any long-term export potential prospects. AC considered the second phase optimistic and the long term definitely well over the top. I reasoned that it was better to be over ambitious with the distinct possibility that it could all fail dismally, than under ambitious with the likelihood of the same result. We agreed therefore not to make any changes. The whole thing was quickly knocked into shape and included details of our professional backgrounds together with a section angled towards our horticultural experiences. This short synopsis included my assistance on my father's market gardens, the success of our allotments and AC's knowledge and culinary and medicinal herbs.

We both considered that this aspect was the weakest part of the overall project proposal but still thought that it should be included. It was factual and no one could accuse us of untrue exaggerations. Soon it was completed to our satisfaction and I was keen to get it submitted. AC was not so sure that this would be the ideal approach. The contents were very professionally prepared, beyond any doubt, but the presentation left a lot to be desired. It was hand written, in English, and in a simple clip type of file. If a glimmer of interest ensued we both agreed that we would pay someone for a typed translation, which would then be submitted in a more substantial ring type binder.

Within only ten days of postage a response was received which gave the Institutes approval in principle and we could not contain our excitement. Once they were in possession of our cheque to cover all their administration and other associated costs, a final decision would be made within fourteen days. On reading this I hugged AC firmly and told her that it was a formality, but she was not so sure. We sent them a cheque by return, and lo and behold, exactly two weeks later the official approval document together with all of the forms that supported it, duly stamped, was in our hands. We were in business at long last and could now make rapid progress. The cost was less than a quarter of the lawyer's fee and had only taken three weeks.

Now that we had permission to import the money we dithered about the exchange rate. When we had originally paid for the land, without being able to own it, the rate was lousy. It had moved against us after the down payment had been made over the time it took to make the final one. This cost us the thick end of three and a half thousand pounds, so we were more than a little concerned especially as the amount involved now, was much larger. The rate still showed signs of minor fluctuations, up and down, so we thought that it would be prudent to arrange a meeting with bank manager. After he had thoroughly checked our newly received documents and telephoned their head office in Lisboa he told us that for the amount of pounds sterling we intended to import the exchange rate would be two hundred and fifty eight and a half escudos to the pound. We decided to go for it and my hands shook as I wrote a cheque for the highest value that I ever had, and probably ever would write out. We asked what deposit accounts were available and arranged to transfer some escudos into a three-month one and the balance into another of six months at a high interest rate. Income tax would be automatically deducted on maturity but we were now in a positive cash flow situation and there was no way in which we could turn back now. Most of that evening our recent successes were celebrated over a few bottles of wine and one of port and we took a long time chewing the fat about where to actually locate the villa.

On one visit to the co-operative we noticed that our pump was no longer there, it had disappeared, hopefully to Lisboa and not just to the back storeroom. We called into the cafe later on for a nightcap and were given two plates of snails each with a safety pin. They showed us how to extract the snail from its shell using these and we found that they were quite tasty. It was just the sight of them that did not turn us on. We managed to clear the plates, aided by large gulps of beer, and the locals were very impressed, as they had thought that we would decline their offer.

The weather had started to get warmer, thirty-five degrees in the caravan before midday and the water temperature in the cistern was sufficiently high enough to encourage me to have some skinny dipping sessions. AC had another Margo day just at the thought of it. After one refreshing dip I had towelled down and got dressed when a couple, obviously English, approached the caravan and introduced themselves. They had seen our car parked by the track and by the registration plates had deduced that we must be fellow countrymen. Cheryl was bouncy, talkative and a physiotherapist, Simon was tall well built but said very little and was an accountant. They had bought some land about three hundred metres further along the track from ours. On it was a small store, more like an electricity sub-station and it was being converted into a two story three bedroomed villa which would have a swimming pool built behind it. We knew the estate agent who had sold them the land, but had never needed to use them ourselves, and it was their architect and engineer who had prepared the designs and drawn up the plans.

Progress was nowhere near as advanced as they had been promised and they were not sure that they would get what they had paid for. Their plans were to hold a beano later on in the year for the whole family but that was totally dependent upon the villa being completed. Although we were not actually asked directly to supervise progress, or lack of it, they would be grateful if we could keep a sharp eye on matters and let them know what the situation was from time to time. There was no mention of any form of payment for services rendered which we did not anticipate anyway. This we promised to do as it could prove to be a somewhat interesting diversion from our normal daily activities so they left us their address and telephone numbers.

I woke up the next day with a spaced out couldn't settle to anything attitude, even more so when told that the fridge had conked out. Not really in the right mood I made a halfhearted attempt to fix it and failed. Gloom and doom as there would be no ice and the milk was sure to curdle.

It was almost the middle of the year and we had had terrible problems with seed germination rates over the past few weeks, sadly it was a very hit and miss basis. We approached a seed merchant in the U.K. about the problem and received a politician's answer. The question was completely ignored but we were informed that the technical term germination rate was no longer an accepted measure of success and had been replaced by "Emergence Percentage". To me it was one and the same difference. I was convinced that it was as a result of lack of water although we often watered two or even three times a day. The soil temperature was very high and it tended to pan after the first irrigation, which made it form a compacted layer. Although it appeared damp and moist on the surface only one and a half centimetre below the ground level it was bone dry. If on the odd occasion water did manage to penetrate, normally as a result of ralo damage the intense heat from the sun caused it to almost boil and the seeds were very sensitive to this form of treatment. It was bad news but a lesson well learnt in that it was inadvisable to sow any seeds after the end of May. On a more positive note, the earlier sown parsnips had been thinned and they had formed long slender roots and the asparagus fern looked extremely lush and healthy.

A visit was made to Cheryl and Simon's construction site up the track. After a quick general inspection all round we came to the obvious conclusion that the promised completion date did not have a cat in hell's chance of being met. The electrical wiring and plumbing installation had only just started and the pool was a big gaping hole in the ground. The builder turned up as we were about to leave, it was M's friend who had quoted us for our villa. He told us that he also had another one under construction behind a cork oak wood nearer to the village than us. That would give me another opportunity to inspect the progress and maybe pick up an idea or two on their building methods. These were the two contracts that he had referred to in our earlier discussions. On the way back to the caravan I pointed out to AC that if he was that far behind on the building we had inspected how would he perform if he built ours, "food for thought" she said grimly.

She had had her nose in the accounts book over the past few days and arrived at a figure, which was the equivalent amount in sterling that it cost us to live here. Our general expenses were as little as three thousand pounds, give or take a few hundred here and there, a year. Both of us were more than a little excited and decided we would celebrate and attend our first village dance at the local sports club. We had no idea what to expect and were surprised that it turned out to be such a popular venue as most of the villagers were there. At around three thirty in the morning totally clapped out as a result of too much food and booze and being constantly whirled around the dance floor at an ever increasing rate we thought that it was time to leave.

It was during the European football Championship that I decided to take a welcome break and watch some matches on the television in M's café. The first game was England versus Ireland and I had made a bet with him, of a glass of his red wine, for England to win. There was a nattily dressed gentleman already in there, and from his accent he was a Londoner, a cockney. When England scored he offered every one there a drink and came over and sat at my table. He had made, so he told me, quite a few bob and had been known as the Dahlia King of Covent Garden and owned a lot of florist shops. Being well versed and practiced in mist propagation it was his intention to set up a business here. The rate of alcohol consumption increased pro-rata to the decline of the England team's performance, I was drinking whisky and his tipple was vodka and tonic. After the match I drove home unsteadily and only just about managed to unload the two water containers out of the boot before I fell flat on my face, not once but twice. AC came to my rescue, she had quickly realised that I was totally out of it, completely blotto and talking to the fairies.

Less than two minutes after she had managed to drag me into the caravan a person, we had often seen in the Council offices and had passed the time of day with, called unexpectedly to invite us to a BBQ on the following Sunday. She managed to keep me quiet and about five minutes after he had left I staggered outside and promptly threw up. It was necessary for her to do her "Flo" role to get me back inside where I crashed out for a very early night.

I woke up and felt as fit as a fart with no trace of a hangover but went down hill rapidly when a lorry load of ready mix concrete pulled up by the car and a telescopic pump wagon stopped behind it. A few moments later both drivers got out of their cabs and sauntered down towards us. After a lot of arm gesticulations from all of us with no one any the wiser, one of the men pulled out an invoice from his pocket. We then twigged that it was a delivery for the villa behind the cork oak wood. All of us walked back up to the vehicles and there I pointed out to the where the building site was situated. After handshakes all round they managed to reverse, turn around and drive off. We were saved again.

The next process to obtain the land was to apply for and pay the land transfer tax. It should not have proved too difficult but we had underestimated the amount of paperwork that was involved. All of the documentation received from the Institute in Lisboa referred to me and not the two of us and it soon dawned on us that it was because I was the sole trader. I then had to obtain a work permit and a license card. After a struggle we found the offices and as we opened the main door we felt an air of tension that we had not experienced in any of the offices we had recently had to visit. The shape of the queue was all too familiar to me, exactly like those I had joined when visiting various Governmental departments in Middle Eastern countries, fifteen bodies wide and almost ten deep in places. What price to be able to find a single file one when it was so desperately needed?

Only one of the four counters was open and behind it sat a stone faced, hard eyed miserable young bitch, the original Hitler in Knickers. She was acting very scathing to everyone, rude and offensive, not at all helpful and had brought one little old lady almost to tears. When it at long last got round to my turn, AC had sat on one of the three seats at the back of the room, she snapped at me and sarcastically suggested that I should return with someone who spoke more understandable Portuguese.

For the first time in my life, under these circumstances, and I had experienced far worse, I completely lost my cool and blew my top. With a very firm handshake I spoke to her in a very calm tone in English and said "good morning" and then strongly recommended that her mother got married sooner rather than later, and that she should take a long sexual walk and learn some better manners on the way. From the look on her face I was sure that she had not understood one word of my abuse as I turned around and calmly walked out of the office.

The next day I returned and she appeared to be more miserable than before. Soon it was my turn and I placed the papers received from Lisbon on top of the counter. Without a word she went to a filing cabinet and pulled out two forms, handed them over to me with a pen and pointed to a table and chair in one corner of the room. Twenty minutes later I had completed them in full, the most important question being the date that the enterprise was to start. I returned to the counter and was given top priority treatment, they were taken, quickly scrutinised and then stamped and after I had handed over a large dollop of dosh, photocopies were given to me. With a lovely smile, which transformed her face into one that was soft and very pretty, even her eyes sparkled, she told me that it would take around five weeks before I would receive my card and also advised me that it would be necessary to obtain from the vendors their tax reference details. There were five of them. I smiled in return, shook her hand and thanked her very much for her assistance.

With our priorities totally focused on ownership of the land, which had already been paid for but was still not ours, social events, unless in doing so we could obtain constructive information, took a back seat to all other to all other matters. However we had to bear in mind that to live here and ostracise ourselves from other nationals speaking our mother tongue would be detrimental in our long-term interests as they were future potential clients. It was very difficult not to be too insular and inward looking.

Another problem was the age differences, AC was only thirty-eight and I was nine years older. We therefore had to attempt to integrate into a much more mature society, to put it politely, a situation totally foreign and unknown to either of us.

As far as we were concerned at the end of the day, sorry to say, that we were only interested in number ones, us! As we had been invited to this BBQ, it would have been extremely rude not to have turned up despite whatever frame of mind we happened to be in on that day. It turned out to be a rather special occasion for us and a very enjoyable event. The hosts were animal lovers, keen on horses and had brought the ones that they rode in England with them. He was also a very proficient sailor. We were introduced to lots of interesting people from different backgrounds and the conversations covered a lot more than the daily local events and gossip and this gave us a considerable boost.

However it was sad to say that when we took full stock of the situation and sorted out the wheat from the chaff over the next few days, no one stood out immediately as being the type of couple or people that we could enter into a long term friendly relationship with. There were several there where an association was worth pursuing and with one couple – Tony and Shirley – there were definite prospects. Perhaps we were too self-centred and with our current lifestyle didn't feel the need to open up to others. We did not seem to have a lot in common with most of them so the chances of becoming close friends were somewhat remote. Our view was that if at the end of one's days you had made a close and long term relationship with four or five people or couples, you should consider yourself very lucky and also that the majority of these would have been formed by the time you reached your mid-thirties.

Early one morning a tremendous thunderstorm woke us up, it was only five thirty. When the curtains were drawn open it seemed to be daytime as the sheet lightning lit the whole sky and the forked lightning zigzagged in more and more frequent sequences. It really was awesome and gave us quite a fright as we lay in bed in our exposed caravan, like sitting ducks, with a television aerial stuck high up in the air connected to a set which always gave a picture which was not a lot clearer than looking through a blizzard.

Every time water was required the dreaded trip down the tunnel had to be made to start up the pump. The swallows, now with their nests filled with young almost ready to attempt their first flight, became more and more agitated as I began to descend down the top steps. In their efforts to see me off they became so brave that the dive bomb attacks at my head got progressively closer and were quite scary. In anticipation of this I had started a few weeks earlier to wear a sturdy type of flat cap, even with AC at the well head bashing a tin tray for all her worth, and our World service radio on full blast at the top of the tunnel entrance, they still kept up their incessant attacks. I once took my golfing umbrella with me held above my head but found that I was one hand short to start up the motor. The noise and fumes when it fired into life made them less bold and gave me a little respite to make my way out at which point they lost interest altogether.

We had a chat to M who knew one of the principal vendors of our land who lived in the village with his family. M was staggered to find out that we had never met but understood as soon as we mentioned the estate agent. He took me around to their small villa and made the formal introductions. After the usual social chitchat I was assured that the information that I required, the tax reference details, would be collected from the other family members and together with his would be available in less than one week.

I felt a little more motivated, "about time too" said AC, and thrust myself into all of the tasks with renewed vigour and managed to cross quite a few off the lists that never ended. So much so that I was able to take some time off to watch the Holland versus Russia match in the football tournament and managed to remain sober at this one.

A decision was made to sample another dance session and this time to have a late supper of chicken and chips there. The weather was conducive to it being held outside under the stars with minimal lighting and surrounded by handmade paper decorations. There was a female electronic organist accompanied by a male vocalist and their performance was very professional considering that they could only have been in their late teens. Many dances later, together, and with numerous Portuguese partners we dragged ourselves away and crashed out into the pit at five in the morning.

The villagers certainly knew how to enjoy themselves, Bobbly hat above all was more than slightly oiled, and have a good time. Even when they overdid it, on the drinks side, they never lost the plot and got too excited, make a nuisance or manage to create any disturbances. They were well practised in the art of pacing themselves for lengthy periods of food and drink consumption. We never heard a voice that was raised in anger or saw any form of a quarrel. Over our positively the last nightcap before we left we were told that a dance was held on every Saturday during the summer. I was far from sure that I could stand up to that sort of pace.

Having promised to keep an eye on the progress of Cheryl's and Simon's villa conversion up the track I made another quick visit and prepared a brief report together with my views on a likely completion date. This was way passed what had been promised even though the pool construction had proceeded rapidly with the timber shuttering fixed ready to pour the concrete for the walls. The builder was there so I discussed our new villa design with him. He wanted to quote so I asked him to call and collect the plans next week.

My priority then was to catch up with the architect, in his office, and collect a full set of drawings. There were occasions when minor miracles happened and I was lucky enough to experience one. He was in when I telephoned and promised to bring all the relevant copies, villa, swimming pool, septic tank and so on the next day which he did. As he handed them over I asked how the design approval process was proceeding and he replied that it was going through, so far, without any hiccups.

We had, after the fat had been chewed over and over again, decided to build down by the new caravan location. When this was pointed out to the architect he just shrugged his shoulders and said, "Obtain the building license for the submission now under consideration and start the villa construction. Then reapply for approval of the same plans but with site plan modified to show the revised position of the villa. It seemed to us to be sound advice and very Portuguese so we decided to proceed on that basis. One nasty though occurred to me however. "Did that mean that two building licences would have to be paid for?"

Over our usual supper in the village restaurant we talked about all the things that were on going and reflected on the jollies that we had had with Lucie and our Fullwood friend. These reminded us why we had fallen in love with the place originally and so over a nightcap in M's café we planned to do them more often even when there were no visitors, it would be nice to make trips out on our own. I suggested as a start that we visit the new golf club at nearby Budens for a coffee and a nose around. A quick survey indicated that the course was hilly and a little tight, it would definitely suit a mountain goat and could prove to be difficult in inclement weather. A brief chat was had with the manager about my handicap. He would be prepared to take my word for it but obviously the handicap committee would expect a letter from my former golf club.

We then travelled to the west coast and stopped in the small village of Carrapateira for lunch. During this a decision was taken to explore and head for the sea. To get there it was necessary to drive along a very rough dirt track. The recent heavy rains had gouged out long and deep furrows, which made the ride a knicker wetting experience. The poor old fart box grounded constantly and twice came to a halt and stalled with a shudder. The alternate use of reverse and forward gears together with a slightly different approach line allowed progress to continue but not before I had thought that it might not have been such a good idea. It was onwards only as a three-point turn was impossible and we soon reached a cliff edge. In front and below us was a truly magnificent sight, which took our breath away.

The beach of Amado stretched out totally deserted except for the incoming tide's huge waves, fanned by the offshore breeze. In the distance breakers formed a dense sea mist up to half of the height of a black rock face. My immediate concern, after the serene beauty of the whole scene had been forever been imprinted on my mind, was to hope that the place would never be exploited as it was a yet to be discovered surfers paradise.

Still stunned we clambered out of the car and down onto the sand and walked the full extent of the beach into the mist. It was an eerie experience everything seemed so still and unreal except for the thunderous noise made by the breakers. Halfway back to the car, with no other living thing in sight we sat on the sand, soaked up the atmosphere and were mesmerised for at least an hour. Our trance was broken when in the distance we saw a solitary figure with her three dogs. It crossed my mind during this dreamy period when our gazes were firmly fixed due west over the Atlantic Ocean, what would be the next piece of land to be reached on the other side? I was not keen to drive back along the track as there was a very steep down hill slope, which would be almost impossible to negotiate with safety. It had been a desperate struggle to climb up to the top. The only option was therefore to continue and we found that it looped along the top of the cliffs and brought us back into the other side of the village.

Along that section, the surface of which was generally in a much better condition than before, a group of old huts with nets and lobster pots outside was passed, they were fishermen's. Opposite these was a bit of a ramshackle building that could, at a stretch, be classed as a restaurant. It was closed and a mental note was made that it could be worth exploring in the future. Only a short distance before the main road was reached there was another magnificent beach on our left hand side. A river estuary had to be crossed to reach it and this would be safest at low tide. It looked like a huge sand dune that had been, and still was, continuously reshaped by the ebb and flow of the tides and storms, it was Bordeira beach.

AC suggested, dead seriously, that we should tow the caravan over and stay for a few days. There were two possible local restaurants, a café and a couple of bars so that we would not have to self-cater. I was, to say the least, far from impressed with this idea as the caravan had only recently been relocated and I certainly did not relish coupling it up again, towing it off the land and after a short break having to manoeuvre it back into position. On that basis I said, "sorry, a complete and utter no no". "Boring old spoil sport," she responded.

It had been a day packed with interest and we took the opportunity on the way home to call into the Council offices in the village to collect the post and were notified that there was a Registered letter at the downtown Lagos post office waiting for collection. Before we left I telephoned and spoke to Simon and gave him some news on the villa. Despite the contents of my letter and this latest update he told me that they would still make a flying visit at the end of the month. A large local villa had been rented and that meetings with the estate agent, architect, engineer and the builder had been organised. I thought that the likelihood of all those meetings actually taking place as planned was too good to be true.

Our final port of call, for the usual before the last leg home, was the café. When M brought the drinks to our table he handed over to me five slips of paper. They were photocopies of the vendors' tax reference details and as this was a bonus, warranted an additional bevy.

Once I had settled down in the caravan, I remembered my earlier thoughts on the beach and eagerly opened my World Atlas and unfolded the map of the Algarve on the table. The Amado beach was found to be at latitude thirty-seven degrees ten minutes north. If this was traced westwards the first landfall would be near the town of Hampton, at the entrance to Chesapeake Bay, Virginia. Over on the west coast of America, it was close to Boulder Creek, south of San Francisco, California. For some unknown reason I had thought that it would have been much further south, nearer to Florida. That just showed how long it must have been since I had had my head stuck in an atlas.

The Registered letter was collected and it contained a Sole Trader card in my name with a permit number on it. All the required documents were now available to finally pay the Land Transfer Tax. An immediate visit was made to the Office and all handed over. They were scrutinised very carefully, afterwards a receipt issued and we were told to return in three days time.

No further progress could be made without the services of a lawyer. Whom could we decide on and trust? The last recommended one had let us down badly at vast expense and we were quite concerned that it could happen again. AC had a bright idea, so we called in on the office of the estate agent who had sold us the land to talk with the new owner's son and his girlfriend who were now running the business. They had been consistently helpful when we had picked their brains on our numerous visits to them since our arrival. For the purpose of drawing up the Deed of Conveyance of the land for Notarisation they strongly recommended a female lawyer they had worked with who was a specialist. Her offices were within easy walking distance and we knew the general location at the top end of the town. Having found them very quickly we made an appointment with her secretary for the following week, on the basis that by then, we would have the receipt for the payment of the land transfer tax.

That weekend was an enjoyable one for us on the social side of things, work and all other problems were put to one side and we were pleasantly surprised how easy it was to completely switch off. There was a Folk Festival in the village on the Friday and a large covered area had been erected next to the Club. Housed in this were many artisans who proudly displayed their crafts. Bulldozer Joe's mother had a fine selection of brooms and baskets and the Alface man showed many of his different rope works and there were numerous stands laden with patchwork quilts, peg rugs crochet and items made from bamboo. Tables groaned under the weight of homemade breads, intricately made marzipan sweets and different brands of honey. All around us up in the hills were dotted groups of beehives, some with up to a dozen in each. It was interesting to see such a lot of local talent on display. The Folk dancing didn't commence until about ten o'clock and by then it had turned distinctly chilly around the edges. So we settled for a couple of quick nightcaps in the club bar and then pootled off home.

Saturday night in Lagos, there was a performance by the Ballet Sovietica, in the open air Auditorium. It was supposed to start at nine-thirty but actually began just after ten o'clock as by then it was sufficiently dark for the stage lighting to be effective. The Lagos Ballet, consisting of a group of youngsters, was the first act and they put on a very professional display. Then it was time for the Ballet Tartania who gave a very polished and well-balanced programme. AC particularly enjoyed the Faust and Romeo and Juliet extracts but for me it was a little too arty farty. The only problem was a combination of a very chilly wind and the hard concrete seats. Despite the two heavy car rugs we had taken our bums were sore and we were frozen by the time we left before the end of the show. Even in late July the evenings could get quite cold.

We had arranged to meet up with M and all the family relatives from Lisbon at the Saturday dance after the Ballet. But this had overrun, and even though we left early it still meant a mad dash back to the village with lots of apologies when we joined them. They had brought cooked crabs along and these went down really well accompanied by some cool beers. The dance floor was sheltered and there did not seem to be as much wind as in the town so after only a few twizzles around we felt quite flushed. Many spins later we extricated ourselves at around four- thirty in the morning, totally bushed. Over the first coffee we both agreed to give the Folk festival, later on in the day, a wide berth.

I had paid brief visits to the builder's two sites along the track and both had progressed as well as could be expected. The site of the villa conversion for Cheryl and Simon was not large enough to flood it with labour in an attempt to blitz it, but the terrace and the coping stones around the pool had been laid and its floor and wall tiling completed. The villa itself was almost in the final stages and the painters, electrician and plumber had all but finished. But, and it was a big but, the septic tank was just a large hole in the ground. The other one behind the cork oak wood had been built up to the first floor level and there were more workers there. At my last visit to this site the builder gave me his quotation and told me that I had saved him a special journey to deliver it.

We finally managed to pay the Land Transfer Tax, fixed at eight per cent of the contract value, on the morning of our meeting with the lawyer. The actual payment ritual had to be carried out in a different office so a bit of paperwork shuffling had to be quickly organised but at long last we succeeded. We gave the lawyer an up to date synopsis of the events so far and handed over all of the paperwork or so we thought. Not quite, she needed the original of the Institute's form, which had been retained unnecessarily by the bank. We chased around there, managed to collect it, returned and handed it over to her. As I was the Sole Trader the land would eventually be registered in my name, which was not an ideal situation for the two of us. The Notarisation process would be performed in Portimao with her, accompanied by me, in attendance and she indicated that it would take place in two weeks time.

Many hours were spent when we poured over the building plans for the villa to refine our detailed utility requirements, specifically the electrical and plumbing locations. The architect had already prepared the details of the waste water pipe work to the septic tank. We had told him that a two-pipe system was essential, one for white water and the other for black, the sewage waste. At every pipe exit from the villa a siphon or water seal was to be fitted. Our bathroom had been deliberately located at the furthest distance from the septic tank and this would ensure that when the bath was emptied it would purge the whole length of the white water drainage pipe-line.

Even more hours were spent as we thumbed through the dictionaries to obtain the correct translations for the preparation of the detailed specifications and general conditions of the contract. The builder's price fitted within our budget, he was local and also employed craftsmen who lived in the village. From what I had seen at his two building sites along the track the quality of their work certainly seemed to be up to standard. Another two things were in his favour and these were, that in all the brief dealings we had had with him he appeared to be genuine and above all, honest. So it was with a good gut feeling that we decided that he should be awarded the contract to build and arrangements were made for early negotiations.

Simon called in on his way to the villa they had rented and appeared to be in a bit of a stew and looked rather frazzled. The planned meetings that they had told me about on the telephone had not gone as they had anticipated, the architect was in Lisboa and the engineer had serious domestic problems so was unavailable, and as yet they had not had the time to view the progress on the villa construction. We didn't believe it when they called in later the next day to tell us that as it was lockable, although unfinished, arrangements had been made to have some furniture for the lounge, kitchen and bedrooms together some soft furnishings to be delivered. We considered that this step was a little risky and told them so in no uncertain terms.

With an involvement in all of these various activities we still had to find the time to attend to the daily horticultural mundane matters such as weed removal, irrigation and the harvesting of the vegetables. Particular attention was, as a matter of priority, paid to the asparagus seed beds. Now at the height of the summer they were taking up a considerable amount of our time. The sweetcorn was picked and proved to be an absolute disaster. We knew that it was a special type of maize and had chosen so accordingly, or so we had thought, at the co-operative. With the application of a high strength fertiliser and constant irrigation the plants had grown to a height of well over two metres with an abundance of huge cobs. These were twisted off about four weeks after the flowering had finished and the tassles had turned brown and had lost their silkiness. When they were cooked, boiled in water or grilled over charcoal, they turned to be as tough as old boot leather. Even when we experimented with varied cooking times it made no difference. Not only were they tough but they lacked any degree of sweetness. In fact they were yukky and inedible.

It finally dawned on us that we had bought sown and lavished attention on maize, the type grown for cattle fodder and not the dining table variety.

The cistern was to have a dual purpose, primarily irrigation and secondly to allow me to have a dunk or even a swim. It had been thoroughly cleaned out and the inside walls given a coat of very expensive white protective paint. Now that it had been refilled it was possible to have a daily dunk with costumes on due to the frequent arrival of unexpected visitors. It proved to be a welcome respite from the heat but AC found the water a little on the chilly side. The water stayed clear for up to five days and then started to go green in colour due to the build up of algae. As the crops were continually irrigated the cistern had to be frequently topped up with more clean and fresh water so the daily dips could be enjoyed.

Some days were good and others totally indifferent but one especially stands out in our memory. The architect informed us that the building approval was imminent and the licence would then be available for collection. The lawyer needed a copy of my passport details and had fixed up the meeting at the Notaries office in Portimao for the following week. That evening we were invited round to the villa rented out by Cheryl and Simon for supper and more excitedly a steaming hot bath.

We had just got ready when the builder arrived and the specifications and the price agreed, all that was left was to settle the payment terms and the starting date. Our soap, towels and smellies had been thrown onto the back seat of the car and I had put the key in the ignition switch when Alfonso 2 tapped on my window. Would we ever get away? He asked if he could make a connection to our main irrigation feeder pipe and extend it to his orange orchard that had been planted in nineteen forty three after he had completed his army service. He only wanted a gravity system and laboured the point that he would not pay for the water but would be pleased to contribute to the fuel costs to pump it from the well. I had no objections to this proposal as long as he supplied and fitted his own stop valve.

We somehow arrived at the villa only a few minutes late and with a stiff drink apiece enjoyed a magnificent soak in the tub. I had forgotten how really hot water could help one to unwind. The meal was superb, the wine excellent and the conversation very interesting. It turned out to be a very late night and we were physically and mentally knackered when we collapsed into bed and I experienced the sleep of the damned.

On one visit to town we called in to see the lawyer but only managed to speak to her secretary. She told us that they had to wait for an updated certificate from the Registry office but that the appointment in Portimao was still on.

Returning to the fart box a large carbuncle was noticed on one of the rear tyres where it had deflated. It was way past the sell by date and in a dangerous condition. As luck would have it a specialist tyre workshop was just around the corner so I removed the wheel and a new tyre was fitted in less than the blink of an eye.

The day before Cheryl and Simon left we met up with them at their villa. In the daylight we could see that not a lot of real progress had been made. He gave us a list of what furniture was going where with a planned programme for completion and a spare front door key. They had been terribly disillusioned on this visit as nothing had gone according to plan, but it was their intention to return in a couple of months time. We sympathised with them but did point out that it was sometimes better to keep out of the way. Even though well intentioned, interference normally cocked up the whole situation and this was a classic example. They were promised further progress reports on an as and when basis.

Being devils for punishment we decided to go to yet another dance. I was dead keen because there was a fellow in the village who owned proper bulldozers. Tracked caterpillar ones with a huge front blade ideally suited for site clearance and levelling. The villas new location would certainly need to have some work done on it before any form of construction could commence. His business was booming so a poxy half days operation to clean up my patch wasn't worth a toss to him. The delivery and removal expenses for the machine would be far higher than the value of the work. However Bulldozer Joe was also there and after my requirements were discussed he quoted an hourly rate. I would have much preferred a fixed price for the job and asked if he would come round to see the exact extent of the works. We were surprised to find that there were many couples there whom we had met at the earlier BBQ invitation and as we were devouring a plate of snails Tony and Shirley asked if they could join us at our table. We had at that time got on quite well with them so we said, "of course, feel free". Before we left they had invited us to join them for Sunday lunch the next day, we accepted thankfully and later fell into the pit well after four o'clock more knackered than ever.

The lunch was excellent, after we had first met them in their local for a jar or two, and was followed by a most welcome dip as I had remembered to pack our bathers. It may well have been the consumption of too much scotch as before we left he invited us to his fiftieth birthday bash to be held towards the end of next month. It was a pleasant and enjoyable day and we didn't leave until way past nine o'clock.

The usual visit, on the way home, was made to the café for a nightcap and a chat with Alfonso 1 and Picasso, who happened to be there. After much small talk about the square root of naff all and more than a few drinks AC dragged me away as I had gotten a little *lipsey* and quite excitable. The bed in the caravan had to be made up before we could fall into it, which for me was a right pain in the arse.

In early September daytime temperatures got hotter and hotter and with the absence of any wind the heat build up inside the caravan reached a distinctly unpleasant level. On most evenings it was necessary to sit on the terrace until after midnight to allow it to cool down, although only by a few degrees. There we were joined by the biggest toad we had ever seen. It always lurched towards us from behind one of the cistern walls, stopped and gave us a glaring stare for a moment or two and then clumped off in the direction of the well.

In the middle of the week Bulldozer Joe turned up and together we paced around the area of the works. He guessed that it would take about two days and I agreed to peg it out more accurately before he started. The high costs to load up lorries and then have the spoil transported away was avoided as I told him to fill in the pond area behind the ruin. It was hoped that he could start straight away but he could only fit in the work over the next week or two.

There were other balls in the air, which needed to be monitored, some important and others less so. The reinsurance of the fart box was successfully delegated to Les, back in the U.K. This was a good move as he had close contacts with an insurance broker and the original policy had been arranged through this connection. In one of our discussions he mentioned that he would like to pay us a visit in the autumn, if his business commitments permitted.

AC suddenly remembered that we had left some shoes with the bespoke cobbler in the village some months ago and that they ought to be collected. They had all been repaired but it had taken him a long time to match the green leather for her stiletto heels, which had been damaged on the cobbled footpaths. They were not at all a practical type of shoe to wear here. My sole and heel renewals had been ready weeks ago so we mumbled our apologies as we handed over a ridiculously small amount of money to settle the total bill.

To keep Picasso amused, one day we gave him the Horticultural manual deliberately opened at the section on asparagus to study and hopefully keep him out of my hair. Alfonso 2 was around at the time and they immediately became self-taught experts eager to impart this newly acquired knowledge to any of the residents or local people that had learnt of our plans through the ultra-efficient grapevine.

There had been quite a few humorous moments over the past few months. One was when I went into the village to watch *"Papillon"* on the television in M's cafe AC was too tired to bother and asked me to take the rubbish to the main disposal bins at the end of the track. There I somehow managed to lock myself out of the car with the engine still switched on and had to run back to collect her set of car keys. When I did finally sit at a table, with a large glass of red wine in my hand, I found it impossible to follow the film as there was too much background disturbance. The café was full to bursting point with highly excited conversations going on all around me.

The day of our appointment in Portimao soon arrived and we met the lawyer at the Notaries office at eleven o'clock. One hour later we were led into an air conditioned room and seated before him where he then proceeded to read out all of the legal details contained in a document. The pages of this were then signed by him, me and the lawyer as a witness. A hefty cheque was handed over whereupon copies of every thing were given to me. Technically all that remained was the land registration, which could take from six months up to a year. As we left the lawyer told us that any residence built on a large area of rural land, such as ours, would normally be referred to as a Quinta. We thought that sounded rather grand and a little bit more upmarket than a plain villa.

It was the first time that we had felt secure since we had signed the promissory contract, which seemed to us to be light years ago. As a result, maybe we could sleep more soundly tonight.

If ever there was a time to celebrate it was now. We had frequented a popular restaurant in Lagos when we were tourists and now dined there on a fairly regular basis. As we were on very good terms with the owners it was decided that it would be the ideal place to have our celebratory meal. My brother and his wife had given us a top of the range bottle of champagne as a wedding present. Although sorely tempted to open it lots of times in the past we had resisted, but not on this occasion. When we reserved the table we asked, and it was agreed, that they would put it on ice and open it at the start of our meal. On our first holiday in the complex at Praia da Luz we had met a young German couple, about the same age as AC, who were residents and lived on the outskirts of the village. We had bonded with them immediately and they had proved to be very help full and supportive. When we arrived on our land it was their telephone number that we had given to our families as an emergency contact. They were always readily available to assist us in as much as they could, which was a tremendous help, so we were pleased to be able to invite them to join us on this special occasion.

They had known the restaurant owners longer than we had and all six of us sat at our table for a glass of champers. As we ordered our meals we were given a complimentary bottle of a superior red wine, it was a nineteen eighty-seven Alentejano "reserva" and we found it to be very moreish so another two were quickly ordered. The place was as popular as ever, fully booked, but we had a magnificent meal. Between courses there was the inevitable dancing, some on the bar, with less versatile people cavorting on the floor as the tables were speedily rearranged. As always we were the last to leave, in the late hours of the early morning. It was a day and an evening to recall forever.

Chapter Nine

We could now crack on with the major construction projects and start to pull all of the loose ends in together. This would mean that we would soon have to fork out mega amounts of our hard earned capital so we thought it would be prudent to take stock of our current financial situation.

Our August 'eighty-six budget included the estimated costs of a house, swimming pool, electricity and telephone connection charges, a borehole and general household items. A generous allowance was made for the latter and was based on the fact that we had almost nothing to start off with. An additional budget figure had been set aside for the land transfer tax, Notary and legal fees and the actual land and building registrations.

This total figure, with a small amount as a contingency, was imported after approval was received from the Institute in Lisbon. Since then we had forked out to the ex-lawyer, paid the Notary's fees and the land transfer tax. The quotation for the villa, now upgraded to a Quinta, and the pool had been requested as separate fixed prices. When all monies were totted up there were just sufficient funds available although we still had to cover our day-to-day living expenses. It was hoped that these could be met by the investment income from the deposit accounts.

Our drafted contract specification, in Portuguese, which we considered to be quite an achievement, was typed out by the builder's wife on the twenty-five lined official blue paper sheets. It was signed by both parties after all the drawings and pages had been initialled. The final page contained the two fixed prices, which included the building license fee. There was a copy for each of us and it was dated the second of September nineteen eighty-eight.

An annexe was prepared that detailed the terms of payment. They followed the normal working practice in operation at the time, almost! The builder wanted an initial down payment on the overall contract value but I would only agree to one on the Quinta's price immediately and another, when the swimming pool construction was about to begin. They would be treated as two separate contracts for payment conditions as I was not prepared to give money up front for a construction that might not commence for several months. In any event I needed that cash on deposit to improve our cash flow. He reluctantly agreed but strongly emphasised that every other client had paid a percentage of the total contract value, which was the standard procedure. "More fools them," I said and told him that my position on the matter was not negotiable.

The stage or progress payments were agreed without any problems with a five per cent retention payable on completion and when the keys had been handed over. He would start as soon as I could hand over a level site as he had men and equipment on standby. This was very encouraging news. The discussions were concluded with handshakes all round and afterwards ours continued to tremble as we felt just a little concerned at this total commitment. We both gave a gulp and thought oh shit, oh dear, what have we let ourselves in for now. It was hoped that the contract documents could remain in a drawer as the builder knew his obligations and we knew ours. It was both of our intentions to get the works completed as quickly as possible. We wanted a Quinta to live in and a pool to swim in and not have long drawn out contractual disputes over trivial matters.

The site area and the drive from the track were pegged out and we could do no more than wait for the arrival of Bulldozer Joe to perform. Ideally it would be in our interests for his completed works to coincide with the end of the month when one of the deposit accounts matured. He turned up one day after lunch and after he had walked around the pegged out area he clambered into his machine, lowered the bucket and got started. Now the show really was on the road as he worked non-stop until half past nine that evening and returned the next morning. By mid-afternoon the site had been levelled, the driveway cut out and all the excavated soil been deposited in the hole behind the ruin, which was now completely full. It was a Friday and the deposit account matured on the next Monday. I would then be able to visit the bank in the morning, arrange a cash transfer to our current account and juggle with the other deposits.

On Monday afternoon the builder turned up for the down payment cheque: the jungle drums must have pounded over that weekend! He suggested that it was time for a celebration and gave us a lift to the café for a few drinks and nibbles. Someone in there mentioned that an earth tremor had been felt in the village earlier at about two o'clock. It was news to us as we had sensed nothing. During the session the builder intimated that the construction of the Quinta could be completed in six months, the contract had included ten with no penalty clauses for delays. I had thought that the addition of these would be a waste of space as they would have been nigh on impossible to apply.

"Great," said we but did not really believe it and assumed that it was the drink talking. "Bollocks thought I," as that would totally knacker up my projected cash flow. We had monies in various deposit accounts over a range of fixed periods at interest rates from eight to thirteen per cent after tax. Should stage payments be called for earlier than he had originally estimated then the interest would be forfeited.

The asparagus seedlings looked really healthy as we continued to weed and water them. They had been fertilised for the third time and some of the fern had grown to a height of more than forty centimetres. It was necessary to buy another sack of fertiliser from the depot at the end of the track. "I can't see any fruit trees on your land", the owner said. He drove past regularly on his delivery runs. "That's because I don't have any," I replied. "Well, why do you keep on buying sacks of this then?" he enquired. I told him that it was for my asparagus seedlings and all the other vegetables we had sown and that it was applied as a top dressing. With a gasp he explained that it was more likely to kill them, it was far too strong and was normally only used in orchards for the fruit trees. To say the least, I was a little bit taken aback. It was too late to be told this now as there was not a thing that could be done to change matters, only to wait and see.

After this conversation I carried out a very careful investigation and everything appeared to be normal, there was no sign of any damage so I decided to carry on as before. In one long weed removal by hand session my back started to twinge painfully. AC was definitely not amused and insisted that I rest and take it easy for as long as it took to correct itself. Her numerous vegetable patch areas gradually reduced in size as the produce was harvested for the table, had gone to seed or died. The tomatoes had started to ripen thick and fast and also the courgettes. In the other areas just a few cabbages, leeks, parsnips and carrots remained.

The spare part for the fridge arrived in the post at the Council offices. The parcel had no name on it only the address and the maker's trademark was visible. That gave me a clue as to what it was. I explained to the girl that it contained a part that I had been waiting for and she handed it over. To fix the fridge was a simple matter but it was necessary to tighten two nipples in the gas supply pipe-line before it would function. We had ice once again, so we added a bottle of gin to the shopping list in order to celebrate its availability. A note was also added to remind us to visit the lawyer and settle her account.

Someone had hinted that it may be possible to obtain an EEC grant to fund our venture. Flushed with my recent success in the application to the Institute in Lisbon we applied to the bank for the paperwork. They were not particularly helpful and insisted that any project must be presented in Portuguese and that it must be prepared by a local qualified Portuguese engineer. With all of the other things being processed and our building construction soon to be supervised, I didn't consider it worth all the hassle and decided not to pursue it any further.

Regular progress inspections were carried out on Cheryl and Simon's villa and a report on my findings sent to England. There was some movement towards completion albeit slowly and as we had engaged the same builder had mixed feelings about it. Perhaps he had overstretched himself, hopefully not as he had said, "that men were ready and available."

Early one evening nine workers appeared all at once under the two cork oak trees. All were mounted on "phut-phut" fifty cc motorcycles, too small to be classed as motorbikes. They were some of the builder's men and we hoped that they had stopped to look at the site of their next project.

It was all go after that. Bulldozer Joe arrived, the next day, with his bill scribbled on a bit of paper. The total number of hours were correct but the rate had been increased from the one discussed at the dance. That rate he now said "was based on a long term contract, not on a short one of less than two days." Was it a con? We did eventually shake hands and settled on his original figure as payment was made in cash. A couple of hours later the builder and his brother drove up in his lorry and dropped off a cement mixer, a lot of steel reinforcing bars and a large quantity of timber stakes and planks.

When we sat on the terrace next to the caravan and gazed down the land we could see quite a steep escarpment beyond the Bensafrim to Barao de S Joao road. About half way up its slope there had been installed a tall concrete electrical distribution support pole. I decided that I would position a stake which would be the datum point from which all the Quinta's measurements would be set out and a direct line between this stake and the pole was as good as due south. This line would mark the outside of the utility room wall that faced west. Our bedroom and bathroom walls would project further westwards from it. As she checked out this alignment AC considered that she had married a genius and told me so. I quite rightly under the circumstances agreed and preened smugly.

All of the profile boards were marked out from this datum, by the builder and his brother, with the stakes and planks that had been delivered with the cement mixer and were in position in a little under three days. I carried out a thorough check each day and found that with my eye, almost as accurate as a theodolite that the north to south alignment was about five centimetres out of line. As it would have no effect on the finished construction I was perfectly happy to leave it as it was. More important to us was to ensure that the overall internal dimensions of each room were as detailed on the drawings and I was pleased to find that this was the case. The price was based on a square metre basis and I was determined to get what we would, at the end, have to pay for.

The location of all of the ground beam footings and column foundations were marked out by white lime powder being sprinkled along them. This enabled Bulldozer Joe to see where his excavation works were to be carried out.

A gang, seven of them, turned up on a Monday morning just after eight o'clock. We were not familiar with the two labourers but immediately christened them, en block, as the *"Magnificent seven"* and as individuals, workers. Four of them sprang into action and quickly knocked up from the stakes and planking something that closely resembled a refectory table at which they all sat and polished off their breakfasts. This was swilled down with a glass of red wine, which they called café frio, cold coffee. In the meantime the other three had cut a channel across the track and a temporary connection of electricity and water to the cement mixer was laid from Bulldozer Joe's mother's small farmhouse. After breakfast our old store in the ruin was taken over as a major holding depot as more materials were delivered.

The table was then used as a work top for the assembly of the reinforcing bars that would form the core of the building columns. Soon it was time for their lunch, a real sit down affair. Not just a simple sandwich, but large vacuum flasks filled with soup which they poured into a dish and this was eaten assisted by the dunking of huge chunks of home made bread into it. A main course followed which was in a large plastic container. One of them had a cold bean stew and some others a variety of chicken and rice dishes and some I failed to recognise and was too polite to ask.

After a quick wipe of their mouths they sped off on their phut-phuts into the village. We found out later that they would normally have a strong black coffee, a Bica, together with a brandy or Bagaceira, a course brandy made from the husks of the grapes, a type of moonshine. Sometimes half of this was poured into the coffee and the remainder drank in one swift swallow, with their heads tilted backwards, or it was savoured with intermittent sips of coffee. Work then resumed after this lunchtime episode which, normally occupied an hour and the afternoon shift had a brief interruption at three o'clock for a small beer. They then beavered away until almost six o'clock.

At the end of the first week, even after I had thrown a wobbler into the works, when I pointed out that the reinforcing for one of the west wing columns was in the wrong position and this then had to be re-positioned. The casting into the cleaned out excavations of all of the reinforced ground beams and column bases on prepared grillages was made. A total of twenty=eight cubic metres of ready mixed concrete had been poured and the foundations were completed.

By the front door threshold I had buried a plastic sack, which contained a full set of English and Portuguese coins. The workers were quite touched at this gesture and there were handshakes all round. It was my intention to symbolise the fact, and remind us, that with this little bit of England and Portugal buried there, we intended to stay and integrate into the Portuguese society. They had been placed there to act as our anchor.

At the end of the day we invited them all down to M's bar for a well-earned celebratory bevy. Before we left, three of the men managed to help me mount the well wheel onto the well-head where I had carried out some minor works to accommodate it. As it was being lowered I somehow managed to badly trap one of my fingers. My shout, a loud scream, alerted them and they quickly tilted it away from my hand so I was able to withdraw it. A brief examination revealed that there were no broken bones, the skin was split and badly grazed with a large piece that hung down loosely. It had already begun to throb and turn black but in the end I only lost the fingernail.

My back was soon as good as normal so I could keep a watchful eye on the building works and still find time to spend on the asparagus seed beds and clear more of AC's vegetable plots. We still had to water daily and had lots and lots bonfires with the piles of accumulated garden rubbish. Our neighbour, a farmer with a herd of cows that often grazed at the bottom of our land, delivered four large truckloads of well-rotted manure. The last one still steamed and was exceedingly rich. As and when time was available it was wheel barrowed and spread over quite a large area. All of the top of the land above the well and a large portion below the asparagus seed beds were fully covered. We intended, after the winter rains or when possible, to have it all ploughed in. The rotavator was unfortunately not man enough to carry out this exercise.

With an excess of tomatoes AC boiled up kilos of them and with some added sugar together with other herbs, produced jars of sweet tomato chutney that was extremely tasty. All of the other vegetables had been harvested except for the parsnips. These had been deliberately left in the ground for Christmas.

On one shopping trip, after we had checked our list, we called in to see the lawyer to settle her fees and found that that she had still not received the land registration documents.

The time soon came round for us to hit the social trail again and attend the fiftieth birthday bash that Tony had invited us to. It was held in the Odiaxere social club and turned out to be a very enjoyable evening. There was a good mixture of Portuguese, English, Dutch and German. The hosts had certainly pushed the boat out, like they always did. A young female organist had been engaged to provide live music for dancing, which as usual, speeded up as the night wore on. We always ended up exhausted and never could understand why, we led an active outdoor physical life so could be expected to be reasonably fit, but apparently we were not. There were more than sufficient amounts of food, including a variety of sumptuous starters and main dishes with the inevitable array of puddings. All of these had been prepared by the wives of the hosts many Portuguese friends. Drinks flowed steadily but all too soon it was time for us to leave, unusually not the last.

There was a pleasant surprise for us one day when a people carrier pulled to a halt next to our car and out jumped a couple quickly followed by four children a mother and father and another child. We were gobsmacked but quickly recognised the couple who we had befriended when we had run the pub in the village in Studley, although we had not met the rest of their family. He owned and ran a double-glazing manufacturing company, also in the village. It was their first visit to Portugal and they told us that they had only called in for a nose around.

We met up for suppers at many restaurants and chewed the fat over old times and about mutual friends and acquaintances. There was a lot of catching to be done but after a few chinwags we were right up to date. On their last Saturday they all joined us at the weekly dance in the village and arrived in two taxis. Two others returned to collect them just after midnight when AC bundled them all in, some a bit the worse for the wear, and we waved our goodbyes. As I was a few sheets to the wind, she then bundled me unceremoniously into our car immediately afterwards, along with Bulldozer Joe's mother and the Alface man whom she had agreed to give a lift home. They were quite bemused by the whole thing. Over an enjoyable evening, entertained by the lively children on the dance floor, the couple mentioned that they would also like to purchase some land or buy a property and would welcome any advice that we could offer. We put this down to the holiday "high" mood and had seen and heard it all before so gave only a few cursory grunts and nods during that part of the conversation.

The clearance of the top portion of the land between the well-head and the track gave us a few problems. It was in a bit of a mess with long blades of a very wiry grass, which had grown profusely. I thought that the best way to treat it was to cut it down first and then get to work on it with the Portuguese hoe. At the BBQ, where we had met Tony and Shirley, I had been given a conducted tour of the garden and stables and had noticed a motorised strimmer with a steel cutter hung up in one of them. It was used to cut the cultivated grass to feed their horses. I called in on them and rather cheekily asked if I could borrow it? They were very nervous about the idea as they had no spare cutter and there were none available in the Algarve. If it was damaged or worse still broken then they and the horses would be right in the fertiliser. Reluctantly they agreed after more patter from me and assurances given that no damage would occur.

It only took five minutes for me to realise that this was not the answer to the problem as the blades of grass just bent over as soon as the cutter made contact with them. Under the circumstances I could not afford to be too heavy handed so after this brief trial period more head scratching was necessary and the strimmer returned in one piece to a very grateful lender. The use of the rotavator to chop off the grass proved to be more effective but the only sure way, at the end of the day, was by the use of hand shears. A very hard and somewhat long-winded labour of love and this still had to followed, to remove the roots, by a demanding physical exercise with the Portuguese hoe.

Another trip up the track, deep down in our minds we seriously hoped that it would be the last, for a progress inspection on the Villa conversion. It was, to all intents and purposes complete now that the kitchen units had been fitted. Only the roof to the septic tank had to be constructed. There was however one small problem, the pool water was pea green. Someone was there and had started the water re-circulating pump and had set down two containers of chemicals by the poolside. The contents of these he gradually poured in and I jotted down on my report sheet their names for future reference. In less than thirty minutes the appearance of the water had greatly improved so we had some good news to tell them during our next telephone call. They told us that their visit had been delayed by a week due to flight problems and that it would only be for three days and could we spare some time to help out as there were quite a few items to be fixed. We thought that was much too short a period to get everything sorted out even with assistance from us.

All the concrete and mortar for the garden shed, our first construction project, had been mixed by hand and there was still a considerable heap of sand left over. Sacks of cement could be bought as and when from the depot down the track. Now on site we had mechanisation in the form of the builder's cement mixer and this was utilised extensively most evenings and every weekend when the workers were not around. There were many landscaping projects to be constructed and also the well tunnel and head had to be repaired. Lots of paths had to be laid and the formation of a herb wheel for AC around the well shaft housing. There were many others and the list seemed endless.

With the well wheel now located in its proper position I was able to construct a cover over the wellhead. This would serve two essential purposes, primarily to stop visitors, especially children, who were bound to peer down it and fall in and secondly to prevent the top access by the swallows. This consisted of reinforcing bars laid close together criss-cross wise over the head opening covered with a small mesh wire netting. It was a simple but very effective solution.

One of the many benefits of being resident in a caravan on our site was that it enabled us to supervise the construction of our Quinta and be readily available if and when things started to go awry. We had heard of many instances where people even when they had employed and paid through the nose for a third party to protect their interests, found that the finished product did not conform to the agreed designs. Worst still, the final payment had been handed over which had left them with no recourse whatsoever.

We managed to prevent a major cock-up. Two of the bedrooms and the lounge were south facing onto the pool terrace. The workers had started to build the walls up on the basis that they would have had windows in them. When it was pointed out that there should be openings for fully glazed sliding doors there was a lot of chuntering but the mistake was speedily corrected.

One balls up could not be rectified. The twin bedded room and the second bathroom were about thirty centimetres smaller in width than designed. The dimensions had been correct when I had checked them off the profile boards and I could only assume that when the workers had taken a line from one of the marker nails the interior face of the wall had been picked up and used as the exterior one. The thickness of the wall including the air gap was exactly this distance, thirty centimetres. It could not be altered as the reinforced columns had already been cast in. Any attempt at a modification would have needed a major excavation of the foundations so we were stuck with it and the profuse apologies offered had to be accepted gracefully. How pleased we were that the planned room sizes had been more than generous.

On the brighter side one setting out error by the builder gave us a tremendous bonus. The four terrace roof support columns had been lined up one metre further from the Quinta than shown on the plans. This gave us a much larger terrace area. I had checked the line and found the error but had decided not to mention it as I thought that it was a good example of swings and roundabouts. I had planned that the roof overhang to the terrace would provide shade in the summer with the sun at its highest and be in full sunlight in the winter when it was at its lowest. The extra cover we now had would improve on this design. Each end was to be left open and not much benefit would be gained at sunrise but at sunset, in the early spring the rays would beam down its whole length. The timber moulds for these columns had already been used on the villa behind the cork oak wood. They were circular and had a slight taper from the middle to the top and the bottom.

Work on all of the internal and external walls progressed rapidly up to the underside of the roof ring beam supports. At this stage all of the columns were cast. As if by a prearranged signal, more likely a telephone call, the roof beam manufacturer arrived to measure up for all of the pre-cast roof beams that would support the roof and the tiles. He was a stocky little chappy, built like a brick shithouse, about one metre twenty tall and the same in width. On a longer second look I quickly realised that his appearance made him the best candidate, by far, that I had ever seen as he was the ultimate hangmans nightmare. The lobes of his ears were only one centimetre above his shoulder blades he had hardly any neck at all.

Cheryl and Simon had just arrived and called in for a chat. At that moment I was halfway through a mix of concrete to lay more stones and paving so it was not a really convenient time as far as I was concerned, they really could pick their moments. Over a coffee we were asked to pop up later in the day for a chinwag and they suggested that we brought our bathers with us.

We felt very refreshed and cooled by our dip after which we discussed their plans for the next couple of days and made a list of the things that needed assistance from us. The tasks were quite basic, mostly fixing jobs such as the numerous light fittings, some curtain rails, pictures and paintings, heated towel rails in the bath and shower rooms and other minor items.

The builder did not seem unduly concerned that the license to actually build our Quinta had not been issued but I had started to twitch a lot and made a point to chase the matter up with the architect. We visited the Town Council in Lagos where we were told that no license could be obtained as the structural plans and the steel reinforcing designs had not been lodged or had been lost. We had signed these almost twelve months previously and did not have a clue as to why the problem had arisen now. The architect was insistent that all of the necessary paperwork had been submitted and withdrew a grubby receipt out of his folder. There was much shuffling of feet, on the other side of the counter, so he promised to produce a duplicate set signed by the engineer that afternoon. Now it was no longer a necessity to have them signed by us. On that basis we were promised that a license should be available for collection in a week's time.

Good progress continued to be made on the Quinta. The top ring beam shuttering to support the roof had been fixed and the reinforcing bars positioned. The pre-cast concrete roof beams had been tied into these and the infill tiles had been located, this knitted the whole of the roof together and all of the different slopes were now locked into position. It was intended to pour the concrete to cast the roof beams and slab on the Friday so the period for it to cure would commence over the weekend.

I did not believe my ears when on the Wednesday evening the first rains for over four months crashed down on the caravan's roof and poured through the unfinished roof of the Quinta. It continued unabated all night, two bloody days too soon!

On our first wedding anniversary AC celebrated and emptied the Porta-Potty, whilst I completed the wellhead projects! The asparagus seed beds had been thoroughly soaked so there was no need for us to bother to water them for the time being. In the early evening we went up to Cheryl and Simon's villa, AC for a steaming hot bath and a shower and a shave for me, they had invited us to use the facilities at any time. The water was heated by the gas heater as the solar panel installation was still not completed. We then dressed up in our best bib and tuckers and went for a pig out in the village restaurant. No expense was spared and grilled king size prawns were ordered as a starter followed by the usual boring but delicious roast fillet of pork. This was washed down with a very up market, not the normal house, bottle of red wine. A nightcap or two in M's café followed where by sheer luck we received a telephone call from Don and Sandra. They told us that they had rung on the off chance of catching us there, possibly by sheer instinct, and they had booked a flight at the end of next week. It was not much notice for us but as we had no other commitments it would be a really good chance to get together again. They had arranged to stay in a Motel at the top end of Lagos and intended to do quite a lot of exploring around the Algarve whilst they were here.

It seemed to get hotter, bloody hotter even by my standards and AC was decidedly co-pooped, more frazzled than usual and rattier than ever. Even I was beginning to feel the strain caused by the heat, the late nights and early mornings. With men who buzzed around five days or more of the week and the constant noise of the cement mixer our precious space had been snatched away from us. There was so much to do but it was too bloody hot to do it. We dreamt of the time when the building works would be completed and our land given back to us. Oh for the days when at least our weekends could be shared solely between us with no interruptions.

Friday was a bright sunny day. It was just as well as in the afternoon thirty four cubic metres of strong ready mixed concrete was pumped up into the ring beams, over the whole roof beams and infill tiles to form the composite roof structure.

I made a point of being on the roof with the "Magnificent seven" the builder and his brother when the pump started to discharge concrete onto it in great dollops. I had taken a position over the East wing part of the pool terrace to watch the antics of manoeuvring the pumps snorkel over the ring and roof beams, it seemed to have a mind of its own as with every splurge of concrete it bucked into the air almost throwing the men off their feet. After an hour of industrious activity all over I felt a tremendous shudder and a movement underneath my feet. The others felt it and all of them rushed off down the access planking as the builder waved madly at the pump operator to stop it. They made their way to the point under where I stood rooted to the spot, some shuttering had slipped. It took all of them about fifteen minutes to force it back into position by which time I had managed to get myself back down on the ground. AC could see that I was visibly shaken and had gone deathly pale but I was able to convince her that I had suffered no physical harm. It was just a vivid memory recall.

As I sat on the caravan step, with a third cigarette alight, I trembled as I thought of the time I had experienced something similar and was lucky not to have been killed.

I was a Project Manager and my company had been awarded the contract to design, manufacture and install an Industrial incinerator plant just to the north of Basingstoke. The local authority had employed a Consultant so the civil works for the installation had been contracted out to another company. The framework of the building that would house the overhead crane and grab had been erected. It consisted of pre-cast columns and roof beams and the bases had been built on top of the walls of a deep pit that would eventually receive the domestic refuse.

As we were to supply the crane it had to be installed before the roof was completed and I had already checked out the level and alignment of the corbels on the columns where the crane runway beams and rails would be positioned. This was carried out by climbing a scaffolding tower at each end of the building for the end columns and the use of a long ladder for the intermediate ones.

The runway beams and rails had been scheduled for delivery a week before the crane so it was necessary for me to supervise their installation. I drove down from Worcester in the early morning in weather that was not at all conducive to outside work, especially at heights. The two towers were still in place and a telescopic crane was in position and the beams and rails had been laid on the ground in their correct places. Two steel erectors took to their stations and the first beam was quickly lifted up and bolted to the column and its corbel as I supervised this operation from the top of a tower. I was very surprised at how smoothly it had gone. As the next beam was offered up I climbed off the tower onto the first one behind one of the erectors. My legs were firmly clamped around it with my Wellington boots planted on the bottom flanges. The corbels were about ten metres above the ground level and the pit about eight deep so I was up a fair depth with no chance of a soft landing. Sat there some eighteen metres above a concrete floor should not have given me any cause for concern. I had once been, very briefly, on the high catwalk as the Severn Suspension Bridge support cables were spun across the river without any qualms, but somehow here I did not feel at all comfortable, in fact definitely nervous.

We completed the erection of all the beams on the north side of the building together with the crane rails and I inched my bum backwards to the tower and made a final check on their alignment and found that it was within the acceptable engineering tolerances. As I started to descend the tower there was a heavy gust of wind and I felt a violent shudder and noticed a slight lateral movement in the first three of the line of columns to which the beams and rails had just been fixed. This should not have been possible as there was no applied load on them, which would be the case when the plant was operational.

I looked back up as my feet touched the ground, something did not seem to be quite right but I continued back to my office. My wellies were kicked off, hardhat removed and then I had a general clean up. It was almost one o'clock and time to drive down to the local village pub for lunch.

Arrangements had already been made there for me to lodge on a bed breakfast and evening meal basis when I started to spend the weekdays on the site. On the drive to the site entrance there was a particularly strong gust of wind and the rains lashed down. Just as I reached the gates there was a loud and tremendous rumble which I thought was thunder and not a good omen for the afternoons work.

It was a very good pub lunch, steak and chips with all the trimmings and a salad followed by apple and blackberry pie with cream and ice cream. I was sure that my portions were much larger than other peoples, maybe because of our arrangements. It was just as well that I did not suffer any indigestion difficulties.

I cannot describe my shock when I returned to the site working area and immediately stalled the car's engine. There was no building standing, only a pile of concrete and steel that protruded from the pit it had collapsed into. As I looked at the mangled heap I realised that it was not thunder that I had heard but the noise of this collapse only minutes after I had descended the tower. Exposed rebar from the columns and the beams that I had sat and worked on only an hour ago, were twisted together like elastic bands. It made the short hairs at the back of my neck stand up on end, my stomach turn over and I could not prevent the knee shaking trembles. I could not believe what I saw in front of me neither could all the other people on the site who were just milling around with dazed expressions on their faces. Everyone had been extremely lucky, myself and the two steel erectors especially. As the collapse had occurred during the lunchtime break no one was injured, not even with a scratch.

A meeting in the Consultant's office was hurriedly convened and attended by their manager, myself and the civil contractor's site agent. These two had actually witnessed the incident. I cynically put it to the back of my mind the thought of a claim for a contract extension period to mitigate any later penalty clause application for delays but made a mental note that we and our subcontractors had a valid claim should any costs arise from the delay. We were all as white as ghosts and it was a good job that there was no booze in the cupboard. There would have to be an investigation and as it was clearly a civil design problem I would not be involved. Once the dust had settled and things cleared up I would be contacted to attend a meeting that would reschedule the programme of works.

I telephoned the office and blurted out the situation to them, somewhat incoherently, but remembered to tell them to put the crane delivery on hold and that a fuller report would be made on Monday.

It was a long drive home after I had got back shakily into the car which was still standing where it had been stalled. Thank goodness I was lucky enough to pass two lay-byes on the way as I had to make an emergency stop in each one. In the first my stomach was emptied with ease of the earlier lunch and breakfast, and in the second I suffered a very painful fifteen minutes in the rejection of what was left of my previous evening's supper. I was truly grateful that my bowels did not voice their opinion in the same way during the journey.

There was quite a long delay before our work on site could begin but my eventual stay at the village pub was for slightly over six months and I quickly became part of the family. Once a week, on darts night, I was found behind the bar to assist in drawing off the beers, supplying the nibbles and pre-prepared sandwiches and snacks and despite my protestations they actually paid me for these services. The landlady repeatedly told me that if after the basic food costs and the overheads were taken into account you did not make a profit of at least fifty per cent then you were in the wrong business.

The incinerator plant was commissioned and I lit the first fire. I had operated the actual furnaces on others many times where the normal mixture of domestic rubbish was as anticipated, and efficiently burnt to a fine ash residue. After this one had been operating for only a couple of hours I looked through the control room windows at the moving grate and saw that most of the end results of combustion that I could see coming towards me were tin cans. That was most unusual and totally unexpected. We were being televised at the time and I said to the crew "that the people of Basingstoke must live off tinned stuff", they had no comments.

I smoked another cigarette as AC made a strong cup of coffee and found that I had no further interest in the events that were going on around me although she did point that everything appeared to be going to plan. The full concrete pour was completed by six thirty and then they all, somewhat exhausted and me totally shell shocked, assisted by AC, buggered off to M's for yet another celebration. We were joined by the plumber and the electrician who had called in to get a feel as to when their services would be required. I believed that the jungle drums had pounded away again. After all this activity we sincerely hoped that we could enjoy a whole peaceful weekend to ourselves.

The composite roof structure and the building columns had been designed to be earthquake proof. What that meant and to what figure on the Richter scale to this day I did not know and was never informed. If it failed and imploded as a result of one then thirty-odd tons of materials would collapse on the inhabitants, who were more than likely to be AC and myself. Any successful insurance claim for the costs to rebuild would not prove to be of any benefit to us.

I accompanied the builder and the architect to the Town Council's offices and the building license was collected, but only after the builder's insurance certificate had been thoroughly examined. It was both good and bad news for us. He paid for a license, which included for the labour and an amount that related to the construction area of the Quinta, terraces and swimming pool. This had been included in his contract price as was his responsibility to ensure payment of the IVA, the value added tax equivalent. We were then lumbered with a payment for the urbanisation, almost four times more than he had just handed over. This was a real shock as we knew nothing about this requirement and had wrongly assumed that he had covered all the license fees. We found out later that this was the normal practice but that in no way eased the pain. As we had changed our ideas the paper chase was bound to have to continue, as we would have to submit more plans for the revised location of the Quinta. Having got this far we had to continue so we politely asked the architect to pull his finger out and push the approval as hard as he could and the matter was placed top of our priority list in capital letters.

On one visit to Lagos we took some time out to go for a coffee and a sticky cake at one of our favourite cafés. As we sat at an outside table we noticed on the other side of the street, obviously window shopping, a couple from Badsey whom we had known from the many evenings we had spent in their pub where they promoted annual asparagus suppers during the season. He was instantly recognisable as he was the spitting image of a typical *Pickwickean* character, with not quite a full head of white hair, but sporting a great grey handlebar moustache with mutton chop sideboards. He was a really lovable person who had a brilliant gift of the gab when he served behind his bar.

I had long held the reputation, not really deserved, to be able to charm the knickers off a nun without the use of any ULO, universal leg opener, but could well appreciate his talents when he had served behind his bar. We had thought that they owned the establishment but were apparently only in a managerial position, or tenants. He had changed the pub's name to epitomise an asparagus theme and it had been changed some twenty years ago to reflect this. They were countrywide renowned for their seasonal asparagus suppers and people from north, south, east and west flocked there. Many reservations were made by overseas visitors, lots of Japanese, and some were made twelve months in advance and it was always fully booked.

The pub boasted a snug, bar and a large lounge. The attached barn like structure served as the restaurant. A fixed price menu included asparagus soup with crusty bread followed by a main course of long freshly cut spears of asparagus accompanied by boiled new potatoes and gammon steaks braised in cider. Puddings included apple pie and custard, ice creams or brandy snaps with fresh cream. The greedy lot there, I was one, had ice cream as well with the apple pie. As was the custom in the Evesham district those days the asparagus was grown in ridged beds so the thick end of the spears furthest from the tip, were white inedible and stringy. The atmosphere over supper with everyone being asparagus freaks was not far short of electric.

One thing I avoided like the plague at this event was a visit to the gents loo, so thankfully missed the distinctly foul characteristic smell of the urine. This was created when asparagines, an amino acid in the spears, was hydrolised by the enzyme asparaginase into aspartic acid and ammonia on digestion. I found my own particularly offensive and the thought of a concentration that wafted from the steady streams by others repulsive. Marcel Proust in *Remembrance of Things Past, Vol.1* was in my opinion exceedingly kind in his recollection when he described this phenomenon, "at transforming my chamber pot into a vase of aromatic perfume".

The pub owners were totally surprised to see us and thought that we were on holiday as well. We invited them to join us for a drink and fully explained about our living inland nearby and of our agricultural plans. He as an annual bulk purchaser handled up to two tons of asparagus over the season all of which was grown and harvested locally. Both of them wished us luck in the venture and he was very excited at the thought that we would be in a position to transplant up to ten thousand crowns early next year. That would be a very good-sized field were his parting comments.

Don and Sandra arrived on the same day as Cheryl and Simon, this could be fun we thought but it ended up as a complicated mixture of events at home, in the caravan and for want of a better word, outside socialising. When they weren't exploring all of our free time was spent with our friends and this still gave us some quite a lot of time to help out the other two. The social side of life was the bugbear. It was impossible to entertain more than two people in the caravan, even that was a little cosy, and the outside seating and table arrangements on the terrace were far from practical. On the infrequent occasions it was attempted the food booze and ambience was first class but there was a drawback. When the jollities came to an end we were always left with task to clear everything away, tidy up and then make the bed before we could fall into it.

It was not difficult to lose track of the number of bars and restaurants we visited for lunch or for dinner, or even both. The combination of this lifestyle together with our physical workload was to be rigorously avoided. To burn the candle at both ends, and somewhat more, left us with little or no wick to rekindle. I became quite cheesed off and became very fidgety and insular much to AC's concern. It was unfair of me as I really did enjoy the company especially that of our friends. Those golden moments were ones to be experienced and shared with all of them so I decided to get a grip and buck up my ideas.

We continued to help out at Cheryl and Simon's villa and, when it was a long session, they always provided substantial lunches and ample supplies of food and drink. One heavy afternoon blitz finished way after seven o'clock so to relax with a gin and tonic with a few nibbles was very welcome. We had no sooner settled down on the recliners by the poolside, bathed in the late sunshine, to enjoy this when a couple, obviously English, appeared in front of us. She murmured a cooey and they proceeded to introduce themselves as Margaret and Bob. They had bought a plot of land on the right hand side of the track about two hundred metres past ours and a slightly less distance from where we now sat. I vaguely recollected that we had seen a "for sale" sign some months before but it had not imprinted itself into our grey matter as being relevant to our situation. They, or she was from north London, an Arsenal supporter, he was from Cheshire. I immediately twigged them to be ex-pats, probably having worked in the Gulf States. Both of them were given a really frosty reception at this unexpected interruption and not even offered a drink. They told us that a house would be built on the plot and it was their intention to live there on a permanent basis, it transpired that they had employed the same estate agent and architect as had Cheryl and Simon. The four of us were not in a position to warn them of the possible consequences of this action but gave each other a nod of pity and I muttered under my breath "the very best of luck". That stint had finished off all the current jobs on the list but back in the caravan we anticipated a new one before they departed.

We had a meal with Don and Sandra on their final day in Lagos. They planned to travel on to Tavira for three days prior to their return to England. The restaurant was the same one at which we had celebrated on the day of our land ownership. Unfortunately the roast duck and the spare ribs were off and the day's homemade pate had been dropped on the floor. I jokingly said to the owner "never mind, everyone has an off day" and his wife was not amused. Nevertheless we all still had a very good meal and an enjoyable but subdued evening. After our somewhat tearful farewells we returned to the caravan and felt as flat as farts.

As anticipated the inevitable follow up list was handed over by Simon on their way to the airport. There was nothing on it, which appeared to be too difficult so I decided to complete all of the items in the quickest possible time. Over a four-day period I was able to cross everything off and felt quite pleased at the end results. After this we were glad to have the chance to be the first to commission the solar panel heating installation, we had been invited to take every opportunity as soon as it was operational. AC had the honour of luxuriating in a hot, very hot bath whilst I took a cooler shower. The system was efficient, almost instant scalding hot water so it was tested again the next day, with equally enjoyable results.

I had examined the use of solar energy for our hot water requirements and had decided not to pursue it as relative to our budget, it was an expensive initial capital outlay compared to a gas fired heater system, which we would have installed. I had calculated that we could operate this type, even when an allowance for an increase in the costs of gas was made, for a period in excess of ten years for the initial cost of a solar panel system. I had ignored, as I had no idea, what the maintenance costs on the panel, solenoid valves and pipe work would be over that period and these could add on another year to my figure. Another major point in my decision, nothing at all to do with finance, was that I considered that the panels were not aesthetically pleasing and were an eyesore stuck up on the roof. At the back of my mind I had considered that if in the future, finances and my attitude changed, it would only take a simple modification to the existing piping to integrate both systems.

The "Magnificent seven" returned and proceeded to strip the ring beam shuttering, but not the supports and these would not be removed for at least a fortnight. Over one morning they had laid a relatively smooth screed, almost four centimetres thick over the whole of the various roof slopes and then the builder arrived and threw a wobbler into the works as he requested an early second stage payment. That completely spoilt my day. It so happened to be the anniversary of our arrival on the land, which I had hoped that we could celebrate happily with some degree of stress free style. The easy answer was to say no and refer to the contract that had only recently been stuck in a drawer. I thought quickly on my feet and considered that that response would not be a positive move. His men had certainly cracked on since day one and he was ahead of schedule, I offered to pay him slightly less than he had requested at the end of the next week and this was agreed. It was an amicable arrangement that suited us both.

It was brilliant from my point of view as one high interest deposit would have matured by then and have been transferred to the current account with no financial loss to ourselves. There was a potential downside however with the strong possibility that other stage payments would be brought forward. Any early maturity of other deposits would certainly be to our disadvantage. Overall we could lose out as our cash flow could be seriously affected. A gloomy day all round and I sunk into a decline. To add to the problems it pissed down after lunch and prevented any further work on the roof.

AC had spent most of the day with her nose in her little red Horta book and had researched from the manual and other information leaflets on the various weed and bug control methods. It made us, me in particular, even more depressed when we read through it. She had started to make entries as soon as we had planted our first broad bean seeds and it already contained a record of everything that we had produced. It included the types of vegetable seeds, the dates sown with germination periods and dates of harvest with weather conditions. To read what we had achieved so far was remarkable and the entry on the work that was entailed with fruit trees in an orchard was unbelievable.

We did, with very little effort, celebrate somewhat boringly on a late trip into the village for supper and a few very stiff nightcaps. If nothing else it took our minds off the problems. Afterwards we lay in bed and chatted about money or the lack of it and finally drifted off into a fitful night's sleep.

Our recent visitors had only just departed when we received a letter from Susie "Q". She had planned a two-week holiday at the end of the month but that the actual timing depended on her work commitments and available flights. It did not give us much notice and could we gird up our loins to stand the pace again? So soon after the hectic times with the last ones. We wrote back to her and gave her our German friend's telephone number that she could use in an emergency, but only if she could not confirm by post. The rains continued on and off with some very heavy downpours but then the weather improved and progress soon got back on course. We were asked to select the roof tiles on the builder's next visit and he had brought samples, two to be exact. It was a choice of red or yellow, not a lot to strain our decision-making faculties. We both preferred the yellow ones as they appeared to be of better quality and free from blemishes but had no idea as to whether they had been kiln fired or dried out in the open air. Whichever had been adopted should not have affected their usage, after all they were only decorative.

Two pre-cast chimney tops were then produced from the rear of his van and two twenty five litre cans of, we could not believe it, "Aquaseal", our roof specification had called for two coats of a proven water sealer to be applied and painted over the screed and this was undoubtedly one of the best. I was chuffed in one respect and bloody miffed in another. Had I known of its availability I would have insisted that a thick coat, even if it had to be painted on by myself, was put on top of the foundations under the internal and external walls and column bases as a type of damp proof course.

The workers were highly amused by our excitement but could not understand the instructions. They were amazed that we could until it dawned on them that they were in English. All of them had a go at the application using soft long-haired brushes and had completed the first coat on the roofs over our bedroom and bathroom, kitchen utility room and the lounge before lunch. When they returned I gave them a full bucket of water and indicated that it should be poured down one of the treated slopes. I was impressed and they were stunned that all of the water ran off and not one drop penetrated into the screed. By the end of the week both cans were empty and the first coat was completed. I asked the builder to collect three more over the weekend and that I would pay for the third one.

That weekend was a peaceful one and we decided that the slope of the roof over the gas bottle and water heater store was not ideal. It was another architect's wet dream. The slope was at ninety degrees to the one over the kitchen which gave it an attractive line at a different level but it was totally impractical as when it rained, and by now we had had a considerable experience of this occurrence, hundreds of litres of water would slosh down past the kitchen window, a miniature Niagara Falls. To overcome this it would be necessary to build up the walls of the store to the level of the kitchen roof and continue the slope of this over them. It was also decided to have a chimney over the water heater section of the store to allow all the exhaust gases from the boiler to escape.

The last time that I had walked around and inspected the asparagus seed beds seemed like light years away with everything that had gone on. It could just have well have been, as then, the mass of elegant fern like foliage had already started to die down. This made the red berries on the female plants even more discernible. Now, only two weeks later the fern had died down completely with berries all over the ground. With a few exceptions it was now impossible to distinguish the male plants from the females. Shit, oh double shit I moaned aloud with my head lifted to the heavens. We had blown it completely!!!

The female crowns would not be as heavy a cropper as the males as energy had to be expended to produce the seedlings. This was an important factor when deciding which sex to plant. We had intended to mark the females in the seed beds and AC had spent hours on the production of marker sticks. When the time came around to transplant the one-year-old crowns the unmarked ones, the males, would have been lifted first using the marked female ones only as a reserve. That future extremely important selection was now impossible. We would only be able to ascertain how many male crowns we had transplanted would be when they produced the fern in the following year. What an absolute cock up! What really pissed me off was that we had known, and catered, for this one off opportunity to select the most productive of the one-year-old crowns and had still screwed it up. All of the beds were now in a real buggers muddle but it would still be possible to cut down all the fern with the heavy duty hand shears that had been recently bought from the co-operative, as the thickest one was no thicker than a size four knitting needle.

The red berry seedlings that had fallen to the ground ripened and split open day-by-day revealing up to six little black pearls in each one. On the permanent asparagus beds these, if they remained, would have a high probability of germination and prove difficult to eradicate. They could then grow on top of the parent crowns which would be masked and smothered and their production capabilities severely hampered and reduced. This was another important factor in crown sex selection as all male plants produced no seeds and therefore fewer problems.

It was now necessary for us to clean the berries and seeds off, as far as was practically possible. They had to be raked up into small heaps and then cleaned off by hand with us bent over double, bums in the air yet again and all of this dross would have to be burnt. We totally ignored all of the chaos that continued around us as this exercise had to be given top priority. It was only after this cleansing operation was completed that we could appreciate once again how large an area the seed beds covered. With a gasp and a gulp I tried to envisage the space that would eventually become the permanent beds when the crowns were transplanted early next year. It was hoped that now with only an occasional weeding session over the winter months, the crowns would remain dormant until the spring.

AC suggested that it would be a good idea to lift some of the parsnips and I agreed. What should have been a straightforward and easy exercise proved to be extremely difficult. I had to use both the fork and the spade to extract some of them as their roots went half way down to Hades. Others had short stumpy roots and had lumpy nodules, and on some of them the roots were forked. Most, we were pleased to find, were of a regular shape and when cut open were not at all woody in the core. Some of these weighed over half a kilo and others were as heavy as one. We decided that if we were to sell on a commercial basis that a more shallow rooted variety would have to be selected and the shorter nobbly ones would be classified as "Uglies", to be used for soup packs, stews or whatever.

A lorry and trailer turned up very early one morning loaded with pallets of roof tiles, about seven thousand of them. Through the caravan window they appeared to be red. It was in a mad panic that I managed to drag on my pants and drape a dressing gown around my shoulders and hurtled through the door where I waved my arms frantically and indicated no, no, no they were not for us. The builder who stood by the lorry smiled, winked and tore off the deep pink plastic covering on one of the pallets. The tiles were exactly as we had ordered yellow ones. I grinned and with an extra firm handshake complimented him on his sense of humour.

The required modification to the roof of the gas bottle and water heater store was agreed with him there and then. It did not represent a problem as the walls had not yet been built up to their designed height and the additional chimney could easily be included at this stage.

As he was in a good mood I asked if I could borrow his heavy-duty electric Kango hammer. He told me that it would be on site when they started to excavate for the drainage and sewage pipes and that I could use it then. This type of hammer worked on a vibratory principle and with the right tool bit was an ideal machine to break up rocks and sandstone. There were many layers of these materials, in varying thicknesses at the front of the Quinta towards the two cork oak trees.

When Bulldozer Joe had levelled the site he had only cut out, on my instructions, the minimum distance from the datum point to enable the building works to be constructed. I therefore had to form the final perimeter of the front driveway to ensure that there was sufficient clearance to enable the caravan to be removed from its present position to a parking space by the east wing of the Quinta. I had drawn up a scale plan on which were shown the outside line of the utility and kitchen walls and had superimposed a cardboard cut out of the caravan on to it. By moving this I was able to determine how far from these walls the driveway would have to be cut back to get it safely out, hence the need to borrow the Kango.

The weather became yet again pretty shitty with lots of rain and thunderstorms. Shades of last year crossed our minds. My mood was made even shittier when AC pointed out that our Residents Permits were due for renewal and that we should do something about fairly quickly. At the offices in Portimao we said, "that we believed that we were entitled to five year permit," and they handed over a list of all the necessary documents to be submitted. There was even more rain as we traipsed round the by now, all too familiar departments on another paper chase and collected everything bar one. It was a new requirement and had to be collected from the Tax Offices, filled in and returned to them for signature. We had considerable difficulty in the translation and the completion but we eventually succeeded, most of the questions referred to my sole trader details. With a duly stamped copy of this and all of the other supporting papers we returned to Portimao, where they were scrutinised and after a long while accepted. As the receipt was handed over they told us that we should collect our permits in two months time.

Our German friends turned up late one Tuesday afternoon quite excited as for the first time since we had arrived they had received a telephone call from England with a message to pass on to us. Some young girl called Susan would arrive tomorrow and spend the night in a Hostel in Lagos and visit us on Thursday. We thanked them very much and apologised for any inconvenience that might have been caused but they were delighted to have helped out. They were always very busy and ran two popular restaurants in Lagos. During the season they had no free time so they had taken this welcome opportunity to take a short break. After a brief tour of the works, where they were surprised and very impressed, we took them to M's café for a quick catch up chat over a drink.

We met Susie "Q" off the bus in the village and returned to the caravan for supper, which we had had the time to prepare. A few good relaxing days were spent together on the inevitable vegetable plot preparations and much chin-wagging on life in the evenings. She seemed more relaxed than before, more so than us. It should not have been a surprise as it seemed that the more visitors we had, the more often whispering death appeared and generally made himself a nuisance. Grubby tangerines or windfall oranges were pulled out of his pockets in return for wine and fags. I never begrudged him the wine, sometimes three full glasses, but he was becoming knackered up rapidly by the fags. It took him only five minutes to scramble down to the caravan but up to thirty for him to drag himself or crawl on hands and knees back up to the track and then make his way home.

We received a prearranged telephone call, in M's café from Lucie, she and Les wanted to come over in mid November and asked us to arrange some accommodation for them in Lagos. Once they had confirmed their flights we could book something up.

Susie "Q" commuted between the caravan and Lagos. It was good to see that she could do her own thing and enjoy a massive degree of freedom and relaxation. This was certainly the place to have unlimited access for such needs.

On close examination of the asparagus seed beds I discovered that many small spears had burst through as a result of the recent rains complimented by the still warm soil conditions. I knew that it was naughty, and was not good husbandry, but I quickly cut three good handfuls of spears and in less than thirty minutes they were placed on the table and gleefully scoffed. They had been steamed and served with fried crispy streaky bacon and the hot fat from this was drizzled over the cooked spears. I thought that it made a delicious and novel starter for this time of the year. AC complained that the spears were a little bit gritty as a result of the downpours and that I had not washed them thoroughly enough. She was right but I still considered them to be excellent after only eight months growth from seed. The flavour was not particularly strong as it had not sufficient time to develop

During Susie "Q's" stay there was a torrential downpour, a really violent storm with water everywhere. It thundered down the gully and again poured off the track onto the land. It had to be seen to be believed. To us it was absolutely incredible and all we could do was to batten down the hatches and stay put.

We were both extremely frazzled the next morning as our visitor went into Lagos to meet her friend from the Exeter area. We had met her briefly some years earlier when we had stayed there for a short break. This friend was on holiday with her two small children and she wanted to bring them all back to see the rancho. As luck would have it there was some sunshine so we did not all have to sit huddled in the caravan. A makeshift lunch was taken on the terrace followed by a rather squelchy meander round the estate.

They were just about to leave when the heavens fully opened and the rains sloshed down. To escape I had to literally pour them into the fart box, all of us soaking wet, which initially fired on only two or maybe three cylinders and didn't fire on all four until we had climbed up the drive onto the track. We eventually spluttered into the bus station in Lagos for their onward journey to Armacao de Pera.

Susie "Q" was to catch the same bus the next day and would stay with them overnight and then they would all catch the same flight back to England. After we had waved her off we felt a sense of relief. We loved her dearly but there were times when she could be difficult to understand in some of the intense conversations. It was nice to see that she was so much calmer and not as serious about everything like on her previous visits and we were pleased for her as she had gone through some difficult times over the past few years.

Chapter Ten

Some years before we were strongly advised that some form of heating would be essential over the long winter months and provision had been made on the plans for a fireplace in the lounge. Both of us agreed that an open fire would be totally inadequate and had examined the alternatives. The obvious one was to install a central heating system with a boiler, a pump and radiators. Heat could be generated by a stove with an integral back boiler, with wood, bottled gas or diesel oil used as the fuel. A liquefied gas supply from a sunken storage tank was not available. One local company had been approached and their engineer had visited to look over the room sizes and orientation relative to the fireplace.

When questioned he stated that wood was the cheapest readily available fuel. The amount of bottled gas that would be needed made it a very expensive system to run, and home deliveries of bulk diesel fuel were not at all commonplace. It seemed like a Hobson's choice situation to us so we asked for a quotation for a log-burning stove, the maximum size that they manufactured, together with all of the ancillary equipment.

He also offered to quote us for a swimming pool heat pump, as they were now available, despite my comments that such a luxury was a long way down our priority list. When the quotation was received and studied it did not generate too much excitement. A decision on the heat pump was, as I had expected, an immediate no!! The installed price was almost of what we had contracted to pay for the complete pool. Our financial situation made the decision on the central heating system an easy one, no again, as the cost was almost three times more than our budgeted figure. We would have to try to sort out another solution.

Over supper that evening we realised that it was more or less three years to the day that we had made our offer for the land. Since that step had been taken, neither of us had ever seriously regretted the decision. There were some momentary occasions when we had wished that matters could have worked out differently but there had been no major traumas. It was no wonder, that some of our friends often referred to us as a couple of "odd balls" that had temporarily slipped over the edge. For me it had not proved to be too difficult. Just another move into the unknown but, this time it had turned out different to what I had expected.

The builder arrived with the carpenter, the same one who had carried out the work at Cheryl and Simons, and we all walked around the Quinta and discussed doors, wardrobes, kitchen and bathroom requirements. It was a useful exercise as everyone, we thought, then fully understood what was needed and more importantly its location. He told us that the electrician would arrive later on in the week. Most of the rest of the day and evening was then spent poured over our previously prepared plans and layouts of the electrical installation and a few minor modifications incorporated.

As promised the electrician turned up and we handed over our layouts. Another walk about followed with a couple of the workers in tow. He studied our requirements in each room and marked in chalk on the appropriate wall the location of sockets, switches light fittings and the conduit runs for the cables. The latter were not like those in England, up and down vertically from the power outlet, but horizontal and curved around the walls not one was in a true straight line. Where he wanted a cable to go through a wall he marked it with a circle surrounding an X. As we progressed I noticed small grins appear on the workers faces and these got wider and wider until at the end they looked totally bemused. Before the electrician had left the workers had already started to cut out the "Charlie Chases", grooves, and holes in the wall for the conduits to be buried and the fittings mounted. In every room they asked why we wanted so many and we always replied that they were necessary and with a shrug of their shoulders carried on. When we occupied the Quinta there would be a lot of wall fixings to be made, paintings, mirrors and other fittings so I made a sketch of each wall, which showed the conduit runs. I could then make holes in the walls without drilling through a live electric cable. The following week all the cable conduits, socket and switch fittings had been fixed and the electrician pointed out that where the conduits terminated for the ceiling lights in the utility room, kitchen, lounge, our bedroom and bathroom a support would needed.

We could not believe the weather, it was wetter than the previous late autumn and early winter period. Rain and yet more rain fell but without the thunder and lightning. One afternoon after I had collected more fresh water supplies from the village there was another real Algarvean downpour. This one gave me serious problems on my return up the inclined part of the track. It was like a river in full flood against me and the fart box stalled again and again. At one point just before the brow, where it started its descent to our land, we just crept over in gear, only because the starter motor turned without a flicker of life from any of the spark plugs. From there it was literally go along with the flow down the slope, in the hope that the brakes would function and that I could turn into the drive by wrenching on the wheel as I had no power steering. The drive had altered considerably in less than an hour and was barely recognisable. The builder's pile of sand at the top, about four cubic metres of it had been washed away. All of this was now deposited down alongside the access on the east wing of the Quinta. This appeared to have been built upon a beach. The sand was piled against the wall to a depth of almost twenty centimetres. It still continued to piss down until way past midnight and the caravan was damp and had a leak over the front window. As we crashed out we wondered whether this nightmare weather would ever end.

Comfortable accommodation had been chosen for AC's Pees at the top part of Lagos, the keys had been collected and the fridge loaded with basic foodstuffs. It turned out to be a real buggers muddle on the day of their arrival as nothing went according to plan. I was not surprised when early in the morning the fart boxes engine refused to fire. It was only after a can of a proprietary damp start had been almost emptied, the contents squirted onto the distributor cap, the coil and the plug leads that it laboured into life. Only just, and it sounded most unhealthy until we had covered a few kilometres on our journey to Faro. We arrived in good time to meet their incoming flight only to find that there was a mega delay. It was still on the ground at Birmingham due to a part malfunction so rather than kick our heels at the airport we decided to go and spend some time in the old part of the city.

We returned some hours later just in time to meet them as they staggered into the arrivals hall completely knackered. Under the circumstances it was decided to drive them straight to the apartment and get them settled in. There we found that one of the electric blankets didn't work but it was too late in the day to do anything about it. AC made a medicinal pot of tea and we left them to their own devices and arranged to collect them in the morning.

It was the weekend and the site was peaceful and free of the "Magnificent Seven" or any other bods, just us two. AC went off to collect her Pees and I started to strip off the shed roof as it leaked like a sieve again, was it any wonder when one considered the appalling weather conditions. On their return Lucie was suitably impressed by the rate of progress and her father was somewhat dazed about it all. He loved the Quinta's location and the surrounding area and was more than excited at what we had achieved in the relatively short time since our arrival. We travelled around extensively with them and visited all of the popular places, some new restaurants were tried and old ones, new to Les, returned to. More often than not we ate in the apartment and at these times treated ourselves to the luxury of a hot bath and a loo that flushed into the mains.

Despite a couple of feeble attempts to get it sorted out the electric blanket refused to function The weather perked up, much to our disbelief, and there were many hours of sunshine to enjoy. One day Les actually stripped to the waist when he wheel barrowed some soil from the front of the Quinta to a position where the pool pump house would be built. Their general assistance around the place during the holiday was invaluable and it gave us a considerable lift.

All too soon it was time to take Les back to the airport. Business commitments had only allowed him to take a one-week break. It was an early morning flight and for a change on time so we were able to wave him through to the departure lounge without any delay. This gave us the opportunity to call into Portimao for almost a full days shopping spree much to Lucie's delight as she wished to purchase some shoes. I bought another two cans of damp start, as I was sure that they would be needed sooner rather than later and browsed around before meeting up with them for lunch.

Their morning's retail therapy had gone well but one or two items still remained on her list. As I also had other items to find we arranged to meet up in the central gardens around four o'clock.

The cable clips for the generator had become distorted by constant use and needed to be replaced. Some were eventually found in the third electrical shop that I visited. In there were two Englishmen whose conversation was quite agitated and loud and it was impossible not to hear most of it. The subject was about a fellow who manufactured log burning stoves to a Swedish design and that they had found that they were extremely efficient. Nothing ventured, nothing gained I thought and introduced myself. When my requirements were outlined to them they became quite excited and promptly gave me his full details and telephone number and wished me luck. One of them mentioned that on some days as his stove smouldered away that he had had to open a window as the rooms got too warm. All in all a very productive day, AC's tolerance level at shopping was at the most two hours so she had borne up much better than she had expected, and we returned to the apartment with a car boot full of goodies.

On Lucie's final evening had we supper in the apartment, a nourishing steak and kidney pudding, her speciality, which was followed by pancakes. It had started to rain as we left for the caravan and a few problems were experienced and detours made to get out of the town as some of the roads were flooded. This was not good for my nerves because we had a run to Faro the next morning so a quick visit to M's café was made for a medicinal bevy or two.

It rained all night long and it still tipped down when we left to collect Lucie. Plenty of time was allowed which proved to be a good move as it took half an hour to get the car engine running. There were floods all along the river Bensafrim's valley and the water level was much higher than last year. A newly planted orange orchard looked as if it had been sighted in the middle of a moving lake that rapidly flowed through it. We were unable to drive the car into Lagos and had to abandon it at a petrol station on the outskirts. The flood waters swirled so angrily and were at such a level that it would most certainly have stalled, and with our luck, in the most inconvenient place. Our Wellingtons were in the boot so we managed to walk through the floods into town. I was very concerned as there was no way the poor old fart box would get us to the airport. It was however a Thursday, a "tourist change over day", hundreds would leave and hundreds would arrive and we knew that tour operators would collect holiday makers from hotels and complexes and bus them on to airport at Faro.

On the way up the hill to collect our passenger we called into the main Lagos hotel and were told that a coach would depart from there just after lunch. No one however could confirm to us as to whether or not there were any spare seats available. Despite our early start we still arrived quite late at the apartment where we found Lucie in an extremely frazzled state as she had wondered what on earth had delayed us. Over a snack lunch, nobody was really hungry, we outlined our plans to her and she was more than a little apprehensive about the whole idea. After the apartment was given a quick tidy over we started the trek back down the hill to the hotel.

As a result of all her shopping the main suitcase was very heavy and after about fifty metres my arm felt as if it was being dragged out of its shoulder joint. "Bugger this for a game of soldiers" I said and with a gesticulation not used since I had left full-time employment, waved down a taxi that was heading out of town. With his foot hard on the brakes and full left lock on the steering wheel, tyres screeching and burning, he changed direction and came to a halt beside us. It was quite a skilful and completely unexpected manoeuvre, but effective. At the hotel I handed over the fare and a generous tip and it would still have been cheap at twice the price. When the coach arrived I quickly cornered the courier and explained our predicament to her. After her clip-board had been carefully scrutinised she said that we were very very lucky, there was only one vacant seat and due our circumstances she could allocate it to Lucie. When I asked her about the fare she gave a big smile and said that nothing would be charged. AC said, "she could have kissed her". "And me," said I, she was after all extremely attractive. There were the usual lumps in our throats, and a deep felt sense of relief, as we waved her mother goodbye. She rang us at the café the next day and told us that the trip was like a nightmare, the coach had to be diverted as Portimao was flooded and there other minor detours, but that they had in the end, got through to Faro. To cap it all the flight had to land at East Midlands airport and not Birmingham as scheduled, a journey through hell!

Despite the awful weather the roof tiling was completed somewhat later than had been anticipated due to the frequency and ferocity of the storms. On some days it was too dangerous for the workers to go up on the roof. We were pleased to find that all of the ceilings were as dry as a bone, which was a good reference for the Aquaseal applications. As agreed, the roof for the gas and water heater store was built to our new requirements and all three chimneys fixed, one over the fireplace, one over water heater store and the other on the kitchen roof over where the cooker hob would be positioned. Everything was ready for the electrician to install the cabling with fittings and to make the connection to the main distribution board, which the carpenter had just delivered and had already been built into the hall wall. On the down side there was no sign of the plumber but I had managed to make contact with the log burning stove manufacturer and arranged to meet him at the Lagoa petrol station.

The internal and external sides of the walls and the ceilings were now ready to be plastered. This was made with a mixture of sand and cement and applied as a rendering and in each individual room the ceiling would be completed before a start was made on the walls. I therefore quickly fabricated the supports for the ceiling lights for the workers to build in.

The garden shed roof had been fully stripped down to the eucalyptus pole supports. These were then boarded over and what was left of the Aquaseal liberally applied all over. Luckily there was sufficient to complete it. The whole roof had then been retiled and as more rain was forecast its waterproofing would soon be put to the test.

It continued to be all systems go a really fast moving whirligig. As quickly as the carpenter delivered the door frames the faster they were fixed into position. We certainly needed our wits about us, to avoid an accident, on our twice-daily overall progress inspections.

We had almost forgotten the architect until he turned up one day with all the drawings, which now indicated the revised site plan of the Quinta's location and the all-important signed structural plan. He drove us into Lagos where they were submitted to the Council and a receipt and reference number obtained.

The discussions with the log burning stove manufacturer proved to be very constructive. On top of the free standing stove would be mounted lengths of stainless steel tubes, an internal chimney, and these would be connected, through a hole in the lounge ceiling, to the outside chimney. They would of course become very hot when the stove was burning and this heat could be utilised. I suggested that if a lintel was cast in over the front face of the stove a thin walled chimneybreast face could be bricked up above this to the ceiling. Behind this the heat from the tubes, as well as the back top and two sides of the stove, would warm up the enclosed air chamber and also the breast face. As the stove was located in a corner of the lounge the other two sides of the chamber, part of our bedroom wall and part of the corridor wall would also soak up the heat. On a purely decorative note a firebrick facing could be built around the stove and a mantelpiece added.

By now, completely warmed to the idea, I suggested that a simple warm air circulation system could be installed to the two guest bedrooms and the kitchen and quickly prepared a draft layout. This showed underground tubing from these to the back of the stove. At a high level in the corridor wall, built into the chamber, would be another tube connected to a hot air extractor fan from which a tube would be laid back to them. Cold air could then be pulled from the rooms and heated air from the chamber pumped back in. I intended to fit dampers to all the cold exit and hot re-entry grills in each tube. This would give me the flexibility to control which room or rooms would receive the heated re-circulated air. In our bedroom wall an opening would be made into the air chamber, covered with a simple fixed grill, to transfer some warm air into it.

He calculated a price there and then which included for the supply and delivery of the stove, the largest one in his range, and a hot air extractor fan. I would source the necessary tubing and fittings and the aluminium backed foam with fibre glass wool to insulate the hot air distribution side of the system. Although his price was higher than we could afford it was a far better alternative than a simple open fire and substantially lower than the other prices that we had already rejected. A cheque was handed over for fifty per cent of his quote and we promised to let him know when it could be installed and give him two clear weeks notice. We did however need the fan for me to fix in position and the electrician to wire up and he indicated that he could deliver it in one week's time. On our return to the site I immediately took measurements for the lengths of tubing and made a list of all the other requirements and then beetled off to Lagos to buy them. Everything was sourced from one supplier and delivery confirmed for the following day.

Despite our previous walkabout with the builder and the carpenter, there was still a lot of confusion on their part as to our exact requirements in the guest bedrooms. We met again and I sketched out what we expected. The light dawned and the workers quickly built the two thin walls that would support a central plain marble dressing table and form the side of the wardrobe. Double wardrobes would be built in either side and to span over all of this would be six storage cupboards. Just to make certain that our bedroom requirements were fully understood we went through them again. Wardrobes were not required on the south facing external wall but were to be fitted on the inside wall to our bathroom. We had been advised never to build anything against an outside wall due to the problems with damp and humidity in the winter, even though we had made provision in our electrical layouts for the installation of sockets for panel or tubular heaters. It was a Friday and at the end of the day all of us, except AC, enjoyed a stiff shot of Glenmorangie to celebrate my imminent birthday.

We had a stroke of luck and the stove manufacturer did not need to make a special journey. He had forgotten that he had an installation to carry out in Barao San Jao and on his way there dropped off all the fittings and the extractor fan. There was no peace for the wicked on the actual birthday, the Saturday, as I spent all of the morning on my hands and knees to hack out channels, from the two guest bedrooms and the kitchen to the location of the stove and fireplace, in which all the cold air tubing was laid and covered with a thin weak mix of concrete, Openings were then cut in the respective walls at ground level and the grills and dampers connected to the tubes. I also took the opportunity to bury a small plastic conduit from the internal telephone connection, provided by the electrician near the front door, to the lounge doorway opening. This would enable us to extend the incoming line all over the Quinta if required.

Flushed with success at the day's progress my mood improved tremendously and on the spur of the moment we decided to celebrate and enjoyed a cosy candlelit champagne supper in a very small but intimate restaurant in Lagos. All too soon it was back down to earth again with a bang as we assessed progress over a nightcap in M's café where he and his wife joined us. She, as always, produced a plateful of home made stickies, which rounded off the day quite well.

The next morning we took the opportunity to take a wander around the ranch and saw some of the damage that had been caused by the storms and were pleased to find that it was nothing too serious at the top and middle sections of the land. Reparation would not prove to be too difficult or expensive but that moment was not the time to worry about it. The bottom area, which we had considered as a possible location for the permanent asparagus beds, was in a dreadful state. Surface water that had surged down the land and from across the fig orchard had converged and had gouged out wide and deep furrows all over before it had finally escaped into the gulley about twenty metres from the bottom of the land.

Quite a large amount of high quality topsoil had also been washed away in the process. It was in a real mess and extremely soggy so that with even a minor movement great care had to be taken so that we did not sink in up to our knees. To see all of this was a stroke of good fortune for us, any asparagus crowns that had been planted there would have suffered massive damage. Some of the furrows were so deep that the crowns and roots would have been fully exposed with disastrous results and some of the smaller ones would have been washed away.

An immediate decision was taken that the permanent beds would be made up below the existing seed beds. Also that as soon as some of these became empty, all of the crowns having been transplanted, they would be converted into permanent ones. The whole area would be bounded on its west side by the six mature pomegranate trees that ran parallel and next to the gulley. We realised that this was not the ideal arrangement as there would be competition for water supplies but as we did not wish to grub them out we would have to live with it. The plan was to have this area ploughed along with all the other ones that had been spread with manure from the four large truckloads delivered by the local farmer. This assumed that sooner or later the ground would have actually dried out sufficiently to enable a tractor to gain access.

At the start of one week it was again an all systems go situation, the workers commenced the floor preparation in the two guest bedrooms, the electrician and his mate had started to pull the cables through the conduits, rolls of them were everywhere. A van stopped at the top of the drive; it was the plumber and his son. They were immediately collared and taken to our bathroom and shown the markings we had made of our revised requirements. The bath and shower positions were different to that shown on the plan. We also asked them to install a supply to an outside cold water shower on the swimming pool upper terrace by the guest bedroom sliding window. A major specification change was also necessary as we did not want galvanised water piping. All the main line distribution pipes and fittings were to be in heavy-duty plastic tubing which had recently become available. It was a bit of a "phew" period, a "trying to keep up with the buggers" time. There seemed to be bods working in all directions and materials arrived on a daily basis.

Just after one of our coffee breaks the builder called in and wanted to take us to choose the wall and floor tiles and select the bathrooms and kitchen fittings In the contract the tiles were defined as high quality and a price per square metre had been specified. At the end of a long day after several suppliers and warehouses had been visited our choice seemed to be quite limited. Anything not in stock was on a medium to long-term delivery period. We had made some progress though as a few ideas on designs and colour schemes had been formed.

Unexpectedly one morning a borehole man arrived on the site. His rig and gang had just finished a successful drilling operation nearby and he could sink a shaft and line it with plastic that afternoon. He was the same fellow that we had met some three years earlier and had impressed us then far more than the other bunch of cowboys. We were aware that he had carried out similar works locally for some people that we knew and this made us feel quite comfortable. The position that he selected for the drill was less than thirty centimetres away from the one where AC and I had tested for water availability with him. In his opinion the borehole would need to be about fifty metres deep and it would then have tapped through three underground veins. The price per metre depth was agreed on the spot as was the "no water no payment" principle.

The rig was unloaded in mid-afternoon and quickly set up. It was a compact machine powered by a diesel engine and mounted on two sets of caterpillar tracks, which gave it considerable manoeuvrability. The drill bits were laid out and one fitted as the engine roared into life and the drilling operation commenced. After thirty minutes water was hit at a depth of only fifteen metres, it was like an oil gusher in full flow. In less than two hours the whole operation was completed and the borehole plastic lining was capped, the actual depth was fifty-two metres. When I handed the cheque over I was advised to position the pump ten metres above the bottom and that the flow rate could be as high as eighty litres per minute.

Once again the builder dragged us into Lagos, Portimao and Lagoa, he was in "hyper mode" and wanted to finalise the tiles and fittings selection and get them all on order. At the end of yet another long hard day, everything except the floor tiles for the kitchen, lounge and the hall and corridor had been ordered and we found out, much to our amusement and dismay, that the toilet fittings did not include the bog seats and had not been included in the contract price. Their cost was a minor issue but it meant that we were then lumbered, later on, to find identical coloured ones that matched. Although outside the specification and our budget, we had toyed with the idea of having marble tiles for some floors, so on the way home we asked the builder if we could visit a marble factory the next day. There, after much umming and arring as there were so many to choose from, we made our selection and ordered tiles of three different colours, each one for a respective floor. They were all in stock and delivery was promised at the weekend.

The jungle drums were as efficient as ever. A young man whom we knew quite well as we regularly filled up the fart box with petrol and had brought many cans of engine oil at a garage, where we had had to park the car during the floods, on the outskirts of Lagos called in. We never knew whether or not he was the garage owner or just an employee. He wanted to take us to meet a borehole pump specialist with whom he had a working relationship. This man could supply and install a pump and pressure tank system with all the associated electrical control equipment. I suggested that it would be far better to have discussions here on the site and after they had measured up the pipe and cable runs a quotation could be prepared for consideration and this was agreed.

We still remained on good terms with the builder. There had been no major *"argie bargies"* and only a few minor wobblers had been thrown, all of them by me! All of us remained encouraged by the fact that there had been no disputes between us contractually or financially. Any differences had been quietly and amicably resolved. This relationship was borne out as we received another invitation to his Christmas piss up in the village.

I had mentioned to AC that when I had visited his other two local sites, Cheryl and Simons and the one behind the cork oak wood, there had been an interchange of personnel between them. It was noticeable that none of these workers ever appeared on our site and I never witnessed any of our "Magnificent seven" at either of those. I therefore concluded that our gang were not on his permanent payroll and were employed on a fixed price for the job basis to complete our Quinta. This would explain their incessant work output in an effort to achieve the earliest completion date after which they would be free to work elsewhere. This gave the builder huge logistical problems to ensure that all of the required materials were always ready to hand.

The Christmas bash was again an excellent occasion; the food and booze were as good as ever, mountains and rivers of it, Although the whole affair was not as frenetic as the one last year. My conclusion proved to be correct as not one of the gang who worked on our site were there, all of the workers sat at the tables were his full time staff.

There was a method of level transfers that the workers utilised that I had not come across before. Theodolites, dumpies and spirit levels yes, but never this one before. At the back of my mind I did have a vague recollection that this principle was used extensively in the Arabic countries I had visited many years ago. Here on the Quinta they used a more or less twelve-metre length of transparent thin walled small plastic tubing with a cork plug inserted at each end. This was filled with just a sufficient amount of water to provide an air bubble. When the tube was placed against a wall in one room at a marked spot, and then offered up to a wall in another one, the bubble would become stable and when it was equal in length at each end, this indicated that the levels were exactly the same.

They marked a level on the wall at the front door threshold. This was at a height of one metre above what would eventually be the finished floor level. I called it "the magical metre line" as it was transferred throughout the Quinta and all references were marked off from it. Door heights, windowsill levels, socket and light switch locations, everything. Everyone worked from it and I was happily surprised how simple and efficient it was.

A delegation of three appeared from nowhere on the terrace outside the caravan early one evening. It was the young man from the garage accompanied his pump specialist and an electrician. They had already paced out the distance from the head of the borehole to the Quinta and had scribbled some figures down on a piece of, what looked to me to be, a bit of scrap paper. The specialist handed over two catalogues, one on submersible pumps and the other on pressure vessels. He asked how deep the borehole was and on my response he placed a steel ruler over a set of pump curves. In less than ten seconds he indicated that a pump with a three quarter kilowatt, one horsepower motor would be perfectly adequate and could supply at least fifty litres of water a minute. This was well within the borehole's capacity. I requested a three phase motor and repeated the borehole man's recommendation as to its location relative to the depth of the tube, to which he nodded firmly in agreement.

I had examined three different systems of pumping water from the borehole to the Quinta and had finally decided on one that utilised a pressure vessel and for our installation this would have a capacity of one hundred litres. It would be situated in the water heater store, which was as close as it could possibly be to the heater and the Quinta's internal water distribution pipe work. It could be pre-pressurised and fitted to its top would be a differential pressure switch. The low setting of this would call for water and would start up the borehole pump and when the high setting was reached switch it off. It was a nice neat and compact operating unit.

A quotation was requested for the whole system to include for all interconnecting electrical cables and the control box. I also insisted that a low water level sensor be incorporated to prevent the pump from running if the level of the water was below it.

Before we really knew it Christmas day hit us. It was a Sunday and we were able to have a late leisurely start as there was no else around. Our pressies were opened over breakfast on the terrace. It was not at all cold but there was quite a thick mist in the valley at the bottom of the land. There must have been a thick fog overnight but the sun had broken through by the time that we had stopped looking at the inside of our eyelids. A table had been reserved for lunch at a restaurant bar in Praia da Luz run by some young brummies, two couples with whom we got on rather well with. We had plenty of time to stroll up the track to Cheryl and Simons pad for a long soak in the tub with lots of lovely hot water. Back at the caravan we tarted ourselves up for the big occasion and were pleasantly relieved when the fart box burst into life at the first attempt.

We had dined at this restaurant many times before and the food, as always, was excellent. Christmas lunch consisted of, a rich vegetable soup seafood vol-au-vents, turkey with all the trimmings followed by the traditional pudding and/or oranges glazed in Triple Sec, a liqueur. Drinks including champagne cocktails, wines or beers, flowed and flowed. It was a lovely meal taken in a relaxed ambiance. We knew quite a few of the couples there who also appeared to be thoroughly enjoying themselves. One young lad of about thirty, in one corner, had become a bit of a pain in the butt as after only a few drinks suffered from a severe attack of verbal diarrhoea. This diminished immediately after one of the owners whispered a quiet word in his ear. At one table there was a group of youngsters who were having a whale of a time. We knew one by sight as he lived in the village with his mother not far from the end of the track. He came over to our table and during a brief chat told us that he was employed as a steward on a cruise liner.

Afterwards we called in to see the owner of the complex where we had spent our first holiday for yet more champagne and stayed longer than intended. It was way past ten o'clock when we arrived back at the caravan.

The next day was not celebrated as a holiday here, so we were blessed with the arrival of the "Magnificent seven" together with the other trades. It turned out, as usual, to be a really "bang crash and get on with it" day and someone called to measure up for all the aluminium doors and windows. He completed his exercise and left, much to my annoyance, as he did not make a commitment on a delivery schedule.

There was heavy rainfall on the last day of the year and the reconstructed garden shed roof stood up well to its first test. A great improvement on my initial effort as there were no leaks at all and the inside was bone dry

In previous years, even in England, we had never got our act together to sort out some form of entertainment for the New Years Eve celebrations. This year was again no different. The square root of naff all had been arranged as we definitely lacked motivation. Keen to whip up some excitement we went to the café about nineish only to find that they intended to close up the shop as they were off out on a jolly. We then drove to the club only to find that it was deserted. Over a drink at the bar the steward told us that there would be a party and dancing later. On our drive into Lagos we found that every restaurant or bar was either shut or had the doors closed. On a close inspection a large notice had been pinned up on them, which generally read "Private Party", and from the sounds we could hear there must have been some rave ups on the go inside. The same was true in town, shut or all full. One small back street bar was found open where we had a couple of beers in complete silence. As we sat there alone we felt a little miffed and totally cheesed off.

It was decided in "bah humbug mode", to return to the club for a swift nightcap and then beetle off back to the caravan and have an early night. We would not even bother to sit up and wait for midnight.

There we found that a real *wing-dinging* bash was in full swing upstairs, the whole place throbbed to the sounds of live music. Yet another private party we thought so made our way to the stairs to go down to the bar and console ourselves. We had not quite reached them when the electrician, who was working on our Quinta, popped his head out through the door and came over and grabbed both of our arms and ushered us inside. He quickly led us to his family's table and urged us to sit down where all the introductions were made. Seated at the next table was the plumber and his family so more introductions followed. We were made to feel extremely welcome by all of them but as it was basically a party for family members and associates, we felt more than a little uncomfortable. All the tables in the room were laden with goodies such as prawns, cold chicken joints, cured hams, sausages, pies, nibbles, sweets puddings and breads. You name it and it was there. Every table groaned under the weight of so many bottles of wine, red and white, most of which had been homemade as had a lot of the foods. Also in abundance were port, whiskey, medronho and champagne.

The festivities had commenced, in true Portuguese style, some hours earlier but there was still plenty of everything left on the tables. We were offered plate after plate they would not accept any refusals and insisted that we freely helped ourselves. The same applied to the drinks, rather large glasses were filled to the brim and it was impossible not to spill a little when the first sip was attempted. During all of this activity three musicians played their piano accordions with non-stop gusto.

At midnight all of the champagne bottles were opened after being vigorously shaken and a shower of corks shot across the room. AC whispered in my ear that she had smoked her last cigarette as the New Year was boisterously toasted in. Everyone stood up, shook hands and embraced whoever was next to them. They then moved on from table to table where the gestures were repeated. We heartedly joined in although we felt a little homesick as there were no chimes from Big Ben or the strains of Auld Lang Syne. It happened to be the plumbers birthday on the day and his daughters had been on New Years Eve so there was much rejoicing and many toasts were raised before and after midnight. We were both dragged to different tables and offered more food and booze and then pulled onto the dance floor many times to be whirled around by assorted partners. It was way past four thirty when we managed to extricate ourselves gracefully and left as the music became even louder than ever. Even then party was still in full swing, where did they get their energy from we wondered?

We eventually woke, what a dynamic duo we had been, just after midday and I had had the sleep of the dead. Over a most welcome cup of coffee, both of us without even a trace of a hangover, readily agreed that the celebrations had been by far the most enjoyable that we had experienced since we had got together. They had been better than any New Years Eve party we had been to in our lives before.

It was just as well that we were awake and in the land of the living as Alfonso 1 turned up and had dragged down the track a three-metre length of what appeared to be a slender branch of a tree. It was in fact a long leader cut from the Wisteria shrub in the French girl's garden and was a New Years present for AC. Rumour had it that the land had been sold to a British person who was still employed in the Middle East. We had seen and admired the Wisteria there as it bore a lovely pale lilac coloured blossom which flowered profusely. We then had to decide what to do with this as it was quite unmanageable in its existing length. AC quickly cut it into three pieces and stuck them in a bucket of water. After we had thanked him we took the opportunity to enquire as to when our land could be ploughed and he promised to speak with his friend.

There was another piece of well-intended advice that had been thrust at us on many occasions which was never, never ever plant anything adjacent to a swimming pool that flowered, such as shrubs, deciduous trees or plants. To do so would ensure that the swimming pool attendant – not many guesses would be needed as to whom that was likely to be in our circumstances – would have to spend endless hours in the summer and autumn cleaning the blossom and leaves off the surface of the water and the dross that had sunk to the bottom of the pool overnight. To plant a Wisteria anywhere near to our pool would be an invitation to long-term problems.

Later that day a worker informed us that only half of the kitchen picture tiles had been delivered. Why he was scrabbling around in the ruin was a mystery as it was a National holiday. We set the alarm clock for an early start the next morning to go into town and try to sort out what had happened to the ones that had gone astray.

On the way in we stopped in the village and offered a lift to the electrician's son and his friend who were waiting at the bus stop. Less than one hundred metres after the café there was a police roadside check point and we were waved to a stop. "Oh shit oh dear", I said to AC, "not really the best of times". All of the car papers were found to be in order as was my English driving license. With this I was able to lie through my teeth and tell them that I was a regular tourist and thus prevented any potential on-going interrogations. The officer then indicated that I should get out of the car and produced from behind his back, a breath analyser kit.

The two lads in the back of the car had by this time almost wet themselves and struggled to contain their giggles. I blew as hard as I could into the small tube and the scale registered zero. AC and I were amazed at this result and the policeman was very pleased. There were handshakes all round and we were given the signal to move on. We then breathed a heavy sigh of relief and were astonished and surprised when the amount of booze that I had consumed over that more than *alchofrolic* weekend was taken into consideration.

At the builder merchant's yard there were none of the picture tiles that we required in stock and the bad news was that they were now a discontinued line. The good news on our return to the site was that the missing ones had been found. They had been mistakenly placed in the wrong store in the ruin. Our journey had not been necessary at all and I was really pissed off about it as matters could have gone desperately pear shaped if the breath test had proved to be positive.

We both agreed where the Wisteria cuttings should be planted, one near to the garden shed and utility room, which could then be trained around the cistern and along the front of the kitchen wall and the other two in the wheeled herb garden around the well.

Early one morning we were rudely woken up to hear "noises off" and looked out of the window to see Bulldozer Joe and his machine had just commenced the excavations for the drains from our bathroom and the utility room. AC promptly forgot her New Years resolution and lit up a fag that she had taken from my packet. After a couple of quick nervous puffs I rather beastily muttered under my breath, "what a weak willed wimp", and she handed it over to me with a sheepish look on her face. That was a very close call she admitted to me later on in the day.

The drainage channels along the front and down the east wing side of the Quinta were soon completed and it looked to all intents and purposes as if a bomb had been dropped there. Joe then manoeuvred his machine to start the excavations for the septic tank.

When it came to the plumbing I stood over the plumber as he connected the internal piping to the outside drains an ensured that at each exit a u-bend was fitted. All of the main distribution pipes had been laid, which included the additional cold one to the external shower, and their joints glued. The sanitary fittings had been delivered and located in their respective positions and we thought that they looked rather smart, when we considered the limited selection there had been to choose from.

The electrical wiring installation had almost been completed with most of the fittings attached to the internal and external walls. I had mounted the extractor fan up in the corridor ceiling above the guest bedroom doors and this had been connected up to a new switch. It seemed pointless to ask for a quotation as the electricians work to date had been more than competent, so I asked him to provide a three phase supply to the garden shed and install a switch and cabling to control an electric pump that I would purchase.

This would be situated down the well tunnel and replace the petrol driven pump which hopefully meant that I would never ever have to descend down into the depths again. Two lights were also requested, one to be fitted inside the garden shed and the other on the outside wall that faced the utility room window. This one was to be connected so that it could be switched on and off from inside the utility room. We could then clearly see the way if we wanted to get to the shed in the dark.

One morning a gang of four men almost fell out of a clapped out old van at the top of the drive, fully clad in white overalls. It looked like a "they were coming to take me away" scenario and when they opened the van's rear doors their dress sense was revealed. It was chock a block full with paint drums, rollers, brushes and dust sheets: they were the painters. In less than a day the whole of the outside had been completely painted although it was a little bit patchy in places. We were not unduly concerned as that was only the first coat and it could be corrected on the second application. The transformation from a dull grey cement colour to a gleaming white building was quite amazing. We had no idea as to why the builder had called them in at this stage and in our view thought that it was a little premature.

The builder still struggled to keep up material supplies to the "Magnificent seven" who continued to maintain their rapid rate of progress. They seemed to be active in every room at the same time and had also started on the septic tank foundations. A six centimetre sized gravel had been spread over the bottom of the excavations and a weak mix of concrete laid on this as a blinding. In my opinion Bulldozer Joe had not removed the excavated soil very far away from the hole. It had been deposited almost on the edge along two of its sides, which had not been shored up. There was the danger that these could collapse and the whole mass slide back down into the hole. I warned the workers of this possibility and strongly recommended that they should scrape the soil further away from the holes edges.

I had not been idle during this partially controlled mayhem and was allowed to borrow the builder's Kango hammer. The hole for the shower base on the terrace and the channel for its drain pipe had been cut out. We had intended to fit an enamelled unit but could not find one of a suitable size or colour. A white shower base would have looked somewhat out of place amidst the sandy coloured terracotta type terrace tiles. AC suggested that it should be constructed from that same ones, I thought that it was a brilliant idea and in a couple of hours had laid them to form the base and sides, and had set and buried the drain pipe from it. The workers could now complete what we grandiosely referred to as the swimming pool upper terrace.

At the other end of it, near to our bedroom sliding door I had cast two steps, which led down to the pool pump house floor level. All the sandstone and rocks had been cut back to the required distance from the front of the Quinta so that the caravan could be removed at a suitable time. All of this spoil had been wheel barrowed around to the back and spread out to form the base of the pump house and BBQ areas.

The top of the well had already been made anti-swallow proof so all that was left to completely deny them access was to fit a pair of hinged doors at the tunnel entrance and this proved not to be a problem once a supplier of the t-type hinges had been found in Portimao. Whilst there we called into the Residents department and to our delight found that our Residents cards were available for collection. It was with a great sense of relief when we discovered that they were, at long last, five year ones so we had a quick celebratory bevy in the café on our way home.

Overnight there were heavy rainstorms and in the morning we could see the damage they had caused. The hole for the septic tank was almost half full of water and most of the excavated soil on the sides had slid into it, exactly as I had anticipated. Why the hell had I not insisted that it be removed? Two more days of rain and it was full with what appeared to be more soil than had been originally been dug out together with a lot more rainwater. The whole area could not have been in a bigger mess and our major concern was that it could set back an early completion.

A quotation for the supply and installation of the borehole pump with ancillary components was delivered and then studied with dismay. Why was it that our budgeted costs never bore any resemblance to the amounts that we eventually had to fork out? It was expensive but we decided to go for it and not spend the time and effort to seek an alternative quote. At the back of our minds we considered that the probability of obtaining a much lower price was highly unlikely so why bother with such a fruitless exercise.

One of the workers asked if it would be possible to use my well water pump to empty the septic tank hole. I agreed as we would not need to use it in the foreseeable future and decided to ignore the fact that it was such a bloody pig to start. He humped it up the well tunnel and I set it up with the necessary suction and delivery piping. Great care was taken when the suction pipe was lowered into the muddy waters and this would have to be continuously relocated during the pumping operation to avoid the removal of just syrupy mud which would immediately block up the pump. As usual the bloody thing played silly buggers and it took almost four hours before a drop of brown water was removed and discharged down the land. By late evening as much water as possible had been pumped out but a terrible heap of thick gooey sludge remained. How this would be removed was anybody's guess.

Most of the internal building works were now completed and the painters had started to paint anything and everything that didn't move. All of the floors had been cast on a thick plastic membrane and fully tiled. In the lounge I had marked out the fireplace and the hearth and firebrick surround for the stove had been built. The wall tiles had been fixed and grouted except those in the utility room, the pantry and the kitchen. The marble windowsills and door thresholds had also been fixed and AC had placed a protective cover over all of them. Internal doors had been hung and wardrobes and kitchen cupboards fitted. It was beginning to look very nice, like a finished Quinta, and we were pleased with the results so far. There were items to be completed however but the builder had at long last lost the race to keep up with the men and they were short of materials.

The levels of three outside inspection chambers for the sewage and drains had been pegged out. I was not at all happy as they were not deep enough to ensure a rapid flow of waste and water and were not as specified in the contract. We had heard that at some building sites some drains had been laid level or even at a slight incline with disastrous results. They were soon corrected to the required depth and the three other chambers set and built to maintain this slope to the septic tank. The two lines of pipes were then lowered into the drainage channels and connected to the chambers whose pre-cast covers were then placed into position on top of them. There was mud everywhere even when the whole of the excavations had been covered with the sand that had been washed down from the top of the drive during the earlier storms. It still looked like a bombsite, a real squelchy quagmire.

With all of the front of the Quinta in this terrible state AC's main concern was that entry to it could only be by traipsing through the mud and that she would have the continuous chore of clearing up all of the resultant mess. She insisted, quite rightly so, that a duckboard pathway be constructed from the used timber shuttering that had been left lying around the place.

This was soon finished and at the end of the day the leader of the "Magnificent seven" told us that they would not return until all of the outstanding materials were on site and that the septic tank area was available. They were not prepared to sit around on their butts, hang about and wait for dribs and drabs of items to be delivered as they had more productive and profitable work to do elsewhere. I told him that in my opinion there were sufficient materials to complete lots of the minor works and requested that someone remained to finish them. Much to our relief one of them volunteered to do so.

The builder had lost the plot a little and got into a right pickle. He had overstretched himself and still had not finished off all of the external works at Cheryl and Simons and was also late on the completion date for the villa behind the cork oak wood. The owners of this had been told that it was completed and the final payment had been handed over. On that basis they had driven from England and found that they now had to live in temporary accommodation. At whose cost we did not know. Although ahead of time on our works his subcontractors, or his lack of organisation skills, had finally let him down.

There continued to be heavy rain with thunder and lightning on and off, so when Bulldozer Joe arrived to clear out the septic tank hole, he didn't manage to fill even half of a bucket and spent a wasted hour before he gave up and drove away.

It was a "gloom and bloody doom" type of situation, especially after a tour of inspection of the land under cultivation, specifically the asparagus seed beds. Here we found that they were smothered in weeds some of which were over forty centimetres tall, with the soil so soggy, that to walk on it, would almost certainly damage the roots. The proposed area for the permanent beds was in an even worse condition. If the weather conditions didn't improve rapidly then there was no way in which we would be able to transplant the one-year-old crowns from the seed beds, always assuming that we could even get onto them safely. We would then be left with the daunting task of transplanting two-year-old crowns in the following year, not recommended in the gardening books that we had studied. If it actually came to that, we gave ourselves little or no chance of being able to lift them out of the ground without causing considerable damage to the more established and larger root system that would have then developed. As such we would be landed in a classical "well and truly up shit creek without any form of paddle" crisis. It was a rather thought provoking "time to slit your throat" moment.

Not only had we to contend with all that, but there were also no external doors or windows fitted to the building. The lounge and front doors were being made by a carpenter in Barao de Sao Joao, the next village along the track. The frames had been delivered and fitted but were minus the doors and the windows were still being fabricated in a factory at Odiaxere. As such we had a major exercise on our hands to temporarily board up these openings to prevent the swallows being able to complete some nests that had been started in one of the guest bedrooms.

The electric pump that I had ordered some two months before, to replace the petrol one in the well tunnel was finally delivered. It had a three-phase three quarter horsepower motor and had a one and a half inch suction and delivery connections. I had chosen this model as it meant that installation into the existing pipe work would only require a few minor modifications. As it was a lot smaller and not so heavy as the petrol ones I had to construct at the bottom of the tunnel, on the flat portion, a plinth on which it could be mounted and fixed.

Arrangements had been made for the log-burning stove to be installed and to have early discussions on the borehole quotation, so it was still all go as far as we were concerned.

The stove was delivered and placed into position. As I gazed at this new acquisition the realisation that I was back on a treadmill hit me quite forcibly. Way back in the sixties, after I had had gas fired central heating installed in my first home, I patted myself on the back and smugly thought that the constant winter days of having to make paper spills and cut up kindling wood and remove the ashes were over for ever. How wrong could I have been as at that moment I was back to square one and had turned a full circle. For about one hundred and fifty days of the year I would have to lay a fire and once a week for almost twelve weeks I would have to rake out the ashes. My only consolation was that these from the hardwood fuels of almond and olives would contain relatively high amounts of potash. The asparagus crowns, in the permanent beds, would thrive on this when it was used as a top dressing, provided that the soil did not become too alkaline. The stove manufacturer interrupted this reminiscence when he recommended that an extra half a metre of stainless steel chimney flue pipe should be fitted. This meant that the outside chimney needed to be extended and I was able to carry out this modification on the roof without any major problems.

All aspects of the borehole quote were agreed and the installation would start as soon as the pump was received from the stockist in Lisbon. A delivery date of one week was advised. It was my responsibility to prepare the channels for the water pipe and electrical cables from the top of the borehole to the Quinta, by the utility room external wall.

We tracked down the builder to be told that the windows were due to be delivered in a few days time, so were the two outstanding doors. When I questioned him about the completion of the septic tank he just shrugged his shoulders, gazed up at the heavens, shook his head and said nothing. An embarrassed hush ensued. He did, however, have the balls to ask for another progress payment and was curtly told only when the Quinta was swallow proof.

I rigged up my electrical extension cables to use the cement mixer and cast the pool pump house and BBQ base slabs. Another base was also constructed around the top of the borehole tubing. A small housing would be built on this after the pump and piping installation had been completed.

On the black side, the shitty weather continued and muddy water now flowed continuously out of the septic tank hole down the land. It had turned into a much larger muck area than before with no short-term prospects of even a minor improvement in the awful conditions.

The pump was delivered from Lisbon and connected to a high pressure plastic pipe, we had refused to accept galvanised ones as a cheaper alternative, and it and the electric cables were then lowered gently down the borehole tubing by the use of a strong rope and a hand winch. It was set at a depth of ten metres from the bottom as per the recommendations. A generator was quickly set up, started, and this section tested which produced a fierce gush of brown muddy water. The piping and cabling were then laid to the Quinta. There the piping was connected to the pressure vessel and the plumber's main internal distribution lines. A control panel was mounted in the gas heater store and the cabling wired in. This panel had already been provided with a feeder line from the main unconnected incoming electrical supply and nothing else could be done until this was energised.

We had totally forgotten that Cheryl and Simon were due to descend on us for another flying visit until they called in and invited us out for supper. They had a friend who lived on the other side of the village and had a telephone installed. He had relayed a message to us but under our current circumstances it had completely slipped our minds. After a meal in the village we went up to their villa and enjoyed a few brandies and sat in front of their large open log fire. They had had a few problems as a result of all the storms but we reassured them that it could have been a darn sight worse. The front of their drive was still being landscaped and the carpenter, who had recently finished his works at our place, was in the process of making some internal modifications, basically in the kitchen and bedroom wardrobes.

A few more social events were shared before the end of their visit and we also attended three meetings at which they had arranged to discuss general matters on their building problems with all of the parties involved. Other than us, no one else put in an appearance so they asked if we could chase up matters after they had left. We had come to dread this situation as it left us in a difficult position but we never refused and always promised to do the best that we could.

Not long afterwards on one extremely stormy evening, as the rain bucketed down, there was a loud rap on the caravan window and when we opened the door saw a poor scruffy looking drenched individual who stood there with a severe attack of the shivers soaked to the skin. He asked us if we could tow his friend's car out of a flood. They had got stuck on an interconnecting track, about five hundred metres past us, between ours and the Bensafrim to Barao de Sao Joao road. It was normally passable in a dry summer across the riverbed as there was only a trickle of water which formed a shallow ford. The river was now a raging torrent and as I was aware of the exact location knew that we could not provide any assistance with our old fart box whatsoever. However I donned my wet weather gear and with the umbrella turned inside out by the gale walked with him to the spot. My assumption was correct as we could not have even driven down to the river without getting completely bogged down. All of the occupants had managed to get out onto the riverbank and what a bedraggled lot they were. The car had only managed to get halfway across before the engine had got flooded and stalled. It had been washed around at a ninety-degree angle and the bonnet now faced down stream.

By luck I managed to find the local farmer, who had taken shelter in his store only a short distance away. After I had explained the difficulties he agreed to help and, thigh deep, in the raging flood that swirled dangerously around him, without the use of flippers or a snorkel, he was able to connect a thick steel wire cable from the front end of his tractor to the towing bracket at the rear of the car. All of us watched on helplessly as he took more than an hour to get the car out onto the bank. Sometimes, as the tractor wheels spun continuously and with the engine screaming angrily, he managed to creep slowly backwards, and at others, when a particularly heavy surge of water flowed past, he lost ground and slipped forward but in the end he won. It was then another struggle to pull the car up to our track. I did not believe it when the driver clambered into it and turned on the ignition but knew the outcome, there was nothing, the motor was as dead as a Dodo.

It remained there for a few days after which it suddenly disappeared and during this period nothing was seen of the driver or the passengers. The farmer was never offered any form of gratitude and this made me very angry and as I had asked him for his assistance in the first place so brought him a large bottle of whisky, which he reluctantly accepted.

Chapter Eleven

We had been surrounded by the workforce for almost six months without a break. A few short but *alcofrolic* social events had been thoroughly enjoyed but something different was required as both of us were under a considerable strain.

There was nothing that we could do on the land as it was too sodden and the construction work was almost at a complete standstill. There was not really any need for the daily walkabouts to ensure that everything was going as planned. The situation had been reached where very little could go horrendously wrong or not be easily corrected if it was only a minor cock-up.

The idea of a "break away from it all for a few days" appealed very strongly, especially to me. The thought of being cleanshaven every day and not having to plod around dressed in my scruffs, (clothes that had been continually de-classified from best down to only just suitable for wear in public, and then ultimately "downright useful for manual work only when nobody else was around"), was something to really look forward to. Another more important reason was that AC would celebrate her fortieth birthday very soon.

On that day she woke up and felt very grotty. Her health had gone downhill for almost a week with a sort of flu bug virus and even though she had received lots of cards and lovely presents she was definitely not in a bubbly and excited mood, just generally fed up and out of sorts. In an attempt to buck her up I took her out for an evening meal in the village and no expense was spared. It was however a complete failure as she was so much under the weather and her taste buds were on another planet. It did not turn out to be the event that I had intended and try as I might there was no way that I could stimulate her interests. In another effort to improve the situation I told her over dinner that when she felt a little better we would take a holiday away from it all and try to fit in a dirty weekend as well.

Even this promise with the prospects of hot baths and loos that flushed did not fully perk her up. I was fighting a battle that I was bound to loose, everything was against an even partial success, as on our return to the caravan it poured down with rain, yet again, to further dampen her mood.

She had, most unusual for her since the New Year, felt depressed, lifeless and physically stiff, generally crappy with a complete lack of motivation. Not able to make any curtains, no machine or electricity and not able to plant any seeds as the land had not yet been prepared.

"Too many nots," she said, "what a bore." I put it all down to, probably most unfairly, nicotine withdrawal. She had heard from her mother that purely coincidentally, she had also stopped smoking on the first of January, her birthday.

There was a gradual improvement in her health as the flu symptoms were overcome. During the next few days we were able to seriously consider a start to the holiday. How strange it felt as we packed, without any scruffs, hers or mine, a solitary suitcase. We managed to place it in the boot but only after a considerable amount of accumulated rubbish had been removed. At one stage we thought that we were not going to get away and that the holiday was doomed but after a twenty-minute performance of squirting damp start under the fart boxes bonnet the engine reluctantly decided to fire.

We drove east, another balls aching slog although nowhere near as dangerous and hairy as when we had towed the caravan, to Monte Gordo. Along the journey we thought how desperately the Algarve needed an east to west motorway. It was hard work, slow, wearisome, very tiring and certainly not a trip to be considered during the main "tourist season". The seaside town was found to our dismay, to be a complete disappointment. It had a lovely long stretch of clean beach, but this was overlooked by a concrete jungle that was still under construction. After a very brief wander around it was decided that it was not our cup of tea and retraced our steps to the town of Tavira, one of the most impressive ones in the Algarve.

The difference was incredible and we fell in love with place immediately. It was strange as we had not felt this emotion on our only previous visit with Picasso. We checked into a boarding house on the east side of the river almost opposite the old market. From our bedroom window on the third floor we had panoramic views of the lovely old part of the town and could clearly see the Roman bridge, now only accessed by pedestrians, a little further upstream from where we stood. This river, the Gilao, divided the town into east and west bank sections. The array of buildings blended much of the Phoenician, Roman and Moorish architectural features. They were beautiful and many had tiled outside walls and wrought iron balconies at the first floor level, far more than in Lagos. With so many varying rooflines and angles in different shades of colour it was not difficult to imagine that the perspectives would constitute an artist's dream. We decided to explore the many little back streets in the town itself and also the surrounding countryside. The numerous magnificent churches, thirty-seven in number, were to be given a miss as we had "done" a couple the last time.

Once we had given the remains of an old fort a cursory once over we discovered a very small metal bashing workshop. It was down one of the tiniest back streets and was a one-man type of blacksmith operation. The proprietor produced extremely rustic hand made weathercocks of different sizes, all fitted with a crude form of anemometer. AC considered that they were original and quite cute and decided on the spot to buy one for me but the size that I preferred was already sold. A price was negotiated and agreed after a very short haggle and he told us that he could fabricate one for collection the next day.

Opposite his workshop, on the first floor, was a restaurant and we noticed that a menu was fixed to a board at street level. It was obvious where we would dine that evening after we had drooled and given it a lip smacking study.

What a pleasure it was to immerse our bodies in the tub, filled with steaming hot water and a glass of wine in our hands before we set out to eat. The ambience and the food was excellent, a delicious spicy fish soup followed by sole in a butter sauce for AC and a huge grilled tuna fish steak for me. There was a party of four at the next table who had ordered a special shellfish dish and when the lid of the cauldron was removed what a splendid sight was revealed. It was full to the brim and the aroma was breathtaking. We called our waiter over and pre-ordered one for the next evening.

In the morning another long soak in the tub was enjoyed, before a leisurely breakfast after which we headed over to Vila Real De Santo Antonio. There we found it still to be very much the same as described by Patrick Smith in his book that we had both recently read. It was not the place for us to dally, so after a quick beer over which we wrote several postcards it was time to travel north along the west bank of the river Guadiana. The views were superb and we became so engrossed in what we could see that we went much further than intended and ended up in Alcoutim.

There its impressive old fort, which faced the Spanish one on the other side of the river was explored as was the village. We had lunch in a restaurant literally perched on the riverbank and were very surprised at how wide it was this far up from the estuary. The food that was being served looked very yummy but we settled for a snack salad, with a small plate of chips, as we both could not face a full-blown meal. Yet more postcards were completed, we really did act like typical tourists, and it was intended to post them all when we got back to Tavira.

On the way back we pootled into Castro Marim to plod over more castle and fort ruins and then called in at St Lucia and viewed the beach at Ilha de Tavira. Unfortunately we found that most of the bars and restaurants were shut and there was not a lot going on, but imagined how different it would be during the peak summer season. Those thoughts made us grateful that we lived in the somewhat sleepy backwaters of Bensafrim.

It rained quite heavily as we returned to our room for a most welcome *zizz* after which we took another bath and had a change of clothes. AC suggested that we should take a short trip inland before dinner, which we did and witnessed the most splendid scenery, kilometre after kilometre of it with the road completely to ourselves. We drove over rolling hills covered with the most luxuriant vegetation that we had seen for a considerable time. It became very eerie the higher we climbed and quite a heavy mist had descended rapidly. Our maps had been foolishly been left back in the bedroom so we had little idea as to where we were. When I found it was necessary to switch on the headlights and drive on full main beam we both chickened out and I did a four-point turn and headed back the way we had just come. We stopped and enjoyed a beer in a very small bar, it only had one table and four chairs, which could truly be said to be right in the middle of nowhere and after this we drove straight back to the town, parked and walked to the restaurant with eager anticipation.

The service was no way near as efficient as the previous evening and the waiter was completely thrown out when we did not ask for a starter. There were several covers to choose from and with the large paella dish this was more than adequate, a first course would have spoilt the experience. We had eaten paellas many times before but none had been as substantial as this one. The ratio of seafood, prawns clams mussels crab and crayfish, was about three to one to the chicken rice and vegetables. It was absolutely gorgeous and could easily have fed another couple. Pigs that we were we scoffed it all and even dunked an extra serving of bread, we had requested, to mop up all of the tasteful gunge.

The whole of the next day was spent as tourists normally did and we just lazed around. The only exercise that caused us a certain amount of exhaustion was to have lunch in a local bar, fish soup and ham rolls accompanied by the inevitable liquid refreshments.

We had dinner on our final evening in a small restaurant that only had three tables. A couple came in and sat at the one nearest to ours. I recognised him straight away, he was, or had been, the sales director of a company in Bromsgrove who had quoted for some mechanical equipment for the contract that I had signed in Iraq. Unfortunately the order had been placed elsewhere. He recognised me also and was surprised to learn that we lived in Portugal. They were taking a mini-break and "doing the Algarve" in four days and had visited Lagos, Albufeira and Faro. This was their last port of call and they would leave tomorrow. An interesting discussion followed over a few nightcaps after which we wished them a safe journey home and returned to our room. Our explorations were completed and we eventually had to leave, albeit somewhat reluctantly, with a promise to ourselves that we would have to return.

We drove west and headed towards Albufeira, before we reached the town I parked the car at a large hotel in Montechoro but a quick about turn was made when we studied the tariff that the receptionist had handed over. The room rates were way above what we intended, or could afford, to pay. Only a few kilometres further on we checked into a hotel on the road to Praia D'Oura. I had stayed there before, in the early seventies with my first wife and two daughters and it was obvious that it had been totally refurbished. It did not take us long to unpack and as we were hungry and thirsty we took a short stroll to a beach bar not that far away. AC and I had found it on our first holiday but the surrounds since then had changed beyond all recognition. The amount of construction works that had been and was still in progress was absolutely unbelievable in such a short space of time. We found it difficult to come to terms with it and compared to my earlier holiday, with the family I could have been on another planet.

A second floor room on the opposite side to the main road had been chosen, its one drawback was that it was single bedded. All the doubles were on the ground floor and faced the main road and after the peace and quiet of Bensafrim we thought that they may be rather noisy as a very popular Discotheque was not that far away. Both of us had a quick *zizz* followed by a luxurious bath, a long soak in hot water that seemed to steam forever, sheer bliss and decadence as some wine and nibbles had been brought for us to sip and munch as we wallowed in the tub.

That evening we attended a reception at the hotel and were offered glasses of chilled white port wine, a rather odd aperitif we thought but very acceptable, and then queued to enter the dining room for the buffet meal. Later on in the night there would be a session of folk dancing. We sat next to a couple who had recently retired to the Isle of Man and she hated it there. Once his soup was finished he excused himself and went out for a fag, never to be seen again. She only managed two mouthfuls of buffet, decided that she didn't like it, and followed him! We were sure it was not something that we had said and if it was I really did not give a hoot as I was in full holiday mode and intended to enjoy myself. We found that it was a splendid buffet with an exceptional range of goodies to choose from and I in particular, as always, pigged myself out. The dancing was given a miss as we had been to similar ones oodles of times in our village. A coffee and a few liqueurs were savoured in the hotel's piano bar to round off a very relaxing evening.

After another bath, this time without any wine, for AC and a shower for me, they were the first orders of the day on this holiday we ambled down to take a leisurely breakfast. The only thing missing was the morning papers, not that we had them back at El Rancho anyway, but it would have been a nice touch. We then drove up to Alte, the small village described by Mitchener in *"The Drifters"*. It appeared to us that it had not changed that much but imagined that life had for the local inhabitants. To obtain a beer proved difficult until a bar that was open and had someone awake enough to serve us was found, it was way past eleven thirty. Two stops were made on our return to the hotel, one in the village of Paderne where we came across a gypsy open-air street market. AC spotted some nice basket weave also some raffia-fabricated rugs and after I had haggled somewhat successfully we bundled our purchases into the boot. My souk mentality told me that I had been robbed, again.

Back at Montechoro village we sat outside a bar and enjoyed the sunshine and a few glasses of wine before we returned to the hotel and crashed out for another *zizz*. We had not slept at all well the previous evening because the beds mattresses were a lot harder than the king sized one that we were accustomed to in the caravan.

My skin had remained rather pinkish but not as a result of any sun bathing. It was mainly due to the ever-continuous soaks in the hot water tub and the never-ending showers. Despite this we had yet another bath after which we drove to the nearby village of Guia. Our sortie was to a restaurant, which had been recommended on our earlier holiday and thankfully had not changed very much, if at all and still served delicious food. The service was as efficient as ever and the fish soup better than we remembered. Both the swordfish steak and the special beef casserole, the dish of the day, with an accompaniment of fresh vegetables was just scrummy.

The next and final port of call that evening was to the centre of Albufiera. This was found to be a very inopportune moment as the main square looked worse than the front of our Quinta as it had been totally dug up and was in a complete mess. It was a nightmare to try and move around anywhere. We did, out of desperation, manage to crawl over some excavations to a Port wine bar, the one visited previously when AC had not felt one hundred per cent. This time she certainly made up for it joined enthusiastically by myself. We didn't dally there for too long and finished up with a few nightcaps in a bar close to the hotel and eventually staggered back to our room. It was literally get up and go the next morning, to have a final bath and loo flush followed by the serve yourself breakfast, a routine to which we had become completely addicted to at the start of the day. Our case was glumly packed and we reluctantly checked out to begin our journey back home.

This was planned to be a casual trip and we were not to be rushed. We stopped in St Bartholomew de Messines for a brief wander around and a coffee and a sticky. Then it was on to Silves for lunch after a visit to the castle. We had intended to call in on two garden centres but found them both closed as it was Sunday. It was certainly not like the hard-nosed business attitude that had prevailed in England before we had left. There they would have been open to attract the large weekend crowds of amateur gardeners and where we lived they were mostly Brummies. It was generally one of their busiest days of the week. Here they appeared to be totally switched off to this potential opportunity.

We now had the time to meander up to Monchique and Foia, the highest point in the Algarve and a vantage point from which to see most of it. On the slow drive up, almost overcome by the strong heady fresh aroma from the huge eucalyptus trees, we noticed an Estalagem, hostelry, tucked away on the left hand side of the road. From its car park there were superb views southward and the Atlantic ocean was clearly visible. Unfortunately it was closed and appeared to have been for some time. It was a great pity as we would have loved to have extended the holiday by another day even though our ready cash reserves had almost ran out. We continued on up to the summit where there was very little to be seen as it had become misty and overcast the higher we climbed. It was our second disappointment in almost as many minutes.

On the run back down to the coastal strip we took a short detour off the main road and called into Caldas de Monchique, a spa village. It was a quaint little place and the bottled water from there was sold all over the country. There were some spring outlets where you could fill your own containers. We thought that it was extremely pretty built into a small valley and on the sides of a hill. AC said that, "it reminded her somewhat of Cheltenham." I said, "Portmeirion", what a chalk and cheese visualisation. How could both of us stand there, gaze at the same buildings, and conjure up in our imaginations places so completely different?

It was an ideal place to have a picnic as a large area had been set out under the massive eucalyptus trees and tables and chairs, cut from the local stone, had been positioned carefully to provide private but sociable places to eat.

We really loved the sound of the continuous flow of water that trickled between the small fish pools with miniature fountains at every level. What appealed even more was the main stream, which rippled loudly as it flowed down past all of the seating places. I was sure that the burbling melodies created by these would wash away the tensions of the day when seated there at any table, over a light snack or a full-blown picnic and this was logged as a must for an early future visit.

Despite the numerous people that wandered around, mainly Portuguese, we sensed an air of complete tranquillity. There were restaurants and a variety of accommodation facilities in the small centre so for a short holiday it was self-contained, every basic requirement was available. We looked at each other and instinctively knew that this would be the perfect place to have our promised dirty weekend, but on some other occasion.

By the time we arrived back at Bensafrim our stomachs ached due to a lack of food so to round off the holiday we visited the local restaurant to sample the dish of the day. We were in luck as only two portions remained of a succulent lamb stew with a variety of vegetables, which was really yummy. As it was the last serving the helpings were very generous. We then managed to stagger over to the café for a coffee and liqueur after which, fully sated, we crashed into the pit in the caravan, which had been prepared before our departure. We were so contentedly knackered that we did not bother to even take a look at the Quinta. The break had been so thoroughly enjoyable but the excitement over the past few days had left us totally exhausted. As we rapidly drifted away the prospects of what we would find in the morning was not over eagerly anticipated. One final thought before oblivion took hold was that it would all too soon be back to reality.

Chapter Twelve

It certainly was with a vengeance as the builder banged on the caravan door at some godforsaken hour in the early morning and insisted that we did a walk around with him. In our dressing gowns, he dragged us all over the Quinta and we were able to see that he had, at long last, cracked the whip to a remarkable extent during our period away from it all and had blitzed the site with some of the outstanding materials. The aluminium windows – without the fly and mossie screens and doors – had been fitted, as had the arched front timber door. It all looked good and gave us a tremendous encouragement. We thought that perhaps we should take another break and trust to luck that these improvements would continue.

With a grin from ear to ear plastered all over his face he asked for the progress payment. A cheque was duly signed and handed over as had been promised. The Quinta was now at last swallow proof although we thought that it was necessary to insist to everyone that windows and doors should be kept closed at all times. With the cheque stuffed into his wallet his mood became more bullish and he asked me yet again to empty the septic tank hole. I agreed on the basis that if there were no further heavy rainfalls he would promptly clear the whole area up and start the construction immediately.

A detailed inspection inside found that progress had again advanced considerably. The carpenter had completed the assembly of the vanity unit in our bathroom and the marble tops had been fitted. It was the last major item on his list. All of the marble work surfaces in the kitchen had been positioned over the units and the two pieces for the dressing table in the guest bedrooms also built in. The recently hung arched double doors into the lounge certainly caught the eye, especially their bevelled glass panels. There was ample evidence that the painters had commenced the sanding and varnishing of all of the woodwork including the doors and cupboards as well as the kitchen units.

A gas fitter had connected up the buried copper tubing to a pressure regulator in the gas bottle store, to "on-off" valves for the water heater connection and in the kitchen for the gas hob.

At the back end of the holiday the winds had blown themselves out and the weather had turned upside down. The sun shone for long periods and there was a mild to gentle drying wind that blew down from a north easterly direction. There was only the occasional brief downpour and a few showers overnight. With the assistance of Alfonso 1 we enquired about the hourly rates to have the land ploughed. He favoured a farmer friend of his whom he considered to be good value for money. The local postman was cheaper at half of the price but it was obvious why, his small tractor only had a single ploughshare compared with the others double one. We agreed to use his friend and that we would let him know when we were ready.

I received an unexpected letter from my sister. This was most unusual as the Collin's clan had somehow failed to develop, over the years, any form of interfamily communication networks. It was as if the individual units existed in complete isolation and information was only passed on at an all too infrequent get together. She amazingly rambled on about everything and nothing in particular but the main topic was that it would soon be our parent's fiftieth wedding anniversary and that they intended to have a celebratory bash, which we should attend, especially as I was the number one son! There was no way that we could be there. It was one of the major disadvantages of living so far away. All that we could do was to send a card, arrange for some flowers to be delivered and to telephone them at the party on the day. When I spoke to her she was not at all happy but fully appreciated our difficulties and welcomed my suggestion that we should all chip in together for a special family present, which she agreed to organise.

As the cement mixer was still on the site I moonlighted and commenced the building of the walls for the pool pump house and the BBQ. The electrician had left the cables and the conduit for the well pump installation. I now had to cut out the channels and lay them in position from the Quinta to the garden shed and from there to the top of the well tunnel. Most of this work was carried out by torchlight and AC had the hardest task of all; she had to sit there and hold it.

It was necessary to inspect the asparagus seed beds on a daily basis to see if they had dried out sufficiently enough to allow us to work on them and commence the removal of the weeds. As and when it was possible, we got stuck in to tackle the problem and spent, what seemed to us a lifetime every day, our bums in the normal arse upward position until we had finished and there was not a weed in sight. Great care had to be taken as we had noticed that there were quite a few new spears that had appeared. Alfonso 1 was immediately contacted to arrange for his friend to come and plough the area for the permanent asparagus beds as soon as possible.

He arrived the next day and proceeded like a bull at a gate. The top of the land and at the side and front of the well did not give him any problems at all as it turned over easily. But below the asparagus seed beds it was a different story. The land was very waterlogged and the further down it he ploughed the rougher the furrows became. Soon his tractor was almost completely bogged down and he eventually realised that it was so wet that that he could not continue and had to call it a day, sixty metres short of where we had planned the beds to finish. "Just our luck, at this stage," we thought. All of the manure that had been previously spread over the area, some months before, had rotted down well and now had been turned in and fully buried. We paid him the equivalent of eight pounds sterling and asked if he could return and try again next week. He agreed, but with a shrug of his shoulders, said, "that a lot would depend upon the weather" and "that he was not optimistic about the prospects of being able to continue".

Not far down from the point where his work had come to a halt, between the pomegranate trees and the gulley, I noticed that some spring flowers were in bloom. There were a few wild daffodils and clumps of Oxalis, Bermuda Buttercup, and a profusion of the violet coloured snap dragon like flowers which I had noticed last year and had still not yet been able to discover their name. Also, if one looked more carefully some orchids, but as these were not in flower not easily identifiable. I thought that they were of the bee orchid genus but could not be sure.

The rotavator was not in use and had not been for some considerable time in view of the foul weather. I trundled it down the track once again. It had gone up and down like a fiddlers elbow since it had been repaired. We would concentrate all of our efforts on the preparation of the permanent asparagus beds. There was a lot of hand digging and weed removal to be carried out before the rotavator could be used to prepare the soil ready for the formation of the beds.

The pump, after many days of intermittent operation, eventually overtook the rain showers and removed more water out than was draining in and the septic tank hole was as empty as it ever would be. Luckily the builder arrived just as I had disconnected all the piping and after a brief look at what was still an awful mess, said that, "work would commence on it in the morning" and he dashed off to make the arrangements. He was obviously successful as Bulldozer Joe turned up early with his machine, just as we had surfaced from a deep sleep. He clambered down from his cab and stood by the hole motionless for the best part of fifteen minutes. He scratched his head and rubbed his chin continuously and then started to prowl around it several times and all we could hear was a low chunter under his breath.

Finally he jumped back into his machine and at full speed started to form a ramp at the southern end. He then drove down this into the depths and removed quite a lot of the muck on his way in. It did not take him long to get to the bottom by which time his machine was completely out of sight as it was fully below the ground level. AC was concerned that more soil would fall in on top of him but I explained that this was highly improbable, as the sides had formed their own natural angle of repose on the first collapse. I doubted that he would ever get himself out but he proved me wrong and in the process removed all of the mess and revealed the concrete blinding at the bottom. It was by now early evening when a lorry loaded up with gravel turned up. Half of it was tipped into the exposed hole and evenly spread around and the remainder was deposited in a pile nearby to be used as a backfill to the sidewalls.

The cement mixer started at seven o'clock the next day and rudely woke us up. We walked around to where all the activity was going on and found that five of the workers had already started to build the sidewalls of the tank. Later on we discovered the other two inside the lounge where they had almost completed the construction of the lintel over the log-burning stove and the chimneybreast. By the end of the day, with only short breaks and no lunch hour, that had been completed, as had all the exterior walls for the septic tank and one internal one, to form two chambers and also the floor slab had been cast. They had also extended the drainage and sewage pipes and connected them to the tank.

It was the same start time again in the morning with a similar work schedule. All the walls were plastered on the insides, pre-cast concrete roof beams laid complete with the infill tiles to form the top of the tank. After provision had been made for an inspection opening in each chamber, with a cover, the roof slab was cast.

A pipe had been connected from the second chamber to a circular rubble drain that had been built up with large and small interlocked boulders, which was then completed up to just below ground level. We asked for this drain to be extended down the land and agreed that the additional costs would be to our account. All of the walls and this drain were then backfilled with gravel from the pile and some of the excavated soil. There were smiles of relief and satisfaction all round and an extra heavy session in the café followed.

A large heap of soil still remained and its removal from the site had not been covered in the contract and therefore was not the builders responsibility. "Oh shit, oh dear," I thought as I realised that I had made a major cock up. The costs would be down to us as would those to remove an even larger amount of excavated soil from the swimming pool. It was an expensive oversight on my part and I could have kicked myself!! A small, very small consolation was that had I not pumped out the water we would still have had to look at the terrible mess, which could have remained there for a few more months and jeopardised the Quinta's habitability.

It had been quite a few years since we had first conceived the idea to grow asparagus on a commercial basis, After extensive research and investigation many plans had been made as had some fundamental decisions and we had now reached the point when the most important phase could be carried out. Two types, green or white spears could be produced from the same plant as a result of them being grown in distinct and different methods. These worked on the principal that spears below ground level were white and those above it became green. We had elected to opt for the green ones.

We planned to use the one-year-old crowns that we had grown from the seeds we had sown with such difficulty and that they would be planted on flat beds to produce totally edible green spears, "Green gems," as we preferred to call them. These would be cut off about one centimetre below the surface of the soil and this white portion would be trimmed when the bundles were made up. I did not like the spears that were widely produced in England. There the beds were ridged, earthed up, and the spears cut off some eight centimetres below the top of the ridge. They were then only two thirds green and the rest of their length was white. This portion, unless peeled, was inedible and therefore wasted. I always felt cheated whenever I bought a bundle from the roadside stalls in the Vale of Evesham and also very much so at the asparagus suppers in Badsey.

Traditionalists argued that this white woody base of the spear was used as a grip when eaten by hand but I knew that this was a complete load of *bollucks* as you could still quite easily pick them up when they were all green. In this condition it also helped the spear to curve effortlessly down into your open mouth.

These were the principal reasons behind my decision to only crop green spears from totally flat beds as I considered that this gave our clients and us far better value for money.

The idea of having to grope a with long bladed knife into a mound about twenty-five centimetres high and cut a white spear, after a tedious examination to locate it's tip, certainly did not appeal at all, even though it was the common practice in most parts of Germany and Holland. We would have to wean potential clients from those countries who were readily familiar with that type and resident here, onto our green ones.

I passionately loved and was more than partial to the "Green gems" so that the opportunity to be able to grow, eat and sell them gave me a considerable motivation to ensure that our venture succeeded.

Many years ago I had read an article in a journal, which had highlighted the many difficulties encountered when attempting to achieve continuous and profitable agricultural production. It also touched on the roles of wholesalers and retailers in the marketing and sales of the produce, which should ideally operate as a separate function. It was our intention to attempt to perform both, and thus cut out the "Middle Man" and we hoped that we had not bitten off more than we could chew.

We had, since the caravan had been parked for the first time, learnt very quickly that our land was in a frost pocket. It therefore was not ideally suited to asparagus cultivation as the young tips of any spears that had just broken through the soil surface would be liable to serious damage, or even worse be totally killed off. Our commitment however was irreversible and as we had recently seen only a few spears on the seed beds and the frosty season was now hopefully behind us, we decided to gamble on the fact that any losses would be minimal. It had to be the right decision to continue on as planned but with our fingers and legs tightly crossed.

The preparation of the permanent beds would be without doubt the most important factor in any success. All of the time and extra special care that we took now was essential as the crowns would continue to produce an annual crop of spears for at least twenty years. This period of time had been taken into account when we made our overall plans, as it would at that point be way passed my retirement age. A few of my father's crowns, the funny little things that I had watched him plant, produced a small crop even after fifty years and over the latter part of these, had not been given a modicum of tender loving care. We certainly had not planned that far into the future.

As the land sloped gradually down from the track, north to south, a different orientation of the rows of asparagus was not seriously considered.

Our somewhat ambitious plans were to cultivate an acre of asparagus crowns, in round terms about ten thousand of them. This would require an area of just under half a hectare, or to be more precise, a plot that measured four thousand square metres, one hundred by forty. We had this area available with the hundred metres distance down the slope of the land and the forty across it but as the weather had been so shitty only a fraction had been rough ploughed and even this small piece had not been harrowed.

Unlike the weather in England the prospects of sufficient rainfalls to promote healthy crown growth here over the months from April to September was basically zero and as such irrigation would be essential. Although the submitted Project had included for an overhead sprinkler system my calculations on the costs had been a pure guestimate as I had not then had the time to carry out a detailed investigation. In a recent exercise I had found to my dismay that the costs were prohibitive and completely unaffordable. We would have to stick with, and extend the already installed gravity or pump pressurised pipe work.

AC was not at all impressed and extremely frustrated as the "cannot afford it", too "bloody expensive" expressions were used by me with monotonous regularity.

We had ample space, but there was no way that we could provide an adequate supply of water down the whole one hundred metre length of asparagus crowns, even with our pump system. It was with reluctance therefore that we had to settle on a split bed arrangement.

It was now necessary to experiment and we formed channels down the slope and watched how slowly and how far, a normal or pressurised, stream of water would flow along them. This gave us an indication of what the ideal lengths of the beds should be and we decided that about seven metres was the optimum.

Many specialist gardening books had been studied and the sections on asparagus made our heads spin in confusion. In each one the recommendations on the width of the row spaces and the distances between the crowns in them was entirely different and varied widely. We often thought that it would have been better and far less confusing had we read only one!

The amount of land ready for preparation was nowhere near sufficient enough to meet our somewhat ambitious planned target. All of the available area was at a premium, so we could not afford to be too generous when the decision was made on the spacing of our crowns. We mused about it for a considerable time before we went for broke and plumped for a ninety centimetre row width and forty centimetre crown spacing along them, slightly smaller distances than advised. Each bed would then be around eight metres wide and seven deep and be spaced with a one-metre walkway at the tops, bottoms and between them.

A final piece of information had been gleaned from our studies. It was that one-year-old crowns could be expected to have up to fifteen succulent roots and each would be about twelve centimetres in length and that these must not be allowed to dry out during the transplanting exercise. Trenches therefore had to be dug out in the beds around fifteen centimetres wide and deep to accommodate them. As we did not intend to earth the rows up we had decided to make them deeper at thirty centimetres.

With all of this information or garbage, it depended upon ones mood at the time indelibly printed on our grey matter we were ready to meet the challenge. On a similar principle to that used when the seed beds were prepared it was decided that only two permanent beds would be tackled at a time and that these would be completed before any more were started.

The first two took far longer to prepare than had been anticipated. The only consolation to us was that we were on a learning curve and that they did appear to have more weeds to be cleared than some of the other areas.

A damp sack would be wrapped around the roots of the crowns to minimise any air exposure during the time that they were dug up and then placed and covered in the prepared trenches. Only two of these would be opened up and down the beds and when they had been filled with crowns and the soil levelled, two more would be made. It was time to "go for it" and I dug out the first and second trenches with the spade as AC. with great difficulty, even with the heavy garden fork, struggled to lift the first one-year-old crown out of the seed bed! She then brought it over and when I unwrapped it had a terrible shock. The crown had almost twice as many roots as we had anticipated and were half as long again as intimated in the books. What a load of codswallop their information had turned out to be.

There was an immediate problem, a big problem. The trenches that I had just carefully prepared were far too small both in width and depth to accommodate that particular crown. It was quickly re-wrapped and we then both dashed over and tried, successfully thank goodness, to replace it in the spot from where it had only just been lifted out of. This was not quite the start that we had expected after all of those years and was more like a scene from a double act farce!!

A brief state of panic and nervous exhaustion started to set in especially when I dug up, with much grunting and hassle, three more crowns from different parts of the seed beds and found that two were slightly larger and one a lot larger still than AC's original one. All of these were quickly re-buried, again with difficulty, and the two trenches then re-filled. To make absolutely sure four other parts of the seed beds were examined. These also produced oversize crowns and our only conclusion was that it was as a result of the strong fertiliser that had been applied during their growth in the first year.

We discovered with mixed emotions after this operation that we had more crowns than could be seen at first sight. Where we had thought that there was only one, there were two or sometimes three with their roots intertwined. This may have been caused by the ralo damage to the beds where the seeds may have been disturbed after they were first sown and great care would be need to be taken when the time came to separate them.

Over a lunchtime beer our panic rapidly dissipated as we agreed that it was not, as had been our initial reaction, a major problem to overcome. The trenches would obviously have to be made much larger and as such only one would be prepared at a time. The work would be far harder and would take a lot longer to complete.

We realised as we finished our second beer that the longer it took, the more problems AC would have in trying to lift the crowns. I had already found it strenuous and difficult and that was during the brief investigation exercise. It did not take long for it to dawn on me that it would eventually, to lift a single crown, necessitate a brute strength and ignorance approach. There would be little time for finesse. If some of the roots were damaged in the process, and this was a stone walled certainty, it would be too bad. From what we had witnessed so far there appeared to be more than a sufficient amount of them to ensure a high percentage of survival.

Our next attempts proved to be very successful in the much larger trenches albeit rather slowly. We only managed to transplant three hundred and sixty crowns over a four-day period.

The roots of each one, after being lifted by AC were rigorously scrutinised by me to check for the fungus disease Violet root rot, a fungus greeny blue in colour. Fortunately for us they were all spotlessly clean. Each crown was carefully positioned, one at a time, in the trench and the roots were spread out, evenly radiated around it and then covered with fine soil. This process continued until the bed was completed. At that stage we then made sure that all of the trenches were filled and that the bed was flat before it was watered and fertilised.

At the exact moment when we covered over our first transplanted crown with soil we firmly believed that it was the first one grown from seed that had been planted in the Algarve for commercial production.

The advice given in the books, that the trenches should only be half filled at this stage and gradually filled up during the summer when the regular hoeing process continued was totally ignored. We had a valid reason to take this approach as our prevailing wind was from the north-west, which swept down off the hills behind us and cut through our little valley right where the asparagus beds were situated. The crowns therefore needed as much soil on top of them as possible for maximum stability to prevent potential problems from wind rock when the ferns were at their full height.

Late one Saturday afternoon Alfonso 2 arrived with a large bag clutched in his hand from which he produced a live rabbit. It was a present for our Easter Sunday meal and he expected me to kill it. We both baulked at this idea so he promptly did the deed on the spot. First a heavy clump to the back of the head and then out with his knife to cut and skin it like a banana. There were guts and blood in all directions and AC was directed to get a large saucepan into which it was thrown and on which she quickly fitted the lid. He then stormed off over to the gulley and threw all the scraps into it and with a wave of his hand went off along the track.

I had only once killed anything, other than the snake and thousands of bothersome insects, and that was by accident. When I lived in the village of Martley I had bought at a jumble sale an old leather cricket ball. It must have had at least six previous owners and had been knocked about quite a bit and was more oval than round. One day during my morning bowling practice, against the pigsty wall before I caught the bus to school, one of my father's very young chicks had escaped out of its run. I hit it unintentionally with my fastest – unfortunately for the chick – perfectly pitched Yorker and then had to find a spot to quietly bury it and fervently hoped that he never carried out a head count.

As we relaxed with a glass of wine on the terrace we decided that we really could not face the prospect of rabbit on our plates that weekend and we were very naughty as it was slung into the rubbish bins on our way to the village for a fish and chips sort of supper.

The farmer friend of Alfonso 1 called in to examine the land below where his tractor had almost got marooned during his initial ploughing session. In less than five minutes he slowly shook his head and said that, "any further work was still not possible" and left us to ponder our position which was painfully obvious. We had all of the land for the permanent asparagus beds that we were going to get and the area was far too small for our overall requirements, At the back of my mind I optimistically thought that the Postman could be used as a back stop if there was no more rain although it was an extremely slim chance. The top piece of land had not been considered ideally suited for asparagus and had been earmarked for other vegetables and some of these had already been planted. It was not really possible therefore, at this stage, to reverse the decision.

As we had been so preoccupied with the asparagus transplanting we had totally missed the boat with the parsnips and it was far too late in the year to sow now. We had different types of seeds but had not made up our minds on the variety that should be grown.

Whatever situation eventually transpired we would be left with far more crowns than we could transplant. As a result I came up with the brilliant idea that we should sell some of them. Absolutely naff marketing was AC's immediate response. Why sell to prospective clients the plants that would supply the same product that I intended to market to earn a living? It was a fundamentally sound argument but I reasoned that any purchaser would be enthusiastic amateur gardeners and would not have the patience to wait and look after them over the three-year-period until the plants were ready to crop. A very risky assumption was her response and we agreed to differ.

The lawyer wrote to inform us that the land registration had been completed and that we could collect the document the next time we were in town. As there were quite a few matters that we had let slide an early visit was necessary. Firstly we called into the local office of the Electricity Board and enquired about the installation of a three-phase supply. Several papers were filled in and all of them signed. We left having been given a special form that needed to be completed. After this had been studied over a cup of coffee and a sticky we decided that this was a job for our lawyer. She then became the second port of call.

The land registration document was handed over together a cheque made out in my favour. It appeared that the registry office had made an initial overcharge. AC took a quick look at it and suggested that we didn't spend it all at once. We discussed the form and she did not foresee any problems and could complete it and use the technical details, signed by our electrician, that we had also handed to her. She would then submit it to the relevant authority for approval after which we would be able to make the final application for the electrical supply.

It was pointed out to us, just as we were about to leave her office, that we must register for the ten year exemption from the Predial Tax, rates on the Quinta, within ninety days of receipt of the certificate of habitation. We thanked her for the advice and told her that the possession of that particular piece of paper appeared to be a long way into the future.

Before we returned home, a few establishments and offices were visited and the owners notified that we had asparagus crowns for sale over the next four-week period and would they spread the word for us. In a couple of cases their eyes lit up, but in all of the others there was just a deadpan expression, although they promised to pass the information on.

There was a terrible clatter on the caravan roof early one morning. It was not a Thursday, Sunday or even a public holiday so it could not have been the hunters shot gun pellets raining down and we had had many experiences of that on previous occasions. AC drew back the curtains and we saw that it was hailstones. From their size had the colour been different, they could have easily been mistaken for frozen peas. The shower quickly ceased only to be followed by torrential rain and it turned out to be a "not able to do absolutely anything at all outside" day because as soon as the rains stopped there were more hailstones. This went on until the late evening and for the first time in ages we found ourselves caravan bound. We did not even trek up to the car for our customary trip into the village. I was extremely miffed as I had slogged away and completed two more beds that were, before the deluges, ready for transplanting. It was now impossible to even attempt to get anywhere near them.

Work on the Quinta continued in a dribs and drabs fashion. The carpenter had fixed the frames for the roller blinds in the lounge and the two bedrooms that faced the upper pool terrace, all the kitchen shelves and the slatted ones in the airing cupboard, so his work was completed. The wall tiling in the utility room and pantry had been finished and the solitary painter continued to plod along inside at his own pace. It was basically habitable but we did not have a single stick of furniture. We decided not to doss down on the floor at night as it would involve the constant toing and froing of the caravan's king sized bed mattress.

The electricity people arrived to measure up for the cable connection. There were two concrete distribution poles nearby and I requested that they ran a line from the one located at the east side of the Quinta. Two quotations would be prepared, in less than a month, one for the power supply cable and the other for the meter and circuit breaker switch. That evening I made a special effort to contact our electrician and was in luck. I explained about the situation on the permanent supply and he arrived early in the morning to link the main fuse board to earth by means of a copper rod driven into the ground by the front door. He then connected the wiring that I had laid in the channels, to an isolator he had fixed in the garden shed, and from this to my new well pump.

The top portion of the land was just about workable so as well as the broad beans, peas and mangetout that had already been sown, we were able to plant some main crop onions, tomatoes, melons and peppers which had been bought on a recent shopping trip into town. A small packet of turnip seeds had also been included for an experiment. If they grew successfully then we were almost guaranteed that there would be no problems in the production of Swedes.

No sooner had we completed this little task than it was "rain stopped play" yet again. Down and down it came and we both regretted that we had slung our Noah's Arc hats away after last year's similar saga. Work on the land was now at a complete standstill as nothing at all could be undertaken. I could therefore concentrate my mind to tackle outstanding items on one of my many lists of things to do.

Between the storms and showers I managed to crack on and make good progress on the pool pump house and the BBQ. When it was too wet even for that I had work to do inside the Quinta. Holes had to be made in the corridor walls at a high level for the hot air distribution ducts and the support brackets had to be positioned. Whilst the hole into our bedroom at the back of the stove was made, I noticed that the timber shuttering for the fireplace lintel had not been removed. Not very clever I thought and was far from amused.

As the rain continued to fall incessantly, it had now got way way past a joke; there was not even the slightest possibility that we could have any more land ploughed. If it ever did dry out sufficiently to enable tractor access, it would be too late in the year and too hot to consider the movement of any more crowns.

At the end of yet another dreary day, I made the dismal calculation, which showed beyond doubt that the maximum number of crowns that we would finish up with on the available land was less than a quarter of our planned target. This assumed that none of them rotted in the waterlogged soil. What really pissed us off even more was when we realised that our second course of action would not be possible. That was to have the extra land ploughed in the autumn before the winter rains and in the following spring transplant the crowns, which by that time would be two years old. We would then have lost no time in the transplanting programme. On the basis of what we had discovered in the operation so far, with sizes of the one-year-old crowns, it would need the services of a small mechanical excavator to dig them up and to form the trenches in which to plant them. The very thought of an attempt to go through that exercise totally put us off, to say the least, so that idea was kicked into touch.

We were stuffed at every turn. An alternative solution was to plant some more seeds now, which would enable us to extend the current operation with one-year-old crowns next springtime. This would mean that three quarters of the beds would be out of phase by one year but we could certainly live with that. Unfortunately even this was not an option for us as there was no prepared land available, not for only a few seed beds.

A lot of encouraging enquiries and orders for crowns had resulted from our initial soundings but again we were stumped. The requirements could not be supplied as it was too wet and impossible to get on the land to dig them up.

This shambolic and messy situation had long begun to get right up my nose and I could have spat blood as there was no short-term solution that sprang to my mind. I didn't say anything to AC but I then seriously thought that it should all be jacked in and that the whole caboodle be put on the market and sold at the first offer, reasonable or not for a quick sale, and move on, to anywhere but here!!

That attitude soon changed, as with our current run of bad luck scenario, the whole bloody lot would have been swept downstream to Lagos before there was the slightest sniff of any interest. So I had a quick change of mind and decided to ride out the storms and stick it out as we had done all along.

I had run out of materials so it was essential that a visit to the co-operative was made. AC asked that as I was in town could I call into the small back street vegetable shop and stock up on our basic requirements. I nearly had a purple fit when I walked into it and saw three bundles of asparagus that had been placed in one of the metal shelving trays. The spears were like English ones, sixty per cent green and the remainder white. They had been imported from Israel, probably from a kibbutz and each bundle weighed about a third of a kilo and were priced at a much lower pro-rata figure than our half kilo ones would be sold for.

We had never ever seen commercial asparagus on sale in Lagos or surrounds, only the wild variety, and this eyesore presented us with a triple whammy. Not only was it cheaper but it was available during the time when we would be in our peak production period. Any form of competition at this time had never been seriously considered as there had been no evidence to show us that it existed.

Thoughts rushed through my mind that surely all these forms of gradually compounded emotional pain and anguish must end sooner rather than later. I reluctantly added one bundle to the list of other items and scampered home. AC was probably more upset for us than me at this turn of events but we both cheered up tremendously after it had been cooked and eaten for supper. It turned out to be complete and utter crap with no flavour at all and as stringy as a Hessian rope. We were confident that ours would be of far superior quality but it was still competition of sorts, which we could well do without.

AC was delighted when she received a letter from her father who could organise some time away from his business and visit us for a fortnight. He wanted to stay in the same apartment as before so we went into town and checked on its availability and as it was, booked it for the dates that he had given us. We then called into the Electricity Boards office and found that the two quotations were ready to be posted to us. A cheque was written out to cover both and we were asked for the outstanding form as they could not proceed without it. A mad dash to the lawyer's office followed only to find that she was in court, although her secretary was convinced that it had been completed and submitted. She made a quick telephone call and was able to tell us that approval would only take another seven days.

Despite the rains that continued the inside of the Quinta remained perfectly dry. This was a tremendous relief as we had heard several horror stories about recently constructed homes where water had dripped, and in some cases poured, through the ceilings and this appeared to be quite a common complaint.

All of the odds and sods that were left to be completed on our building were slowly but surely ticked off the rapidly diminishing list. The roller shutter blind supplier arrived on the site measured all three windows up and they were fitted within a day on the outside of the terrace sliding glazed doors. To our dismay on a close examination in the morning, the aluminium side guides were found to be dark green and not black to match the frames. The all, important mossie screens were installed and all of the steel security grills fixed around the windows. The only things that remained to be completed were some internal wall painting and the varnishing of some of the woodwork. Two ladies, from the village, had, by means of lots of heavy elbow grease, cleaned off, almost all of the floor and wall tiles, the workers general muck and debris.

It all looked very nice and we felt justifiably proud of the end result. As we walked from room to room there was a resonant echo from our footsteps as there was no furniture or carpets to absorb any sound. We now had to concentrate our minds to correct this situation.

Les's plane arrived slightly early, for a change, and he was soon settled in the apartment where we enjoyed a hot bath. He had eaten during the flight so we were all happy just to have a snack supper. The drive home in the fart box suddenly became rough and very bumpy as a rear shock absorber decided to give up the ghost. We had planned to create a rockery on the land that sloped from the cistern up to the two cork oak trees, whispering deaths favourite access way, and this would be an ideal project for him. Les preferred to catch the first bus from town every morning and stroll along the track from the bus stop at the end of it. That suited us as we then didn't need to make a collection journey. In spite of the weather, with a little help from AC, a remarkably swift progress was made and the transformation was quite dramatic.

At long last, after a four-week delay, I was able to get back to some asparagus transplanting but with little hope of the lost time ever being recovered. With all three of us involved, under the watchful gazes of Picasso and Alfonso2 on their first appearances for many weeks, we managed to peak at one hundred and fifty crowns in one day. Subsequently my back had started to twinge, a very bad sign and we suffered all sorts of other aches and pains, which slowed us down considerably. The lesson was quickly taken on board, keep at it little by little and just plod on. It had developed into another almost never-ending labour of love.

I was glad of an excuse to take a break from the ordeal and that was to take the fart box to be fixed. It would have been, if not impossible, extremely uncomfortable to drive over to Faro and back in its present state. The back seat passenger would have suffered agonies all the way there. The garage foreman told me that it would take ten days to obtain "original parts", those manufactured by Ford, to which I replied that any make, as long as they were compatible, would be ok. They had some in stock and two were fitted in under an hour.

As the garage was on the outskirts of Lagos I called into the lawyer's office and collected details with regard to Portuguese driving licenses and the completed approved form for the electrical supply. In the Board's office I handed this over, together another cheque. I was then told that my application could now be placed in the installation work file and that other connections were scheduled in the Bensafrim district, but that they could not be certain when the work could be carried out. Before I returned home all of the places where we had spoken about asparagus crowns were revisited to inform them that we were now back in business and that we would welcome any enquiries and, better still, orders. The whole morning from my point of view had been extremely successful and I had worked up quite an appetite for lunch which was ready and on the table as I entered the kitchen.

In mid-afternoon we learnt that Cheryl and Simon would make a snap short term visit in a couple of days time and would bring some of their friends with them. With some degree of apprehension, we wondered what to expect this time!

Les had an early morning flight so we drove over to Faro the evening before and booked him into a hotel in the city centre for the night and he would catch a taxi to the airport in the morning. We stayed a while and had a drink and some nibbles with him in the hotel bar before we said our goodbyes and both thought that he hadn't look too well on this trip. Good use of this journey was made as we called into Portimao on the way to collect some certificates from the Consulate that would be needed for the car and our driving licenses. In Faro we were also able to visit the offices of the agency who would arrange for the legal importation of the car and its registration to Portuguese number plates.

My back improved sufficiently for me to gingerly get back to the asparagus beds. A grand total of nine had been completed already and contained almost a thousand crowns of which all but ten had shown vigorous growth. It was still miles way from our original target of over nine thousand, a horrific shortfall. At this current rate we would never make a fortune, not even a very small one. As I had anticipated it became more difficult for AC to lift the crowns, one in particular was massive with almost one hundred roots and a spread across it of sixty centimetres and I certainly did not relish the thought that there could be many others of the same size. Eventually she had to give up as the shear physical effort was far too much for her.

We made our first sale, the princely sum of ten pounds, when an English couple called in and collected five crowns, which were lifted by me as AC made a pot of tea. They were both very surprised at the size and quality and promised to recommend them to some other people they knew who appeared to be particularly keen gardeners as well.

Halfway through a rather heavy session, when one of the beds was almost completed I was interrupted by Simon who had arrived very late the day before. There was a problem with their water supply system, which had gone "off" so there was not a drop in the villa and could I fix it for them? It was an inconvenient time but after a brief investigation I was able to sort it out. There followed, a most welcome, invitation for supper with their friends, over which they wished to chat about their short-term plans and matters with which they required our assistance. We looked forward to the meal and the company, but dreaded the "after eight" discussions.

I was pleased to finally finish planting that particular bed in the mid-afternoon and was a bit annoyed that I had been called away. AC had brought a cup of tea over when we both heard loud funny droning noises and looked up to see thousands of relatively large insects that flew around over our heads and almost smothered us. She feared that they may be locusts, as she had heard on the World Service radio that they were swarming in North Africa. If they were she would, as promised, high tail it back mum. I knew, from a similar experience many years in the past that it was an extraordinary large swarm of wild bees so I grabbed her by the arm and dragged her over to the caravan. Only her toes touched the ground on the way there and I was very relieved when the door was shut behind us. We were very lucky as the swarm decided to leave us alone and buzzed off down the land.

Evenings were the time to sort out the paperwork and all of the forms for our driving licenses were filled in and submitted. Attached was a statutory medical report based upon an uncomplicated examination by the local doctor, who smoked continuously during my interview and found that everything appeared to be in order.

AC had read a notice in the village that there was on offer a free analysis of well or borehole water. Full advantage was taken of this and three samples were taken directly from the well. After the requisite number of tests had been completed we were notified that it was "sufficient" as it was very low in nitrates, potable and that the pH value was neutral.

We had almost finished a somewhat scrambled lunch on the caravan terrace when a car pulled up by the cork oak trees. It was M from the café and with him, to our amazement was the couple with their young son, who owned the pub in Studley, which we had – for one never to be forgotten fortnight – ran for them. That short experience had weaned us off forever the notion or ambition to run in any way, shape or form a bar or restaurant. It seemed as if it were many far away moons ago. As was always the case on these impromptu visitations there was, a distinct shortage or even worse, a complete lack of either liquid or solid refreshments.

After we had showed them round an almost completed but empty Quinta, a partially started market garden area, except for the asparagus beds, an almost non-existent landscaped garden zone, only the rockery was of any note, we drove them into the village to have lunch, over which we were able to have a really good long chat. From the little we had been able to show them they must have thought that we had been completely inactive since our arrival, little did they know the truth. They were on a short package holiday in the eastern Algarve and were staying in Monte Gordo. We declined to make any comments on the locality. They had taken the train and then a taxi to Bensafrim but had misplaced the instructions that they had been given by the double-glazing man, but were determined to find us.

It was good to chew the fat about old times and to catch up with all the news on mutual acquaintances. Their pub business was, as always, still very busy and they now offered bed and breakfast accommodation. All too soon it was time for them to leave and a taxi picked them up at around five o'clock to take them to the station to catch the train back to their resort. Once again we suffered the brief pangs of a lost contact with our past. It was lovely to see them, but a great shame that it could not have been for a longer period of time and that they had not booked into a hotel on this side of the Algarve.

Someone had told us that there was a furniture exhibition about to open in Silves so we decided that should be a must to visit. It peed down with rain on the day that it opened and as there was nothing that we could do on the land we drove over only to find that the stands were still being erected. They were not ready to be staffed and did not contain any display items. It was a complete waste of time although from the limited amount of information we were able to collect from the organiser's office the designs were not suitable to our tastes and the prices certainly weren't.

The sixteenth and final asparagus bed was finally completed so we went out for a celebratory meal. Cavaliers that we were, we ended up as usual in the local restaurant. With the delays caused by the rains it had taken slightly over three and a half months and we finished up with the pathetic amount of only two thousand crowns, about a fifth of an acre and far below our planned target. All those that had not survived the cruel wrench from the seed bed to the permanent one were replaced with great difficulty. We took some encouragement as the losses only amounted to around two per cent, forty plants, it could well have been much worse. Under the circumstances this was a remarkable achievement.

Some more crowns were sold to customers that called in after they had heard the news on the grapevine and two deliveries were made. The overall income from these sales more than covered the initial outlay on the seeds, fertiliser and the petrol for the pump that had supplied the water.

In one postal collection I received a letter from the Finances Department, which notified me that, as a Sole Trader, the submission of a tax return was obligatory. The I.R.S. forms were therefore purchased and completed. To fill in my tax returns in England had never presented me with any problems, but here, all of the questions being in Portuguese gave me quite a few headaches. Many hours were spent, yet again with the open dictionary before it was filled in. I declared an overall operating loss as the costs of the garden shed construction, borehole and pump and all of the irrigation equipment far exceeded the miserable amount of income that had been generated. To rub salt into the wound I had to pay a small penalty as my forms were submitted late.

One needed eyes in ones backside as on one inspection of the rapidly growing asparagus fern I noticed small sticky grey balls that moved, attached to some of them. I removed one and on a closer examination I could clearly see that they had a black head and legs. A quick dive into the manual gave me the answer. They were the grub of the asparagus beetle. The adult one, about one centimetre long, would have reddish wing cases that bore a double black cross. It also pointed out that there could be several generations over the course of a summer. The constant attacks on the shoots and foliage could result in the plants being seriously weakened. What I failed to understand was that if our asparagus plants were the only cultivated ones around, where the hell did this pest come from???? This for me was positively the last straw. We had proceeded almost exactly in accordance with the books detailed instructions and recommendations but our crop had somehow been afflicted with an inbuilt perennial parasite. That was a real and most unwelcome kick in the teeth.

As a member of the co-operative I had automatic access to their Agricultural Advisory Department and they proved to be extremely helpful. A discussion with the chief engineer on a Friday morning examined whether or not it was an asparagus beetle or moth problem. He made a brief telephone call to Lisbon and told me that a tome would be posted to him that day. When I called in at midday on the Monday it had arrived and the information contained in the relevant section was specifically clear, in its recommendations on the type of chemical spray antidote and the optimum method and time of any applications. The chemical was thankfully in stock so we bought a one-litre bottle together with a shoulder harnessed back pack hand operated pressure sprayer.

There was only a very slight breeze down the land on our return so after we had translated, from the extremely small print on the bottles label, the correct ratio of chemical to water, it was absolutely miniscule, the beds were then thoroughly sprayed. It took three completely full sprayers, each of ten litres capacity to finish the operation.

AC entered into her little red book all of these details for future reference. I happened to notice that it now contained an incredible amount of information that she had accumulated from research and practical experience. One section outlined all the various application times of the chemicals that we had had to use to date, the strength of the mixtures and most importantly the periods of safety before the treated produce could be harvested.

What amazed us was the potency of the chemical that I had just sprayed onto the asparagus fern. In diluted form our one-litre bottle would last us, even if we had to spray three or four times a year, yonks past its sell by date.

The next morning I went on grub patrol and to my relief found not a trace and was so chuffed that I made a special journey into town to thank the engineer. He was also very pleased at the outcome but offered some words of caution. "Never ever drop your guard," he said, "always maintain a rigid inspection procedure and be prepared to carry out the operation at least once every year". Thank you very much I thought.

On this walkabout AC noticed that many new green gems had burst through the soil on the old seed beds. I had given up the ghost on the prospects of ever being able to increase the number of permanent asparagus beds and on that basis these old crowns would not be of any use next year. They would be too large to dig up and transplant them so every day I went round the beds and cut each green gem that appeared, It was good practice for me and we were able to enjoy many "pig out" asparagus suppers over several weeks and we found that the flavour had definitely improved.

A man who we had often seen standing with his hands in his pockets on the track called in one day and asked if we wanted to sell the cork from the oaks. He had spoken to M in the café who had suggested this direct approach, as he was the local "cork baron". A price per arroba, approximately fifteen kilos in weight, was quoted. I told him that I would consider his proposition and give my answer the next day. That evening I scuttled into the café and asked M for advice. He thought that the figure was slightly above the average for good quality cork and that I should accept his offer. The next morning I sauntered down to Alfonso 2's land and asked the same question. His response was also positive. When the Baron returned I shook his hand and told him that the deal was on. For us it was another little bit of income out of nowhere, even better, for doing nothing.

The cork was stripped from the trees and stacked in a large pile adjacent to the track and the exposed trunks were a rather sharp lightish brown, very similar to the colour that I had painted tree trunks as a child, much to the anguish of my art teacher. We were notified that it would be weighed at the end of the summer. At that time, just as I had predicted, our income had halved as the cork had dried out considerably.

We had faffed around on the question of furniture for the Quinta but now as it was basically habitable it was necessary to pull our fingers out. As we had to start from scratch even all the minor but essential items such as light fittings, bulbs, mirrors, curtains and rails together with the fixing plugs and screws had to be purchased. White goods like a fridge and a washing machine were required as was a cooker, hob, water heater and two gas bottles. The top priority for me was a double bed, either for ours or the guest bedroom, complete with mattress. We had sheets, blankets and pillows in the caravan but additional ones would have to be obtained. Kitchen and lounge furniture, not forgetting two toilet seats, had to be selected as soon as possible. All of the other requirements for the guest end of the Quinta were pushed to the bottom end of our urgency lists.

A mega search was embarked upon and we dashed around like blue arsed flies. No problems were encountered with most of the minor items but intensive searches in warehouses at Almadena, Portimao, Chinicato and Fonte de Boliqueime produced a very limited choice. It was exactly like the time when we had to select the floor and wall tiles; if it was not in stock then the delivery was long term. As our tastes were, more or less, on the same wavelength the selection from what was available was not too difficult. Most of the priority items were ordered on a payment on delivery basis, which was always the next day. We were not asked for any deposit only for our telephone number, which we could not provide. This did not appear to present any supplier with a problem and we left them all with fingers tightly crossed.

Whatever the outcome we had decided to "move in"! Our torch bought from the AA shop in Halesowen, fitted with new batteries, and our Kermit coloured paraffin lamp, bought here, were set up just inside the utility room door. This was to be our principle access in as it was the closest and most convenient to the caravan. Our supper was nervously nibbled at on the caravan terrace and we had almost given up hope when a delivery van careered down the drive with a load of goodies at around seven thirty.

We had to give the two man crew full credit as not a breath was wasted until everything had been unloaded and placed into position. They even assembled the double bed, the one in the guest bedroom as ours had not yet been chosen. After they had left we had a mad scramble to get things and ourselves organised. We only managed to finish by judicious use of the lamps to get from one room to another but had ended up with a made up bed that we could crash out into. The Quinta was now our home and the caravan would only be used as an office, shower unit and kitchen with a dining area facility. Earlier that afternoon I had made, for the umpteenth time, another hole so that AC could empty the contents of the porta-potty which was then given pride of place in the guest bathroom next to the toilet. This could have been used but without a continuous supply of water on tap we decided, in the short term, to stick with what we had.

The electrical company's engineers had laid the underground supply cable to the villa behind the cork oak wood so I wandered up to have a nose and by luck met, and was able to speak with the area installation manager. I asked him about the programme for our connection and after a brief look at his list he said that, "a Mr Collins is listed down here for next week".

"Are you sure," I said and as he shook my hand he nodded and said "for sure". I skipped back to the caravan to tell AC of the good news.

All the hot air ducts and lagging had been ordered delivered and had festered in the garden shed for quite a considerable time. It had been my intention to install this as a priority exercise but now it would have to wait as there were far more important things to do.

Another mega shop was now even more urgent for the items that we should have bought much earlier but had not got our heads around to do anything about them. I thought that it would be a straightforward exercise for a load of non-personal inanimate items like gas bottles, water heater, gas hob, electric oven, fridge, deep freezer and washing machine. How wrong could I have been! There was no difference of opinion, there could not have been really on the gas bottles and the selection and rating of the water heater. It had to be the largest in the range in terms of litres of hot water it could provide per minute. We did not quite come to blows over the decisions on the other items but it took visits to four electrical appliance shops before AC could finally make up her mind.

The main problem was that there were too many models, all in stock, to choose from. Delivery and fitting charges were included in the prices and as we had already experienced, this service had been extremely efficient. It proved to be the case again as on our return home we found that the two gas bottles had been placed in the store. A flexible rubber pipe, with an isolating valve, from each bottle had been connected to the pressure regulator so an easy change over from one bottle to the other was possible. We had arranged for all of the appliances to be delivered after the electrical and or, water supplies had been laid on. All that would be necessary was a telephone call.

True to his word the area installation manager with his crew turned up and proceeded to fix a cable from the concrete distribution pole to the Quinta. After a quick break for lunch they returned and completed the wiring to the main incoming switchboard and the power supply was switched on in the late afternoon. I had connected Bakelite light fittings to the bare cables in the bedroom we were using complete with one hundred watt bulbs and indicated to AC to flip up the switch. Bingo we had light, luz in Portuguese, and we were delighted.

The older generation of Portuguese who lived out in the country areas, around us, referred to electricity as light. This was because when the only recently installed distribution system was connected to their farmhouses and their small cottages it was singularly used for only that purpose, as they owned no other electrical appliances whatsoever. The distribution poles along our track had only been in place for about six years.

I almost had tears – a mixture of delight and relief – in my eyes as I humped the petrol pump up the well tunnel for positively the last time. The electric one was then carried down, quickly rigged up, primed and fixed onto the plinth that I had built. It was a hectic mad scramble back up the tunnel and then into the garden shed where it was my turn to give it a try. I paused to catch my breath and then counted down three, two, one and then flicked up the starter switch. There was only the sound of the motor turning for about three seconds, as the delivery pipe was being filled, and then there was the emotive sight of cool clear water being spewed into the cistern.

We had intended to lash out and enjoy a slap up meal in the village as a celebration but both felt too mentally exhausted to do it justice so we ended up at Cheryl and Simons for a long hot bath. Cheeky devils that we were, we took with us a bottle of wine and nibbles to enjoy as we soaked in the tub, glasses were already there. It felt like we were on holiday again. Hopefully we thought that it would probably be the last time as all we lacked at home was a water supply.

First thing in the morning I drove into Lagos to find the young man in the garage and was very pleased to find him there. He was told that we now had power and desperately needed the water supply to be connected. After a quick telephone conversation he promised to commission the system that afternoon and indicated that it would only take half an hour to get everything sorted out. I then called into the electrical appliance shops and requested delivery of our items for mid to late afternoon. That did not present any problems for them as it fitted in with scheduled programmes. Vans were available over that period.

It was a real nail-biting time as we waited for things to happen. We had a snack lunch but could not settle down to do anything. We were very nervous and fidgety until the team turned up, the young man from the garage and his electrician. After only twenty minutes AC was asked to turn on the cold-water tap in the kitchen. There followed a few agonising moments when all that happened was a series of spits and farts as the air in the pipes was expelled. Then as if by magic we had water, very brown and shitty in colour but water nevertheless. In less than a minute it became clear, sparkly and wonderfully cool. She was almost in tears with the sheer excitement of the occasion.

About an hour later two delivery vans almost collided as they drove down the bottom of the drive. Before the cabin doors were opened both drivers and their mates made sure that there were no large vicious un-tethered dogs around that could give them any degree of balls aching grievance. Once assured they got out of the cabs and as they all knew each other there were handshakes all round. Soon all the equipment was unloaded and installed, the last item being the water heater, which was quickly set up and the gas supply turned on. I tossed a coin and called heads, heads it was so I turned on a hot water bath tap and the heater fired up. After many never ending seconds the tap spat and farted and then produced even shittier coloured water, which soon became warm and then hot. AC became more and more ecstatic as the water gradually cleared so she fitted the plug and watched as the bath began to fill.

At the sight of the dirty water one of the drivers advised us that as it was being circulated for the first time, it would be prudent to check and thoroughly clean the washing machines inlet filter after three or four operational cycles,

We still had to fully settle in but both of us now considered ourselves well and truly domiciled in our Quinta. As a celebration I prepared our first evening meal and in the process commissioned the cooker and the hob. It was my Collin's special, an excellent as always, dish of super spicy, but not an ass blaster, chilli con carne with a more than basic Collin's style baked potato.

There were many reasons why we should have, but didn't, open more than one bottle of port that evening. It was a very special occasion, a major success and milestone in our development. The events and the many problems, overcome one by one, that had brought us to this situation had been hard fought over and we were thankful, blissfully happy and as always totally knackered both physically and mentally.

As we were always completely exhausted and bolloxed I suggested strongly that we should try, at least for a short or medium term period, to cut down and reduce our activities on the horticultural front. AC completely disagreed with this idea and as an alternative proposed a different approach. We agreed to mull it over and knew full well that whatever we decided in the end would be totally theoretical, as we had no past experience to guide us.

Before we finally crashed out into the sleep of the dammed we suddenly realised, with a great degree of sadness and lumps in our throat that the caravan, our home and substantial base for the past twenty or so months, had been made redundant, as once had we so long ago. On a brighter side we could put it up for sale to generate some much needed cash into the coffers.

Chapter Thirteen

We quickly settled down into a routine but found it difficult to get used to all of the space that we had and to start with, seemed to rattle around quite a lot. Three lists were made, one for agricultural work on the market garden, another for all of the fixing jobs that were needed and further items that had to be sourced and bought. This appeared to be very extensive so it was necessary to prioritise it. The third was all of the outside construction projects and again this appeared to be never ending.

One priority, although it was a very minor task it needed to be sorted out immediately, was to replace the light bulb fittings. The Bakelite ones fitted with a one hundred watt bulb tended to overheat and had given off an awful pong. I quickly realised that the maximum bulb rating was only sixty watts and these would not give out sufficient light. Metal or porcelain ones would be essential in most locations.

I collected the painting of the ruin and the land from Picasso's studio. Before I left I removed it's dust sheet to have a quick peep and remained impressed with the composition. It was the first real item to be fixed and we decide to have it mounted, in pride of place, on the chimneybreast above the firebrick mantelpiece.

As the carpenter had not made provision for air circulation from the wardrobes to the overhead cupboards, despite my instructions, it was necessary for me to drill holes in all the wardrobes chipboard ceilings.

A major two-person fixing job was the installation of the hot air circulation ducting at high level in the corridor onto the brackets that I had already fitted and this was carried out with only a little blaspheming. The connections to the hot air extractor fan, the back of the chimney-breast and the openings in the two bedrooms and kitchen, as was the fitting of the lagging and foil, a straightforward single person exercise. The airflow dampers also proved not to present a problem. Upon completion as I glanced upwards it reminded me, although on a much smaller scale, of the lagged lines of steam piping from a ship's boiler room to the engines. Attractive to me in its "as installed" position, it would certainly not be to people who would visit us, especially the ones who would pay for the privilege. Some form of cover or overhead screening would be necessary to hide it from view.

Alfonso 1 called in and asked if the caravan was for sale and if so how much money did we require. His face fell when I told him the amount and he shuffled off with shoulders slumped.

I had no sooner closed the door when the builder's wagon pulled to a stop in the driveway, he jumped out and rushed over and when the door was reopened, he thrust a sheaf of papers into my hand, they included his final invoice and a typed list of "the extras". With a grimace on my face I suggested that we would contact him as soon as we had had the time to study them carefully.

My outside construction projects continued on a "little bit here and a little bit there" basis. In an effort to keep all the balls in the air it appeared at first sight that not a lot of progress had been made. This was far from the truth. The pool pump house walls had been completed, the pre-cast concrete beams had been heaved into position, the infill tiles laid and the reinforcing bars fixed, so all that remained was to concrete the roof and fix the tiles. Built out from one of its walls was the BBQ and this had been built up to hearth level with a work surface on either side cast in.

All of this work had been undertaken with the use of the builder's cement mixer and this had now been removed. Now it was back to hand mixes only so progress was painfully slow.

I had been employed in the distant past as a Project Manager by a company that designed and manufactured incinerators for hospitals, municipal and industrial uses. Before I had been promoted to that position I had been a part of the design team and some of the basic Principles of Combustion still remained implanted in my grey matter. It was therefore not difficult to carry out simple on the "back of an empty fag packet-engineering calculations" for the BBQ. The hearth and grate surface area was fixed and a proportionate chimney size and height determined. This had to be sufficiently high to create an adequate flow of induced draught to maintain a good distribution of heat over the coals. Two push you and pull me firebrick dampers were fitted under the grate, to control after a fashion, the amount of air that passed through it. Two slots at different heights were made in the sidewalls above the grate into which the actual grill could be located when the BBQ was lit. The astute use of these two levels, could to large extent, control the time the food would take to cook and eliminate the all too often burnt to a crisp, charcoal black end result.

The rear wall of the BBQ was the back wall of the log store and was built up to a height to give it a volume of five cubic metres as I had assessed that this amount of logs should be enough to last us over a winter.

There was one small cock-up by the builder. It was impossible to open the door to the water heater store as it fouled the kitchen window security grill. It was not difficult to correct, the door and frame had to be re-fixed slightly further into the store and this then allowed it to open freely.

During one of our evening paperwork sessions we studied the list of "the extras" and felt that we had to resolve this as soon as possible as there had been no indication from the builder as to when construction of the swimming pool would start. They were fully discussed with him and his wife whom he had brought along and I firmly believed that she was present to gain a sympathy vote. We had no problems in accepting all of them bar two, where we considered that we were being totally ripped off. These were for the vanity unit in our bathroom and the boxed shelves inside the fitted wardrobes. However, in the end after a long drawn out haggle we agreed to pay the full amount as the overall cost was well within our budget. Sad to say but it was the one and only thing that had been.

We were not prepared to accept the green guides to the window shutters and required them to be replaced with black ones to match all of the other window furniture. Also the handles on the doors to the water heater and gas bottle stores had to be changed. Until these had been carried out a sum of money would be retained. The final cheque for completion and "the extras" was handed over less this amount and they both looked relatively contented with the situation. When I questioned him about the start of the pool construction he was a little vague and mumbled maybe in two weeks time and that he would use his full-time employees and not the "Magnificent seven". He then had the cheek to ask for a down payment and was politely told that it would not be available until there was an earnest degree of activity about the pool area.

The vegetable sections of the market garden were always watered on an "as and when" basis, but for a long time now it had been a very infrequent exercise due to the almost continuous rains. All of the crops had grown at a rate that never ceased to amaze us. I found it necessary to go down to Alfonso 2's plot to discuss a broad outline rota for our water use during the summer months. He had extended my main irrigation pipe with one of his own and had fitted a stop valve. His requirement was for a gravity supply only, direct from the cistern. He did not need to use my pump for a pressurised one. A rough guide was agreed and made as flexible as possible although I retained priority on the times of use of both of the systems. He had a small well on his land and the petrol pump which had at one time been seen down our well, so why he needed to use our water I did not know and thought it best not to ask.

I had decided to water all of the asparagus beds every fortnight by gravity for one and a half hours and then with the use of the pump for another hour. This appeared to be more than adequate as most of the dense fern was now well over a metre high. AC harvested our first tomatoes and a melon, which was not quite ripe.

When I called into the co-operative for yet more bits and pieces for the irrigation system I noticed that the well pump that I had originally bought was on the floor. It had been repaired as new gaskets were clearly visible but some ten months had elapsed since I had returned it to them. When I suggested to the engineer that I took it away with me and brought the replacement back on my next visit, he replied that it would be better if the other one was returned first.

AC received a registered letter from the car agent in Faro which enclosed a letter stamped by the Customs Department which legally enabled us to drive the Cortina in Portugal, after all this time, and that she would be notified shortly of the date and place of its inspection and registration to Portuguese number plates.

Cheryl and Simon arrived midweek for their usual quick chaotic visit, and as always invited us up for supper. We were now in a position to reciprocate so invited them down for a meal on the Saturday. They would be the guinea pigs for our first social event in the Quinta with a brand new, barely christened, electric oven. It all went really well and we felt that they were quite impressed with the place. AC and I had decided months earlier, as on their visits they could without any difficulty create a fair degree of confusion and a certain amount of dreaded anticipation that often bordered on panic, that we should give them a nickname. Over a few glasses of brandy, some port with Stilton and digestive biscuits, we told them of our decision and gave a full explanation. They would be known as "The dreadeds", their children as "The Junior dreadeds", their grandchildren as "Mini dreadeds" and their friends who visited as "Honorary dreadeds". They hooted with laughter and appeared to be tickled pink with the idea.

The jungle drums in England and Bensafrim must have pounded away as lots of our friends and relatives all wished to come and visit us to see what we had been up to. It was easy for our Portuguese friends, who lived in the village, as all they had to do was take a stroll along the track and call in. Many did for a looksee a chat and refreshments. With the English contingent however we decided that relatives should have preference over friends and Lucie was to be our first guest. A major bonus for us was that any one from overseas would be able to bring with them lots and lots of housey items that were unavailable here.

We had performed very well and had crossed off almost three quarters of the fixing and purchases list and I had managed to obtain a Portuguese railway line sleeper and intended to make a proper mantle piece from it and to put it on top of the firebrick one.

Lucie was collected from the airport and it was a good job that we had an estate car as she was laden down with goodies. She was impressed with the Quinta and really enjoyed the open-air Saturday bop at the club. It was a completely new experience for her and one that she thoroughly enjoyed so it was with an extreme effort that we managed to tear her away. It was not a "must dash around" holiday, but a more relaxed one, although several trips were made into Lagos to shop and visit familiar restaurants. Most days we walked into the village and back and this was a good form of exercise to work up an appetite for the evening meals.

The fortnight sadly passed by all too quickly and was marred by electrical power cuts in the evenings. There was not much of a chance of entertainment by candlelight and we experienced a major problem, which was with the supply of water to the Quinta, or more to the point the lack of it. Once the pressure tank had been emptied, it would stay empty until power was restored to operate the borehole pump to refill it. Complete overnight failures were inconvenient and made things a little difficult but we did have the sense to take precautions and fill up a few water containers and the two from the caravan we found particularly useful in the toilets.

One morning with the power still off, we could have killed for a cup of coffee, but we only had an electric kettle. It was quite a long period of time before someone woke up, it wasn't me and had the savvy to pour some water from the container into a saucepan, place it on the gas hob and light the ring with a match.

We had a power cut on the last of our morning walks into the village with Lucie and found that they had power there. I assumed therefore that our supply must have been from a different substation. A letter from number one daughter Sharon was collected from the Council offices asking if she, her boyfriend and Michelle could come out and stay with us. On the way back we saw Nora Batty, obviously in difficulties as she struggled to carry two five-litre plastic water bottles. When we caught up with her she had placed them on the ground. I walked over and offered to carry them to which she snorted with indignation, snatched them up and trundled off.

A request had been made to the Local Authority to have the borehole water analysed. One morning their technician arrived with sterilised bottles to take the necessary samples. Unfortunately there had been a power cut overnight and electricity was still off, so there was not a drop of water in the whole system; it was absolutely bone dry. He left in a complete huff, never to return, and we didn't bother to pursue the matter any further.

We had asked the builder about the swimming pool construction so to be one step ahead of the game I staked out the four corner points of the inside dimensions of its location. We agreed that there should be at least a three-metre terrace to the front of it and one and a half beyond. The centre of its ten metres length would line up with the middle of the lounge which was central in the Quinta and flanked by a bedroom on either side. These proportions appeared to be reasonable when compared with the size of the upper terrace.

An early wake up call was suffered one morning as from out of nowhere telephone linesmen appeared, one scrabbled around on the roof with a ranging pole. What actually woke us was the sound of a loud explosion. This came from the bottom of the land and had made a hole for the installation of the first pole. We had not realised that the incoming connection would be from the Barao de San Joao road and had blissfully assumed that it would be fed in from along the track. It was plain to see that they intended to place the poles in a direct line up the land and one would be just behind the pool and only ten metres from the Quinta. We could not tolerate that as it would be such an eyesore. It took a lot of heated discussions as we argued constantly about the problems that we would suffer to effectively plough the land before they reluctantly agreed to a change in the line of entry. Even so we had an unexpected row of poles across the land. I was not a happy bunny, but required a telephone, which they informed me as they left, would be installed the next day. A cream hand-set was duly connected despite the fact that I had ordered a red or green one. I noticed that included in their paperwork was a copy of the original application form that I had submitted in Portimao so many months before. Three days later the switchboard link was made and we then had an operational telephone and AC immediately made a call to her mother and I telephoned Sharon and told her that we looked forward to their visit and awaited details of the dates and flight details.

Bulldozer Joe sauntered down the drive from his mother's cottage and asked if he could see where the pool was going to be constructed. Apparently the builder had spoken to him and had enquired about his availability. Before he would make a commitment he wanted to view the working area. He had excavated for many pools in the past so that was not a problem but he needed to reassure himself that there were no restrictions on access, in our case he could see none. We asked him when he could start and he indicated that if the builder agreed it would be possible next week. I told him to tell the builder that the down payment cheque was available for collection. That information provoked an immediate response and it was handed over on Sunday. We then waited with bated breaths to see what would happen on the Monday.

Come the Monday morning at around eight o'clock the activities started, two men checked out my stake lines and then proceeded to lay a line with lime powder outside them. Joe then clanked his machine into position and started to cut out the soil to form the pool outline. By late evening the whole of the excavations had been completed and, as directed, they were dumped at a good distance from the sidewall that was furthest away from the Quinta more or less level with the pile that remained from the work on the septic tank. It all looked like a small mountain. To round off the day's events one lorry unloaded a load of reinforcing bars, sand, sacks of cement, and importantly for me a cement mixer. A second one arrived not long after and tipped its load of rocks into the east end of the hole.

The first of the sweetcorn was sampled and it was not bad but not brilliant. A mental note was made to try another variety next time although we discovered that the flavour was much better if they were picked when the tassles were only slightly brown and not really dark brown and shrivelled. It was certainly better than the maize that we had grown the year before. We were now up to our ears in courgettes, tomatoes, melons, peppers and a few kilos of beetroot had been pickled. The melons continued to ripen at a ridiculous rate, even after many had been given away in the village a lot were left to rot.

I had almost completed the BBQ as the floor and the two work surfaces had been cemented ready for a tiled cover and the chimney had been capped with an ornamental Algarve fancy top, it looked great.

Five hundred cement blocks had been ordered for various walls and delivery had been promised within the next few days. With no workers around I found the time – how one had to pick ones moments – when the weather was reasonable and with assistance from AC to utilise the cement mixer and lay the roof to the pump house. She helped to lift the many buckets of concrete up to me and overstretched both her neck and shoulder muscles and finished up in a great deal of pain. On a dry evening I was able to apply two coats of Aquaseal to waterproof it.

One particular Thursday was a red-letter day tinged with economic gloom. We accompanied the architect to the Council offices in Lagos and obtained the official approval to build the Quinta to the "as built" design and in its present location. The sting in the tail was, as we had anticipated, the cost of another building license had to be paid for. Although over-budget and almost broke we took consolation that the amount was only a tenth of the inflated building costs had we started the construction then. As we parted company he suggested that we immediately apply for the Certificate of Habitation but when we pointed out that the pool construction had only just commenced he agreed that this action would be a little premature.

Sharon rang to tell us the details of their planned visit, which was not that far off and it fitted in with our limited movements so we eagerly awaited their arrival. Our friends the surgeon, Peter, Mary and the family had booked a holiday much earlier in the year but as we could not be sure that we would be able to accommodate them in a completed Quinta they had booked into a complex at the top end of Lagos as part of a package deal.

Bulldozer Joe drove his machine, which was followed by two lorries from the bottom track up the land to the rear of the mound of excavated soil. Twenty-six loads later, each of about eight cubic metres; all of the septic tank and most of the pools deposited soils had been removed and tipped at the depot at the end of the track and in their neighbour's garden opposite. A smallish pile had been deliberately left and this was to be used as a back fill for the outer pool walls and as an under fill for the surrounding terraces. He must have made a few bob out of the deal as a round trip for the lorries was less than one and half kilometres and he had charged them for the material and delivery, and me for its removal.

Sharon and number two daughter Michelle, loveably known as Shaz and Shelle for short, together with Shaz's boyfriend Eddie whom I had not met, were our second wave of visitors to arrive. I had not seen the girls since just after our wedding so there was a lot of news to chat about and also to catch up on subsequent events. They had brought two additional large suitcases with them, which were crammed full with goodies for us and the Quinta. Shelle had collected quite a lot from Lucie who had made, and enjoyed, numerous shopping trips after her visit when we had discussed some of the major requirements, which we couldn't find here. Eddie seemed very nice for a solicitor, relatively quiet, maybe as a result of meeting me in the flesh and Shaz and he appeared to get on very well together which I was extremely pleased to see. Both were outdoor types and a session at a local horse-riding establishment was soon organised as were some scuba dives at Praia da Luz, even a night one was included.

I made a lot of BBQ's and each time AC complained that it was too efficient as the meats were cooked and ready before the food in the kitchen was available. As we all sat on the upper terrace with a glass of some form of alcoholic beverage in our hands we gazed at the hole in the ground and tried to visualise what the lower level would look like if and when the pool was ever completed. Since some materials had been delivered we had not seen hair nor hide of the builder or any of his crew.

Many meals were enjoyed at various hostelries and a lot more boozy sessions with the inevitable late nights resulted.

I suggested that we all go to the beach at Amado. They took their swimsuits but AC and I not being beach lovers, didn't bother. It was still as beautiful as the one and only time we had been there before but on this occasion there were a lot of

Portuguese people there. We seemed to be the only foreigners. All three had a dip and Shaz, who was a really good and strong swimmer, thought that it was quite dangerous with a very strong undercurrent but in the right weather conditions would be an ideal place "to surf".

"Ugh," I said.

We walked up to the small restaurant by the fishermen's huts for a few bevies and found on a closer inspection that it was a ramshackle sort of place with crude and very basic toilet facilities. I stood at the makeshift bar and spoke to a young girl to order some drinks. There I noticed two women, in a small room at the back that appeared to serve as the kitchen. They had prepared different types and quantities of food. One was her mother as the facial likeness was uncanny and the scruffy fellow at the BBQ on the outside was obviously her father, for the same reasons. In one tucked away corner sat a tiny grey haired old lady, it could have been her granny, and she had peeled some potatoes and prepared a huge pile of chips, proper big thick chunky chips, not like the squitty little French fries all too often dished up in most eating places. I called the gang over, pointed to them and suggested that we try a couple of platefuls. "Cor yes," was the immediate response. When I asked the young girl for the menu she pointed to a tatty bit of paper that was pinned on one wall, fixed by a drawing pin, it was a hand scribbled one

Shaz didn't fancy anything much but could not resist the chips when a plate was put on the table. Shelle and Eddie selected the grilled sardines with chips and AC and I ordered the tuna salad, also with chips. We sat on a bench at a trestle-supported table and the standard cover of bread, butter, olives, cream cheese and sardine pate was set out on a paper tablecloth. Another round of drinks was ordered and these came with the food. My salad was one of the best that I had ever tasted lettuce, onions, peppers, cucumbers, tomatoes and olives were topped with tuna steak meat obviously from a tin but the flakes were thick and juicy, and all of this was surrounded by sliced boiled eggs and smothered with homemade mayonnaise that had been drizzled over it. The plate was huge as were the ones that had the lovely big chips piled on them. It was a magnificent scoff and I suggested that the restaurant be named the "Chippery". AC after a quick loo fix disagreed and suggested sarcastically the "Ritz or the Pitz". When I asked to settle up the bill the young girl handed me a slip of paper with some figures on it, it was the same writing as on the menu fixed to the wall. The total came to the princely sum equivalent to eight pounds sterling.

We then returned to the beach where everyone crashed out but after an hour the gang plunged in for another dip and a splash whilst we were glad to just lie there and doze. To complete the round trip we then went to Cape St Vincent and then stopped off at Sagres. Not a lot seemed to be going on and we found it impossible to find anywhere to have a refreshing cup of tea. I thought that it was a bit of a one-horse place and fully expected to see John Wayne dismount from his mangy old steed outside one of the few bars. We only stayed for a quick beer at one of them and then it was back to the rancho. All in all it was a thoroughly enjoyable day and we were pleasantly knackered at the end of it.

On the Saturday we all had a ball at the dance. AC Shaz and Eddie left at about one thirty and AC came back to prise Shelle and me away just after four. AC went straight to bed but Shelle and I had a few cheese butties, a morning cap and then crashed out about six o'clock.

There was a very slow start by some of us later on but I somehow managed to prepare a cooked brunch around midday. The gang then hurtled off to Praia da Luz for a swim, snorkel or just sunbathe. They found that the water was very cold and that the planned night dive had been called off as the underwater visibility was extremely poor.

In Lagos we bought some highly expensive but extremely pretty sheets and pillowcases for bed. It was their treat and I was very miffed when a requested discount was refused by the shop assistant who was a little snotty when she told me that the price on display was fixed!

Shelle, as the youngest, wanted to try a Disco and we managed to find one that was open early, at one o'clock in the morning. I threw a complete wobbler when asked to pay four hundred escudos, about one pound fifty pence for the first drink and three hundred, just over a pound for the following ones so told them to stuff off. The others told me that I was totally out of touch but I stubbornly refused to budge. Instead I dragged them off to visit a few more bars with sensible prices and we arrived back home around three o'clock and dived into bread, ham cheese and biscuits. After another morning cap for Shelle and me it was finally off to bed.

We met up with Peter and the family at the complex in Lagos, their flight had been delayed by two hours, and were staggered to find how the children had grown. After they had checked in and found their villa they unpacked lots and lots of goodies for us food wise with many gifts for the Quinta. After a drink we arranged to catch up with them in the morning and they could meet up with our gang.

I collected them and with the youngest one tucked into the uncovered boot drove to a restaurant not far away from the Quinta. AC and Shaz had managed to drag Shelle out of her pit into a cold shower and they were all there when we arrived. Our German friends and their two young children had also been invited as we thought that it would give them a welcome break and other children would be present. They turned up late as their dog had been in an accident and had not forgotten as AC had surmised. It really was a superb lunch, aperitifs were taken on the terrace where the sun was so hot that AC and I sat in the shade, whilst all of the others took full advantage and sunbathed.

We had pre-ordered one of their specials, a fillet of pork roast and two large ones were presented surrounded by lashings of potatoes and individual plates filled with a variety of vegetables. I carved at the table much to Peter's amusement at my cutting techniques. The specials had to be ordered twenty-four hours in advance and were exactly as described, special and this one certainly was.

After a long session it was back home for a lot of idle chatter and lots of chin wagging about everything and nothing in particular with more liquid refreshments. The Dorset brigade were then driven back to the complex and I caught up with AC and the gang in the village for another bevy before we drove home again for a latish nights snack of bread and toast and whatever happened to be left in the fridge.

It was the gang's last day; they had an evening flight and had only just closed their suitcases when a taxi appeared at the top of the drive and who should pop out but the double-glazing family from Studley. They had returned for a working holiday and intended to look around the Lagos district and possibly purchase some land a villa or an apartment.

Shaz and Eddie went off to Praia da Luz for a final swim and AC and Shelle popped into the village for some bread and provisions as I set up the BBQ. The newcomers just sat around and gazed at our hole in the ground. From the original five of us for lunch there would now be another six so it was a bit of a scrabble to find sufficient food and drink to satisfy everyone but we managed admirably.

Around mid-afternoon my girls and Eddie loaded up their hire car and we all had lumps in our throats as we said our goodbyes. A wonderful time had been experienced by us all and AC had been given a golden opportunity to get to know my daughters a little better. For me it had been an exciting and very emotional period during which I was chuffed to naffy breaks to have my "bambinos", as I still called them, around.

A subdued conversation followed with the Studley crew and we eventually drove them into the village around seven o'clock to order a taxi. As they piled in we suggested that if they required any help, assistance or advice then they should feel free to contact us.

Later, as we sat in the lounge, we really felt as flat as a couple of wet farts and were in a deep gloom and doom mood with no voices heard to say more bread please, pass another slice of melon and from Shelle the immortal words, "I think that I can just about manage one more bottle of beer". There had still been no sight of the builder and no progress on the pool construction and this certainly did not help to improve our frame of mind.

Peter as head of the Dorset brigade decided to hire a car, which gave us all a much better degree of flexibility. There was a water problem in their villa; there wasn't any, it was that time of year. Our two bathrooms then came into their own for the next few days, as did the hire car. We managed to arrange a few days out with them to the beach at Arrifana on the West coast, Monchique, Foia, the highest point in the Algarve and a few more.

The Saturday bop in the village was a must, AC and I put on a magnificent spread at our BBQ that evening. We had prepared hot and cold dishes that included a wide range of Arabic delights and a variety of cooked meats. As usual there was a large assortment of different hot and cold beverages. The Studley crew had been invited but could not make it as they had to meet someone to discuss the potential purchase of a villa and were booked on a plane home the next day.

An absolute beano was had at the bop and we left with the children who would stay the night, or what was left of it, with us at about four o'clock completely shattered and exhausted. It was a very slow start when we eventually surfaced and I didn't make the first cup of coffee until almost eleven. The others were even slower to get their acts together and as we all felt slightly peckish I lashed up a mongrel style late brunch with the BBQ leftovers and a fry up. It all went down very quickly after which the children asked to be taken to a different beach and we really couldn't refuse them. AC and I just sat on the sand and went along with the flow as they all had a whale of a time in and out of the sea non-stop although we were both bored stiff. Again all too soon they had to leave and another emotional time was experienced by everyone. As we waved them off on the tour operators bus AC was exceedingly choked.

Later that afternoon I was in the kitchen to make a pot of tea which we would drink on the terrace as we gazed into our hole. As I glanced through the window I saw another taxi draw up and stop at the top of the drive and shouted to AC. After a double take I recognised the couple who got out. They were long standing friends of hers, Jean and Derek, an interesting pair from totally different backgrounds. When we had last met them they were unmarried, had always intended to but had never got around to it. AC rushed up the drive to greet them as I got another two cups out of the cupboard. Over tea and biscuits they told us that they were on a mini four-day visit arranged through a tour operator and had been booked into some multi-story hotel in Alvor. We persuaded them to stay the night as the double bed had been made up and we had spare toothbrushes towels and other things so that it would not be too difficult for them to conduct their normal ablution routines. A BBQ was quickly laid and a supper of sorts cobbled together.

After breakfast we took them on a conducted tour of the village and then drove around the area and visited Praia da Luz, Burghau and lastly Lagos where we had a sardine lunch down by the boatyard in a converted garage. All of the afternoon was spent back on our terrace where we chatted away most of the time. We were just about to take them into the village to arrange a taxi back to their hotel when to our amazement one turned up and stopped in front of us. In all of the months that we had lived in the caravan not one single taxi had ventured along the track. Now it appeared to be a weekly event. You could have knocked us both down with a feather when the occupants turned out to be "The three Musketeers", the lads that we had got very friendly with when we supped a few drinks in the pub in Studley.

As Jean and Derek got into the taxi after more tearful farewells the driver gave us a huge beaming smile and shook our hands vigorously. It must have seemed to him that it was his birthday. To pick up a fare along a dirt track this far out in the sticks was a minor miracle. I agreed the cost of their journey on the spot so that they would not be sat in the back seat at the end of the trip and, as tourists, get ripped off when asked to pay an excessive charge.

The five of us had just started to walk down the drive when a wagon turned in and drove down to the bottom. I thought that it was the builder but it wasn't, it had on board my new toy, a second hand cement mixer. M at the café had purchased the small house next door and had carried out major works to the ground and first floor levels as an extension to the cafés existing living areas. He had employed local artisans and had brought the cement mixer for the construction. I had asked him on one occasion if he would sell it when his works were completed and his response was "yes, at the right price". With so much concreting to be carried out around the Quinta hand mixing was now out of the question and I had looked around at prices for a new mixer in the co-operative and other stockists in the Lagos area. He mentioned a figure, which I thought was very reasonable so I shook his hand and wrote out a cheque for fifty per cent of it as a deposit. Now it was mine and there were many hands to help offload it. In future therefore, I did not have to give a monkeys toss as to whether the builder's one was on site or not. If I wanted to I could work twenty-four hours a day seven days a week and felt a real sense of satisfaction with this degree of independence and made a mental note to settle up with M as soon as possible.

The lads had only called in for a quick visit as they intended "To Do" the Algarve and were prepared to slum it on the floor overnight. "Not in this five star establishment" I said and in less than thirty minutes all the beds had been sorted out and a few bottles opened and downed. None of their circumstances had changed at all and none of them had married, or even considered it as a possibility, they were still as mixed up as ever. We thought that each had some plus points in their favour but obviously apathy ruled as far as marriage was concerned. Foodwise we were almost out of supplies so I nipped into the village and returned with what I believed were ample loads of booze and a chicken and chips take-away for seven. That should have been more than enough and for the amount of food I was only just right but I had seriously underestimated, in fact totally forgotten how these fellows could knock back the beers, ably assisted by me and we soon ran out completely. The four of us went into the village to restock and have a few whilst we were there and I took the opportunity to give M a cheque for the outstanding balance on the mixer. AC as always the wise one, stayed at home.

We didn't travel around very much with them, as they were not really sightseers but spent many hours in all the local pool bars and played the occasional game of darts when a board could be found. Most of the evenings were spent at our pissy arsed BBQ's after which we played card games, backgammon and on one evening in desperation Trivial Pursuits, sometimes until three o'clock in the morning. They gave me a present of a bottle of Glenmorangie, my favourite malt whisky tipple, and for AC a large bottle of Rive Gauche perfume. Soon they started to become a little restless and wanted to move on and hit the nightlife of Albufeira so we dropped them off at the bus station in Lagos and declined an invitation to go with them, even for one night. By chance we found out that they would on the same return flight to Birmingham as Jean and Derek.

After all these weeks of more or less continuous visitations we had to quickly get back to reality. There was work to be carried out on the market garden, construction and other projects, more purchases to be made and most importantly to chase up the builder to complete the pool. With the excitement of all the visitors this had taken a back seat but we now had to make a concerted effort to catch up with him and get him to pull out all of the stops before the rainy season was upon us. When we finally did he cheekily asked for the next stage payment. I was quite blunt and told him there would be nothing until the base had been cast and the brick sidewalls had been built.

It had been over five weeks since any work had been done on the pool but it restarted with a vengeance. After the plumber had sited the sump with a fitted length of plastic pipe that ran to a spot outside where the west wall would be built large rocks were hurled into the bottom and then placed and set to a string line level. These were then covered with a steel mesh and a double layer of reinforcing bars the ends of which were bent upwards to a height of one metre at a point just inside where the outer brick walls would be laid. As if by magic three ready mix concrete wagons then arrived and the whole base of the pool was then cast. The outside pool brick walls were quickly thrown up and the steel fixers then attached a double layer of reinforcing bars inside them. Alternative vertical ones of these were tied to the bars that protruded through the recently cast base slab. Right on cue, two lorries arrived loaded with timber shuttering, which was then deposited around the pool perimeter. It was the same timbers that had been used to construct "The dreaded's" pool and the one at the villa behind the cork oak wood. The builder called in for his cheque that evening and although questioned we never found out where he had been or what he had done over those weeks when he was away from our site.

Rain, real heavy rain slashed down over the weekend, which made it impossible to do any outside work so we commissioned the log burning stove. This proved to be very efficient and it got so hot that the shuttering for the lintel that had been left in position soon started to smoulder from the radiated heat so we had to shut it down earlier than anticipated. The next day I had no choice but to attempt to remove the shuttering. I was glad that I did, it was not too difficult but very fiddly and a task not to be trusted to a "bull at a gate" approach by the builder or one of his men.

We lit the stove for the second time and after a couple of hours the chimney breast was warm to the touch so I switched on the hot air extractor fan to test the hot and cold air distribution system. Two hours later it seemed that the chill had been taken off the kitchen and the two guest bedrooms. To obtain a reasonable temperature in these would take a considerable time due to their high ceilings and the stove might have to be fired on a continuous basis but for our immediate requirements the system functioned to our satisfaction.

As the pool pump house was waterproof another little inside job could be tackled, the rendering of the inside walls and ceiling. The walls were relatively easy and I considered that the finish was far more professional than the outside walls to the garden shed. I toyed with the idea of showing them to Alfonso 1, but I didn't. However the upside down cementing to the ceiling and the door lintel I found to be a pig to apply. The lintel was a relatively small area so a reasonable job was made of it in the end, despite blobs that continued to drop off, but the ceiling was a nightmare. I could not get the mix to stick into position, as fast as I slapped it on it slowly peeled off. After several attempts it was completed but by no stretch of the imagination could it be described as up to the same standard as the "Magnificent seven's" finished ceilings in the Quinta. I classified it as artistic in that it was applied in small patches and the end result was similar to the whorls on the outside of a wasp's nest.

When I had finished the BBQ I also cast the base to the log store behind it. Onto this had been placed all of the logs we had obtained when the olive trees had been so drastically pruned and the other woods that had been collected since that time. It had no roof but we had covered them with a sheet of plastic so that they remained quite dry and would serve as our first winters fuel supply.

When the carpenters arrived on the Monday morning they took one look at the watery mess in the hole and after ten minutes shrugged their shoulders and buggered off. I told them that I would empty it during the afternoon and that they could return tomorrow to carry on the works. My original well pump, the kerosene and petrol driven one, which had been collected from the co-opertiva, was dragged out of the garden shed and set up by the pool. This and the other one had been, thank goodness, extremely versatile in their operational locations. As I looked up to the heavens I wondered why when every time that I had a hole in the ground they always opened. To my surprise the pump started easily and by late afternoon most of the water in the hole had been pumped down the land and it was almost empty. It turned to a completely wasted exercise as it pissed down all night so the un-shuttered hole had even more water in it by the morning.

In view of the monsoons no one turned up on the Tuesday but I proceeded to dash around like a character in a Benny Hill speeded up movie. I had my own cement mixer and was able to take full advantage of an unexpected brief lull in the stormy weather.

Over the previous weeks many car boot loads of rocks from the surrounding hills had been collected and had been laid to replace the soil and other materials that had been washed away from the land that sloped up to the track. More had been used as a base for the foundations of a wall that would be laid at the top of this slope along the whole length of the track from the gulley to the west of the driveway entrance. Another wall would be constructed on the east side of the drive but this would require a much less substantial base. A weak mix of concrete was poured over the rocks on the slope, just to key them in, and a very strong one along the foundations. These were covered in heavy duty plastic sheeting to minimise the possibility of damage from further downpours.

At the top of the drive small stones and gravel had been rammed into place across its width which then made it higher than the level of the track. This was intended to ensure that any raging floodwater would flow safely past and not down the driveway.

More rain followed but a dry spell was forecast so I set up the pump for another attempt to clear out the crap from the pool hole. It turned out to be a successful operation and when the builder's brother delivered some more materials he could clearly see that the hole was almost empty and that work could proceed. It took only three days for the carpenters to assemble the internal shuttering and by late on a Friday afternoon it had been finished and it looked like a fortress had been built inside the outer walls. When asked, the builder told me that the ready mixed concrete had been ordered and that it would be poured on Monday morning.

The ordered cement blocks were delivered first thing on the Saturday and AC helped to unload them, it really was a foolish thing to do as she was still in pain from the pump house roof exertions. I laid sixty of them, each twenty centimetres high, on the prepared foundations along the lowest part of the track and thought that I could easily be a hundred a day man. The excruciating aches and pains on the Sunday told me otherwise.

The daytime temperature was still warm; low to mid twenties centigrade and with the constant wet weather some of the asparagus fern remained a lush green although a lot of it had died off. This was obviously not the right time to cut it down and in any case the ground was waterlogged and very squidgy, too wet to even walk on.

Again there were more heavy rain showers in the early hours of Monday morning which made the ground even soggier but it did allow the "Goon Show", the ready mixed concrete brigade, and "Fred Karno's Army", the builders gang, to present a two act comedy drama, which I did not consider to be at all amusing or funny at the time.

At seven thirty the builder arrived with eight of his men. His brother turned up soon afterwards quickly followed by Bulldozer Joe in his machine. They all swung into action and proceeded to backfill the pool outer walls with the soil from the small pile that had not been removed. He told me that the concrete pour was scheduled for nine thirty and that they were normally very punctual. I had seen one of his workers at "The dreaded's" villa and had named him "fag in the mouth" as one continually dangled between his lips. He was bad value for money as although he always appeared to be industrious, if you studied his movements carefully it was plain to see that he actually did the square root of naff all. He also did not resemble a wide hunk of a fellow as he had runaway shoulders that sloped over forty-five degrees downwards from the nape of his neck.

I decided that it was prudent to point out the builder that some important items were missing, such as the skimmers, two tubes for the recirculation pipe work and the vacuum tube connection. A look of anguish appeared on his face as he had forgotten them. His brother was immediately despatched to collect them and returned with only the tube fittings. We then witnessed for the first time a Portuguese person totally loose his cool. The builder ranted and raved at the top of his voice with arms that waved like a windmill at high speed. The brother, who was in a complete state of shock at this outrage, then buggered off and finally returned with the two skimmers and all of these were quickly fitted into position and the back filling continued with Bulldozer Joe in control. His machine had to move all of the soil as the gang had not one shovel, Portuguese hoe or a wheelbarrow between them. This exercise was successfully completed, after a fashion, and much to my dismay most of the soil that I had carefully saved for the terrace under fill had had to be used in the process.

The "Goons" boss man arrived and started to discuss with the builder the location of the pump and the concrete wagon access. He had strong facial features and I thought that his ancestors were probably North African, maybe Moorish. The thing or two things that really stood out were his ears. He was the original "Wing Nut," they were larger and more extended than Wallaces. It was decided that they would set up the pump on the land area adjacent to the ruin much to AC's and my relief as our east wing drive would have been seriously damaged as would the drain and sewage pipes that ran under it. During these discussions the skies blackened and a few drops of heavy rain fell ominously.

Act one of the drama now commenced as the "Goon Show" participants arrived at ten o'clock with the pump unit. This should have been driven in forward from the track and then turned to the right to get down into a position that faced the pool. What happened was that it reversed in up the slight slope to the ruin and then tried to turn left to reach that position with the result that it got stuck across the slope at an extremely dangerous angle, mistake number one. Timbers, planks, gravel and sand were liberally strewn around and eventually it managed to extricate itself out of the ruts that it had made and get manoeuvred into the ideal position.

I gave them eleven marks out of ten for their next move even though it racked the nerves to witness the performance, AC could not face it so went indoors. They had to manipulate the pump's boom under the telephone cables and over the Quinta's guest double bedroom roof. I estimated that the maximum space or clearance between these was less than twelve centimetres but they were successful in their initial attempt.

The first ready mix concrete wagon then drove in forwards up the slope to the ruin and then tried to reverse down to the pump. This was the second mistake (would they never learn) as it got itself stuck in the shit, ruts and mire created by the pump's entry. The concrete wagon that was waiting on the track then had to drive in forwards and managed to pull it half out. After a lot more planks and gravel had been thrown around it was released and was then able to line itself up behind the pump unit. Thankfully the distribution of this pour of concrete went smoothly as it was a strong mix with a hardener accelerator additive. "Fred Karno's Army" ensured that it was spread evenly around the pool walls with the continuous use of long poles which they used to agitate the mass, with the builder down in the depths with his Kango hammer, hammering against the shuttering for all his worth. "What price a bog standard vibrator?" I thought. The now empty concrete wagon with its rear wheels spinning furiously somehow managed to reverse until it reached a patch of level ground and then made it back onto the track.

At the insistence of the driver of the second concrete wagon, a clever bugger who showed some semblance of common sense, more sand and gravel was deposited all over the churned up area and the ruts filled in. He then cleverly reversed into position with no difficulty at all. This load of concrete, again with the additive, was distributed in the same way although there was a slight interruption as some of the Army had to rush to shutter up a part of the outside wall where they had not quite finished the back filling. At the end of the pour, as the driver successfully made his way forward up and onto the track, the rains began to fall quite heavily.

Then began act two, the site clearance. "Fred Karno's Army" cleared away what little they had brought and the two concrete wagons had been hosed down and were ready to leave. As the skies got darker and the rain became heavier the pump unit tried to reverse up the slope. It did not have a cat in hells chance. There was no more sand or gravel left to repair the churned up mess and it got well and truly stuck in the deep ruts made on its entry and those made by the two concrete wagons. One of these returned in an attempt to tow it out but failed dismally and got itself stuck with mud up to its back axles. Bulldozer Joe came to the rescue and pulled it out quite easily but had tremendous problems with the pump unit. He could not pull this up the slope but eventually managed to drag it behind him at a sharp angle across it until he reached firmer ground. It then gained sufficient self-traction to reverse back onto the track.

The heavens then really opened and it seemed to me that they had never ever closed. If it had been five minutes earlier then the pump unit would have had to remain there for several days. The churned up mess that they had left behind them next to the ruin, down the slope to the Quinta and on their way out to the track, was strewn with mangled pieces of timber and mixed up sand and gravel appeared to have been randomly plonked all over the place. It resembled a World War One scene. Similar I pictured in my mind the aftermath of the battle of the Somme.

After a late lunch we fell onto the bed totally bolloxed, mentally and physically knackered. An exercise that under normal circumstances should have been completed in one and a half hours had taken almost five and I was not prepared to pick up any of the associated extra costs.

In the midst of this shambolic escapade a man had appeared and enquired about the generator. I had put a for sale notice at the top of the drive which included full details and the price. It was a really inconvenient time to call and I nearly told him to return some other day but as he was the only person to have shown any interest and the notice had been up for a few weeks, I didn't. The shed was opened, the cloth cover removed and it started with the first pull on the rope. There was no time to haggle so I told him that the price was as on the board and that he could basically take it or leave it. To my surprise he said "ok" and that he would call back with the cash in the morning. For the only deal in my life, with the exception of property sales, I had sold something for more than I had paid for it. He noticed the water pump and asked if that was for sale as well. "Yes, but not until that bloody hole in the ground at the back of the Quinta is completely finished" was my emphatic response. I mentioned a price and he agreed to it immediately. It was my second profitable deal in as many minutes, so telephone numbers were exchanged.

After a somewhat restless *zizz*, we had become a little less frazzled, the rains had also stopped so we went on walkabout to see what other damage had occurred. Both of us were relieved to find that where the blocks had been laid along the track no water had washed down onto the land, a major achievement. That sense of satisfaction didn't last for very long as we discovered that torrents of water had flowed off Bulldozer Joe's mothers land opposite the top of the drive and then straight down it. What a mess, it was in a sorry state and in need of a great deal of repair. All of my hard work and efforts that had been carried out over the past few weeks had been undone in less than an afternoon. The materials that I had carefully placed at the top of the drive were a shade too low and from what could be seen, with the waters in full flow, needed to be at least another five centimetres higher to prevent a reoccurrence. The small slopes that I had graded in the front and alongside the Quinta had, thank goodness, proved to be more than adequate as none of the waters had penetrated inside.

I then girded my loins and went onto the east wing roof to view the damage the "Goon Show" had caused from an elevated position. It was not a pretty site and appeared to be much worse than could be seen at ground level.

Sharon had told us earlier that she and Eddie had booked to go on a Safari trip down through Africa later on in the year. I had almost forgotten until she rang to tell us that the party would sail from Algeciras in Southern Spain and that the planned ferry date was some time over the weekend after next. I was dead keen to meet up with them there to wish them a safe and trouble free journey and even keener for us to escape this place and recharge our batteries. I suggested to AC that we leave on the next Monday and travel via Sevilla, maybe Granada and Gibraltar and then return back to Algeciras to be there at the ferry terminal on the Friday and stay over the Saturday and Sunday. We would treat it as our second holiday and we well deserved one.

Chapter Fourteen

That evening after supper, when more than a few glasses of red and white wine had been downed, we poured over our new up to date and larger scale maps of Southern Spain and Portugal. The old ones that we had studied when we made the poor decision on the route selection to the Algarve, whilst we were on the ferry to Santander had long since been slung out. It was obvious that a visit to Granada would mean quite a detour from our intended destination so we agreed an itinerary, Bensafrim – Sevilla – Jerez – Cadiz – Gibraltar and then return the short distance back to Algeciras. There we would wait for the Safari trucks, charabancs or whatever, to arrive. We were so excited that we packed all of our things, except toiletries, before we went to bed.

We had been warned that the theft of car contents was a common occurrence in Spain, especially from those with foreign registration plates. To combat this possibility when I loaded our two battered suitcases into the boot they were covered with empty plastic fertiliser sacks. Another touch was to throw in two pairs of very dirty wellies and a Portuguese hoe with a lump of dried up Bensafrim mud stuck to it. The fart box itself looked dreadfully tatty so the whole package would not attract too much attention from any would be thieves as it appeared to be owned by a very poor farmer.

Before we started our adventure I positioned my pump and pipes together with a full can of fuel on the terrace so that if the builder showed any degree of initiative he could empty the hole as and when required.

Now we could escape and as we would have to pass through Lagoa we had decided to drop off all of the paperwork that AC had amassed in connection with the importation of our tea chests and her piano. These were handed over at the removal company's offices and after a few more bits and pieces of paper were stamped and signed the Baggage Certificate for the Customs clearance was finally prepared.

We caught the car and passenger ferry over the river Guardiano into Spain at Villa Real St Antonio and decided to drive on for a few more kilometres before we stopped for our prepared picnic. This was eaten at another one-horse town called Lepe where we sat just off the main road. On either side of this were numerous warehouses that had piled up on full display, every conceivable type of fitting and pieces of equipment that one would need to establish any form of modern irrigation system. It was mind boggling in the extreme.

Our next stop would be Sevilla and we were amazed at how the land along the way had been so intensely cultivated and also at the many different methods by which water was distributed over it. That quickly explained the vast range of items we had seen during our picnic. There were orange orchards, olive groves and even one large bed of asparagus that was, like ours, still in fern. Hectare after hectare had been formed into ridges and covered with black plastic sheeting and we could clearly see strawberry plants, in flower, poking through the top and the sides. What absolutely gob smacked us was the sight of a large area of peach trees all festooned under clear plastic. We had read about the agricultural methods that had been adopted in this part of Southern Spain but to actually drive through the district was something else.

Mine and AC's first impression of Sevilla was not a very encouraging one. We disliked the awful smell of petrol fumes and the roaring noise of the traffic. To find a vacant parking space proved to be impossible so I had to drive some way out and then we walked back to the centre where we found the Tourist Office. The relevant bumf together with a city map was collected and these were mulled over as we sat outside at a nearby bar. We opened the map to look for Hostel locations, Hotels would be far too expensive, and there was a small block not that far away with quite a few marked on it, which showed potential. One was found almost in the city centre and after a brief inspection we booked in. The bedroom was pretty poky and the bathroom contained a hip-bath, a style that I had never come across before. It was spotlessly clean and decidedly shabby but would suit us for our brief stay. We wearily trudged back to the car and intended to drive back to the Hostel and park as close to it as we could. The trip turned out to be quite a slog as it poured down with rain and there was an endless traffic jam. I thought at one stage that we would never find a suitable parking space and there was the distinct possibility that we would get lost. However a little man jumped out into the street and waved his arms around madly and proceeded to guide us in to a spare parking space which I would probably have passed by. For that piece of assistance he promptly demanded some money.

I was prepared to tell him to sod off but AC convinced me that as the car would be parked there overnight it would be prudent to pay up. We did not have too many spare Peseta coins between us but gave them all to him together with a few escudos. He was not at all pleased at this but I shrugged my shoulders, turned out two empty trouser pockets and said, "no more". He then spat on the ground, turned away, and reluctantly shuffled off.

After he was out of site I opened the cars boot and unloaded our suitcases. We then double-checked that all the doors and the boot were locked and humped the cases the short distance to the Hostel. After a bath of sorts, AC managed much better than I did, and a quick change of clothes it was time to hit the high spots of the city. We had long since forgotten what "City Slickers" looked like but they were here in droves dressed in smart suits and ties, some actually carried brief cases. All of them appeared to move at a gallop with eyes fixed firmly to the ground so that any forward motion was purely by instinct. AC soon realised that she had dropped a booboo as she gazed down at the well-worn and fairly knackered espadrilles on her feet. They certainly did not come up to anyway near city standards but they would have to do for the evening.

There were many restaurants and one in particular caught our eye. It prided itself that it was one of the oldest in the centre and their specialty was paella. The meal did not come anyway near up to the standard that we had anticipated. It was an unappetising and a real below par soggy mess, which contained only a miniscule amount of shellfish. We were not impressed and I was even less impressed when the waiter angled strongly for a fifteen per cent tip, as he presented the bill, which I refused to even consider, in fact I left nothing. In most of the interesting small back streets we found London type pubs crammed with people who all stood at very long bars. We had a drink at one and were almost deafened by the noise from the continuous chatter and finished off a somewhat disappointing evening with a couple of night caps just around the corner from the Hostel.

The double bed sagged badly in the middle so we were unable to have a decent night's sleep and the noises outside until the early hours of the morning made us wonder if the Spanish ever went to bed. I jokingly hinted to AC that we could be in the middle of the red light district at which she was not very amused and was pleased that she had checked out the cleanliness of the bed linen before we had checked in. Breakfast consisted of coffee and hot croissants and was most welcome after the previous evening's experience.

Still embarrassed by the sad state of her footwear our first port of call was a shoe shop where the sales assistant looked down her nose at the offending articles AC kicked off her feet. She eventually settled on a rather smart black pair, which she kept on and put the others in the empty box with the intention of leaving them behind. The assistant would not have any of that and promptly handed it back to her and indicated in no uncertain terms that she must take them with her. We soon found a rubbish bin and quickly dumped the box into it and began our big city tour. The number and size of the department stores was amazing and the variety of their contents and the professional layout of the displays were mind-boggling. We were like two children in a sweet or toyshop, with so much to choose from and too many things to take on board. It was actually possible to pick things up and examine them in detail, a real upmarket improvement to Lagos, where if AC wanted to buy a pair of tights she had to ask and then wait until they were taken out of a drawer.

We had not intended to visit any historical sites only the Cathedral but when we arrived there the length of the queue was so unbelievably long that we reluctantly decided to give it a miss. A two hour mooch around followed and then we had lunch sat outside a small Tapas bar where three different types were sampled and found to be very good value for money especially as a glass of wine was included in the price.

I did not believe it as the same little man magically appeared when we returned to load up the car to continue our journey and certainly could not get over his cheek when he demanded more money as he had looked after it all night and muttered only Pesetas, not any foreign money. After our suitcases had been placed in the boot and AC had clambered into her seat I grasped and shook his hand as hard as I could and smiled as I saw him wince. I then said quietly, "Piss Off", decided not to give him a kick in the crutch, which is what he deserved and got quickly into the driving seat. We swiftly accelerated away and left him standing there totally gobsmacked as he realised that he was not going to get a cent.

In Jerez there was not a lot to get excited about so after a very brief walk around a central shopping area and a beer in a bar we decided to leave and continue our journey. That was the plan but the town's one-way traffic system confused even my highly tuned sense of direction. I must have driven past the same Sherry Baron's gateways to their estates several times and no escape progress was made at all, much to AC's amusement. I knew exactly which way we should go but could not get there. Finally in desperation I drove through a garage forecourt straight across the two northbound lanes of a four lane highway and then over the central reservation, breaking every rule in the high way code, onto the two southbound lanes, turned left and we were then on the road to Cadiz.

The outskirts of Cadiz were like a typical seaside front in England and did not appeal to us at all, but we drove on and found a place to park, without the assistance of a little man. We were not far away from the real old part of the town. This appeared to us to be a big improvement on what we had just driven through and we liked it much more. We booked into a small Hostel only a five minutes walk away from the car and this had a room that was a lot better appointed than the one in Sevilla and was also much cheaper. The streets were narrower and cobbled with the buildings on either side like Medieval England with high balconies that jutted out and almost touched each other. It was very quiet as we sat on a concrete bench in a small square and found that it was not possible to watch the world pass us by as most of the streets were completely deserted. One or two restaurants had been earmarked for supper but both were closed.

Back at the Hostel after a welcome *zizz* and then a bath, which I found much more comfortable and did not feel that my knees were permanently stuck up under my chin, we dressed and wandered out into the midst of a bustling crowd. The streets now hummed with bodies all on a walkabout and the atmosphere was, to say the least, extremely lively. There was a continuous hubbub of conversation and we were surprised at the transformation from only a few hours ago. All of the shops were open and there were numerous stalls to potter about in but we finished up as usual empty handed.

The evening meal this time was excellent; shrimps in a garlic sauce followed by lightly grilled swordfish steaks washed down with a couple of bottles of very palatable white wine. A few more back streets were discovered on our meander back to the Hostel and we did not need much persuasion to call in to a bar and sample yet another nightcap. The whole place seemed to get more rowdy as the night wore on but we felt tired, shattered and totally pooped so crashed out onto the bed for a somewhat unexpected early retirement.

After a leisurely breakfast we checked out and I loaded up the car ready to set off for our planned day trip to Gibraltar and found that a parking ticket had been fixed under a windscreen wiper blade. As AC got into the car I removed it and started to examine the official piece of paper when an attractive, raven haired and smartly dressed young girl with jet black eyes, aged about twenty came over to me. She gently took my hand, with the ticket in it, and proceeded to wave it backwards and forwards as in a no no signal. At the same time she said in excellent English, "as your car has foreign number plates you should throw it in the nearest waste paper bin and ignore it". With a seductive wink she then turned on her heels and with an exaggerated waggle of her hips walked away. After a few paces she deliberately turned her head back to me and threw a swift glance with a really infectious smile on it. After a much more suggestive wink with rounded lips she continued to walk on. I had not had the time to utter a single word during these bizarre moments and AC had missed the whole performance.

We arrived at Gibraltar well before lunch and had no problems with delays at the frontier and luckily found a place to park that was relatively central. I was familiar with the "Rock" as the company with whom I had at one time been employed had built the refuse incinerator there. Although that had been many years ago nothing much had changed. Again we decided to give any historical sites a miss and definitely did not want to fraternise with the apes. After a quick lunch we spent the rest of the afternoon in all of the main shops and soaked up some retail therapy. We just looked around Marks and Sparx. BHS, Safeway, which once upon a time had been Liptons, the Body Shop and last but not least a book shop that sold English books and this gave AC a real fix as she hadn't bought a book in years.

It was then necessary to obtain more cash as we had not budgeted for any major expenditure so a visit to the local branch of our U.K. bank was made for additional funds. With purses full we went our separate ways, AC back to the bookshop to buy four novels and then some items from the Body Shop with me then lumbered with the boring task of finding groceries that were unavailable back home. I finished up flushed with success, the proud possessor of, among other items, suet, Shredded Wheat, mincemeat, Colman's English mustard powder and Bird's custard powders. We met up inside the bookshop where AC was still in a slight trance. I managed to drag her away and drove back to Algeciras again with no delays at the frontier.

A car park was found just outside the ferry terminal with a Hostel handily placed on the other side of the road. It was the best one we had stayed in so far and also the cheapest. By the time we had sorted ourselves it was quite late and we were starving. In a small back street behind the Hostel we found a restaurant with some yummy smells that wafted out of the doorway. We decided not to explore any further and went in to find that there was only one vacant table to which we were quickly ushered. The paella was absolutely delicious, it knocked the spots off the one in Sevilla and the house wine was exceptionally moreish!

After breakfast we strolled over to the ferry terminal buildings and sussed out the times of the ferries to Cueta and Tangiers. There were six and the last one was at nine o'clock in the evening. We then shopped for some food, soft bread rolls, butter, cheese and the locally produced chourico for our picnic lunch and then spent most of the morning sat on the car's bonnet as we waited for Shazz's party to arrive. Every ferry departure was checked but there was no sign of them and I felt a bit dejected. The only consolation was that it was still only Thursday and she had mentioned that it had been planned to sail over the weekend.

Steak, chips and peas were ordered for supper with a couple of bottles of house wine in the same restaurant as the night before. We got there a little earlier and had no trouble in choosing a table and the standard of the food was again first class.

Halfway through the next morning I decided that the town should be called Algesoreass as we had both started to suffer from numb bums. The same routine was followed as before but again there was no sign of them and our bums got even sorer. The vigil was briefly interrupted as I needed to get some more cash and there was a bank just down the road from the Hostel. It was not as simple a transaction as I had imagined, because, after I had signed all the paperwork, they had to telephone their head office in Madrid with the details to obtain approval and the lines were continually engaged. I threw a bit of a strop when they suggested that the money could be collected after the weekend and was then asked to return in an hour. At that time the requested amount of money was handed over so once again we were solvent but only for a limited time.

Saturday was no different to the previous days. We watched every departure but it was another no show day. During our evening meal, having made the same food selection, as the steak had been so tender, at the same restaurant, we decided to wait and see the early afternoon ferry depart on the Sunday and then reluctantly begin our journey home.

As we sat on the bonnet or stood as our bums ached so much we began to recognise various people, the attractive long haired blond who continuously pestered people, us as well, for money to get home and the dark curly haired girl who just asked for money for services that could be provided, together with many others. They worked the terminal every day and obviously made a living from it. What amazed us was the large volume of traffic, people and vehicles in both directions.

We finished our picnic lunch as we watched the ferry pull away, without Shaz and her party and then sadly got into the car and began the long trip home. By using the bypasses we avoided the towns and the city of Sevilla and eventually arrived at Ayamonte in time to catch the second last but one ferry into Portugal. It was then a mad dash and a long slog to get to the village in time for supper in the restaurant, a nightcap in the café and then on to the Quinta. It was pitch black as there was a power cut so I hurled the suitcases into the lounge and left the rest of the gear in the boot. We didn't bother to light a candle but fumbled to get undressed in the dark and both eagerly crashed out into our little bed.

Over our first coffee of the day we both agreed that we were happy to have experienced our initial taste of Spain but totally pissed off to have failed in the principle object of the visit, to see Shaz and Eddie off on their travels. I especially, was even more pissed off when we received her first letter and found that they had been delayed in France and that she had telephoned to tell us of this on the afternoon of our departure for the holiday. They had made up some time however and had caught the last ferry on the Sunday that we had returned home. We had missed each other only by about six hours. It made me pig sick as in my haste to get away we had started our journey one day too soon and as I had completely cocked-up the day to day ready cash requirements we had been unable to stay for that extra night. All in all it was an absolute and utter cock-up on my part. It did not make me feel any better when I read what she had written in the last paragraph that as they were late for the ferry she and Eddie would only have had a couple of minutes to stop and talk. As far as I was concerned that would have been much better than missing them completely.

Chapter Fifteen

There had been hardly any progress on the pool only that the shuttering had been stripped off and removed and the enclosed hole was reasonably dry, but not for long.

I inspected the asparagus beds and saw that the fern had died down considerably as most of it was a light brown in colour and that lots of red berries had fallen to the ground. There were also traces of the dreaded asparagus beetle, which had returned so I decided, rather than spray yet again, to cut it all down and burn it. Bed by bed, in an uncomfortable position, with the heavy duty hand shears, the fern from one crown at a time was cut and then removed by AC to bonfire locations and burnt on a daily basis. After each bed was cleared of fern we gathered up the berries, as many as we could with a lawn rake and those that remained were picked up by hand and thrown onto the fires. There was no guarantee that we had achieved a one hundred per cent success rate in this operation and my mind flashed back to the time when we would have been in the prime position to select only the male crowns.

AC's Pees hoped to visit over the Christmas period and Lucie had telephoned to give us their flight details. We could not afford to take time out to go back to England so it was the best arrangement. They knew that Don and Sandra would be with us soon and as Lucie had bought a lot more goodies from the list she would take them over to Alcester so that they could be brought out earlier. Any items that were left she would bring with them when they came.

Alfonso 2 called it to tell us that olives would be collected at the end of the week so we set about to pick as many as we could. Our sack was taken up to Alfonso 1's shack and at the weigh in we were credited with twenty-five kilos.

It was now a daily exercise to pump out the pool to allow some oh so slow progress. The coping stones were laid but when they attempted to fix the spacers which would set the thickness of the rendering to the inside of the walls, the rains continually washed them off so they packed up their gear and buggered off again. As they left one of them told us that there were a few outstanding internal fixing items to complete at the villa behind the cork oak wood, which could be finished despite the awful weather. Later on that day the cement mixer was loaded onto a lorry and driven away. There was no reason for that action and I made up my mind that no further payments, a substantial one was due, would be made until a programme to completion was agreed between the builder and myself. These would be, in any event, rescheduled.

Sandra rang to tell us that our tea chests had been collected from their house, gave us the flight details and asked us to arrange a hire car for them.

As far as our car was concerned the car agency had given us a date on which we had to take it to Faro to be legally imported. We collected some paperwork from them and then drove to the Customs offices where two people peered under the bonnet and checked the engine and chassis numbers. They then disappeared inside and came back with the papers duly stamped. The car could now be legally driven in Portugal. It should have been carried out many, many months before. It was then back to the agent to be told that for the registration process they would need another weighbridge certificate which had to show the weight on the front and rear wheels of the car together with a photograph of its front, rear and a side view.

There was more torrential rain and how. The drive had taken another hammering, as I had not got around to making the top that little bit higher. Great channels had been gouged out by the waters that had flooded down from the track, though the Quinta remained dry and warm. The waters stopped their flow as the rains eased and between the resulting showers I managed to pack materials and cement, hastily covered with plastic sheets, across the top of the drives full width. Hopefully that would cure the problem. I then laid some of the five hundred cement blocks to complete the small walls, on either side of the drive, along the track on the already prepared foundations. During this exercise there were many nods of approval from the locals that passed by. They had witnessed the damage that had been caused when the rains had poured down throughout the years.

Once in the past I had been distracted by all the confusion and the events that were being enacted around me. So much so that my brain did not function, it was blinkered and only managed to work in a forward direction with no lateral capability, "a dead brain mode". Now I had completely overlooked the fact that with all this rainfall the ground water level would rise significantly and that my new electric well pump situated down the tunnel, was slightly over three metres below the ground.

On an immediate inspection I found that the well water level had risen sharply and was at the foot of the pump base, which thankfully stood on the plinth that I had cast. Knee deep in water with my wellies full, I had to disconnect the suction pipe and secure it, next the delivery pipe and then hump the pump and motor up the tunnel into the garden shed. I remembered that I had had to make this trip many times in the past with the petrol unit and it was not a very happy memory. If and when the rains ever stopped and a pressurised irrigation system was needed then the pump would sit at the top of the tunnel fitted with a longer suction and a shorter delivery pipe. My luck was really in as when I checked the water level three days later, it had risen to a height that would have totally submerged the pump and knackered it, had it remained in position on the plinth.

It was my fiftieth birthday and the heavy rains had started around six thirty in the morning and the noise as it drummed on the roof woke us both up. I had just made the coffee when there was a power cut, what a start to the day. As soon as it was daylight, with brollies at the ready, we walked up the drive and found to our relief that my last efforts to raise its top level and the newly laid walls along the track had prevented the water from pouring onto the land or down the drive. It now raced on past us to the lowest part of the track and then spewed into the field on the opposite side.

I had intended to treat AC to an evening meal in the village but as the power stayed off all morning we decided to go there for lunch instead and hoped that they had power on. It was still raining so it needed half a can of damp start, squirted all over the engines plugs and distributor cables before it gradually fired into life on all four cylinders. We drove slowly into the torrent to the top of the rise in the track and then literally drifted downstream on the other side and reached the restaurant without any problems. There we found that we were the only people to have ventured out as everyone else had had the sense to stay at home. They had electricity but on a very low voltage so we had our lunch surrounded by candles and a gas lamp. The food was as good as ever and an extra bottle of the house plonk was quaffed with consummate ease. The owners were quite concerned for our well being due to the awful weather, they could not remember conditions as foul as these, but we were able to assure them that we were in no danger, only fed up with the continuous and never ending rain. We then went over to the café, where else, for a coffee and too many glasses of port for AC and far too many brandies for me.

The car started at the first attempt and we floated, us two on a high and the car on water, back to the Quinta where I attempted to light the stove. It took quite a long time, as the logs were slightly damp so it was a struggle to keep warm. There was a tremendous deluge at five o'clock and then the rains stopped as quickly as they had started but we still had no electricity. The telephone was also on the blink so I never received one congratulatory birthday message. Under candlelight we played cards until AC lost her temper, not because she was losing but solely due to the day's events, around ten o'clock and stormed off into the bedroom with a candle clutched in both hands. I still had a large slug of Glenmorangie to finish off and it had to be savoured and not just gulped down. Fifteen minutes later also with a candle in both hands on my way to bed, I happened to notice a slight drip coming from the kitchen ceiling which would have to be investigated as a priority. There was nothing that could be done about it at that moment so I carried on into the bedroom. As I went through the door the power was restored and the lights came on. I suggested to AC that we take a nice hot bath and try to relax for a few moments before we crashed out after a long and stressful birthday. I could not recall some of the previous forty-nine ones but none would have been so memorable for all the wrong reasons. It was certainly not what I had expected but reasonably enjoyable never the less.

After a slow start we collected some more logs as it had been decided to keep the stove alight all the time the weather was so shitty. I then had to sort the problem of the kitchen drip and was very pleased to find that it was much easier to fix than I had anticipated. Every tile had been hand carried by the workers to the various sloped sections of the roof and the strip above where the drip had occurred had been used as the main access way and some degree of damage to the water sealer must have taken place. When I was up on the roof I noticed that water had backed up behind the chimney for the water heater store. It had seeped under six of the overlaps on one row of tiles onto this area and then through into the kitchen. It only took a few minutes to seal these overlaps and then point them up with cement.

It rained so heavily one day that there was no way that I could get the car engine to burst into life. There was not a flicker of a spark even after a whole can of damp start had been liberally sprayed all over the cables. So I spent most of it sat in the kitchen with eyes firmly fixed on the ceiling where the drip had been first spotted. Nothing was seen, not even the slightest sign of a leak and my repair work had been severely tested.

AC telephoned the furniture removal company and was excited when they told her that a delivery would be made the next day. They duly arrived around mid-morning but were only able to reverse their wagon halfway down the drive before it got stuck. All of the tea chests and bits of furniture, which included Lucie's unwanted Hostess Trolley, were then humped in through the utility room but there was no sign of the piano and it was not listed on the delivery advice note either. Quite a performance followed when they attempted to drive away although it was not as desperately comical as the "Goon Show" one. They managed in the end without the need of a tow but left me with a really sickening mess to clear up once again. AC rang the office and was told that the piano was still in store in England and would be shipped with the next delivery provided that there was sufficient space. The first thing that was unpacked was the Hostess Trolley. This had been taken from Lucie's house and stored in Don's garage along with some of our belongings. When AC opened the door to the warming compartment out popped her old teddy bear, which her mother had asked Don to pack as a surprise and it certainly was. The bits and pieces of furniture were soon spread around various rooms but the tea chest we decided would be opened on an as and when required basis.

A few days later Don and Sandra arrived with two huge suitcases, which had belonged to his former employer; one in the boot and the other on the back seat. Both of them were crammed full and most of their contents were for us. They had travelled lightly and had only packed the minimum for themselves. Once they had settled in it felt strange for them to see our bits and pieces of furniture here. Everything had been in their home for a long time and they had got used to them being there.

With the additional pairs of hands the number of logs that were collected on an almost daily basis was impressive and the log store was soon filled to the level of the underside of the roof that had still not been built. Another bonus was that lots major and fiddly fixing jobs were crossed off the lists, which by the time they left was on only one sheet of foolscap paper. We were all sad when the time came, all too quickly, for them to leave.

The weather improved slightly as Christmas fast approached but it rained on the drive to Faro to meet AC's Pees whose flight had been delayed. We were impressed with the new airport as we thought that it looked rather splendid and was architecturally very pleasing on the eye. Don had suggested that it was reminiscent of the new supermarket in Studley and we tended to agree. As they unpacked there was a surprise present for me from Les. It was a petrol driven chain saw and would make log cutting that much easier. The bow saw would stay in the garden shed and my right arm and shoulder could take a well-earned rest. Lucie unpacked one suitcase, which contained all of the other items that she had bought and her list was now completed; pro tem I thought.

Again we had more hands to help us out and to which tasks could be delegated, another opportunity not to be missed. The poor weather returned with more torrential rain, once all day and all night. I thought that it would never stop, the market garden area was like a shallow lake filled with weeds and the rest of the land looked just as bad. It all generally had that unkempt and unloved look about which made us very depressed. After one breakfast Les and I stood with our hands in our pockets and gazed through the teeming rain at the escarpment in the distance. We felt quite a violent shudder under our feet and could not believe our eyes as we watched a fifty metre section of grassed over earth, about halfway up its slope, slip slowly down a depth of one metre to expose a large gaping gash of dark brown soil.

The open market in Lagos had sold out of Christmas trees so I drove up into the hills and cut down two small branches from a pine tree. I used the bow saw as I did not want to make any chainsaw noises. These were then tied back to back and made a very presentable tree, which the girls decorated.

The whole Christmas period was extremely enjoyable and it did not rain on the day so we were able to sit out on the upper terrace in bright sunshine for a nibble and a drink as we looked down on our full but unfinished pool. The company, food and the surfeit of refreshments made it an occasion to be remembered.

A local restaurant, where we had had the splendid lunch with my daughters, the Dorset brigade and our German friends, had advertised their New Year's Eve party details and as we were all keen we had booked a table. The time was indicated as eight for eight thirty but when we arrived at eight fifteen everyone was sat at their tables and had started to eat and we felt rather foolish. The first course was Rice Valencia, hot and delicious and we quickly caught up with the others. Our hearts sank when the main course was laid on the table; it was chunks of cold fatty suckling pig. We had expected it to be hot and served with small roast potatoes and vegetables as it was one of their specialties.

A young girl sat at the next table was a vegetarian and had pre-ordered a plate of mixed vegetables. These looked extremely appetising and nicely presented but she whispered to us that they were stone cold. With the exception of the food, starter excepted, it was a good evening. There was lively music and the wine flowed continuously although Les found the food disgusting and the music far too loud and wanted to leave right away. It was Lucie's birthday on New Year's Day and we had secretly ordered a cake to be presented after midnight, so we could not all walk out before then. It seemed to take forever for midnight to arrive but it eventually did as did the cake. This was quickly cut and slices handed all around the room. AC then discretely spoke to the manager and as he knew that we lived locally and had eaten there before, it was arranged that we could pay the bill later on in the day so we were able to be on our way. By this time the party was in full swing with the music much louder and I had mixed feelings as we left through the only open door as I was thoroughly enjoying myself and didn't really want to leave.

It was a pretty tired and lethargic continuation to the day as we all surfaced at various times before noon. The Pees completed their packing and were driven to the airport in the late afternoon and checked in without incident. We watched them through passport control and with the usual tearful waves of goodbye we left to return home via a brief stop at the café. I had prepared a considerable amount of bumf relative to the advertisement for B&B's, which Lucie would be able to distribute in her local supermarkets and this had been safely packed in her handbag.

The next day we did not feel in the mood for any breakfast so only had coffee on the terrace in our dressing gowns. We were far from happy at what was seen before us. The hole in the ground was chocker block full and when the north westerly wind blew the water overflowed onto the, as yet to be constructed, lower terrace area and then on down to the sodden land. What we knew to be our carefully prepared asparagus beds would be to any casual onlooker appear to be just a patch of cultivated buttercup plants, the type with a knotted clump of roots under the soil surface and tentacles that dangled from it which thrived in these damp conditions. I was more concerned at the survival prospects of the asparagus crowns as they, we had read in the many gardening books that we had studied, preferred a soil which was well drained.

When the beds had been originally ploughed to make them up the conditions were far from ideal and the end result was that the natural slope of the land had been altered and a ridge had been formed below them that prevented any surplus water run off. Despite my attempts, when I had cut out numerous drainage channels to allow this water to escape, it had stayed very water logged and looked like a paddy field. Maybe a rice crop would have been a more successful alternative. We had no options, it needed a full-scale operation to remove all of the weeds and we would have to wait and see if the crowns had been drowned or not. The biggest profusion of weeds was on the bottom beds and these were too wet and boggy to work on so we carefully selected the driest ones to begin the painstakingly long exercise.

When I returned to pay the bill for the New Years Eve bash I told the owner that I and several other people were not impressed with the cold pig!! They explained that this was the traditional way that it was served in the north of the country. I then pointed out that as we were in the southernmost province I did not consider this to be a satisfactory answer and there must have been an Algarvean alternative as they served the same dish of the day hot, if one pre-ordered a special. I then suggested that the menu should be made specifically clear in the future, for these special occasions, to avoid any future misunderstandings.

I did not have to go down the well tunnel to check up on the water level as it could be clearly seen behind me as I opened the garden shed door to get at our tools to start the asparagus weeding exercise. It was almost up to the second top step level.

On our cushioned kneelers we began the slow process to clear the beds and after almost an hour I glanced up and noticed a motorcycle that drove very slowly past us on its way into the village. Less than five minutes later it returned at a very fast rate of knots, hotly pursued by a police vehicle. The policeman in the front passenger seat with his head and shoulders hanging out of the open window fired two shots as they careered by. We thought that he must have missed because the sound of the two engines gradually dwindled to nothing. In any event our eyes stayed concentrated on the weed removal, as we did not wish to get involved in any way as a potential witness to whatever the problem may have been.

After a seven-week delay the builder called to tell us that he would restart work on the pool next week as some dry weather had been forecast and that he would bring some sample tiles with him. When I asked for a firm completion date he indicated four weeks and added it would be better to allow for six. I promised to pay him fifty per cent of the outstanding price after two weeks of continuous and productive work and not one escudo before that time. He was not particularly impressed with this and I sensed that he might have had serious cash flow problems.

Over the weekend I cleared the rainwater from the hole, continued work on the asparagus beds and prepared an area for AC to begin the year's market garden programme. She had already sorted out the broad beans, pea seeds and garlic cloves.

Alfonso 2 turned up and handed over three litres of virgin olive oil. We both considered that we had done rather well out of our very brief olive picking exercise. The return was one litre of oil for every eight kilos of olives and AC noted this in her little red book, which by then contained a wealth of information. She had actually sorted out the basic format for a four-year crop rotation programme.

True to his word five of the builder's workers arrived complete with gear and the cement mixer and hurtled into a frenzy of action. They firstly set up their equipment and then started to clean out the hole. The builder showed up after lunch with a selection of tiles. We chose the randomly spaced light and dark blue two centimetre square ones with white grout between them. Each main tile was made up of fifteen by fifteen of these and was thus thirty centimetres square. I required a different style of tile to be fixed, a smaller patterned one, immediately under the coping stones and on top of the main ones. These had been ordered and delivered many weeks earlier.

AC and I continued to work on the asparagus beds and made good progress. We even managed to clear two of them in one day. She noticed some buds on one of the Wisteria cuttings so transplanted it close to the garden shed. During this period the workers had also made substantial inroads to the work outstanding on the pool. They had formed the curve at the bottom of the four walls, cast the steps fixed my top tiles and about fifty per cent of the light and dark blue coloured ones. Overnight there was more heavy rain and I could not get the pump to start so they had to bucket it all out.

It seemed that we were in the middle of a large construction site as there was continuous work on our pool, the last bits and pieces at Cheryl and Simon's villa were being finished off, a start had been made to the rebuilding of the French girl's old farmhouse and the roof of an old cottage opposite was being retiled. The daily movement of lorries laden with materials had churned up the track into a quagmire to such an extent that it had become an absolute nightmare to drive into the village or even get anywhere.

As good steady progress had been made on the pool I handed over a cheque to the builder and suggested that the tiles to the steps should be just plain dark blue ones so that they would stand out and be more easily recognisable. He thought that it was a good idea and would bring a couple of spare boxes he had from one of his other sites. When I questioned him about the pool equipment, pump, filter, pipes and valves he told me that these parts had been subcontracted to a specialist company and he would enquire about their work forces availability.

One letter in the post was from the car agency in Faro and this notified us that the new number plates for the old fart box would be UF-80-17. We were to have them fitted and then, together with all of the bumf and photographs they had told us to collect, attend the Inspection Centre in Lisboa for its registration. The date fixed for the inspection just happened to be AC's birthday, what a pain.

We finished work on the asparagus beds, the last one solely by AC as I had strained my back. Purely by coincidence the workers completed the finishes to the pool on the same day, all it lacked now was the equipment. There was great excitement when on our usual inspection walkabout we noticed that little green gems had broken through the surface of the soil on the old seed beds. Sad to say there was nothing to be seen on the recently weeded ones.

After weeks of regularly pumping water out of the hole in the ground it was now time to fill it. I connected a pipeline, with a stop valve, from the main irrigation line to the side of the pool. The electric pump was then positioned at the top of the tunnel and fitted with new suction and delivery pipes. It only needed a slight modification to the original delivery line and we were back in business and could now extract water from the well as we had done so before the pump had had to be disconnected. AC switched the pump on and I opened the stop valve to the pool, which gradually started to fill.

When the pool was half full I rigged up the petrol pump with a short suction and delivery pipe then dosed the pool water with chlorine and acid and started it up, much to my amazement, without difficulty. This set up served as a simple form of water recirculation and would avoid, I hoped, the problem of the water turning green. With a full pool more chemicals were added and after another recirculation session I used my water testing kit for the first time. The results for the pH figure indicated neutral. We knew that it would be as an analysis on the well water had already been made. The test for the level of residual chlorine was found to be well within the acceptable limits, which must have due to a large slice of beginners luck.

I then telephoned one of the local swimming pool equipment suppliers and obtained a price that would cover the items that were required to complete the works and was happy to find that it was far less than what I owed the builder. If things did eventually go pear shaped then I could employ someone else and not be out of pocket. It was just as well that I had checked this out as when he called to collect all of the timbers his workers had dragged up to the top of the drive he came down and asked for a cheque. With no hesitation I handed one over as the outstanding balance was still comfortably in my favour. He could not give an answer as to when the equipment would be delivered but under the circumstances I was not unduly perturbed.

My back was still not up to scratch so I had to pootle around and only work on light tasks, so I laid the green marble tiles on the floor and to the two work surfaces to the BBQ. The same style of tile to those at the top of the pool walls were also laid around these and along their front faces.

It was time to concentrate the mind and get the car ready to pass the inspection. Many odds and sods of things caused problems, the passenger door handle was difficult to operate from the inside, the side front lights only worked intermittently, the main beam headlights needed to be adjusted, a replacement brake light bulb had to be fitted and the new registration plates made and fixed. What surprised me was then when I collected these no one asked for the original English ones in exchange. I therefore fixed one of them to the outside of the utility room wall on the right side of the doorway. There were other niggly little items that would have to be sorted out but only if time permitted.

Last but not least was my number one hate job it had to be cleaned inside and out. We had not realised just how filthy it was until the vacuum cleaner sack had to be changed twice before the interior looked anything like reasonably tidy and the seats almost new. Then I washed down the outside and polished up all of the chrome work. It was the first time in many years that I had worked so hard to tart up any car's appearance.

We had mentioned to M that it was necessary for us to travel up to Lisboa to have the car inspected and his wife asked if she could come along and visit her two sisters. One of whom we had met two or three times when she had visited on holiday and on the last occasion, some months before, we thought that she had lost a lot of weight and looked quite ill. We picked her up after lunchtime together with the assorted plastic sacks of oranges and other goodies that she had gathered from their Quinta up in the hills that surrounded the village. It took around four hours to reach the one sister's apartment in the western suburbs of the city where we were all greeted as family. Her health had deteriorated since we had last seen her and we quickly realised that she was seriously ill. Although we had intended to book into a cheap Pension or Hostel for the one night her other sister and brother in law insisted that we stayed with them and informed us that supper had already been booked at a nearby Chinese restaurant.

The next morning was spent shopping in a Jumbo supermarket, which was quite a novel experience for us. It was huge and much larger than any of the ones we had shopped in when we had lived in England and completely dwarfed the *squitty* little ones in Lagos. Lunch was taken in a small but typically high standard fish restaurant on the Avenida da Liberdade in the centre of the city.

Before we set off for the inspection I decided to check on the engine oil level and noticed that top screw that should have secured the offside headlamp assembly was missing. The whole sealed beam unit was only retained, more or less, when the bonnet was lowered. I had only a vague idea where the inspection centre was so the brother-in-law named Rui, who was on holiday, accompanied us. He knew exactly where it was as he passed it every day on his way to work and on our arrival at two o'clock we found a queue of cars and lorries parked outside the closed and locked gates. Most of the drivers were stood by their vehicles and I chatted to a Nigerian fellow who pointed at the fart box's rear wheels and asked why there were no fitted mud flaps as they were obligatory.

That information put me into a state of blind panic but Rui had a friend who owned a small back street garage nearby. He directed us to it as there was no way that we would have found it without him. The mechanic shrugged his shoulders and apologised when he told me that he didn't have any genuine Ford spare parts in stock. I told him that it was not a problem, any make or style would be acceptable if he could fit them. It was then my turn to apologise profusely because when he lay on his back to attach the first one, almost half a bucketful of rich Bensafrim soil and half a kilo of rusty metal dropped from the wheel arch and covered most of his head and shoulders. He did not make the same mistake with the second one and belted the outside of the arch panel with a heavy type of lump hammer and waited for an equal amount of crap to fall onto the floor. This side was so rusty that the hammer almost punched through the metal, it seemed that it was only the metallic paint that held everything together. I paid him in cash with a generous tip and then we made a mad dash back to the centre where found that there were five more cars in front of us, than before we had left and that we were the last in the queue.

As we progressed slowly forward I discovered that one side light still played up and only worked intermittently and needed a hefty thump to make it operate. There was not a lot else that could be done at this late stage of events and I doubted if the car would pass unless we had some desperately needed stroke of luck. We did as when it came to our turn it was quite late on the Friday afternoon and the technician must have had an extremely hard and heavy week. He was so pleased to see that we were the last that his inspection was cursory in the extreme. I was asked to open up the bonnet so that he could check the engine and chassis numbers against the English logbook which the car agent had forwarded to the centre. He immediately signed a piece of paper which was then handed over to me as he told me that that the Portuguese log book equivalent would be posted to us in the next few weeks and we could then apply for the ownership document. That was it, there was nothing else and I was surprised and very relieved as we got back into the car to be waved off.

Rui navigated us back to the apartment all flushed with success. I had brought a bottle of *champers*, which had been placed in the fridge and this was opened to celebrate the car's new status and more importantly AC's birthday. The family were aware of this and had produced a homemade cake with one lit sparkler and after a chorus of happy birthday, in Portuguese, she blew it out and what was left after everyone had taken a slice was wrapped up for us to take home. Our return journey commenced in convoy style as Rui drove in front to guide us in the right direction to the Twenty-fifth of April suspension bridge over the river Tagus. We stopped for some petrol at the first service station we came to and a quick pee at the second. There we picked up a young air force cadet hitchhiker who wanted a lift to Portimao. He was very happy to be dropped off in the village where we arrived around nine o'clock. En route we drove down some stretches of the road on which we had towed the caravan and found that they had been improved out of all recognition, A quick meal in the restaurant was followed by an extremely stiff double nightcap in the café after which we very gladly crashed out into our own bed quite exhausted by the whole affair.

I had always parked the car halfway along the Avenida in Lagos by the petrol station, once and often twice a week, with its English registration plates in full view. The first time that I parked it in the same place after the inspection with the brand new Portuguese ones fitted we found that a policeman had fixed a parking ticket under one of the windscreen wiper blades. It had only been left there for twenty minutes whilst we carried out some basic shopping so I was hopping mad and could have kicked the cat had it been there. I had a hopeful vision of another discussion on the merits of the famous Benfica and Manchester United European Cup Final and AC chuckled at the thought of it. However when I examined the details that were written on the ticket it was with a deep sigh of relief to find that the registration numbers did not match those on the car so it would not be possible to link the two together. It was quite a let off, we had been very lucky and from thereon we would have to sort out another place to park.

The following week I pegged out the lines of the pool terrace outer walls and thought that it was time to pack it in for the day when a plumber and electrician turned up with the pool equipment. The cables from the garden shed to the pool pump house were quickly laid and the timer control panel fixed in position. All the plastic tubes that connected the sump suction, the vacuum, drain and delivery lines to the pump and filter were completed in no time at all. With the exception of the coupling joints, that would enable the pump or the filter to be removed for maintenance or replacement, all of the others had been glued. As they left the plumber told me that he would return within forty-eight hours to commission the whole system. Although everything appeared OK there were some small but essential items missing such as the two skimmer covers, two director jet eyelets and the vacuum hose connector. I pointed this out to him to be told that they would be fitted when he returned. It was quite dark by the time all of this had been finished and I surmised that they had moonlighted.

The commissioning went without a hitch and was very straightforward with no sign of any leaks. This was good news for me as it meant that I would now have the whole of the lower pool terrace area to work on without any interference from other people. At that moment it dawned on me that at the flick of a switch the pool water could be re-circulated as and when I thought it necessary. It would no longer involve skirmishes and problematical procedures to start up the petrol pump. This pump was now a liability and the sooner I could get rid of it the better. It only needed a brief telephone call to the man who had bought the generator and the deal was completed. He called in the next day to collect it and hand over the previously agreed amount of cash.

It was the end of an era as after eighty-two weeks of toil, agony and very little ecstasy we had a completed Quinta and swimming pool. Although the contract had specified fixed prices I half expected the builder to ask for an extra to the pool price when the time came for its final payment to be made. I was relieved and very surprised when he appeared to be happy to accept the amount written on the cheque and he was obviously more than a little pleased that he had, at long last, finished the works. During this period we had been taught a sharp lesson, one we would hardly ever forget, it was that in the Algarve never ever have a large hole excavated between the months of September to March.

Chapter Sixteen

The rains had damaged the bottoms of all the permanent asparagus beds and some of the topsoil had been washed down onto the separating pathways. As such there was a lot of extensive repair works to be carried out. I had to rake out this soil back onto the beds and then reform the mound at their bottoms to retain the irrigation waters that would be applied in the summer. As this painstakingly slow work progressed we could see that a considerable success rate had been achieved as all of the forty crowns that we had replaced showed signs of new growth. On the down side however there was an overall loss of eighty of the others. Some of the new spears had become shrivelled and had turned yellow, I put this down to the recent spate of quite heavy frosts and hoped that it was not more serious than that. A quick telephone to my father confirmed that this was the problem as he had witnessed the same type of damage in the Vale of Evesham many years earlier. There was nothing that could be done about it just sit it out and wait for the warmer nights to prevail.

Despite the lousy weather I had hand dug a patch below the beds and had made up some new ones and intended to transplant the now two-year-old crowns into them. Firstly, as a priority, we needed to replenish the existing beds and this proved to be an extremely difficult exercise as the crowns were by now very large and had become almost impossible to get out of the ground. After a lot of heavy sessions all of the replacements were finally planted although a tremendous amount of root damage had been done during the process.

As a result of this balls aching task we had a long and serious discussion over quite a few fairly stiff alcoholic bevies. We somehow managed to remain sufficiently sober to agree that enough was enough and any further attempts to increase our asparagus production was by now, well and truly bolloxed. A double bonus resulted from this decision in as much that firstly the two-year-old crowns now had no commercial value so we were able to cut and eat as many of the green gems as we wished and did not have to worry that the plants would be weakened. Secondly the golden opportunity was taken to give small sample bundles, as part of our preliminary marketing strategy, to selected restaurants and potential private clients one year earlier than had been anticipated. The bundles were tied with two pieces of raffia exactly as the traditional manner employed around the Evesham and Badsey districts.

I was staggered by the number of spears that were produced as we had broken every rule and continued to cut from under developed crowns and by all accounts, that should have more or less knackered them up completely. What was even more incredible was that we were able to carry this out for a period of eight weeks, from the end of February to the end of April, longer than in the U.K. In England the harvest time commenced very late in April or early May, depending on the weather, and ceased in the middle of June, only just over six weeks. Their harvest was also from more established and much more mature crowns than my little babies as they would have been four years old or more. A lot of traditionalists advise that nothing should be harvested after the thirteenth of June as there was the distinct possibility that the buds would become paler and less tasty.

When in England we had to pay two pounds for a one-pound bundle of asparagus, normally from a roadside store, it was too expensive to experiment with unknown and untested recipes so I always cooked it in the standard and simplest way. I used an asparagus steamer and placed the whole tied bundle, buds upwards, into its basket with a sprig of mint or summer savoury and sometimes added a few cracked peppers. Water was poured up to a level about two thirds of the way up the spears and the lid loosely fitted to avoid the possibility that the water would boil over. I always attached a loop of raffia to the upper of the bundles two raffia ties to enable it to be easily lifted out of the basket, when it was cooked, to ensure that there was no damage to the delicate little buds. The two ties were then cut and the spears then served with melted butter drizzled over them or with a mayonnaise sauce to which a smidgen of curry powder had been added, both accompanied with brown sliced or crusty bread and butter. It was an easy method and one in which not a lot could go wrong other than to overcook the spears.

Other people I knew obtained equally good results by just boiling the loose spears horizontally in a heavy based frying pan slightly offset over the heat so that the thicker ends were in the hot zone and a cover placed over them. I tried this method and was pleasantly surprised at the quality of the end result. It was certainly less elaborate than with the use of the steamer but just as effective. That was the limit of my then often tried, tested and well-appreciated self-imposed asparagus culinary skills. When we entertained the asparagus helpings were always eaten with much gusto and many compliments were received accompanied by requests for secs. Not a suggestion for any physical male, female bodily contact only second helpings. As we were meanies these had to be turned down as we considered that we had the priority to finish off, as a cold dish, anything that was left after very generous amounts had been served up in the first place.

Now as we had asparagus by the so-called ton we could afford to be much more adventurous. AC suggested that we make some asparagus soup, in England it would have gone down like a rat sandwich although here we could certainly give it a try. It was our intention to produce and sell totally green spears that were one hundred per cent edible. If two centimetres were to be cut off the ends of each spear then this could be used to make a flavourable soup and still leave plenty to savour for the main course. A basic recipe was developed which included thin strips of chicken breasts, the asparagus spear bottom ends, potato, onion, plain flour, butter, the boiled asparagus water or good chicken stock, I preferred the latter. This was all cooked, then processed in an electric blender and served with a small dollop of plain yoghurt placed on top in the centre of the bowl. On this a small leaf of freshly picked and washed mint was carefully positioned. I experimented further and stir-fried some spears in virgin olive oil and fresh lemon juice and these were then served with salt and ground black pepper sprinkled over them. This resulted in an excellent feast, especially here with our own new boiled potatoes and young unpeeled carrots that we cooked whole.

Subtle differences were noticeable when they were cooked on a hot griddle for a couple of minutes and turned over once or twice. When they had become nicely charred we then dressed them with salt, pepper, a squeeze of lemon juice and drizzled on some virgin olive oil. Freshly grated Parmesan cheese was then sprinkled over the dish. I preferred to use a hand crumbled Dutch cumin cheese, it was a much better topping and gave an improved flavour to the whole dish.

One sample bundle had been given to the owner of the holiday complex at Praia da Luz in which we had first stayed some few years ago. She was Dutch and an enthusiastic lover of asparagus. My word to describe people of that ilk who had already tasted, and therefore were experienced and had become connoisseurs in the delights of the green gems was asparaguseurs. Over one of our many foodie conversations she explained that a simple but very popular dish of asparagus, frequently prepared in Holland, consisted of cooked spears dressed with thinly sliced strips of fried ham and the hot butter from this preparation poured over them. It was then served with chopped up hard-boiled eggs. This was similar to a meal that we had eaten at the Pickwickean character's pub in the U.K.: There they had served streaky bacon fried until it was crisp and added a Parmesan cheese topping instead of the egg.

An idea sprang to my mind as a result of this unsolicited information and I hoped that it could be put to good use. Over a very short space of time we had put together and more than tripled our experiences in the preparation of this delicious vegetable for the dinner table. A good topic of conversation with *asparaguseurs* would be by means of an exchange of recipes.

We had to make a decision on the type of parsnip we would grow to sell on a commercial basis. The roots of the Albino improved marrow, which we had sown initially, seemed to go down to hell and back and were extremely difficult to lift out of the ground intact. There were three types of cultivated ones that we were aware of, short rooted with a conical shape, medium length and blunt ended and long with tapering ends. It was decided to experiment with Avonresister, a canker resistant variety and White gem, a short rooted broad shouldered one with a reputation as a high yielder. The seeds were sown in a part of the area that had been earmarked for the additional asparagus beds. The same method was adopted as that on our two allotments, the old Victorian way. They were sown in drills at a depth of two centimetres with two or three really fresh seeds placed in stations twenty centimetres apart and the drills again at this same distance between them. As we had planted parsnip seeds before we knew not to panic when nothing appeared for three or even four weeks later. AC duly noted the information in her little red book and made lined columns to enter the end results.

Although the crappy weather continued I managed to build up the walls down the driveway. One continued past the Quinta on the east wing and finished level with the septic tank and the other curved round to form the car parking space in front of it. Portals were constructed in these almost at the top and were intended to house the entrance lights and support the double electronically operated gates. The pool terrace external wall foundations had already been cast and were ready for the blocks to be laid and I could now fix the pool pump house roof tiles.

The log store roof had to be constructed as we had a pile of semi dry logs, covered only by a plastic sheet. The quantity of stored logs increased weekly as my newly acquired toy, the chain saw, proved to be a godsend. It only needed a single support column as one side was built into the pool pump house wall and the other was integral with the back of the BBQ. I thought that it would be quite novel to build this from the small flat rounded pebbles that I had collected from the river banks on the other side of the village. Progress was very slow but sure as, if I built it up to more than a fifteen centimetre height at any one stage, even with a somewhat dry concrete mix, the whole of that construction slowly crumbled and slid down to the ground level. In the end it was completed, another labour of love but an enjoyable one and it gave me a complete sense of satisfaction to have designed and built, out of natural materials, something that looked different and quite unusual.

All track of what was required to complete the legalisation of the Quinta had been lost until one day the architect called in with a pile of documents that had to be signed and submitted that afternoon. At that time he intended to apply for the official inspection of the completed project, Quinta and pool, to obtain the Habitation certificate. That would be his last commitment under our agreement and he wanted to get it settled as soon as possible, somewhat discombobulated we fully agreed. When he left he suggested that we be on call over the next seven to ten days and we replied that this would be OK.

On another daily walk about around the asparagus plants it was obvious that the dreaded beetle had returned with a vengeance so a full spray operation was obligatory. This was not a problem, only a pain, as I had now become very proficient in the preparation of the chemical mix and the use of the sprayer. The whole exercise to dowse all of the beds took less than an hour.

We did not believe our luck as after a very brief telephone call the architect and three inspection officials arrived and conducted their full survey. They had in their files all of his drawings, which included the ground floor plan, and proceeded to view each room, one by one and then went out to inspect the pool, pump house and terraced surrounds. All three appeared pleased, and somewhat relieved, to find that it had all been constructed in accordance with designs. We had been told of many cases where the inspector's powers of imagination had been sorely stretched to decide if, in fact, they were at the correct location and inspecting the same building that was shown on their plans.

I had ordered a black aluminium door for the pool pump house, with a louvered top panel and a plain bottom, like the ones for the water heater and gas bottle stores and this had been delivered just after the overall inspection had been completed. On the drawing I had made for the fabricator, I had allowed for a gap of one centimetre between the top of it and the underside of the upside down cemented lintel. When offered into position I was pleased to find that it fitted perfectly. On a postal collection trip into the village I had handed the carpenter details of the window frame required for the pump house and ordered lengths of door architravings that I would fix to act a supports for the false ceiling in the central corridor and the hall. These had been delivered, as had the glass for the window and it did not take long to fit this and assemble it into the opening in the pump house wall that faced the swimming pool. The pump house was now fully secure.

Over the previous months I had squirreled away many pieces of timber shuttering off cuts that were no longer of use to the builder. Quite a large amount had been salvaged from the mangled debris that had been left over from the pool "concrete pour debacle" and both lots had been neatly stacked by the log store. I cut to length carefully selected ones and constructed a useful work bench in the pump house on the wall opposite the filter and pool and another in the garden shed along the full length of the wall that faced the utility room. Neither had a metal vice fitted to them as both had been foolishly sold long ago, at given away prices, at some car boot sale or other. The saved shuttering was too thick to be used as shelves so thinner planks were bought from the same timber yard that had provided the materials for the garden shed door and these were quickly installed.

Underground works on the lower pool terrace continued and electric cables were laid to the outer wall corner lights and the waste pipe from the pool filter backwash was extended to a point below the septic tank. I was now able to crack on with the backfilling and levelling of the lower pool terrace and the construction of all the surrounding walls. AC required some form of cold frames so I was able to build four of them next to the log store integral with the East terrace wall. With more rainstorms the water level in the well had risen even more and I was glad that I had not left the electric pump on the upper tunnel steps.

We received a letter from the Council that notified us that the Habitation Certificate was available for collection. I was terribly disappointed when it was handed over as I had expected something scroll like with an impressive seal and tied with a red ribbon. It turned out to be just a simple computer print out on continuous paper. However with this we were then able to apply and obtain the ten years rate's exemption on the Quinta, from the date of the certificate but the rates for the land remained payable. This certificate with all of the other required documents were handed over to our lawyer to put in motion the registration of the Quinta into our names.

Even with the difficult, and sometimes horrendous, weather conditions we had managed to prepare beds and had sown a large variety of vegetables. Broad beans, garlic, parsnips, peas, onions, leeks, chillies, tomatoes, red leaved lettuces, yellow courgettes, peppers, beetroot, spring onions and many more, as well as many types of herbs. Basil, curly leaved parsley and Dill being the main ones. When we looked down onto the land from the track, the overall impression of a thriving small market gardening enterprise, gave us a lot of satisfaction.

We had not sorted out our policy on any individual prices for the various veggies and there was no yardstick here to give us even the slightest clue. Lucie had been asked to collect and list prices, during the seasons, from vegetable shops that sold the same produce that we planned to. She had produced a wealth of information from shops in Evesham, Worcester and Pershore. All of these towns were literally surrounded by the local growers so the information was sure to give us the best possible guidance. Across the full range of vegetables the individual prices from shop to shop only differed by a matter of a few pence, once we had changed them from pounds in weight into kilos. Each highest price was taken and then converted into Escudos at a very favourable exchange rate in our favour. I then added a "Collins factor" which took into account that the produce was unavailable elsewhere and a full list of prices was compiled.

This was slept on for many weeks and although some appeared to be expensive we decided to stick to our guns and if some clients thought that they were too high then it was tuff (tough) for them, they could either pay up or go without. Our policy was that all prices would be fixed and no discounts would be offered, also all transactions would be on a strictly cash basis, we would not issue invoices.

The villa up the track for the London couple, Margaret and Bob, had recently been completed and we were invited to a celebratory party. Instead of taking the usual bottle of cheapo *plonko* we harvested a few salad crops to give away as freebies to them and the other guests together with a priced list of all the other various vegetables. It was an extremely shrewd move and as I just happened to have a pen and some paper with me quickly jotted down some advance orders. There were lots of orgasmic ooh's and aah's when parsnips, spring onions and the future planned swede were spotted on the list. Unfortunately asparagus lovers were conspicuous by their absence. The principle that vegetables could be pre-ordered was eagerly accepted. Also the fact that on the day that they called in to collect them they would have been freshly cut, lifted, cleaned and ready for them. Everyone was requested, at the end of a great evening, to spread the gospel to their friends. AC and I considered this concept to be an A1 sales tactic, as we would not have to make delivery runs and returned home in a very relaxed and contented mood, not in any way due to an excessive consumption of alcohol.

The backfilling of the lower terrace was completed together with the building of all the outer walls. A central four-metre opening was left in the southern one so that when we sat on the upper terrace we had an uninterrupted view straight down the land to the escarpment in the distance. An open archway was built into its west corner and I fixed roof tiles to the top of this to give it a "Carmen roller" effect. It served no useful purpose, only as a short cut to the asparagus beds, but I had built it just to prove that I could.

One evening as we sat on the upper pool terrace and took full advantage of the south facing view, a couple turned up and introduced themselves as Jack and Jill. They were from Devon and had completed the purchase of a run down old ruin in the centre of the village. Their neighbouring Portuguese had told them, in a very complimentary manner, about an English husband and wife who lived in Hortinhas, just outside the village. They also explained that we had started to grow strange and different types of vegetables. Based upon this information they had decided that they must try and find us and that was the reason for their visit. Both appeared pleasant enough so we agreed to meet up with them to look at their new acquisition. It turned out to be a typically long and narrow building in the middle of a row of single story houses, with the animal's quarters still intact at the rear. Although it was pretty basic we thought that it had a lot of potential for a future conversion.

Some weeks later we were invited to a plant sale at a large villa on the Funchal Ridge just outside Lagos and met a fellow who helped out there in the garden. We had often seen him around the town where he worked as a general type of odd job man, painting and decorating appeared to be his main occupation. It seemed that we saw him everywhere and always struck up a conversation with him as we passed by. From the types of works he did, basically on his own, we decided to call him "Do it yourself David," DIY Dave for short and this stuck for all the time that we were acquainted. He showed us an old rotavator that was for sale at a knock down price. I sensed that it had been brand new when it was purchased by the current owner and gave it a quick once over before I started it up. The engine ran smoothly and the gearbox was easy to operate with just two forward speeds and a reverse facility. The cutting width of the blades was ideal to work in small areas and would be more than adequate for my purposes. I decided to buy it there and then and would have been prepared to pay the asking price. However with my haggle mentality I made an offer, which to my surprise was accepted.

Arrangements were made to call in and collect it the next day. I would now be able to work independently, just as I was when the cement mixer had been purchased, and not have to wheel the borrowed one backwards and forwards up and down the track. I gave it a cursory service, a new spark plug, change of the engine oil and air filter and a quick clean up of the top of the solitary piston. The engine started easily so I was in business and ready for action, so much so that the whole of the top part of the land was rotavated in less than a morning. It would have taken at least four hard weeks work to have hand dug it over.

Vegetable orders started to trickle in and Margaret from up the track called in regularly. She was a good P.R. person and had spread the word around, so lots of her friends telephoned and collected. Often she would collect on their behalf. The dreaded's villa was a holiday let and in their information bumf our activities and telephone was prominently displayed. There was never ever what one could describe as a mega order. Always collections on a regular basis, which meant that overall we were able to sell almost all of our surpluses. It was a very encouraging start to this side of the venture.

Michelle was in the process of preparing her thesis for submitting to the University of Strathclyde for her degree of Doctor of Philosophy. At one stage she was given the opportunity of a field trip to the University of Oporto. This was brilliant news for us as when she had finished her work there she could bus down to us, take a brief holiday and then fly out from Faro. We met her at the bus station in Portimao and over supper we exchanged lots of up-to-date news. She had had a fantastic time in Oporto and had even managed a weekend in Lisboa. When I asked her what she would like to do here the response was just to chill out for the next few days. We both took the welcome opportunity to relax with her and only worked on the essential things.

The weather was sufficiently warm for her to sunbathe and swim and for us to enjoy lunchtime and evening BBQ's. It had not occurred to us until we went in for a dip that it was the first that we had been in the pool for many months. One special trip out was made to the "Chippery" for a tuna salad and large plates of proper chips. Shaz telephoned from South Africa the day before Shelle left and spoke to all of us. She and Eddie had to return to England shortly as they had run out of money and were basically broke, although both were prepared to rob a bank to get the money to be able to come out and visit us. The possible dates were left open and they would be in touch when they had settled back to normality in the U.K. We drove Shelle to the airport and there was a rather subdued atmosphere, as usual, when we said our goodbyes.

After this brief period of self imposed inactivity I cracked on to lay the screed for the terrace tiles and had almost forgotten how large an area it was. I did manage to console myself with the thought, although not specifically associated with building projects, that great works were performed not by strength but by perseverance. AC had almost filled all of the cold frames with potted tomatoes, lettuces and basil and I was glad that I had made up wooden framed plastic covers as the night time temperatures fell quite sharply. Most of the plants were ready to be transplanted and the land had been prepared. Everything grew like crazy especially the parsnips, which needed watering almost constantly, unfortunately we had a disaster on the pepper germination – basically nothing – so we had to cheat and bought twenty-five very healthy specimens at the Lagos Saturday open market.

AC's Pees had booked another fortnight and would arrive fairly soon. On the airport run, just for a nose, we called into a new hypermarket at Albufeira and found that by and large it was much cheaper than anything around Lagos. The flight was only slightly delayed and they were quickly chauffeured home, both of them a little knackered. This time they did not want an energetic type of holiday, more of a meander around one and be able to potter or pither about and that suited us down to the ground. We had a real treat at our first breakfast with them, kippers courtesy of Lucie.

Sandra from Alcester rang to tell us that all of the tests had proved positive and that everything was OK. She had told us some months earlier that she was pregnant and that they wanted to visit us after they had received the test results. We told her that the dates for Shaz and Eddies visit had not yet been finalised and that we would get them sorted out soon and then get back to her. That same evening one of the "Manchester mob" from Fullwood rang to see if it would be convenient for her to visit in the autumn so we made a mental note to keep our calendars up to date. The next day Shaz rang to give us their flight details, they would land at one o'clock in the morning and the day was the same one as when AC's Pees were due to leave. In my diary I wrote, in capital letters, that it would be necessary for me to polish up my chauffeur's hat that day.

Lucie was a keen gardener and had worked daily on the vegetable plots and also in the garden, As a result her back had begun to give her a considerable amount of gyp. Oh how I could sympathise with her. Les spent many hours on walkabouts and lazes in the pool. He did not seem to have a particularly good appetite and appeared quite drawn and pale although when we had lunch at the "Ritz or the Pitz" he thoroughly enjoyed the proper chips. Both of them somehow managed to go down with a miserable cold although we were able to avoid it. Their last two days passed uneventfully when we all did our own things. I left for the airport at ten and rang AC when Shaz and Eddie walked into the arrival hall just after midnight. It was an easy drive back with less traffic on the road than usual and we made it home in just less than two hours. AC's Pees had already packed their suitcases before Shaz and Eddie surfaced, when introductions were made over an AC prepared brunch.

With my polished hat on at a jaunty angle it was back on the road to Faro to see the Pees off. They checked in and we watched as they cleared customs without any problems and then it was another return journey home, this time hatless. We had *champers* with supper followed by a film show of all the slides that had been taken on the trans-African safari. Needless to say I drifted in and out in a very dozy mood and eventually fell fast asleep long before the show had ended. They all left me on the sofa to come too some hours later somewhat confused.

Eddie was young fit and a hardy outdoor type so I had prepared a list of tasks that needed to be tackled. The two principal ones were to clear out the gulley from the point where the torrent flowed out under the track and to move the caravan. The gulley had not been cleaned in over thirty years and had become completely overgrown. Armed with the chain saw, a bow saw, a large and small axe and a pair of secateurs we clambered over the manmade retaining wall and promptly set about the problem. The amount of rubbish and debris that had been washed down and was now caught up in the brambles, olives and other bushes beggared belief. All of the obstacles were either sawn cut or hacked out little by little and at the end of each day dragged over to the spot where it was intended to have a bonfire. We seemed to remove ton after ton and it took four full days to clean up the worst affected section of the gulley, a length of about thirty metres. The end result was that the floodwaters now had a clear width and height across the gully, which they could speed through as it was almost twice as wide as when we had started the exercise.

Some large holes had been uncovered at the bottom of the retaining wall so substantial repair works were required. These were carried out whilst the huge bonfire blazed fiercely away. I crossed my fingers and legs at the thought of the caravan removal. That evening I found my cut out model and sketches that had enabled me to fix the distance of the front wall from the Quinta and we would soon discover if they had been accurate. The caravan was turned around so that it could be manoeuvred out backwards. I pushed on the grab handle at the front and Eddie pulled on the one at the rear and we slowly inched past the corner of the utility room wall, the narrowest section that had to be negotiated. It was parked and jacked up on the east wing drive adjacent to the swimming pool in less than five minutes. The whole operation had been a resounding success and as it faced up the drive towards the track it would be a simple matter to have it towed away. I had amazed AC many times in the past but this achievement surpassed them all. It did not take long to paint a "caravan for sale" sign on a piece of old timber which was then securely nailed to one of the cork oak trees at the top of the drive.

One day before we took them back to the airport we enjoyed a lunch, after a long swim for them and a rest on the beach for us, at the now very popular "Chippery". Our pet name for the establishment was a classic case of word association as when it was my treat it was called the "Chippery" and when it was AC's, the "Ritz or the Pitz".

In view of what seemed to be continuous downpours of rain over the winter, one could have easily assumed that and further application of water would not be necessary for a considerable time. This however was not the case as after the last of the season's storms the top two to three centimetres of the soil had rapidly dried out. We had many beds of seeds that had already germinated or were at some stage along the process so water was essential. It was therefore fortunate that I had already rigged up the well pump to fill the swimming pool so the irrigation system was fully operational it only needed the flick of a switch.

Due to circumstances entirely beyond their control Sandra told us that they could not visit as planned and that the baby was due in October. We brooded about this situation somewhat wistfully for a few days. Despite the fact that our funds were in a more than usual dire state, at the back of our minds, the outside possibility of an earlier than anticipated return to England for a holiday was given careful consideration.

I had finished the screed over the entire area of the pool lower terrace and scoured the length and breadth of the Algarve to try and find some tiles that matched those on the upper one which were Santa Caterina air-dried ones. The exercise had failed dismally and around two thousand were required. In the end I had to settle for a yellowish rather than a red tinged type as there was no other choice. This did not cause me too much concern as they were bound to weather over a period of time and the difference would then be hardly noticeable.

This bottom terrace construction had, in itself, become a major project. Two double seats were formed against its east wing wall. Three sets of steps were constructed down to it from the upper terrace. A single width one gave access from the outside of our bedroom, another gave access from the guest bedroom and the third, which was of double width, direct access from the lounge. With those completed I was then able to commence on the long-winded task of laying the tiles onto the screed and to finally grout in all the gaps that had been left between them.

During the search for the tiles I found a builders merchant who stocked a variety of concrete balusters. These small pillars would support a parapet coping to form a balustrade on the upper terrace and these were constructed between the access steps and the roof supporting columns.

The old Cortina Estate laboured at least twice a week when it was heavily laden with smooth river stones that we collected from the same place as the small pebbles for the log store column. It groaned even more so when we drove up into the surrounding hill above the north side of the track. There we found that wide tracts had recently been scarified between the large expanses of citrus shrubs. These had unearthed an assortment of coloured flat slabs, which we loaded into the boot on a regular basis. The stones were used to form the terrace by the utility room and the garden shed and a footpath down the west side of the Quinta to the pump house, log store and cold frames. A pathway was also laid around the wellhead beds which were to form an herb wheel. Paving behind the well water flume and around the cistern was constructed with the slabs. Eight circular concrete columns had been cast on top of two walls of the cistern with slab constructed ones opposite them. These had been linked together at the tops to form a portal walkway. It all had a natural look and feel to it and of course had cost us nowt except the cost of a minimal amount of petrol.

The asparagus had been watered and weeded on a regular basis and had certainly reaped the benefit from the two applications of a liquid fertiliser that had been sprayed over the fern. In general, food wise we benefited enormously, as we ate freshly cropped home grown salad ingredients at lunchtimes and most of the vegetables for our evening meals were collected, prepared, cooked and served on the table in next to no time at all. Every one of the veggies that had been specifically grown for sale sold well, much better than had been anticipated and there was not a lot left in the ground. The only main crop that remained was the parsnips. There were also a few beetroot and the odd tomato and lettuce plant together with four rows of spring onions that had died down before I had had time, to harvest them.

The experimental turnip crop indicated that we should have no problems in the production of swedes. This exercise had been a complete and utter farce as during the later stages of our crops development we had seen turnips on sale in every mini-market vegetable shop around, as well as the Lagos open market. All that we had proved was that they would grow in our soil, which was no big deal. When to sow the seeds was the big question. As a vegetable it was normally considered to be a winter crop sown in the springtime. We did not relish the thought of the continuous applications of water during the hot summer months to have them available before Christmas. We therefore made the decision to sow as soon as the first autumn rains occurred. Hopefully we could then lift and harvest them, sooner than the normal maturity period of five months, from early in the month of January onwards.

One of the "Manchester mob", our friend from Fullwood was collected at the airport to begin her flying visit. She just wanted to relax and had already done the tourist scenes on her previous holidays. This situation suited us down to the ground as we had gone through a fairly stressful few months of building works and vegetable production so lazing around times were eagerly accepted as the order of the day. Out of one suitcase she produced her handmade quilt for our double bed that had been sewn in a log cabin design and from the other lots more goodies.

One extra special highlight of her stay was that we were all invited up to M's Quinta in the hills just outside the village to celebrate the beginning of that years wine production. I had been asked to join in the ceremonial grape treading session and was told that it would be the final year of dealing with the grapes in this traditional way, as mechanisation would be introduced from thereon. Whilst I squelched round and round and breathed in aromas never before experienced I was convinced that a vintage year, albeit locally due to my leg and feet involvement, was bound to be declared.

The barbequed food was something to be savoured. Home reared pig, slaughtered that morning, had been professionally butchered and selected choice pieces were cooked to perfection. AC and I particularly relished the crisp parts of belly draft, the cubes of fillet and the deep fried chitterlings. M's wife had baked several types of bread in the oven at the side of the Quinta, they were presented hot and proved to be delicious with many different flavours. Her garlic one was crude but thoroughly enjoyable and consisted of two very thick slices with lots of butter spread all over them and whole cloves of garlic crushed and sandwiched in the middle. M's red wine, treaded last year, flowed continuously.

Almost at the end of the festivities several of M's friends turned up with lots of freshly caught large sea bream. The coals on the BBQ were therefore quickly stoked up and the party spirit rekindled. We had already stuffed ourselves silly so we found it difficult to fully join in this additional gastronomic feast. I did manage to share half of one fish with AC, which was delicious, but our friend declined as she had already eaten herself to a standstill. We left way before the party ended and I slowly, very slowly drove the car down the steep hillside track back into the village and then home.

It had just started to rain, not heavily but steadily, as we entered the Quinta and went straight to our bedrooms. Over a morning coffee, taken on the upper pool terrace, the smells were heavenly as there had been more than a sufficient amount of rain to wash off all the dust from the leaves on the trees. The sharp smell of the eucalyptus and the softer one from the pines combined with that of the cork oaks had created this really heady fragrance. Our friend commented that if we could bottle it for sale then we would quickly make a small fortune. On a more practical note I suggested to AC that if we cleared the last of the tomatoes and rotavated the bed, it would be an ideal time to sow some swede seeds and we managed to complete the exercise before lunchtime.

The following day the return trip to the airport was in the late afternoon so the morning was spent in Lagos where we called in on a printer's workshop to order some business cards. I had sketched out the format, which included our names, the telephone number and a small map together with the principle types of vegetables that would be available. In large print at the bottom it read that telephone orders for collection from the Quinta would be welcomed. Another highlight, in print, stated that pre-ordered vegetables would be available for collection from the Lagos open air Saturday farmers market between the hours of nine o'clock and ten thirty.

After some heavy discussions in their offices we agreed on the layout and style of the card and ordered the minimum quantity for collection within seven days. We then visited a travel agent and enquired about the availability of flights and costs to the U.K. There was not a lot to choose from and the cost of a British Airways return flight to Birmingham was an extra thirty-five pounds per person than the one to Gatwick. AC quickly agreed when I suggested that we go for Birmingham as we had both flown into Gatwick many times on business trips and had always found that the journey up to the Midlands was extremely tedious. Also had we had to pay for them then it would have been very expensive, and must have been more so nowadays. I considered that the extra monies to fly direct to Birmingham to be cheap at twice the price.

After a snatched lunch we set off for Faro with our Fullwood friend and narrowly missed a horrific accident. We must have arrived at the scene moments after the ambulances had left. There was still debris all over both sides of the road and two cars involved looked like mangled concertinas and I very much doubted that the occupants had survived. It was no wonder that the E.N.125 had the reputation as being one of the most dangerous roads in Europe. We however managed to deliver her safely to the airport and in the end we saw her off again with more tears.

I wanted to dig up some parsnips and this was a good excuse to have a roast dinner, which did not happen very often. We decided that it would be a loin of pork with all of the trimmings. A few of each type were lifted and it was clear to see that the White Gem were superior in overall shape to the Avonresister. Their roots were shorter and the shoulders much broader. Most of them weighed around half a kilo and some were slightly heavier, as good a cropper as the original Albino improved marrow. It may well have been a pure coincidence but from these small samples there appeared to be fewer uglies in the White Gem variety, another factor to take into account when a decision had to be made. The whole meal was delicious and the different parsnips showed little sign of woodiness in their cores and had been roasted separately. We found that it was almost impossible to distinguish any differences in their flavour, both were superb, but in the end with shorter roots and less uglies, we decided to give the White Gem variety our vote.

We had argued quite forcibly on many occasions, always in different pubs in the U.K. that the flavour of parsnips improved immensely after the autumn frosts. Most of the garden books that we had studied were also of that opinion but after this roast dinner both of us were far from convinced that this was in fact true. I had never before tasted anything quite as nice as those that I had cut open and prepared that morning.

The uglies weighed around a kilo each and as an experiment I peeled and cut them open, into chunks and again found almost no traces of hard cores. What little there was I removed and boiled the edible part until they were cooked. They were mixed with an equal amount of boiled potatoes and then mashed up together with a sprinkling of AC's fresh finely chopped herbs added. A portion of this rather sticky mixture was then spread out onto the kitchen marble work surface and flattened to a thickness of about two centimetres, lightly floured and with a pastry cutter formed into "parsnip cakes". The process was repeated until of the mixture had all been used. Half a dozen had been roasted for the meal, but could easily have been lightly fried in a little olive oil, and had proved to be a tasty winner. The remainder were then frozen individually.

One morning I had quite a shock when I drew back the bedroom curtains and saw what appeared to be a large area of black film on the surface of the pool water. It looked like an oil slick and a wave of panic spread over me as I wondered what could have gone so horribly wrong overnight. With my dressing gown untied I rushed through the sliding door and on a close inspection found that it had been formed by a mass of thousands of flying ants. Most had already drowned but many whirled around and around in the water as their wings continued to flutter wildly. Hundreds and hundreds more zoomed in and crash-dived on an apparent suicide mission. I felt quite relieved that it was not more serious and waited until well after the kamikazes had ceased to arrive before I cleaned them all out with the pool net.

There had been a distinct change in the weather and the evenings had cooled down considerably. That gave me a massive headache, as the pool water had turned cloudy and green. No matter what I did in terms of chemical additives and continuous recirculation of the water I could not regain a stable balance. It was technically far more difficult than the simple ant removal. Despite freely offered advice from some locals in the village who were associated with pool maintenance I carried on in my own sweet way and failed, again dismally. The pool water test kit did not offer a solution to the problem. In the end, as I eventually sifted through my accumulated pool information, I discovered that a water coagulant would have to be utilised.

"Why are poxy engineers always wankers and never listened to advice or read the instructions?" said AC as I had been given this free information a fortnight earlier. The water was immediately flocculated with the newly acquired chemical and the pump run for twenty-four hours. Five hours after it was switched off all the crap had sunk down to the bottom.

The next stage was to restart the pump and with the vacuum hose equipment connected remove it through the filter. This turned out to be a disaster as all of the collected rubbish was returned back into the pool, which indicated to me that there could be another problem. I therefore had to swallow my pride and speak with "The dreadeds" Portuguese pool serviceman. He called in the next day and said that, "my filter needed to be topped up with sand and the water had to be re-flocculated for a further session after the addition of a nominal amount of algaecide. I should then "vacuum to waste and bypass the filter". It proved to be sound and relatively inexpensive advice, which would be born in mind for the future.

Over the years on the late Friday nights or early mornings that we had left Lagos after heavy sessions on the town we had noticed lots of activities in the open market area. We did not understand why the marketers had to be there so early, perhaps the spaces were allocated on a first come first served basis or it was a general free for all to grab what was available. We eventually discovered that this was the case and with no allocated spaces this led some degree of confusion when attempting to find the farmer you had bought produce from the week before. It was far from an ideal arrangement, as no one could guarantee a regular position. Growers from all over region, even as far away as Aljezur battled for prime positions. This certainly did not fit in with my planned sales strategy.

The Saturday after our business cards were collected I went to the market and after a general walk around positioned myself in front of the co-operative. I deliberately stood next to the open backed truck of the man who sold a variety of fruit trees, as well as shrubs and plants for the garden. He attracted lots of clients, mostly ex-pats, and it seemed to be an ideal location for me. Whilst I waited for my potential clients to arrive he told me that the chaotic space arrangement situation was under review. It was planned that only farmers from the Lagos district would be allowed to sell their own produce and that spaces would be allocated on application, Identification cards would be issued, carry a photograph with the holder's name, the space number and the general produce for sale. As to when it would be implemented he did not know.

I accosted every foreigner that passed me either on their way in or out of the market. A card was offered and I politely explained in less than fifteen to twenty seconds all of the advantages they would gain if produce was purchased from me. I finally said that, "parsnips would be available for Christmas, Swedes in January and asparagus in early March". This tactic seemed to work as the cards were not all thrust back into my hand or shoved into a wallet or handbag but studied with nods and grunts of approval.

It came as quite a relief to us as over the past months most of the heavy construction works around and about had now been slowly but surely completed and those noises had been replaced by the sounds of DIY activities such as, masonry drills, angle grinders, orbital sanders and many others. When I met any neighbour after a particularly noisy session I suggested that they had shown off and had put their Black and Decker D.I.Y tape on full volume. This always raised a wry smile and the comment, "I wish it could be that quick and easy".

AC had arranged for Susie "Q" and her friend to "Quinta sit" whilst we were on holiday and they arrived the day before we left and had caught the train from Faro and then a taxi from Lagos. I had agreed an extension to the fart boxes insurance policy to enable Margaret, up the track, to drive it for a one-month period. She could then take us to the airport, have the use of the car and collect us on our return. The cost of this was far cheaper than an extended car park stay at Faro.

Chapter Seventeen

Our flight to the U.K. was trouble free although very strong cross winds made the descent a rather hairy experience and we were pleased when the female pilot safely touched down. I thought that she had handled the difficult conditions extremely well. We had had a swim at eight o'clock that morning in glorious sunshine, so it was rather a shock to the system to have to walk with heads bowed down into a bitterly cold east wind across the tarmac to the arrivals building.

We cleared customs and collected our baggage and were very pleased to see Don and Sandra waiting to meet us. She was definitely pregnant although by no means huge and I whispered to AC, "that it would be a boy because all of her bump was in front". We had a very pleasant weekend with them where we caught up on all of their latest news and re-discovered the joys of English ales, Indian and fish and chip takeaways. AC was in her element as on the mega shopping expedition to nearby Stratford-upon-Avon she spent, what seemed like hours, in the many bookshops and bought several novels.

Les collected us from Don and Sandra's and drove down to Broadway. He had arranged for a car to be made available and it was parked in the driveway to the house. We stayed for a few days pleased not to have to do a thing, just to relax unwind and eat remarkably well.

The advertising bumf to attract paying visitors had produced a zilch response so we decided to revamp it over the holiday. Some interest had been shown in the brief details that Lucie had pinned up on supermarket notice boards. However when further information was posted on to interested parties not one booking had resulted, sad to say. We referred to them as potential poxy paying guests, Poxy P G's, and could cater for two or more preferably four people. Whether they were golfers or not we thought that the expression twosomes or foursomes was very appropriate.

Next it was time to speed down the M5 to Bristol and catch up with Shaz and Eddie. They lived in a lovely two bedroomed flat with a bathroom, kitchen and a large lounge in a rather "up market area" of the city. After lunch we took a trip into the centre and an extended visit to Park Street and its bookshops was a must. AC was in seventh heaven again and bought lots and lots in them. As it was still early in the holiday I thought it prudent to remind her of the airline's baggage allowance on our return journey as the way she was going we would need a separate suitcase just for her books. In the evening we had a delicious meal at a Mexican restaurant and the waitress at our table was Portuguese. She came from Vila Nova de Milfontes only sixty-five kilometres from us and had relatives who lived in Bensafrim. We knew the small street and the little house where they lived but were not familiar with and could not recognise them. She was quite impressed when we ordered in Portuguese although a little confused by our accents.

We then travelled on south via a ball aching cross-country route to Dorset to visit the surgeon, Peter, Mary and the family. The littlies had grown even more, much to our surprise. That weekend AC had some more retail therapy, I opted to play two rounds of golf with our host and won both! I thought that I played well as I had not played or even practised for a few years. I gave him a stroke a hole, used borrowed clubs and still managed to beat him.

All too soon it was time to return to Broadway and we anticipated yet more lashings of home cooked food. AC and Lucie decided to have another full shopping session and spent the whole day in Cheltenham on the day that I had arranged to play golf at Droitwich, when our original fourball Saturday partnership would be made up. Again my game was on form and I literally carried my partner, as I had done so often in the past and we won comfortably by a four and three margin. What amazed them, and also me, was that I had only dropped eight strokes during the course of the round. There was still an excellent selection of food available for lunch in the clubhouse and my substantial meal was washed down with a couple of pints of Bank's Bitter. After this I visited my partner's workshop to see his collection of Jaguar cars, which had almost doubled since he had repaired the old fart box. From that time he had specialised in the repair and rebuilding of this "marque" and had built-up a considerable reputation, nationwide.

That evening, after AC had weighed all her current purchases on the bathroom scales, we re-drafted our advertising bumf and AC typed it all up. Some spaces were left between the texts for the addition of the photographs that we had brought with us. Late on Don rang to tell us that Sandra had produced a baby boy, Mark, which came as no surprise to me, so it was congratulations all round as we clinked together our glasses over the phone.

I had a friend in Evesham who ran a printing business so we handed over our newly created promotional literature, agreed a format and then ordered one hundred copies to be run off on his express production line.

The Collins clan had always and still did, meet every Saturday morning at our mother's house, so AC and I drove over the short distance from Broadway to join up with them. It was just a simple get together with no agenda but only a general free for all chat. Mum and Dad, my three brothers and sister with their respective other halves and children and us two completed the full compliment for the first time in many years. My brother Ray, next down in age to me was a confirmed bachelor. He once seriously courted a pretty blonde haired girl who had trained as a hairdresser and ran her own salon. For some reason, probably in an attempt to live a more exotic life style, she sold up and decided to continue her profession on a cruise liner. He never got involved, to my knowledge, with any females afterwards. I wished that I could have joined him as he made his excuses and left the small talk to go to the local Banks's pub after less than thirty minutes. The family had put on a substantial cold buffet lunch which included my mother's special cheese straws and afterwards we all, especially me, felt quite replete.

AC reminded me that an evening meal had been arranged with Karen, an ex working colleague who had suggested that she should apply for the flat in Redditch, and her husband Norman. They had recently moved from Stourbridge and now lived in the nearby village of Ombersley so in the late afternoon we said our goodbyes to my parents and drove the short distance to her house. She had always provided wonderful meals and that evening she excelled and we all really pigged out. Norman, at the end of a feast that would linger in ones memories for a considerable time, cocked it up completely. His attempt to open and then serve a bottle of vintage port wine proved to be a total failure. I then tried to rescue the situation but even after I had strained the contents through a very fine muslin cloth some sediment still remained to cloud the port in our glasses and this completely destroyed it's flavour. The tastes of the many different cheeses however were up to scratch, especially the Stilton.

After a pub lunch in Birmingham with other ex working colleagues we called in at a nursery and bought a Portuguese laurel tree as a present for Don and Sandra's new arrival. We then made a slight change to our route and dropped it off in Alcester on the way home.

We had arranged to re-register on the National Health with Lucie's doctor and had fixed up an appointment for our tetanus jabs. After this we slogged up the M6 to Fullwood just in time for lunch. Shell had travelled down from Glasgow on the train so I picked her up from the station and we all spent the next couple of days doing the towns. Preston, Blackpool, Bolton and Blackburn and spent money as if it was going out of fashion. All good things had to come to an end so on our final day in the north we dropped Shelle off with only about two minutes to spare before her train departed and then had a horrendous journey back down the motorway. It was like a trip down to hell. There were repeated lane closures that created long tailbacks and to cap it all we passed the scene of two fairly serious and recent accidents on the southbound carriageway. It took us over four hours to reach Broadway where, as some form of consolation, a delicious meal was soon set before us on the table.

I contacted the landlord of the pub in Studley and arranged an evening when we would visit and he promised to let everyone know about it. Lucie drove us there so that I could down a few pints of Banks's Bitter. Almost all of our old friends turned up, including the double-glazing gang, and a thoroughly pleasant evening was enjoyed especially as the buffet that was laid on was more than up to scratch. We were the last to leave, well after closing time, for another horrendous journey as it bucketed down with rain all the way home and I was glad that I didn't have to drive.

Our new holiday information leaflets were collected from the printers and the photographs pasted in. When they were completed we all considered that it was an ideal and economical place to spend a quiet and relaxing one or two weeks break away from it all. As well as all of the surrounding supermarkets it was decided to place an advertisement in the local "Why" magazine and to send a copy to close friends, who could show it to their colleagues at work.

There was one final trip to see the baby, Mark, and his shell-shocked parents and then we were off to the airport to catch our return flight home. Over a glass of red wine on the plane we suddenly realised how totally knackered we both were. I had driven well over two thousand miles and our feet never seemed to stay on the ground for more than a few minutes. In an attempt to please all our family, friends and ourselves, we had overdone it by far. After a second glass we agreed there and then never to make the same mistake again. Instead of feeling refreshed and full of vitality, which was the whole purpose of the holiday, we felt tired, weary and very flat.

Margaret picked us up at Faro and it was a fairly easy drive back to the Quinta. We were still in hyper mode and the Quinta sitters had to leave early in the morning so we had supper in the village restaurant. They had had a whale of a time only marred by noises on the terrace in the evenings. On most nights, not long after they had lowered the blinds to the two bedrooms and the lounge, there was the sound of the poolside furniture being moved. I suggested that it was possibly a stray dog or animal, wild boars roamed in the hillsides less than a kilometre away but they were not convinced. On our return I fully closed all of the blinds, as was my usual custom, and was just about ready to hit the sack when Susie "Q" told me that they had always left the top two or three slats open. I then readjusted the ones in the lounge to that position and in less than fifteen minutes we heard definite sounds of activity outside.

Two upper terrace lights on the lounge wall could be switched on from inside so I told AC to slowly count to twenty before she did so. I then crept round the outside of our bedroom and had just reached the steps up to the terrace when they came on. I could clearly see a figure perched on a chair with his nose pressed against the blind obviously trying to peer in. It must have been one glass of red wine too many as I made a slight noise when I approached him. His reaction was like a streak of lightening. He jumped off the chair and in the same instant turned in mid air so that his back faced towards me. As soon as his feet touched the ground he shot off like a bullet before I could get anywhere near to him. I did not see his face but from his build, dress and agility instinctively knew that it was the same person I had encountered outside the caravan all those months ago.

Back inside the lounge I explained exactly what had happened and after a general discussion we came to the conclusion that we had a Prowler, cum voyeur to contend with. AC and I were not the obvious attraction, well we thought not anyway, as we had been around all the time. It must have been the arrival of foreign female visitors who had unwittingly paraded around the swimming pool in skimpy bikinis or had sometimes even gone topless. How he could have known that they were there was a complete mystery. We assumed that he must have lived locally to be so familiar with the layout of the land and to react so quickly to visits as soon as strangers arrived.

It was lovely to be home as it seemed that we had been away for ages and one task had to be given a top priority treatment and that was to vacuum the accumulated dust off the bottom of the swimming pool. I went into the pump house and turned the valves into their respective positions and then switched the pump on. As I was about go outside I happened to glance up and saw a snake, half of which was still coiled up in the gap between the top of the door and the lintel, the head and the other half had uncoiled since I had entered and was almost level with my eyeballs. I almost wet myself as its forked tongue flicked in and out and did so when it hissed loudly less than twelve centimetres from my face. I reeled backwards and picked up a towel, which was there for the primary filter cleaning operations, and waved it wildly in the snake's direction. It then, much to my relief, dropped to the floor and slithered out through the doorway.

Although I was badly shaken by this incident I still had the presence of mind to dash over to the garden shed and grab hold of the spade. The snake had not moved very far and I found it, again coiled up, on the floor of the BBQ, so with a deft stab it's head was cleanly removed and as I watched its writhings I quickly calmed down.

The next major exercise that had to be tackled was to cut down and burn all of the asparagus fern. This was almost two metres high in places and there were many stems. Even the old seed beds showed remarkably strong growth. I had borrowed a heavy-duty electric hedge cutter in the hope that it would avoid the laborious hand exercise and be much quicker. Well that was the theory but it did not work out at all. Most of the stems were much too thick to sever and until these had been removed it was not possible to get at the, far less in number, thinner ones. The cutter even struggled with these and tended to tear rather than cut them cleanly so, fed up to the teeth and really cheesed off, I oiled the hand shears.

I saw Margaret walking her two dogs along the track and told her that we had spring onions and parsnips for sale and could she spread the good news around. The four rows of spring onions had produced new green foliage after the early autumn rainfalls. I had not anticipated this at all and had fully expected to find that the white bulbous parts would be soft and slimy. A few samples were lifted from different sections of each row and I found that when the first layer of skin had been peeled off they were in fact very firm and had a lovely sharp taste.

A lady telephoned to ask if the parsnips were ready and if so she would like to order one kilo for herself and four kilos for her friend and collect them at the Saturday market. I hastily agreed and we arranged to meet, before ten thirty, in the same place where I had stood when I had handed her our business card; next to the Portuguese shrub and tree seller.

I was there at nine o'clock with this my first market order. She was already there waiting eagerly and scuttled off, clutching the two plastic bags, with a beaming smile on her face. On a speculative basis I had also taken two spare kilos of parsnips, four bunches of spring onions and three packs of uglies. Three bunches of spring onions were sold in less than ten minutes and I could have easily sold the fourth but kept it back to show to other prospective clients. This tactic worked well and lots of orders were taken for the following week. I adopted the same principle for the parsnips and the uglies and retained one of each and more orders were jotted down. Every person who wanted to buy the remaining bunch or kilo was told that it would be offered for sale at exactly ten thirty on a first come first served basis. I was not surprised when at ten twenty five two people returned and hovered nearby. Exactly on time a woman bought the spring onions and a man collected both the parsnips and the uglies.

I could not have wished for a more successful start to our market sales. It was a most profitable one and a half hours work after which I was able to identify two important aspects in our sales tactics. The first was that ordered vegetables, which had been pre-packed at the Quinta meant that a 0 to 5 kg set of weighing scales would not have to be lugged around with us, especially on Saturday mornings. Secondly if we did not overdo the surpluses then there would be no wastage. How many times had we seen crates of unsold vegetables loaded back onto the trucks at the end of a session, only good enough to be used as an expensive pig fodder.

Over a few weeks one middle-aged client had collected two kilos of parsnips every Saturday, one for herself and the other for a neighbour, who she told me jokingly called me "Parsnip Pete". I asked her what pseudonym she or they would be likely to use in the asparagus season. She threw her head and shoulders back and flashed me a wicked smile. "My dear" she said, "we have already decided that you will be known as "The asparagus man" and chortled as she left me feeling in a bit of a daze.

I did not know why or how but a nasty red rash had developed on my hands, forearms, and even on the sides of my body around the chest region and right armpit. It was extremely itchy, painful and formed bulbous lesions, which eventually ruptured and caused the first layer of skin to progressively peel off. As well as the discomfort it was very unsightly. The only relief from the constant itching was to firstly treat the affected zones and then apply a non-adherent dressing and then apply a creamy thick white gunk to dry off the eruptions. This took for ever to be absorbed into the skin and was used extensively for nappy rash on babies. It certainly did the trick although we remained at a loss to understand the problem. It was obviously some form of allergic reaction.

We had decided to select a variety of swede named Marion as it was resistant to club root rot and mildew. The seeds had just been sown and before we had had the time to water them in, the Algarve rains returned with a vengeance and once again the torrent roared, unhindered now, through the cleared section of the gulley. One day when it never seemed to stop the waters overflowed the lower end of the retaining wall and in the process washed away most of the recently sown broad beans together with a lot of top soil. When it finally ceased we inspected the drive and found that it had stood up to the deluge remarkably well. It was in a much better condition than the track which had deep gouges cut into it, down to the bedrock, and the field up to whispering death's cottage was a lake.

The water level was up to the top of my block wall along the track, which had certainly not been constructed to act as a dam. I crossed my fingers and hoped that it would not breach as, if it did, the asparagus beds would suffer serious and irreparable damage. The well water level was also very high, the highest it had been since our arrival, only half a metre below ground level. As soon as the floods had receded I collected and laid another layer of blocks to increase the height of the wall. More boulders were then gathered from up in the hills and cemented behind it to form buttresses three metres apart along the whole of its length. The six expensive hand painted tiles for the house plaque had been delivered and these were fixed to this wall at the top of the drive. It contained the name "Quinta da Hortinha" and in the top left and right hand tiles was a picture of a small, raffia tied bundle of asparagus.

It was too wet to do anything on the land so I fixed the architraving as supports for the false ceiling that would hide the lagged ducting. There were numerous bamboo thickets down the gulley and we both agreed that their poles would make an ideal screen. These were then cut to length, cleaned up and unvarnished lifted into position onto the supports. The mantelpiece was then made out of the old railway sleeper. Its ends were cut off to a paper template I had prepared and it was then offered up into position on top of the firebrick one. Two holes were then marked on the chimneybreast and drilled so that it could be secured. There followed many hours with an orbital sander before it was ready for the application of three coats of dark wood stain. Finally it was fixed into position and we then had a proper mantelpiece.

Our finances, or lack of them, were frequently discussed and we still had not attracted any Poxy P G's. A reluctant decision was taken to prepare some bumf to let out the whole Quinta in the peak season of June to September in an attempt to make some real money. We would move the caravan over to the cork oak wood and operate from there. It would not be an ideal arrangement and we were certainly not wild about the idea. However the details of our proposal were posted to Lucie and we waited with baited breaths. Deep down I hoped that it would turn out to be a no-no venture as I had had enough of life in a caravan and would have to remove the "caravan for sale" sign, which was now in a very dilapidated state.

AC received some bad news that Les needed an operation. England suddenly seemed so far away but we agreed that she should fly back for a part of his convalescence period and the availability of flights was looked into.

With the rotavator still at the bottom of the area that had been reserved for our orchard, as it was too wet to attempt to remove it and work elsewhere, I commenced more construction works on the pool terrace. Two tables were cast adjacent to the seats against the east wing wall and columns cast from their tops to support a light roof structure that would provide some degree of shade. The other two support columns were built behind the wall that formed the back of the seats. The pathway was extended from the log store along the entire length of the south side of the pool to the septic tank.

AC flew into Birmingham, to be met by blizzard conditions and heavy snowfalls, and rang me on her arrival in Broadway. Les had been discharged a few days earlier and appeared to be well but weak and very tired. It would be a slow road to a full recovery.

On my own on Carnival day I thought that I would have a bit of fun. Most of the children wore fancy dress costumes and as I was still a kid at heart I donned all my Arab regalia from head to toe. After I had visited Margaret and Bob to have my moustache and eyebrows blackened with mascara and to borrow a pair of dark sunglasses I drove into the village to M's café. As I entered through the back door, with a string of worry beads nervously thumbed in my right hand, I could see that it was absolutely full. When I forced my way into the main room you could have heard a pin drop and there was a deathly silence for what seemed to be an eternity. Under breath muttering followed and people moved nervously out of my way as I headed for the bar and asked for a beer in the Arabic language. Some wag then called out loudly, its Saddam Hussein and I suddenly realised what a prat I had been. The costume that I wore was vibrantly striking and a very clever disguise. M, his wife and number one son nor any of the regular clients had recognised me and strangers there were just dumfounded and a little uneasy. It was certainly the wrong type of gear to dress up in here during the middle stages of the Gulf War. I quickly ripped of my headdress and glasses and I don't know whose sighs of relief were the loudest, mine or the Portuguese. My first beer went down in no time at all and much backslapping and laughter followed as did a few more beers.

On a drive into Lagos to sort out the application for a patch in the Saturday open market there was a big bang and flames shot out from under the bonnet. I thought that the exhaust manifold had blown but continued on until I could stop in the garage forecourt. With the bonnet raised I could see that the exhaust was sound but it took almost ten minutes to discover that a plug lead, with the plug attached dangled down from the distributor cap. How it had unscrewed itself from the cylinder head remains a mystery. It was promptly screwed back in tightly and there were no further problems. That was not the case with the market patch as there were no available spaces.

Les continued to improve as the days went by and AC managed to spend a lot of time with him. All too soon she had to catch her return flight, which was delayed due to Air Traffic Control difficulties over France and an unscheduled refuelling stop at Bordeaux. She was certainly not amused at the delay or by the torrential rains that greeted her and was very tired. So much so that it took her quite a few days to get back into some form of routine.

We had decided to plant fruit trees and create our own orchard and the man that I had stood next to in the Lagos market had a nursery in nearby Casais. Between storms we paid him a visit and found him extremely helpful and knowledgeable. He was given a list of our requirements for lemons, oranges, grapefruit, apricots, pears, almonds, plums and peaches. We already had olives, figs and pomegranates. There were about fifty in all and he promised to deliver them next weekend after he had finished his market stint.

The ideal preparation of the soil for fruit trees was to have a JCB or any other type of digger loosen up a one metres square and one metre deep hole for each tree. We could not afford this mechanical operation so it was left to muggings to hand dig out at all the tree locations with a spade. It was a mammoth task and I had to work until late in the evenings to turn over and loosen the fifty tonnes of soil, about one tonne for every tree. They were delivered as promised, with their roots in damp sacking. It was not intended to plant them straight away and as there was a strong Algarve breeze blowing we were advised to store them in a sheltered place. The pool pump house was obviously the best available so they were carefully carried in. All were arranged to enable the sacking to be dampened if any showed signs of drying out.

Asparagus spears, both on the permanent and old beds, started to appear and I was soon able to assess the successful survival rate of the transplanted two-year-old crowns moved last year. I was surprised to find that ninety-five per cent had, which was remarkable as it had been almost impossible to lift them out of the ground and horrific root damage had occurred. As the crowns were now three years old we decided that a light cut could be taken and eaten or better still sold as part of our long term marketing strategy. The marker tabs that AC had so laboriously made to identify the male crowns on the old seed beds could be used to mark and indicate where and how many spears had been cut. A basket weaver worked in the doorway of his cottage in the village so I prepared a sketch, which showed a shallow oblong basket with a handle in the centre, a trug, and asked if he could make one for me. He nodded slowly that he could and held up the four fingers of his left hand and pointed to my watch. It took me quite a while to realise that it would take four days. I called back after five and found it completed. As I paid him he lifted up his left hand again with four raised fingers and nodded more vigorously which I took to be a form of rebuke as four meant four and not five. It was a present for AC's birthday and I had sized it to comfortably accommodate two kilos of loose cut asparagus spears.

With regard to a pricing policy we were a bit out of date, except for Lucie's information on the current prices in the U.K. so we took a stab at a figure. We decided that we would charge a thousand Escudos a kilo, five hundred a bundle. This was more or less equivalent to the roadside charges when we emigrated, of two pounds a pound.

We found ourselves in a bit of a dilemma. It was easy to leave spring onions, lettuce, swede and parsnips in the ground, tomatoes on the vine and peppers on the plant if they had not been ordered. Asparagus however had to be sold as soon as possible after it had been cut. We could not go for a full-scale push at sales as we anticipated that demand would far outstrip the availability and most people's memories were only short term, unless they were asparaguseurs. So we adopted a slowly, slowly technique and relied on the news to be spread by word of mouth.

Even though I knew that it was a bit naff I had ordered three "T" shirts, one green with "Asparagus" in black letters printed on, the second white with "Parsnips" in green lettering and the other a very light yellow with "Swede" marked on it.

Asparaguseurs had already started to ring up to enquire if the season had commenced and fell over each other to collect what had been cut. The Saturday market was attended every week with the bundles that had been ordered and any that were spare, these had to be sold! I stood where the business cards had first been handed out with the relevant "T" shirt worn embarrassingly. There were not that many spare bundles and they sold quite easily, with more orders for the next week jotted down. Most weeks we had completely sold out before ten o'clock when we thankfully packed up and left. Many weekday cuts were distributed through Margaret up the track, together with kilos of Swedes, to her friends.

One Saturday a young blond haired man came up to me before I had time to fully unload. I had never seen him before so quickly handed him a business card. He examined the asparagus carefully and gently broke a small piece off one of the spears, at the thicker end away from the tip, and bit into it. "Excellent quality" he said and then asked for four bundles. I told him that it was his lucky day as that was all the spare ones I had. He had not appreciated that orders could be placed and immediately asked for the same number each week for the rest of the season. I was very excited as it was my first bulk order. He nearly knocked over my next client, who stood close behind him, as he rushed off. I asked her if she knew who he was and she said that she thought he was a Dutch chef and owned a restaurant in a nearby village on the road to Portimao.

When I cut the asparagus I quickly disciplined myself not to walk across the beds. This action invariably resulted in short spears bring trodden on and or broken off. It may only have been a small loss but financially we could not afford to lose anything however small. The only safe way was to slowly move up and down between each row and cut the spears to the right and the left.

After one midweek cut I had two bundles unsold so I suggested to AC that we went into Lagos and did a bit of touting, she reluctantly agreed. We ended up with me in my asparagus "T" shirt, which stood out like a sore thumb, sat at a table outside a café, which we had never visited before. It was on the Avenida close to the entrance to the vegetable and fish market. Coffees and two rounds of toast were ordered and the perfect bundles of ambrosial asparagus were prominently displayed in the centre of the table. There they stood pert and sentinel like and really showed off their best characteristics. The spears were about the thickness of my index finger, iridescent in colour and the buds were nice and tight. They really did represent an early taste of spring. There were many gasps and oohs and aahs as people passed by although no one ventured over to speak to us.

As I ordered another cup of coffee four females sat down at the table next to ours and I whispered to AC that they had passed by twice in as many minutes. Cheeky bugger that I was I eavesdropped on their conversation which bemoaned the lack of good quality asparagus for sale locally and I winked at AC and indicated that we had some new clients. One of them leaned over to me, apologised for her intrusion, and asked where we had bought them as she pointed at the bundles.

"Buy it," I said with over exaggerated indignation, "I grow it and sell it and these two have already been sold". At this news we saw four disappointed expressions and AC threw a withering quizzical glance at me. After roughly fifteen seconds, I switched into my overdrive sales mode, turned round to the lady and said that my client was late and if she had not turned up by the time that I had drunk my coffee, it would be for sale if you wanted it. There were four smiles and an air of pregnant anticipation prevailed. They were obviously asparaguseurs as there was a lot of squabbling between them as to who would have what, one shouted out loudly that she had seen the bundles first and therefore had a priority choice.

I calmed them all down and when my coffee was finished handed the bundles over in exchange for the cash, how they sorted out who had what I did not know. Someone had to go without so I suggested that more could be collected from our Quinta the next day. They all lived at a nearby golf complex and had many friends that adored it. I gave them business cards and one said that swede was her mother's favourite vegetable and that she could have often killed for one. I jokingly responded, only if he was two metres tall, that quip went down really well. I gave them all a sketch map of our location on a paper napkin and they agreed to call in around ten the next day.

Six people turned up just after ten o'clock and were pleased to be given a conducted tour around the asparagus beds and even more delighted when handed the long handled knife to cut, under my instructions, their own individual spear which was limited to only one per person. I cut the remainder to make up the bundles. They had also brought with them a mega order for Swedes. Burns night had long since past but the earthy taste of the vegetable still remained with many of their neighbours.

Swede collection was an absolute doddle as many weighed well over a kilo. They were short rooted and to top and tail them took only seconds. I could harvest and prepare over twenty kilos in less than ten minutes so the requirements for our visitors took no time at all. To start with not many people ordered swede for collection at the market but this situation soon changed. Lots of local ex-patty type of restaurants started to add to their typical English Sunday lunch mashed swede on the menu, to compliment the roast beef and Yorkshire pudding. Their requirements of up to ten kilos at a time, was money for old rope.

A new client introduced herself, in the market, as Maureen and asked that if she collected orders for her friends and associates could she qualify for a discount? We breathed in deeply and decided that to stay in line with our earlier agreed strategies the answer had to be a no! I did suggest that she was free to add on whatever margins that she thought appropriate for herself.

There was a small wine shop in the centre of Lagos where we had bought many bottles and also a lot of spirits. A small sample bundle of asparagus was given to the owner's wife, she was a Geordie and we had christened her Daffers. With another stroke of luck we discovered that we had found another two avid asparaguseurs, they both adored it. I then handed her two thin and long white roots with green leafed foliage, they were parsnip thinnings. She squeaked with delight, put her hand to the side of her mouth and whispered, "They can't be, they can't be, but they are, they are baby parsnips". I nodded and said "of course". She had never seen them in the Algarve before and during our discussions became more excited when we told her of all the other crops that we intended to grow. At the suggestion that we would accept orders and deliver in midweek or on a Saturday she became over the moon with delight and ordered two kilos of asparagus for the weekend.

We were just about to leave when who should walk in through the door but the Pickwickean character with the grey handlebar moustache from Badsey. He recognised us and gave a slight gasp as he noticed the asparagus. He nervously asked if it would be possible to pick up the bundle. Daffers indicated a yes and it was gingerly grasped in his huge hand. After a few seconds he turned to us, shook our hands, and said "Bloody hell this is prime sparrowgrass, and I really mean prime stuff". A comment like that from a person who had handled the green gems for over forty years was praise indeed and Daffers was suitably impressed.

He asked if he could see the beds on our land so two days later I collected him at the shop and drove him back to the Quinta. The more he walked around the beds the more excited he became and we could feel his energy levels surge. He had retired some ten years ago and had not got as close to asparagus in season as this.

His one small criticism was that some of the small pieces of fern stems which had been cut down the previous year had not been fully cleared away. We gave him an asparagus lunch and served up "Proper country portions" like he had done all those years ago when he had run the pub in Badsey. He considered that the flavour was excellent, equally as good as the spears he had cooked. I drove him back to the bus stop in the village with two freebie bundles, tenderly held, one in each hand and waited to see him get on the bus. He had difficulties when it came to pay for his fare as he was reluctant to put either bundle down to get some cash out of his pocket, he somehow managed and was soon waved a sad farewell.

AC at the sharp end of the asparagus bundling preparation, had experienced difficulties when the spears had to be actually tied together. They needed to be raised above the work surface to enable the raffia to be more easily looped around them so I designed a "Bundler". This was a simple "H" section made in timber with its length shorter than the spears. These could then be placed inside the top section of the "H", above the work surface and when one end of the bundle was tied with the raffia around it. Then it could be turned through one hundred and eighty degrees to enable the other end to be completed. It was very effective and certainly speeded up the bundling operation.

On the last Saturday delivery of ordered asparagus to the market I asked the young man, who had regularly collected his four bundles a week, if he was a chef and owned a restaurant. His answer was yes to both and that the restaurant was in the nearby village of Odiaxere so I booked a table for two that evening at seven thirty. When we arrived it was quite full and after an aperitif at the bar we were escorted, by a pretty young woman who we later discovered was his wife, to our table. In its centre was a hand written reservation card with the simple wording of "The Algarve Asparagus Man plus One".

During the eight-week period of making a selected cut, we sold over seventy kilos of asparagus, had also eaten quite a lot and all without undue effort. Dependent upon the weather, which could make it a week earlier or later, we had sussed out that the months of March and April would constitute our asparagus season. This would be some two months before that in the U.K. Some small degree of sales and marketing tactics had been developed but these needed to be expanded and consolidated.

I had always bought my cigarettes in cartons of two hundred, ten packs of twenty and one Friday lunchtime was no different. The first pack was opened over a beer in M's café. For many months I had developed a tickly throat and a nasty cough, which started every morning when I lit up my first fag of the day. On Saturday morning there was no exception, in fact it was worse, so I resolved to do something about it. AC said on the Sunday evening, "you are certainly chewing through the cigarettes at the moment and it is not doing you any good at all".

I lit the last one out of the last packet and said to her, "when this one is finished I will never smoke a cigarette again" and never have!

At the end of the asparagus season the poolside lower terrace was extended where we had left the gap in the wall and a step was made down to the newly laid footpath to the septic tank. The area in front of this had been reserved for DC's folly, otherwise known as the bandstand. Four large columns were constructed from natural stones to form portals, which would support an open timber roof and under this a paving was laid with collected river stones to increase the width of the footpath over part of its central length. A slightly curved balustrade with short columns was built onto this to form the front, which separated us from the orchard.

From the upper terrace we could now look down through the portals over this balustrade directly into the orchard and then upwards to the escarpment. Here the concrete electrical distribution support pole that I had used as a marker to set out the Quinta, still remained clearly visible. All of the fruit trees had miraculously survived the transplanting process and had matured slowly. When they were first planted they had to be watered by hand with bucket after bucket, now we had only to open three stop valves and it was automatic as irrigation pipes, connected to the main system, had been installed.

Don Sandra and baby Mark came to stay for a brief holiday and it was lovely to see them and the baby, he was a real cutie. He had his first dip in our pool and I still remember the look on his face when he paddled in the sea on the beach at Amado after we had had lunch at the "Chippery". I had forgotten how time-consuming babies were and the fact that they monopolised the day's events. However we all still had a wonderful time and on their wedding anniversary Margaret and Bob babysat so that the four of us could go into Lagos and celebrate in style. Before they left they surprised us with some presents, eight poolside chairs and matching table.

In an attempt to stick with AC's crop rotation and to tie in with her already prepared watering charts which specified the vegetable, its zone location and dates and times of application I sowed a large bed of spring onions in an area above the well. The seeds had been treated and were a vivid green in colour. I had just finished the last row and was about to clear my gear away when I noticed a movement of seeds on the soil surface. AC had brought a cup of tea over and we both gazed down at a double-filed column of ants. Each one that moved away from the bed carried with it a green spring onion seed and the ones that moved towards it had nothing. We followed the trail of ants for about ten metres to where a hole in the ground was seen and as one ant went in another came out. I was being systematically robbed and although I had sown the seeds quite thickly it would not take too long to lose most of them. Three teaspoons full of the granulated insecticide that we had used to control the ralos were tipped into the hole and my size eight Wellington boots used to crush the ants in the file coming towards us all the way back to the bed. I did not bother to recover these stolen seeds and was satisfied that the thieves had been killed. To be on the safe side it would now be necessary to mount an "ant patrol" in the early mornings and late afternoons.

The Saturday market sales continued to do well although despite a promotion, orders for cherry tomatoes and mange tout peas were few and far between. It did not really matter as the restaurants ordered loads of them by the punnet.

Lucie notified us of our first Poxey P G's who had booked as a result of the local *"Why"* magazine advert. We had to pull our fingers out as there were no light fittings or curtains in the double bedroom due to lack of cash. They were fitted on the morning of their arrival, in the *knicker* of time so to speak. They were a couple, a twosome, from Bromsgrove and had booked for only one week. It all went very smoothly and the breakfasts were a complete success. The design of the Quinta's accommodation, guests in the east wing and us in the west, had worked very well with family and friends and it did so with them.

We did notice however that early morning work on the land and cooked breakfasts were not an ideal combination. When the asparagus season came into full steam we realised that it would be inadvisable to have any visitors, even family or friends, unless they were fully prepared to muck in.

A letter from the lawyer reminded us that the outstanding paperwork was finally to hand as the Quintas registration had spewed out of the system. The land had already been put on record. She apologised for the delay when we collected the documents but AC was quick to point out that it was still a lot speedier than the equivalent procedure in England.

In no time at all we had our second lot of Poxy P G's courtesy of a couple who ran a villa management business nearby. They had two English couples, a foursome caught up in a three day cross over mix-up at two different villas. Could we help out and accommodate them for that period? "Gladly" said AC and arrangements were made to bring the four over. Two came from up north, as we midlanders called anyone who lived north of Stafford, and the others worked for an airline and were based in southern England. After the first morning's breakfast we made an offer to do a BBQ, and join them for the evening meal, which they were very pleased to accept. They then went their separate ways for the rest of the day.

It was agreed that we would provide a three-course meal, followed by coffee and liqueurs and that they would bring their own tipples. They all, and us two, thoroughly enjoyed the meal and despite being complete strangers the evening went down well. Our holidaymakers were in no rush to go to bed. We on the other hand had work to do on the vegetables patches early in the morning before we could even think about their breakfasts. Late nights for us were another combination that was not ideal.

Based on the discussions at my digs in the pub near Basingstoke we calculated the basic costs of the items for the six of us and then included an amount to cover for the BBQ charcoal and firelighters. This figure was doubled and both of us thought that it seemed too cheap so it was trebled and it still compared very favourably with the prices of restaurants standard "Tourist Menus". As we had provided a much higher quality of fare than those, cream of asparagus soup was the starter, we added quite a bit more. When the two bills were presented on their last morning both couples said, "what an excellent value for money the evening had been and wished they could stay longer and do it again". The profit was placed in a tin labelled "for poolside furniture, recliners and umbrellas".

There was a spate of visitors on one occasion and the Quinta was so full that the sofa bed had to be used. My Droitwich golfing partner had driven down to southern Spain in his red soft-top "E Type" Jaguar, which he had completely stripped down and rebuilt just for the fun of it. He called in for a couple of days before he and his wife continued their journey up to northern Portugal to attend some Jag collector's reunion. It was really great to see them both and I relished the two short trips in his open topped car. I had forgotten the thrill of such frightening acceleration.

They were the last to arrive and made up a full Quinta. Shaz and Eddie had been collected from the airport by Margaret and Bob, as they happened to be in Faro, two days before. This assistance had been a bonus it saved us a journey as we had picked up Lucie and Les only one week previously. They just lazed around as Les was not too well. Shaz had brought out with them a new set of rotavator blades and shocked me when she said that she had taken up a post in Malawi, at the University, for two years. It was fairly hectic and crowded with bods all over the place and for a short period we had nowhere to escape to. Meals and BBQ's presented no problems as there were many pairs of helping hands and overall we coped remarkably well. It was sad to see the Jaguar drive up to the track as my friend and his wife left. There he tooted its horn and then must have gunned the throttle to the floorboards as the tyres screamed and a large cloud of dust was left behind floating in the air.

I really dropped a clanger when we took Lucie and Les back to the airport. I thought that I would be clever and save three hundred escudos by not using the car park. Whist we waited for them to check in a young policeman stuck a parking ticket on the windscreen. It was a fine for two thousand escudos as I had left the car in an area reserved for coaches. I was not amused and AC certainly wasn't. The following week Margaret and Bob had to return to Faro, as luck would have it, on the same day as Shaz's and Eddie's flight, so we were thankfully saved another trip.

The bedrooms had only just been sorted out after the last of our visitors had departed when the front door bell rang. It was two of "The three Musketeers" who stood there with a suitcase and a set of golf clubs apiece. As soon as they were sat down with a beer they asked if they could stay with us for a few days and they insisted that they pay. It was their golfing holiday and they intended to play a few courses over the breadth of the Algarve before they moved on into Spain. Obviously they were welcome, with payment or without, but it meant a visit to the village and M's to stock up on the liquid refreshments. On their first full day they put in a tremendous effort and completely cleared the section of the gulley, below that which Eddie and I already finished and now needed some urgent attention.

The second day they had booked a round of golf on one of the local courses and asked me to join them so I humped my bag from the pump house to check on the state of my clubs. The woods were all ok but there was still some dirt left in the groves of the irons since the last time that they had been used and that was long, long ago. My round was a personal disaster. I had a terrible time and it was like living a real life nightmare. During all of the games that I had ever played I had never reached double figures on any hole or gone round with a score of over a hundred. That day I lost a ball on the first, which was a very poor start, had only three pars, scored twelve on the ninth, lost two more balls and took one hundred and four strokes to complete my misery. Maybe because of this I was not over enamoured with the course. I might have played better if I had had legs like a mountain goat as a lot of the fairways were on the side of the hills. My partner's scores were even worse and I swore that if ever, and it was a big if, I played there again I would use a buggy and take a few tinnies with me. AC had watched as we approached the last green and she could see by the look on my face that something was not quite right. After we had showered and changed she quickly ushered us into the nineteenth hole for some cool beers and sandwiches. I didn't join them for their bash the following day at the course near Portimao or the other two at Villamoura. They appeared to have enjoyed themselves and took us out to supper in the village the night before they ventured off to Spain.

After six weeks of visitors, on and off, it was nice to be back on our own and have the Quinta to ourselves again. A whole pile of post was collected one day, which included a letter from Sandra who told us that she had taken back home more than she had brought with her, she was pregnant. We were absolutely delighted and rang her to say that it must have been the Bensafrim air.

Les had never fully recovered from his operation and had gone down hill rapidly after his holiday so AC was booked on the flight to Birmingham, on her own, for four weeks. It was far too expensive for us both to go back and there was a lot of work to be done here. Sadly he passed away on the anniversary of our arrival at

Hortinha and to cap it all my youngest brother rang and told me that our father needed an urgent operation to remove a tumour on his chest.

Orders continued to trickle in for parsnips, Maureen, who had told us that she had not intended to add on any mark up to her purchases, collected three five kilo sacks full every week and Daffers chipped in with orders for her wine shop clients. Eventually we sold out completely and all of our business cards had been handed out so we had to order some more.

Again the nasty itchy red rash appeared, this time on my thighs as well. It was still hot enough to wear shorts and the only common factor that we could think of was that it only occurred when I dug up and handled the parsnips. Surely I could not be allergic to them. I had dug them up in England for years without any problems so we remained not any the wiser.

A German couple had purchased some land further along the track and lived with their young children in two small caravans. It was their intention to build a villa but in the meantime wanted another caravan to accommodate some of their family who would come out on holiday to visit them. They had seen the "caravan for sale" sign and the parked caravan at the bottom of the drive. After a thorough and efficient inspection a price was agreed, in Deutschmarks. The conversion rate on the day into Sterling proved to be another deal where we received more than we had paid out although Lucie and Les had offered the caravan to us at a really knock down price. We agreed that it would be collected after lunch on the Sunday. It was then hitched up to the fart box, for positively the last time, towed up to the track and left parked there under the cork oak trees.

AC became very agitated as by the late afternoon no one had turned up. Eventually however they arrived in the early hours of the evening, apologised profusely and handed over the cash. As the caravan was towed away AC shed lots of tears as it represented a nostalgic memory of her father. It took only seconds to tear down the "caravan for sale" sign, which had, by this time almost disintegrated. Then only a few minutes to telephone Lucie and tell her that the whole Quinta rental lets potential was off as we no longer had cheap alternative accommodation. The caravan had been sold and I was quite relieved.

A lot of the cash from the sale was soon frittered away as the clutch cable on the fart box and a part of the exhaust system had to be replaced. It was a hairy drive into Lagos, to get it repaired, stuck in second gear and I very nearly had a collision on a roundabout. Materials for the compost bins and the utility room porch projects had to be purchased which meant that there was a negative amount left. To overcome this small problem I sold the cement mixer to a neighbour for almost the same price that I had paid for it. AC did not consider this to be a shrewd move as the mortar for the two immediate projects, and any future ones, would have to be hand mixed. Our financial situation however, showed that there was no alternative. Progress was slowed significantly for a while as it was a "go everywhere on foot" time as the car remained in the garage.

During this period I walked into the village to collect the post, some supplies and noticed that both Nora Batty and her husband, Happy Harry stood in their drive just off the track. I had not seen her since the incident with the two five litre water bottles when we had returned from the village along with Lucie. I had almost got level with them when she folded her arms, lowered her head and turned her back on me. He as usual gazed firmly straight ahead without so much as a facial twitch. I asked her what the problem was. She then snorted loudly and scurried up to their villa, which left me extremely flummoxed. I had a beer in M's café before returning and his wife told me that her sister in Lisboa was in hospital and that prospects did not look at all encouraging.

The side and rear walls of the four compost bins were built from concrete blocks with small holes made in them for air circulation and their bottoms consisted of criss-crossed reinforcing bars built in them twenty centimetres above the base, again to allow air circulation. Similar blocks were used to build the small porch, which had a sloping tiled roof. An arched gateway was left in the main wall, slightly offset from the utility room door, to screen us from any passers by along the track.

My father's operation proved to be a complete success and the tumour was not malignant. The old bugger remained as cantankerous as ever and had started to smoke again!

Our third request for manure, from the farmer up the track, produced four trailer loads, about six tonnes of pretty rich stuff as most of it still steamed and ponged a bit. We managed to spread it on all of the permanent asparagus beds, around and between the orchard trees and all over the area above the well. After the winters first heavy rainfalls it was rotavated in on the latter areas.

With winter only just around the corner it was time for the annual logging sessions. Mid-way through one the chain saw motor smelt a bit hot and suddenly died. I could not restart it as the pull-start rope would not move, not even a fraction. It was taken to the workshop in Odiaxere where the mechanic stripped off the head and found that the piston had fused itself to the cylinder block. He thought that the problem had been caused by some dodgy two-stroke fuel. It was not repairable so a new motor was required. The cost of this and the labour involved was more expensive than if I bought a completely new one. This was out of the question in view of our finances so I would have to find a log man.

In one DIY shop we saw for the first time, laminated chipboard suitable for shelving and AC was over the moon at this discovery. All of her books had been stored on the floor since they had been unpacked from the tea chests. I prepared a sketch, which met with her approval and bought the necessary pieces and knocked up two temporary bookcases for her. They were not up to cabinetmaker standards but perfectly adequate and solidly made. She was delighted to find that there were some spare spaces after the floor had been cleared and the books displayed in them and eagerly awaited her next book fix.

Some weeks after we were told that M's wife's sister had passed away we received an invite up to the café for a "pig kill" supper. The pig had been killed that morning at his Quinta in the hills. The meal was taken in the garage where there were two long tables surrounded by bits, some large and others small, of pig. There were many bowls of marinades filled with different pieces and fat was being rendered into lard. We stood around and started with chitterlings on thick slices of home made bread, cooked in the large bread oven at the Quinta. Then sat down to be served from a huge tureen of chicken and pea stew followed by small balls of pork cut from the loin, all of course washed down with M's red wine. The remainder of the family from Lisboa were there so there was a lot of commiserations all round and much to talk and reminisce about. Also the deaf and dumb man, who we understood had killed the pig, but we did not have much to say to him.

Lucie had been invited to come over for a long Christmas holiday, which was an ideal arrangement for us. AC had suggested that rather than we sat around and moped about the best years long since past, we join with M's family to share with them their loss, and have a good old jolly English wake on the Christmas day. I spoke to M, at the pig kill supper, and it only took a few moments of discussion with the family for it to be agreed.

Olives had been collected over a few weeks and one day as I was cutting down the asparagus fern Alfonso 2 called in, to drop off a large sack of fresh oranges. He told me that as there had been only a small collection at Alfonso 1's shack last year it had now taken place in the village, we had missed the boat. He appeared a little embarrassed when he saw the amount that we had picked. I had forgotten to renew my club membership in the village and when this annual fee was paid I asked whether or not there would be another collection. The answer was no but they told me that I could take them to an olive pressing factory near St Bartholomew de Messines, at Portela. We took a day out and took the two plastic sacks of olives there where they were put on the scales and we were then handed a weigh ticket. Like a couple of hicks from the sticks we then just hung around until someone guided us to the end of the production line where there were four huge stainless steel vats. From the bottom tap of one of them, after handing over our ticket, fifteen litres of pure virgin olive oil was poured into our containers to take away.

Although the rear wall of the BBQ was an ideal place to construct the log store it was North West facing, straight into the prevailing wind. Some form of protective screen was therefore needed to keep the contents dry. There remained lots of bamboo canes down the length of the gulley so I was able to make up two widths which when hung gave it some crude form of weatherproofing curtains.

A bit of a soiree had been arranged for the Christmas Eve, which went very well. Mulled wine had been prepared together with plenty of nibbles, carols were sung around the piano and it didn't finish until around eleven o'clock. It was just as well that most of the food for Christmas day had already been organised.

Lucie and us two had buck's Fizz on the upper pool terrace quite early and opened our presents. I was particularly impressed with the weathercock, AC with her perfumes and Lucie over the moon with her blouse top outfit. The turkey was put into the oven with plenty of time to spare and the prepared vegetables cooked in readiness for the feast. The Hostess trolley then came into its own. Thankfully there was not a power cut and the voltage remained constant so no major traumas were experienced.

We started to panic as at a quarter to two the Portuguese contingent had not arrived. One thirty had been agreed but it was just on two o'clock when they turned up. There were fourteen of us, including DIY Dave and the kitchen table had had to be moved into the lounge. A good *stuff* was had by everyone and they thoroughly enjoyed the typical English meal especially the roast parsnips. All of this was accompanied with M's wife's homemade bread and his fairly potent newly brewed wine. As the table was cleared away, Rui, M's wife's late sister's husband did his party tricks with strings and cards and we thought that he had a lot of natural talent that had yet to be tapped. The youngsters cleared off for a couple of hours and then returned with a large dish of tiger prawns to compliment our provision of the Stilton and digestive biscuits. These combinations proved to be an absolute winner and were wolfed into by all. They all left at nine thirty and I for one, felt the need for an early night.

Boxing Day started badly as, when AC opened the oven door, she discovered that the substantial remains of the turkey were covered with the dreaded ants. I cut off most of the meat from the carcass, and this was given to Margaret for her pets.

The downside was that we had no turkey sandwiches to eat at our picnic on the beach at Amado and also my special savoury turkey pie was now a last year's memory.

The remainder of Lucie's holiday passed quickly and without incident. We went to a New Years Eve party at a local sports club and she was amazed that when we left, at one thirty in the morning, that I had to spend almost five minutes scraping the ice off the windscreen. We were less than two kilometres from the sea. A dozen people had been invited round to the Quinta to celebrate her birthday on New Years Day. The weather was marvellous; cloudless Algarve blue skies with warm sunshine, and we were able to eat on the upper pool terrace and laze around to almost four thirty before we all went indoors.

Before she left I spread around another two loads of manure that had been delivered and started the daily hoeing and weeding of the asparagus beds. AC was understandable very choked when we drove to the airport to see her mother off and felt extremely low when we arrived back at the Quinta.

She quickly bucked up the following morning and I was very encouraged but also disturbed as on a walk around, we sighted the tips of fresh asparagus spears on the old seed beds. This meant that my progress of hoeing and weeding the permanent beds would have to be accelerated to avoid any possible damage to the newly emerging spears. It seemed like only five minutes ago that I had laboured to cut the old ferns down and the rest or dormant period, for the crowns, was less than three months. This fact did not bode well for the longevity of their useful productive life.

Chapter Eighteen

This was to be the season's first full cut and we had prepared for this time as best we could. Both of us were extremely nervous of the outcome, success would mean that we could continue to live in Portugal, failure meant a return to the U.K. and I could not bear the thought of that possibility. What the hell would I do there? Our financial situation was in its worst state since we had got together and if our income did not improve then our outgoings would continue to exceed it by a considerable amount.

We had already tapped, with more than a little luck, into asparaguseurs who resided around a local golf complex, which had given us the potential of a domino effect. There was also another golf complex close to Portimao which had not yet been targeted. The private holiday complex where we had spent our first holiday in Portugal had shown good prospects and there were quite a few others not that far away from it. Only the restaurants where the chef was the owner had been approached and a mid-week delivery service offered. We had deliberately steered well clear of those with only managers in charge. It was suggested to the chefs that they could get some kudos and me some brownie points, when they informed their clients that the asparagus had been freshly cut that day, to foreigners by an English couple and to Brits by a compatriot.

More enthusiastic asparaguseurs needed to be winkled out to extend the domino effect. We considered that the exchange of different asparagus recipes should be encouraged in an attempt to pass the good news on of its availability. Any discussions about recipes with restaurant chefs was to be avoided at all costs as we had concluded that they lived in a world of their own on that particular subject. Our efforts in the Lagos Saturday open market had proved to be very fruitful and two other collection points had been earmarked. One was on the sea front at Praia da Luz and the other at Quatro Estradas, a cross road on the EN125 to Sagres just to the West of Lagos. Any mini markets that specialised in provisions to ex-pats were also considered to be prospective outlets. Door to door sales were not seriously contemplated as it was thought to be too time consuming and a very hit and miss approach.

I thought that it would be a good idea to advertise at the collection points and the Quinta and also have a display unit for the market. From some of the remaining timbers that I had amassed during the building phase I made up two "Asparagus for sale" signs. One was just a single sheet of hardboard which we hung on the wall at the top of the drive and the other comprised two small sheets hinged together which could be mounted like a triangle on top of the estate car and quickly folded flat if there were any police around. Two "A" frame trestles with hinges at the tops, to enable them to be flattened for transport, were also knocked up and these together with loose boards formed a table that could be easily assembled in the market to display our produce. The table length was designed to fit into the extended boot as the rear seats of the estate car could be lowered to form one.

A few spears had been cut for lunch for AC's birthday in late February and the flavour was exquisite. In the season's first week there was only a moderate yield; anything up to one kilo we ate and above that was sold locally through Margaret up the track. We defined the actual start of the season when the first daily cut of over three kilos was harvested so the overall season worked to be for a period of seven weeks and not eight.

The yield increased so rapidly that it almost caught us on the hop. Two people from the golf complex and the Dutch chef had already enquired about its availability so it only needed a few phone calls to start the whirligig in motion. These three called in to collect and as they departed, bundles clasped in their hands, all looked like the cat that had licked the cream. The word spread like wildfire and orders flooded in for the Saturday market, the telephone calls never ceased. AC was always bullish and said yes to every telephone order, I was more cautious as I didn't want to let anyone down by overbooking. I need not have worried as we had a few surplus kilos when we set up our stall at nine thirty.

As every spear had been cut including the sprue and some thinnish ones where the bud had opened slightly I suggested to AC that she cut these into small pieces and make them up into packs. We could then offer them for sale as "Soup packs". The assembled table was set up and was an immediate success as it presented the produce at exactly the right viewing level. We were surrounded in less than five minutes by excited clients, all English, and the ordered bundles were collected and paid for in just under fifteen with repeat orders for the next week jotted down. The "Soup packs" were put on offer at a fraction over half price and were snapped up like hot cakes and proved to be very popular. Again lots of repeat orders were taken and one woman actually requested six of them.

Some German and Dutch people handled the bundles uneasily because they were more used to the white spears, grown in their countries, which had to be peeled off from the buds downwards and was quite a fiddly preparation to carry out. I had to explain that the green spears did not have this tough outer skin so this exercise was not necessary. Although they bought some I did not think that they were totally convinced as not one of them placed an order for the following week. Some people viewed the bundles very suspiciously and told me that they had had a bad experience and had been caught out when they had bought some before. When they had cooked it the taste was very bitter. I explained to them that that variety was different to mine, it was wild asparagus and quite different from the bundles in front of them. After an excited chinwag about the matter I handed over four bundles and told the recipients to take them home to try them and I insisted that they would find the flavour far superior. If they found this was the case then they could pay me next week.

We had sold out completely by ten o'clock so the table was dismantled and packed into the car boot. Both of us thought how tatty and dilapidated it looked compared to all the other vehicles around it but with a shrug of our shoulders then visited a small café around the corner for a most welcome cup of coffee and a round of toast.

Every client was politely informed that all ordered produce not collected before ten thirty would be made available for immediate sale. During a friendly discussion with a new client she happened to mention that her husband had been employed in the Emirates and that they had lived in an ex-pat compound not far away from the small village of Al Fujayrah. I asked her, with tongue in cheek, if frozen chickens and fresh eggs were readily available in the locality. Of course they were she responded as there was an all-purpose built integrated chicken farm just a few kilometres away. How in the world did you know she enquired? I told her that I had visited the area years ago when my company had prepared a tender for the project. It was the one where the client had apologised for not awarding the contract to me.

The old fart box was giving me some cause for concern as its bodywork condition continued to deteriorate rapidly. Mechanically it performed very well but the ageing electrical systems proved less and less reliable. State of the art vehicle inspection centres, up market MOT depots, were being installed throughout the country. They were extremely sophisticated and all checks were linked into the centres central computer and one was due to open shortly in Loule near Faro and the inspection was obligatory. One day as I parked the car in a vacant space on the Avenida, which by now had become very difficult to find, far away from the petrol station. AC said, as I switched off the ignition, "I cannot open my door". We discovered that it would only open from the outside, which was not a serious problem until we had an accident.

There was a large scrap yard by the Estrada Nacional 125 at the village of Espiche some seven kilometres west of Lagos and on the many occasions we had passed it on our delivery runs I had noticed some old Cortinas piled up inside. Back at the Quinta I stripped off the passenger door internal panelling and found that a link rod that connected the door opening mechanism failed to engage as a part had broken off. So I set out with my fairly small bag of hand tools and asked the scrap yard owner if I could rummage around to find a replacement. He pointed in a general direction and indicated that I should help myself. One Cortina was totally knackered, hardly recognisable and not worth a second look but another showed a definite promise. It did not take long to obtain the wanted part and in the process I salvaged a considerable amount of other operational spares all at a cost of less than one pound.

I was not new to scrap heap sorties as years ago I had made many visits to "Scrappy Harrison's" yard by the canal in Worcester. Once on top of a five-car heap I successfully removed a cylinder head from a "Gold Seal" reconditioned engine and fitted it to the first car that I had ever purchased. I was the sixth owner of an Austin A40 Devon and this replacement head extended its on road performance by almost thirty thousand miles. It was paid for out of the three hundred and fifty pound winnings at my one and only visit to a racecourse. This was at Cheltenham during the "Gold Cup" week. Four of us went there. One we called "Neddy" as he was a serious gambler on the nags and dogs. That day he lost all of his winnings, of over one thousand pounds on the last two races.

The daily harvesting of the asparagus continued and AC's trug was a boon to me as I plodded up and down the rows and stooped to cut the spears. It soon filled up and contained slightly over two kilos. The spears grew at an astonishing rate, up to twenty centimetres a day, and if I stopped for a second or two I could have sworn that I had heard them growing as they rose ever upwards.

One day on my third delivery to the utility room I found AC there in a bit of a pickle with about six grades of spears all over the top of the freezer, the draining board and the table. I suggested that she should not be so pernickety and not sort out so many different sizes. She really snapped back at me and forcefully reminded me that quality control was solely her responsibility. When the next trug full was delivered I discovered that she had had a touch of the *mulligrubs* and had continued the grading her way.

"I haven't got the room for them yet." she shouted at me. "One bundler is definitely insufficient. I need at least two more". I had to agree and that evening made up three, which transformed the speed of her bundling operation so that she was able to keep well ahead of my deliveries.

Our first sizeable order for the holiday complex in Praia da Luz was delivered after which we parked the car on the sea front opposite the paper shop. Spare bundles of asparagus together with "Soup packs" and ten one kilo sacks of Swedes had been covered in the boot. The "A" frame for sale sign triangle was then placed on the roof so that it was in full view of residents and tourists coming down from or going up to the church. The reason that it had been made collapsible was that I was not in possession of a license to trade there and had never followed up my initial application. If one of the regular police patrols came by and noticed my clandestine operation I could have been in serious trouble. At first sight of any official uniform the sign was slammed shut and shoved into the unlocked boot.

Everything was sold very quickly, with not one policeman in sight, mostly to resident ex-pats and orders were taken for the same time and place next week. Some tourists who were holidaying on a self-catering basis seemed quite surprised to find fresh asparagus on sale so early in the year and it made a good topic of conversation as I wrapped the bundles up for them. One holidaymaker was due to return back to the U.K. that evening and wanted two bundles to take with him.

On my fifth visit to the lay-by at Quatro Estradas with the asparagus for sale sign in full view, I failed to notice a police car that had approached on the road from Praia da Luz. The driver obviously saw me and the sign so drove over. Two officers got out and asked to see my licence. When they realised that I did not have one they proceeded to give me a mild bollocking and told me that without one I was trading illegally. I decided not to offer them a free bundle as that may have been construed as a bribe. The thought crossed my mind at that moment that they were quietly amused to see a foreigner, with vegetables for sale, in that particular spot. In the end they just told me to clear off and not return and then sped off in the direction of Lagos. I still had some ordered bundles left in the boot but thankfully these were collected within the next ten minutes.

My dilemma was explained to these clients and future arrangements were made for them to collect their orders down by the sea front. I then beetled off back home pig-sick as a result of the past fifteen minutes. Due to the fact that I had not been born with eyes in my arse the incident had arisen and had effectively killed off that particular very busy profitable collection point and with it any potential new sales.

The asparagus yield continued to increase and in two peak periods of seven days I found that it was necessary to cut the spears three times a day, early in the mornings, at lunch times and in the late afternoons. AC rang Lucie to explain that we would not be at all able to cater for any Poxy PG's before the middle of May and was relieved to learn that there had been no enquiries. She also told her that visits from family or friends would be far from ideal as it would impossible for us to dance attendant services on them. However they would be very welcome to visit during the months of February and May as long as they were prepared to muck in and give us a helping hand and lots of assistance.

We were stretched to the gunnels and had to encourage clients to collect in mid-week whenever possible. Too much of our valuable time was spent on deliveries to restaurants. A circle had been drawn on our map to define the limit of our range to these, which was Sagres to the West and Portimao to the East. At a pinch for bulk orders only, we would consider deliveries to Lagoa further on from Portimao. Longer distances were out of the question even if it meant that we lost lots of orders.

There was only one restaurant in Sagres, seven in the Lagos district and surrounds and three in Portimao.

Once ten kilos were delivered mid-week to Sagres where we found out that they only wanted ten bundles. The order had been misunderstood as it had been given to us by a third party friend of theirs. Fortunately for us they took the whole lot and explained that it would not be a regular order. Their requirement was normally for weekends only and I suggested that it would be in both our interests if they collected their order from the Lagos Saturday open market. This suited them down to the ground and us, especially, as they did their major shop in the city that day and they gladly agreed.

One of the restaurants in Portimao had an Italian chef who as well as his own requirements was happy to pay for, and take in, the bundles ordered by clients who lived in the Monchique area and they would collect them from the restaurant. He told us that it was good for his business as they normally collected in the evenings and more often than not stayed on for dinner. There were many phone call orders from as far away as Faro and even beyond. All had to be declined as deliveries were out of the question. A few really keen asparaguseurs collected but many did not. It was no great loss to ourselves as we managed to sell all that we cut anyway.

I suffered badly as one early Saturday morning cut was carried out after a really heavy overnight ground frost. The spears were thankfully undamaged but many had a thin layer of ice on them. The tips of my fingers had become numb before the second trug full had been filled. By the end of the cut, even after constantly immersing my fingers into almost boiling water to regain some sense of touch, I could feel nothing and the pain was excruciating. Unpleasant memories of my experiences as a child picking the early morning frozen hard Brussels sprouts were quite vivid. Later in the market, in my usual unofficial position, I wore an anorak over a thick winter sweater with my Russian fur hat, with ear flaps fully down, firmly stuck on my head.

Not many Saturday market days passed by without some sort of serious or comical incident. On that very cold day a complete stranger came over to me and in an aggressive manner demanded two kilos of asparagus. The line of his lips was not quite horizontal, the left hand side was much lower and he spoke in a muffled way. I did not like his attitude and decided to call him "Fuffel chops". There was none spare so I explained that they had to be ordered a week in advance.

At this he completely blew his top, "order, order, bloody order, I have never heard anything so ridiculous in the whole of my life," he hollered at me and became quite abusive. Eventually he calmed himself down and asked for six bundles next week. A fairly large audience of waiting clients had by now gathered during his insulting performance and were shuffling their feet with a mixture of slight embarrassment and impatience.

I had had enough and thought stuff you so said to him with my face less than ten centimetres from his, "take a sexual walk I don't want your bloody custom". After a few seconds he turned on his heels and stormed off. AC thought that I had been rather rude to him but I told her that I would never ever tolerate that type of behaviour from him or anyone for that matter. The adage that the customer was always right certainly did not fit in with my ideas of a client supplier relationship. I worked on a take it as it was or leave it basis.

We lurched from crisis to crisis on a daily basis. One day it was a panic as we could not fulfil the orders and the next we had a surplus and had to come up with new ways to offload it.

I came up with the idea of providing asparagus lunches, similar to the suppers we had enjoyed back in England. We could cater for up to fourteen covers in the lounge if both of the dining and kitchen tables were placed together. Gammon steaks could be purchased from an English butcher in Lagos and we had the asparagus and grew the new potatoes. Three courses could be offered, asparagus soup, asparagus with grilled gammon and boiled new potatoes and a lemon meringue pie. Red or white wine and a coffee and liqueur would be included in a set price. This was quickly calculated in the same way as the BBQ ones for the Poxy P G's and for what the diners would get seemed very reasonable to us.

AC rang Margaret who said that, "she would be glad to help out in the kitchen". It was decided that the minimum number of people at any one sitting should be six as there was not much point in catering for less. An advertisement was placed in the local paper for a three-week period. One client in the market said excitingly, "had we seen it and thought that it was a brilliant idea". She hadn't realised that it was our advert so I kept mum and as anticipated, she did not telephone to make a reservation. The response was terribly disappointing with only four enquiries and three of those were from people who lived on the other side of Faro and the other way up north, almost on the border with the Alentejo, the next region to the Algarve, so it never got off the ground.

The weather was very fickle and I could start to water the asparagus and other vegetables in the late afternoon dressed only in shorts and with sandals on. Within thirty minutes I had to go back indoors and put on a tracksuit, a thick sweater and socks and then Wellingtons to complete the ensemble.

On one memorable market day we had almost geared ourselves up to shut up the shop when a very trim attractive and smart looking blonde suddenly appeared around the wall of the ladies bog. She walked towards me, as I stood in the road outside the co-operative next to the fruit tree man, with a snotty nosed little boy who hung onto her rather short skirt.

"So yourrrrrrrre the asparagus man," she remarked as she approached. I recognised her immediately as one of my first girlfriends she was "thunder thighs'" sister. Her recognition of me was somewhat slower as perhaps I hadn't worn too well over the years. Our relationship had not been that serious and did not last for very long as she was a bit of a *flibbertigibbet* and had the reputation of being cheap to run as no U.L.O. was ever necessary.

The young boy who I assumed was her grandson kept licking his nose and kicked the table trestles repeatedly until I shouted at him to stop and threatened to clip his ear. She thought that that attitude was a bit over the top. He was a snot-gobbling little git, a classic example of a modern "stick job at birth" type of child. One kilo was requested for the next week and between the arrivals and departures of our last few clients we managed to cram in quite a detailed chat. Mine was easy to explain as she knew of my marital split up and subsequent move with AC to live here. I had completely lost touch with her and she told me that she had been divorced three times, had one daughter and this grandson and now lived alone in Birmingham. It was her first visit to the Algarve and she had been told of an Englishman who sold freshly grown asparagus in the Saturday market, hence her visit and she had had no idea it would be me. For some unaccountable reason the

Algarve didn't suit her and she did not think that she would return. As they walked slowly away I felt quite sorry for her but nothing for the little brat.

As most of my clients that came to collect were females and as I always entered into a bit of patter with all of them AC politely referred to them as DC's ladies.

Just as we were finished and about to load up the car one of these rushed over, quite breathless and asked for her half kilo. I told her that I was sorry but it had already been sold and pointed to my watch, which showed that it was almost a quarter to eleven. She was fully aware of the ten thirty collection deadline and apologised. After she had regained her breath she ordered two bundles for the next week and promised not to be late.

The asparagus sales, highs and lows, were a bit like a whirligig, which went faster or more slowly pro-rata to the yield. Our existing clients were locked into their weekly treat and there was no way that they wanted to get off. The down side for new clients, who we were always on the look out for, was that it was a devil of a job to get on. Somehow we seemed to manage, more by good luck than judgement, and only very rarely did we have to limit the number of bundles anyone could have.

At one super peak period there were some unsold bundles so I drove into Lagos with these stacked in the trug covered with a brightly coloured Algarvean tea cloth and wandered around the centre in an attempt to sell them to anybody that looked the slightest bit foreign. I would gingerly lift up a corner of the cloth and ask them if they wanted to buy freshly cut asparagus. At that exact moment I felt like a Parisien spiv dressed in his flasher mac who when he slowly opened it said, with pursed lips from one corner of his mouth, "do you want to buy some feeelthy pictures?"

A Portuguese man, who had a couple of pitches in the market and always appeared popular, came over and bought one bundle and asked where we lived. I told him and he apparently knew the district like the back of his hand. He would give the bundle, as a sample, to a female friend of his who had a stall in the covered market nearer the centre of the town. He was sure that she would be interested in expanding her vegetable range and sell some asparagus on. We were sitting on the terrace with glasses in hand on the Sunday evening when the front door bell rang and we found that it was the Portuguese market man and his friend, they had called in to discuss a business arrangement with us. He left soon after introductions had been made. Her name was Dolores and we took her on a quick walkabout to see all of our vegetables. She expressed a keen interest in the asparagus, spring onions, coloured lettuce and peppers, courgettes and the cherry tomatoes. She was not at all interested in the parsnips or Swedes.

We explained our pricing policy and this presented no problems for her. What was ideal, and suited us down to the ground, was that she or one of her family would always collect from the Quinta. They did not want produce delivered to the market as they preferred to keep their sources to themselves. The collection times in the early evening on Wednesdays and Sundays suited us all, especially us, and she basically inferred that within reason she would take all that was available. If she required mega amounts the she would telephone the day before. There was in a container in the utility room, a couple of kilos of asparagus that I had cut that afternoon which she paid for and took away with her. This verbal agreement so quickly arranged was to us a minor miracle that had come out of nowhere, so we went into the village to celebrate and as I drank more than was good for me, AC had to drive us home.

That seven-week period was the most physically intensive time we had ever experienced. Asparagus was the main crop and we had cut almost five hundred kilos and we had also taken to the market, delivered or prepared for collection many kilos of swede, dozens of pots of herbs which included various varieties of basil, sage, curly leafed parsley, tarragon and many others. One Danish client repeatedly asked for dill, which we had had no success at all in growing so we could not satisfy his demands.

On top of all this we had sowed watered and weeded over one hundred four metre long rows of parsnips, sown thirty rows of spring onions at twenty one day intervals, potted up tomatoes, peppers, chillies, courgettes and pricked out of seed trays hundreds of coloured lettuce and transplanted them into individual pots. The potatoes planted earlier had to be mounded up and broad beans, peas, beetroot and carrots harvested to eat or be prepared for the freezer. The only plus side was that the visits to the bank were to make, by our standards, fairly substantial deposits. I now understood why, as a child, my father never had the time to take the family on holiday. Our relatives and friends had been severely warned, under penalty of death, not to do so during this period as we would not have the time to attend their funeral.

We had deliberately sown more parsnips and spring onions than before and based upon our delivery experiences with the asparagus knew that we had to have assistance if we wanted to sell further east beyond Lagoa. An advert was therefore placed in the local paper.

Lucie came over for a short visit, which was great because she mucked in and enabled us to catch up with all of the things that had been put to one side and gave us the time to spend some brief tourist moments with her.

Only one response was received to the advert, from a man who lived in Bordeira, not the village on the West coast thank goodness, but the one just to the north of Faro. As we had to take Lucie back to the airport, we arranged to meet up with him at the information desk. Over a beer he introduced himself as Stephen and we discovered that he was a singer and had, in the past, had his own rock band. He had led a very nomadic life but now lived with his ageing parents due to a mistake on his part. Instead of moving on after a brief temporary visit, he had stayed with them and had bitterly regretted the decision ever since. He bumbled along and traded at the many car boot sales in the Eastern Algarve. By his account he was very well known and if so, it was very good news for us. Spring onions, parsnips and swede interested him as they were veggies that had a shelf life and could therefore be stored in his customised camper van. The prices were discussed and in line with our policy no discounts were given. We shook hands on a verbal agreement to co-operate and we were very pleased on our drive back from the airport to know that we now had an agent-cum-representative to open up a whole area of the Algarve which was impossible for us to cover.

Don rang excitedly that evening to tell us that he was a father again, another boy who they had decided to christen Alan.

There were two consecutive periods of Poxy P G's and we had arranged the car hire for both of them. One couple were neighbours of Lucie and the others lived in a small village on the outskirts of Evesham and had seen the advert in a local supermarket. The first travelled extensively every day and always returned around five o'clock when, whatever we had on the go, we had to down tools and join them for a really stiff gin and tonic with slices from the lemons that had been picked from our own trees, on the pool upper terrace. The second lot landed very late in the evening so they had to pick up their car in the reserved car park. Next morning we received a telephone call from a very irate manager of the car hire company, apparently our visitors had driven off in the wrong car. The problem was soon resolved to every ones satisfaction. The husband loved poached eggs on toast for breakfast and although this was not a challenge to our culinary skills he asked if he could cook them himself. I answered that it would be OK as long as we were responsible for the toast and there was an immediate agreement.

AC's ex working colleague Karen and her husband Norman, stayed with us for a fortnight and told us that they had purchased a time-share in Southern Spain. They had also acquired an old ruin ripe for modernisation, basically flatten it then carry out a total rebuild job, in France about a forty-five minutes drive away north from Toulouse. We thought that we had been mad many times when some of our decisions were made but their plans really took the biscuit. They gave us a tremendous amount of help to plant the shrubs in the east wing and contributed generously towards the cost of the irrigation equipment, which I installed as an extension from the main pipeline that supplied the water to top up the swimming pool.

The log store was almost empty of the logs cut from the trees I had been able to saw or chop down. When the store had been completed and originally filled with these logs I had had to make up two removable bamboo cane curtains to keep them dry and the bamboo was collected from the thickets along the gully. They now looked in quite a sorry state and needed some major repair work done to them before some logs were ordered.

I had seen a large log pile when I hawked the asparagus at Quatro Estradas and another one on the Lagos side of the village of Portelas. Both had quoted me the same price for a cubic metre. There was another one on the road out of Bensafrim to Barao de San Joao, less than half a kilometre away in a direct line from the Quinta. His price was attractively lower and delivery was easy for him. The "Log man", as we called him, only had to drive his tractor and trailer over the dry riverbed, along the track between the bottom of our land and that of Alfonso2's then turn left straight up our land through the orchard and then reverse into a position. There he could unload the four cubic metres that I had ordered immediately in front of the bandstand which left me the shortest distance possible to travel with my fully loaded wheelbarrow to stack them in the store.

I thought that the trailer would have been a front tip up type, which would have meant that the unloading process would have taken less than a minute. It was not, so every log was thrown off by hand and took considerably longer. The dead eucalyptus trees in the cork oak wood, ones with a trunk girth that I could not possibly cut down were pointed out to him when the trailer was emptied and I made a suggestion to him. He walked over to have a closer look and returned fifteen minutes later, grabbed my hand and shook it enthusiastically, grinned and nodded his in agreement. Three days later four men all armed with large chain saws cut every single eucalyptus tree down. The dead ones were cut into small logs suitable for our log-burning stove and tossed over the gully. It was then easy for me to collect them all up and make a considerable sized log pile that was placed on and covered with heavy-duty plastic sheeting. From previous winters consumption I reckoned that there was a sufficient quantity to last us for at least four years.

Five days later the two metre long logs cut from the live trees had been loaded onto huge trailers and driven away to the pulp mill over the border into Spain. I was the recipient the week after of a large bottle of Medronho so assumed that he had also done very well out of our deal.

Our agent, Stephen rang to tell us that at his recent car boot sales great excitement and an air of disbelief had been generated when he had mentioned the availability of swede and parsnips with some orgasmic swoons at the prospects of bunches of proper spring onions and fifty of these had been ordered. These were lifted, bunched and handed over to him when we met at a small café close to the petrol station in Lagoa.

Maureen had proven to be an absolute super star. She had not bought any asparagus, only soup packs for herself, but had excelled with all of the other produce. Sacks full and kilos were collected from the market every week and on one Saturday, with her mega order and all of the others plus the table even the Cortina estate could not accommodate AC as well, so she had to catch the bus into town. I suggested that as AC went to choir practice every Friday in Praia da Luz that Maureen's order could be delivered en route which would save her the trip into Lagos on the Saturday market and she thought that it was a very good idea.

There were the other superstars who made asparagus sales their priority and their efforts on the other vegetables also clearly showed remarkable results. Daffers regularly accepted between seven and ten kilos of asparagus, which were delivered in two weekly deliveries. Dolores never failed on her collections to take whatever amounts that were left over. The continuous demands from the golf complex residents and the tourists in the Praia da Luz holiday apartments ensured that we managed to flog it all.

We had made a contact with these five principles and they actually did all of the selling for us. The domino effect through them gave us a back door access to third party clients that numbered over seventy. It was a wonderfully simple procedure and we benefited enormously as there was no way that we could have succeeded without their combined efforts.

I had coerced one bundle of asparagus onto a real Colonel Blimp character at the Sunday sea-front sales. He had a waxed moustache, was dressed in baggy long shorts with knee length socks and outdated plimsolls. His face was very jowly and it reminded me of my late uncle who had been a professional glass blower by trade. His favourite party trick was, with his lips sealed, to blow up his face until the cheeks formed two almost transparent pink orbs either side of his nose. Rude elements of the family called him, in this his classic pose, "Bollock chops". I even more wickedly suggested that had his nose been that little bit longer it would have made a more spectacular impact.

When our Colonel Blimp character collected his second bundle, he told me that the memsahib had tasted better. The reason was not difficult to understand as her parents had grown asparagus when she was a child. It had been cut, cooked and presented on the table in less than fifteen minutes. However he did order another bundle and his complaint was the only one we ever received.

Don, Sandra Mark and Alan, the Alcester foursome, arrived and they had brought their own baby car seats with them. The younger tot was a chunkier version of his elder brother, with the same coloured blue eyes and mischievous smile. They both enjoyed their dunks in the pool and went down to sleep at night without a whimper. Margaret babysat twice so that we could visit our favourite restaurants. I had stacked most of the logs in the store and with the extra willing hands it was soon crammed full. We all had a nice lunch at the "Chippery", Sandra had pre-prepared food for the boys, afterwards, we decided to let the four of them go down to the beach without us and made an early return home. On the morning of their departure they presented us with an all singing and dancing ghetto blaster, a stereo radio and cassette player. Needless to say we were delighted. Most of that evening we listened, at long last, to decent music with some tone and depth and had not realised how much we had missed the experience.

We met up with Stephen in Lagoa, on two further occasions, and handed over yet more bunches of spring onions. AC had luckily found a source of the elastic bands, which she used to bunch them. It was a paper shop in Lagos close to the café where we had our toasts and coffees after we had finished at the Saturday market. They were size fourteen, ideal in AC's opinion, and by now I was sure that we were by far the biggest consumer of these in the Algarve or even Southern Portugal. The shop assistant was always too polite to enquire why we continued to buy so many packets.

There was a mini-market in Praia da Luz so I crated up six bunches of spring onions and polished up my sales pitch. One was taken inside as a sample and I was in luck as the owner was there. I explained to him that it was a special type of salad onion much loved by Northern Europeans, especially the British. We agreed a price per bunch and he decided to experiment and initially try with three of them. The sample was left, in the small vegetable section, on one of the shelves, which had a very limited space and I went outside to collect the other two. As I walked back in through door the sample bundle came out clutched in some woman's hands. She waved it wildly above her head and shouted to her friend who was sat in her car, "have a look at what I have found inside," she shouted. By the time that I had made out my payment chit, written on a small piece of scrap paper, the other two bunches had been picked up and were on their way to the check out tills.

I quickly told the owner that by pure chance I had another three bunches in the car and he nodded a yes, shook my hand and then gave me the thumbs up sign as he grinned from ear to ear. These were then placed on the shelf and two were grabbed immediately as we agreed that deliveries would be made on Tuesdays and Fridays. I had suggested these days as they fitted in with our normal shopping routine and AC's deliveries to Maureen.

Another outlet used was a roadside stall set up by a local man on the main road out of the village to Lagos. An agreement was made for me to receive a fixed amount per bunch on a no sell no pay basis. It was easy for me to check on the number of bunches sold and to top up when necessary as it was so local. The stall owner and I were very pleased when thirty bunches were sold in the first full week.

Often in the past I had heard people who had stopped smoking bemoan the fact that they did not seem to be financially better off. In my case it was different as I managed to save up sufficient amounts to purchase the arched porch gate and the one for the east wing side of the Quinta. Both had the letters "AC DC" welded to the vertical bars. The latter was not, as had been my original plan, fitted to the portals up the drive but down by the wall of the twin bedded guest bedroom. An asparagus plaque, of hand painted tiles to be mounted on the outside of the porch wall. was commissioned. The artist was dyslexic but she designed a magnificent picture of asparagus arranged around the wording of a poetically phrased speech made at the banquet held by the Baghdad Caliph Mustakfi circa A.D. 945. It was to celebrate the arrival of the long awaited caravan of asparagus from Damascus.

The Lagos council had only recently decided to accept "foreign" growers and I was one of a small handful of them so a licence to trade was received with my photograph attached. It was only valid for one year and it specified a space in the open market at Rossio S Joao by the central bus station. The patch/plot number was number 89 and it was not in the most salubrious location as it was situated behind the ladies and gentlemen's loos. It's measurements were two metres long and one and a half deep and if I stood behind my table with my back against the external wall of the co-operative I commanded a good view and could see everyone that entered and left the market.

There was only a small blind spot and that was due to the corner of the ladies loo wall. I was now, at long last, legally licensed to sell agricultural products. There was also a Scottish girl who sold in the covered section together with an ex diplomat from H.M.G. The plot next to mine was occupied by a very slim and attractive young girl. She and her husband owned a Quinta not far south of Bensafrim. They had a smallish vegetable garden and some orchards and their main produce was fresh fruit, principally apricots and peaches. They suffered identical problems to ours as, like the asparagus, when their fruit was ripe, it had to be picked and sold immediately. We both appreciated each other's problems and a strong bond was soon established between us. Most weekdays in season found us in a muck sweat in Lagos on deliveries, me with bundles of asparagus, bunches of spring onions and other things and her laden down with boxes and boxes of fresh fruit.

I rang Stephen to tell him that we had started to lift the parsnips and was surprised when he ordered one hundred kilos and asked for more spring onions and some swede. In the past we had pre-packed the produce in plastic sacks, which at a pinch could hold only up to five kilos, so I visited the co-operative to try and find Hessian sacks of twenty kilos capacity and was miraculously in luck. The whole of a sunny and bright Friday morning and half of the afternoon had been spent in the preparation of parsnips to fill up five of these Hessian sacks. I dug them up and wheeled them from below the asparagus beds up to the cistern where AC top tailed scrubbed and sorted them. They were finally weighed out and put into the sacks in four five kilo batches, the sack tops were tied with raffia and then loaded into the fart boxes boot.

In the early evening we met up with Stephen in the usual café in Lagoa and humped the sacks and the other vegetables into his camper van, which, with all the other bits and pieces already crammed in did not leave him much room to doss down for the night. I happened to notice a very small set of kitchen scales on the floor which had probably a weight capacity of only two kilos and as a lot of the parsnips were around a kilo each he would have a major problem to weigh them out accurately.

Only a few kilos had been ordered for the market the next day, thank goodness we thought. One regular client, an accomplished pianist, was aware of AC's interest in the instrument and offered to give her some lessons. Her first one was taken almost thirty years after her last one.

A few minutes after supper on the Sunday evening the telephone rang. It was Stephen who said, "There is a parsnip emergency I have another one hundred kilos on order". Oh shit I thought but set the alarm clock for an early morning call. We managed to lift, scrub bag and deliver them to him in Lagoa late on the Monday night. We thought that surely that this pace could not go on in the same manner, how wrong could we have been, with all of our other clients that had to be supplied, it did. By the time that I had dug the last parsnip up we had sold one tonne, a staggering one thousand kilos, had frozen fifteen in quarters, three as parsnip cakes and one large sack of shavings that could be added to stews to enhance their flavour. We had also scoffed them in our evening meals on a regular basis.

I was definitely not a happy chappy as half way through this hectic period the itchy red rash had reappeared and it was worse than ever. We had decided that it was some form of allergy connected with the parsnips but did not have a clue as to what. That was until one evening as AC was browsing through one of her many gardening books she found the article on parsnips very interesting. The book was "Kitchen Herbs and Spices" where it stated, "The plant contains a high quantity of chemicals, furocoumarins". The clever girl remembered the cutting she had taken out of a Weekend Telegraph. An outdoor article titled "Battle joined against the evil Russian giants" on the dangers of the water-loving giant hogweed, referred to its sap. This also contained furocoumarins which could cause severe rashes and blisters which drastically reduced the human skins resistance to sunburn.

It spelt out my problems to a "T" and was confirmed in a copy of a report received from Shelle a few weeks later. She was aware of my problem and had come across an article in a medical journal, which suggested that further research had shown that people who handled parsnip leaves, especially when exposed to the sun, could suffer from a skin reaction. Sunlight could cause phytophotodermatitis because some vegetables, parsnips amongst them, contained the furocoumarins compound. The report also stated that the affected skin could remain sensitive for several months and in extreme circumstances pose a real threat, as the skins ability to absorb sunburn was seriously reduced.

The income generated from the BBQ's we gave to the last of the years Poxy P G's foursome was sufficient to complete the purchase of the poolside furniture. We had hired a car, group Type E for them and they turned out to be very good sports. It was roomy enough to sit the two lads with us in the back together some furniture although it took two trips to Macro to ship it all back. Not only that but I was only allowed to be an onlooker as they quickly assembled the four recliners.

Our only television set since we had got together was the apology of a thing in the caravan, which had a small twisted wire aerial. Parked in a dip close to the shed the only picture we ever saw, whenever we bothered to switch it on was frizzy snow. Margaret intended to upgrade her set and when she gave us first refusal to buy the old one we jumped at the opportunity and bought it on the spot. We had aerial connections in the lounge and our bedroom and the latter had been fitted to enable us, if we did not feel like socialising with the Poxy P G's, to sit and watch the television in isolated splendour. Our new, to us, TV was connected up in the lounge and switched on with eager anticipation, only to see more frizzy snow. The electrician who had installed the wiring in the Quinta was requested to supply and fit an aerial and even after that it still needed a signal booster to be connected before we had a perfect results but bugger all was on to make it worth while watching. What a let down after all those years,

Shelle had some time ago received her Doctorate and she telephoned us to say that the Pharmaceutical Company with whom she was employed was to close its U.K. offices and laboratories and had offered her a big promotion if she went to work for them in America. She needed time to consider it especially in view of her next and more important news, which was that she was getting married and an invitation was in the post. We congratulated both of them and gulped when she told us the date as a twosome Poxy P G's had already booked for that time and had paid the deposit. The eldest daughter of Peter the surgeon and her boyfriend had also arranged their flights to be with us over the same period. I asked AC to speak with her and float the suggestion that they "Quinta and parsnip sat" and look after our guests at the same time. Despite the fact that the boyfriend despised parsnips, she readily agreed to the arrangements and thought it would make a somewhat novel holiday.

We immediately visited the travel agent and managed to buy return tickets to Birmingham and were lucky to be able to sit together on the outbound flight from Faro. I would only be able to stay for ten days but AC could take a three-week break. The poxy P G's arrived and the situation was explained to them over their first breakfast that halfway through their stay they would be left in the tender care of the two youngsters they had met the previous evening. They were quite happy to go along with this but seemed a little bemused at the idea. He was a professional scuba diver and she held a high-powered position in an Evesham bank. I had prepared a plan of the whole irrigation system that showed the locations of all the isolating valves and what pipes served which areas and on a walk about with the boyfriend pointed out the specific ones that needed attention. A keyboard had been made and fixed to the wall in the utility room and all the keys labelled and hung up on it, this was self-explanatory.

The wedding went extremely well, the sun shone and the reception meal was excellent. There were no awkward moments despite the various in-laws, out-laws and step-laws and the happy couple seemed to be devoted to each other. We stayed at the house of one of my brothers, which was a brilliant move. It enabled us to relax after the reception and before the evening rave up. As his wife did not drink there was no problem in selecting a chauffeur for the night. Shelle mentioned to me, during one bout of mad bopping on the dance floor, that she had been head hunted and received an exceptionally good offer, based in England, from another major international drug company so America was a no no as far as she was concerned.

We travelled around a lot as was usual, to visit as many family and friends as possible and AC agreed to leave her book fixes until after I had returned. Before then we called in at a bank in Evesham and spoke to the guest we had left in the hands of the two youngsters and were relieved to find that everything had gone very well and that we had not been missed at all. The time flew by so quickly and I soon found myself at the airport waiting to board my flight.

The cistern was home to dozens of frogs and there were times in the summer and early autumn that during the evenings their croaks reached a tumultuous pitch. It took quite a while, after my return, for me to realise that the tone was much more subdued. I needed a hoe and went to collect one from out of it and got quite a shock. There in the water just under my nose was a long snake with its jaws firmly fixed on a frog, only half of which was visible. It lay motionless but slowly and surely was gradually devouring the frog. I quickly grabbed the trusty spade from out of the shed and with one swift downwards thrust decapitated it. Then in calm fascination I witnessed its death throes and was surprised to see that the frog had miraculously survived. All of my wooden handled implements were kept in a corner of the cistern with the metal heads immersed in the water to keep the wood tightly expanded on them. The snake had obviously used the longest handle to slither down into the water, swallow its meal, and then slither out again.

It must have done so on a regular basis as the frog population had been seriously diminished, I was annoyed, as since I had fitted a removable mesh grill to the entrance to the irrigation outlet pipe the population had gradually increased. No dead frogs had been found since that time trapped and drowned at the isolating valves to the pipe laterals, from the main irrigation pipe, which effectively blocked them completely. That situation was not a case of a frog in my throat but a frog up me pipe.

AC returned to Portugal and had definitely benefited from her extended stay. I could have done with a longer break but it had not been possible. Jack rang to tell us that they had booked a ferry and as they had lots of things to bring over would tow his trailer. There would be some spare space so it was up to us to let him know if we wanted anything delivered. I measured up the log store opening as the bamboo curtains needed to be replaced with a tarpaulin sheet that I would suspend on hooks. AC then rang back and passed this information and also requested a punch and eyelet kit to go with it, some smellies from the "Body Shop" and a book that had only just been released but was not available when she was there. She also asked for some shallots and five litres of malt vinegar if there was sufficient room.

More land had to be prepared to meet the demands for the spring onions and to fit in with AC's crop rotation chart. The yield on two of the old asparagus seed beds was not enough to waste any time on them so I started to dig up the old crowns. Their roots were huge and had interlocked with adjacent ones and a session to remove only six was extremely hard work. It was again a question of slowly but surely.

A store in Portimao had opened a musical section and we were able to purchase a stereo digital "Midi" system, which included a turntable. We spent a little extra to obtain better quality speakers. Now, with a lot of rubbish still on the TV, we would be able to listen to our LP's, of which we had many that we had collected over the years and had not been played for ages.

AC arrived home in a bit of a tizz. She had made the two deliveries in Praia da Luz and the choir practice had gone very well but she had been stopped by the police on her way home. All of the car documents were in order but after they had compared the registration plate numbers with a list in their booklet they notified her of the last date that the Obligatory Inspection, an M.O.T had to be carried out.

The reason for her agitation was that she knew, as well as I did, that the old reliable fart box did not stand a cat in bloody hells chance of getting through and we did not have sufficient funds to buy a reasonably decent second hand one.

Chapter Nineteen

We were in the wrong business and location to be without wheels and therefore could not afford to scrap it immediately. The exhaust and alternator had only recently been repaired and in general it had been pretty cheap to run.

When we had been made redundant a "Deferred pension Certificate" was received and amongst other benefits it gave us an option to take early retirement with an immediate pension.

As the saying goes "every cloud has a silver lining" and this was mine. I applied for and was accepted as a retired ex-employee.

Asparagus sales were excellent, as were those of swede and early spring onions, and many orders had been received before the first commercial cut. This was as always after our initial "pig outs" and more recipe experimentations. As soon as word escaped that asparagus was available and on the market, there was a continuous stream of collectors, with cars, vans, all singing and dancing vehicles, pedal cyclists and motorbike enthusiasts momentarily parked at the top of the drive.

The peak periods were almost the same as the year before so it was necessary to cut three times a day again. I had made a graph of the daily cuts over the previous years and found when this current yield was superimposed over it, there had been a significant increase, but we managed to sell it all. AC requisitioned for a mobile phone. The nearest landline to the utility room was in our bedroom and it never stopped ringing when she was in full bundling mode there. It was even worse when she was in the bathroom.

Our five superstar salespersons, as they were called, performed better than ever throughout the season and we had serious problems, on occasions, to meet their requirements. We certainly did not have to over exert ourselves to suss out new clients as they did all of the donkeywork for us. AC's Friday deliveries now included another two restaurants near Burghau, for swede and spring onions, and the mini-market took thirty bunches on each delivery day. Stephen was ill for some time with jaundice so swede sales to the east of Lagoa took a bit of a knock. One market day we had an absolute mega sell out and got rid of thirty five kilos of asparagus as well as a lot of Swedes, spring onions, lettuce and pots of many different types of herbs. Three kilos of asparagus should have been delivered to a restaurant in the centre of the town but filled with adrenalin I had classified them as spares and sold them. The owner, an ex-professional footballer, rang at midday and asked where his order was as he had laid on a lunchtime party for some of his old teammates. I had boobed, and how, as I had thought that they only served meals in the evenings. I carried out a very quick cursory cut across the beds and broke all of my rigidly adhered to rules and AC speedily and efficiently bundled the spears. The order was delivered to the restaurant's doorstep just before twelve forty-five and as the owner was completely happy no apologies were offered.

After a weekend when some of my fingernails got broken and what were left clogged with grease and oil, I finally decided, with more than a tinge of regret, that the old fart box definitely had to go. I had stripped down the carburettor and sorted out the automatic choke that continually stuck in the half open position, fitted a new top radiator hose, repaired a leaky fuel line but had failed on the front sidelights. I thought that it was about time that we should drive a car in a reasonable condition, not in a knackered old banger. We had a chat with the car hire company through which we had booked cars for our Poxy P G's to see if they might have any for sale towards the end of their rental usage and were told that the chances were extremely remote. The search for a replacement proved difficult as the number of second hand car dealers between Lagos and Portimao could be easily counted on the fingers of one hand, there was only one.

Our garage man friend who had organised the borehole installation, we had not seen him in years, called in and told us that there was an amnesty for us to register the borehole. At the time they had not applied for the license to execute the works. At least he had had the decency to notify us as we were blissfully unaware of the problem. It meant a visit to the lawyer and more additional expense and was another typical example of sods law. As soon as our finances started to look on a better level, somewhat stabilised, the drains opened and the money quickly disappeared.

Our first Poxy P G's of the year had arrived, some months earlier, with their son. It was the couple who had collected the wrong hire car and were our very first repeat visitors. That evening, not long after I had lowered the blinds in the lounge there were noises on the terrace. By the time that I had got around to go outside and investigate, whatever or whoever had disappeared. The thought crossed my mind that we had had a return visit of the Prowler who had plagued Susie "Q" and her friend when we had holidayed in England.

To our knowledge he had not been around for yonks. The next evening after our guests had gone to bed I crouched down behind the pool south perimeter wall, dressed entirely in my all black gear, from head to toe in a dark top and trouser outfit whilst AC waited in the unlit front hall. She had almost given up hope when she saw, in the light thrown by an extension to the track lights, a slim tallish figure with a hat, jacket and trousers in a light coloured material stroll down the drive and then move into a position where he could lurk, as far as he was concerned, unnoticed in the east wing shrubs and trees. There he had a direct view to the twin-bedded room window, the curtains of which had fortunately been drawn too.

She switched the front door outside light on and off rapidly which disturbed the intruder who then raced across the upper pool terrace towards the gully. I only managed to see the shape of his outline and gave chase. It was to no avail and he sped off like a shot.

We believed that he called every night afterwards but totally ignored him and slept content in the knowledge that by doing so we had spoilt his little game of catch me if you can. Holidaymakers up the track, at "The dreadeds", had also had visitations on their first evening and most others and had coped very well. One lot almost garrotted him with an astutely thrown rope from the pool covers.

I had to speak with our lawyer about another matter and mentioned the problem to her. Consequentially we had a visit from the Police who were very sympathetic but could only recommend that we hit him hard over the head, drag him inside the Quinta, secure him and then telephone them. He must have had eyes in his backside and seen the police because he did not put in an appearance anywhere along the track for a long time after their visit.

AC's Friday deliveries beggared belief. It was the sheer volume of produce that we had to load into the car. Ten kilos of cherry tomatoes, twenty-five oak leaf lettuce, three kilos of yellow courgettes, two kilos of coloured peppers and one hundred and ten bunches of spring onions. Eighty of those were for the mini-market where the same amount had been delivered on the previous Tuesday and all had been sold. What had started out to be a simple delivery for Maureen's order had now developed into a much larger operation and only the asparagus sales in the season generated a more profitable income. The deliveries contributed much more to the coffers than most of the sales at the Saturday markets.

My sister telephoned to tell me that dad had decided to change his mind and would not visit us with mum, as had been previously arranged. I was not at all surprised as the cantankerous old bugger loved to throw a wobbler into the system at every opportunity. I told her to speak with Lucie and suggested that the mums came out together and left the silly old sod on his own, at home. A second call from her confirmed that the mums would travel without him.

Stephen's health had improved and he rang to see if we could provide him with some early parsnips. One of his best clients had arranged a typically English roast luncheon at their vast holiday complex and the principle chef had, for some unknown reason, decided that the early out of season parsnips would be lavishly presented in various dishes.

I had to soak a patch thoroughly in order to get the fork into the ground and even then to lift them up was difficult. The temperature was still in the upper twenties and the sun blazed down. I must have looked a strange sight dressed in a long sleeved shirt under a cagoule, rompers under bright baggy plastic trousers with vivid yellow gardening gloves and green Wellingtons. Sweat poured into my eyes after the first kilos had been placed in the wheelbarrow, so AC had to wrap a towel around my head to act as a makeshift sweatband. That must have made the vision even stranger to any casual passer by on the track. I had to continue and had never felt as uncomfortable as I perspired through every single pore and was thank full that the order was only for twenty-five kilos.

They were wheel barrowed up to the cistern where AC started to top and tail and then scrub them as I pulled off my gloves which were soaked and sweat poured out as it did when the Wellingtons were removed and turned upside down. My shirt, rompers, pants and socks all had to be hand wrung before they were spun dry and then pegged on the washing line. Every body hair was matted so a quick shower was essential. All of this had resulted after less than thirty minutes of labour.

Maybe it would have been easier to have suffered the rash. Over my third ice-cold beer I decided that there was no alternative as the rash was so painful. Even though the article had not indicated any long-term effects when suffered year after year I considered that it was prudent to play safe and not risk potential future problems.

The yellow tarpaulin sheet had been stuck in the shed ever since Jack had brought it out so I decided to put it to good use. It was laid out on the lawn and with the eyelet kit I made the reinforced holes and when it was hung up on the existing hooks it presented a far superior rain proof solution than the old bamboo curtains.

A reasonable exchange rate was obtained when the money for another car was imported and this tied us into a maximum price range. There was no hire car for sale so we had to dash around the limited number of car show rooms. In one of these was a sludge green Renault Clio. I did not mind the colour as we thought that the price was attractive and in line with that in a "used car guide" for this, so we had been told, two years old model. When I examined the documents it was found to be almost five years old and was surprised that the salesman got so shirty when we stormed out.

Another showroom, very small, was pointed out to us by DIY Dave. It was near to the bus station and we had driven past it hundreds of times without even noticing it. They had a racing red coloured Ford Fiesta car only fifteen months old. It was an ex hire car with only four thousand kilometres on the clock and the registration was 11.66.CD. After an extensive drive we put down a deposit and walked to the insurance companies offices, which were only around the corner. Fully comprehensive cover was expensive, the Cortina's was only third party but the refund from this helped to ease the burden.

Jack had agreed to meet us at the car graveyard at Espiche and AC was a little weepy as it really was the last link with father. I was upset as well because the old fart box had done us proud and had been an old and, most of the time, trusty friend. The engine still ran as sweetly as on the day it had left the factory, even after two hundred thousand miles. Bits and pieces had fallen off, some of them important and essential but they were always replaced. What had doomed it to a premature death was the introduction of the Obligatory Inspection. I had seriously considered at one stage of defying them to fail it but had known all along that it was a lost cause. The transfer of car ownership document, our section completed was given to the yard manager and I removed the Portuguese rear number plate, which meant that we had retained a small piece of a part of our lives. With a sad last look over our shoulders Jack drove us away and we thought that it looked so forlorn and lonely.

The final payment for the Fiesta was made and the transfer of ownership document completed. As we left the car showroom we noticed, in the window of the building opposite, a large sign that indicated that an Auction would be held in the afternoon. The doors were open so we entered and were given a list of the lot numbers and the conditions of sale. There were some nice things but, in our view, most of it was Tat. Two pieces caught our eye, a cabinet for the kitchen and a unit for our bedroom. We were still short of certain items, which was not surprising as we had started out from scratch. I had never visited an Auction and neither had AC so we decided to come back in the afternoon.

I proudly drove our new toy home and marvelled at the quietness of the engine. When we got back to the Quinta we found that Jack and Jill had tied pink balloons to the porch gate and there was a bottle of champagne and a card on the utility room doorstep to celebrate the cars arrival. I then quickly fixed the old Cortinas Portuguese number plate on one of the Quinta's walls inside the porch immediately under its original English registration plate. Unbeknown to me, AC had hidden in the porch a bottle of car shampoo together with a sponge and shammy leather and expected me to clean the damned thing on a regular basis. She had her first drive in it to the café in the village where, over a few beers, we decided that any car cleaning exercises had to be joint ones.

We returned to the Auction rooms. It had only just started and we found it quite amusing. The opening asking price for the lots that interested us started at double what we had in mind and nobody bid anyway so they were withdrawn, not a really auspicious start we thought. None of the big items seemed to attract any interest but awful Chinese vases and most of the Tat, when put up for offer, stimulated considerable excitement. In the end we finished up thoroughly disillusioned and left empty handed. The Auction was on for a period of one week but we never bothered to go back again.

The mums were collected on schedule and my mother had enjoyed the flight so much she wished that she had done it years ago. It was the old man that had kept her back. As it was her first visit we had to do all of the tourist trips, which she found exciting although it was a bit of a bore for the rest of us. Lots of work was done on various parts of the garden and by the time they left everything looked all neat and tidy, better than it had done in ages. The return journey to the airport was hellish as the rains pissed down all the way there. They were seen safely through to the departure lounge and we drove home in even heavier storms. It didn't stop all that day and night and in the morning the parsnip patch below the asparagus beds was like a large lake.

Heavy rains continued on and off for over a week and after they had abated, orders for parsnips came in floods, as was the state of that particular parcel of the land. This was in the main due to the ridge created in the early days when the land was ploughed and despite the numerous drainage channels that I had hacked out this area was particularly prone to becoming waterlogged. Over the years on every previous occasion I had had to soak the plot to remove them. This time I stood on planks, like duckboards, as they were slurped out of the ground. Most of them were a nice shape, well rounded, with a good colour and size but some had started to go rotten and ponged like hell. To make up the first market orders we had to lift twice the weight due to the wastage. I telephoned Stephen and told him the bad news and suggested that he pass this information on and warn his major clients. It was a huge struggle to supply all the orders and the season proved to be very short although it made a nice change to have weekends to ourselves. The local clients were very sympathetic as they fully appreciated our problems with the difficult wet weather conditions. Most of Stephen's clients were chefs, in large complexes, who spent all of their time in the kitchen and were totally oblivious to the weathers effect on deep-rooted crops. For some unknown reason Stephen failed to react quickly enough to my bad news and this created a great deal of agro between him and some of his bigger clients. They claimed that now they did not have time to find other local sources. I told him to tell them that that excuse was an utter load of bollocks because I was the sole supplier. Their only solution was to import them.

We had some excitement one evening, something that I could well have done without. The log-burning stove had been lit and we had finished supper in the kitchen and were just about to wash up when AC smelt something like burning rubber. We dashed into the lounge and found it full of smoke. I had left the stove door wide open, the chimney damper fully closed and the logs blazed away cheerily. Back in the kitchen I grabbed a damp towel, told AC to open the front door and returned to the lounge with it held to my face. I then managed to open the damper and close the door but badly burnt my hand in the process. With my eyes smarting badly I managed to slide open the lounge door and we both then stood outside the front door and gladly breathed in some fresh air. After less than five minutes there was a considerable draft of air through the lounge and the smoke had started to disperse. AC also with a towel to her face then helped me to take off the mantelpiece. This was achieved by simply removing a screw at each end. It had caught fire at the bottom so we carried it out onto the terrace and slung it into the pool. Luckily the smoke was not black or acrid so the three-piece suite material did not smell but it took two days with doors and windows wide open to remove all traces of the smoke.

My youngest brother telephoned to tell me that dad had been admitted to hospital with a chest infection and kidney failure. He sadly passed away six days later. He had had a good innings and survived many kicks in the teeth. A major one

256

was after he had signed on to join the army for six years in nineteen thirty-three and had then expected to return to Civvy Street. Ironically at a stroke, due to some German tosspot, six further years were then taken away from him. I had never got really close to him except during my last four years in England when he opened up quite a lot. He was a complicated individual and a bloody cantankerous but likeable old sod.

Convenient flights to Birmingham were a thing of the past as B.A. no longer operated on that route but flew daily into Gatwick, what a bloody pain. I eventually flew into Heathrow, Don had agreed to meet me and I would stay with him and Sandra.

The funeral went off okay as far as I was concerned though I had not attended many. The last had been with my brother Ray. His blonde girlfriend's brother, who had been an usher at my first wedding and three of his friends had been killed in an horrendous car accident after a dance at the Malvern Winter Gardens. They were on their home to Worcester and had crashed, at high speed, head first into an immoveable tree. Ray was lucky as he had been offered a lift in the car but had declined. We both listened to the eulogy at the crematorium and agreed together that the wrong body was in the coffin. Although dad had not been too well for many months I don't think that he ever got over the shock of mum coming on holiday to see us with him left at home on his own. His will was quite contentious so arrangements were put in hand to make mum the sole beneficiary.

A regular asparagus client told us that he had an almost brand new microwave for sale at a cheap price as they intended to sell up and return to the U.K. It did not take us too long to sort out the operating techniques despite the fact that the instructions were in Italian.

As we were early to bed people, too knackered to stay up and watch the late night films on the TV, we bought a Video Tape Recorder. After I had manually tuned it in to the respective channels I tried to insert a tape. I tried and tried as did AC but this simple operation was impossible to carry out. We were baffled and thought that we might have missed something very simple. I vividly remembered the embarrassment that I had felt in the U.K. when I had had to ring up a tyre company to remove a wheel from a car to have a tyre changed. I had exactly the same feelings as I walked back into the shop with the unit under my arm. The problem was explained to the person who had sold it to us and I could not miss the slight smirk that got broader and broader as he calmly listened to me with his arms folded together. He un-wrapped a tape and I was pleased to see that he had the same difficulty. No matter what he tried there was no way that he could he could get it to load. I had a very large smirk on my face as I left the shop with a more expensive model, at no extra cost, after a tape had been inserted, ejected and inserted again and then left in, another small bonus.

I had rotavated the land below the existing asparagus beds when it had dried out sufficiently. This area was extended down from the space occupied by the disastrous parsnip crop by some thirty metres. Many hours had been spent with my head stuck in various seed merchants catalogues and although a decision had been taken, due to circumstances beyond our control, not to increase the number of asparagus crowns, there was an article on one page that caused me to reconsider. I with tongue in cheek suggested to AC that we could utilise this space to plant some more asparagus crowns. After she had picked herself up off the floor we examined the recently prepared land and decided that there was more than enough room for four more beds and that this still left a large amount for crop rotation. The asparagus seeds selected were a F.1. Franklim hybrid variety. They were all male, light green in colour and an early cropper. The information contained in the catalogue inferred that it could be cut in the second year and that it was an ideal companion to Connover's Colossal. These points greatly influenced my decision even though the seeds were terribly expensive. We asked Lucie to order them and post on to us.

As we were self taught experts the dismal germination rate came as a complete shock to us so more seeds had to be ordered. There was only a marginal improvement with these but a quick tally up indicated that we just about had enough to fill the new beds. These were prepared based upon our vast previous experiences. The rows were double dug and the bottom layer refilled with a mixture of well-rotted farmyard manure and finely sifted soil. When the one year old crowns were eventually lifted to transplant them we found that the number of roots and their size were nowhere near as many or as large as those planted in the old beds. The whole process was therefore much easier and was completed in a far shorter period of time. That was a bonus but I was not happy with the quality and robustness of the crowns and doubted their productiveness.

What had concerned us, very much so, was that some of the original crowns might have to be replaced after the first few years. We had been told by some commercial growers in the Evesham district that crowns only had a useful life of between three to ten years and that some might even die off during this period. There was no indication, as far as we could see, that this was the situation in our case and with these new beds we had developed a fall back position should the necessity ever arise.

We had discovered that the name of the man who had introduced us to Dolores was Mario. He put the cat amongst the pigeons one day when he called in and asked for fifteen kilos of asparagus for another lady friend who sold in the Portimao market. His visit was a little premature, as we had not yet started to cut for our lunches and suppers. We promised to notify him when it came on "full stream" and he promised to collect on a regular basis.

Asparagus production peaked that year and six hundred kilos were sold and we did not starve either. The maximum cut in one day was twenty-two kilos and in one week one hundred and eighteen. All of this was achieved when, for the first time, there was competition in the central market from Spain. It was sold in smaller bundles and was therefore cheaper than ours. Some gullible clients, who did not notice this subtle difference, found the price more attractive. Despite this Dolores collected twelve kilos one evening and had sold out by the following lunchtime and telephoned us to collect ten more in the afternoon. Market days were more frenetic than ever and we had nearly always sold everything by ten thirty. On the very rare occasions when someone failed to collect, it only took less than another five minutes before the goods were snapped up. By now we had exchanged over a dozen different recipes with asparaguseurs.

An article on foreign growers in the market was published in the "Discover Lagos" magazine and, I quote "Portuguese farmers don't go in for: kiwis, avocados, asparagus, swede, parsnips, spring onions and organic vegetables. The Brits, as one can imagine, practically worship the swede and parsnip seller". Both of us considered that we had arrived, fame at last!!!

Sales of all of our vegetables, except parsnips, increased at a steady rate. We had worn and clapped ourselves out on that front. As I still had problems with the rash I was not that really too fussed with the downturn in their sales. The timber framed plastic covered greenhouse, which I had built from the materials that my mum had paid for, had really come into its own. The internal staging, around all of the sides and the floor area beneath it were continually filled with pots and trays of all the salad stuffs, many different herbs and everything was in the various stages of development ready to be planted out. Also everywhere we looked there was a patch of spring onions, one half cleared, another almost ready to be harvested and one only just germinated.

Although we had experienced at times, heavy periods of rain, in general the recent winters had been relatively dry. As a result the ground water table level had been lowered. The amount of water that we extracted from the well to maintain our crop production had gradually reduced the level to a depth too low for the pump to operate efficiently. The level was now back to the pre-wet winter period so I had to hump it down the tunnel and reconnect it to the original pipes exactly as it had been before the water levels had risen so drastically.

Somehow we managed to cope, although it was a tremendous struggle, with all the visits of Poxy P G's, family and friends. There were many occasions when we did not have the spare time to offer much tender loving care after the intense sessions of watering, harvesting and deliveries, but everyone seemed to have enjoyed their stay. By pure luck we avoided the embarrassment of having to entertain any obnoxious or difficult types of Poxy P G's and if this situation had ever arisen they would have been given a cheque for a full refund and promptly shown the front door and the key taken off them. Some were very boisterous and stayed up very late by our standards but we were able to escape, if we wanted to, into our bedroom and the TV set.

During some evening chats over a soothing drink, mostly a very stiff one, we discussed the pros and cons of living in and exploring the local countryside. Any idea of them hacking up into the nearby hillsides dressed in shorts and wearing open toed flip-flops was not recommended as there were wild boar and snakes in the vicinity. The snake situation did not appear to perturb anyone, except my mother who immediately when the topic was raised, left the room. I did not believe that no one, except me, had a deep-rooted phobia about them. In a detailed investigation however, it transpired that no one had actually come across a snake in real life. They had all seen them on the television or behind a glass panel in a zoo and they had never experienced an actual snake slither over their open topped sandals. The mere thought of that made them shudder.

The recently transplanted all male asparagus crowns had started to look decidedly sick, almost overnight, and had turned a yellowy brown rust colour. I thumbed through the gardening bible to the section on asparagus, which gave a clear description of the problem. It was "asparagus rust" caused by the first seasonal change in the weather, as we were now into the Autumnal season the fern would eventually fall from the branches and the main green stems die off. The only cure was to quickly cut everything down and burn it. This set back pissed me off no end, the bog standard Connover's Colossal, which had cost only peanuts, had never succumbed to this problem but this very expensive new variety had, in their first season. Perhaps their genetic development had created a more sensitive and less hardy robust specimen.

At the same time all of the other fern was cut down and burnt, even though it was a little earlier than I had planned. After the first winter rains new green gems appeared on the old beds and some were cut for our table and the others sold at an astronomical high price to selected asparasguseurs. This stupid action, we failed to realise then, was the cock-up of the century.

That particular year we achieved, by far, our most profitable income and boy, how we knew it. We had suffered both physically and mentally with all of the strains on top of the additional efforts involved with our visitors. The only way in which this could be increased was to employ someone and as this had never been our original intention we decided not to change our minds.

During the following years the seasons seemed to merge into one and became quite predictable. More clients and therefore more to produce, the same family and friends but fewer Poxy P G's. One year spring onion sales exceeded the income from the asparagus, despite the fact that I had fallen out with the local road-side stall owner. He, with his eye on the main chance as sales had continued to increase, wanted to pay me less per bunch and pocket the difference. AC was not surprised when I told him what to do but thought that I could have been a little more polite about it.

The all male asparagus crown production had certainly not lived up to its expectations. The flavour was good, the colour a lovely light green, but the spears were mostly sprue like and the yield could only be described a pathetic. It was, as an attempt to increase our asparagus production and subsequently our income, an absolute disaster. There had been others but none of them would have been too detrimental to our financial situation over the years.

Despite quite a few attempts we failed to produce any normal size firm and tight Brussels sprouts. Even though they were watered well, the hot dry summers seemed to inhibit the plant's capacity to produce tight sprouts in the autumn. Ours were small with the leaves always opened out and though they were very tasty, not really marketable. Both the winter celery and the self-blanching summer variety we found did not perform at all well. They were a dead loss really. We also had no luck whatsoever with transplanted rhubarb crowns. They were kept well watered, with copious amounts of manure applied but very few healthy stems developed so after four attempts we gave up. The spring winds that whistled down off the surrounding hills to the north of the track killed off newly transplanted healthy runner bean plants every year. When we grew them from seed the leaves still turned brown, shrivelled up and fell to the ground.

AC followed in my footsteps, applied for and was accepted as a retired ex employee and this certainly helped the old piggy bank. A decision was then taken not to advertise for any more, or encourage, Poxy P G's. If any requested a return visit then we would do our best to fit them in. Family and friends would of course, always be welcomed. I suggested to AC that we no longer tried to attempt to maintain such a ridiculous level of activity and gradually run the business down. She, I was extremely pleased to learn, was of exactly the same mind.

The cock-up of the century had weakened the crowns to an extent that although the yields remained reasonable they never ever approached that one years record total and production gradually reduced as they became older. Even when I delayed cutting the fern down until mid December every time the early rains came new spears were produced but they were never ever again cut to eat or to sell. Stiff competition developed in the market on some lines of vegetables from other local growers and some of our clients shopped elsewhere.

We had just finished another asparagus season with a better than average yield and had easily sold all that we had not eaten. During this it had been decided that the recent sowing of the spring onions would be our last commercial crop. It was not to be as of the six hundred grams of seeds sown, not one bloody onion appeared. Never had we had a crop failure as disastrous as that before. Was it a message from above I thought? Other things made me think that it was time to call it a day, our his and hers wheelbarrows were shafted, mine totally as the one handle had rusted through and had fallen off and AC's had holes in its base caused by over use and rust. It was just about useable but on a very iffy basis. The long term effects of the parsnip rash suffered in the early years meant that I now had to wear light weight surgical gloves just to thin out the seedlings and even peeling them in their preparation for cooking gave me problems.

I invariably made our early morning cup of coffee, which we always drank in bed as we put the world to rights, everything and everyone was out of step except "our Jack" we debated, sometimes quite seriously. AC occasionally did the honours and she had on one very notable day as after my first sip, I turned to her and said, "as of now I have retired". She asked me to put it down in writing and then decided it would be great idea if she did as well.

Her little red Horta book was chock a block full and even had many loose pages crammed into the back and the continually re-used watering charts had almost fallen apart. At one stage four foolscap sheets of these had been pinned to a cork notice board in the utility room.

We had worked our butts off over all of the years since our arrival so the concept of retirement was very difficult to adjust too. AC suggested that now was the time to be more positive and take Portuguese lessons from our young neighbour on the other side of track. I had no desire to return to any form, even informally of schooling. To spend my new found leisure hours that way was certainly not my idea of fun but she was obviously free to do as she wished. My theory was that in retirement you had the complete opportunity to pace yourself. One should be able to do, or not do, whatever you felt like as and when considered necessary.

On a short-term basis we would have to return the Quinta to a non-operational establishment and a start had already been made. The greenhouse had been deliberately reduced to a third of its original size and the compost producing capacity was now only half of that constructed and the cold frames had been removed.

Everything pointed to a change of emphasis; the question was what and where. Our sense of relief when we came to the decision, some years earlier, to write to the Institute in Lisboa with regard to a project/proposal was more than matched by our current feelings. The years of self-inflicted toil were over. It was now time for us to really start to enjoy our life here unhindered by the timetable restraints of wholesale vegetable production with the never ending watering and delivery schedules.

We both agreed how lovely it felt to be rid of all the *"toos"*.

Too discombobulated to give a toss.

Too shagged out to put any effort into solving any of our problems.

Too knackered to bother to have a shave.

Too bloody hot to even break into a muck sweat.

Too lackadaisical to do sod all.

Too tired to give a damn.

Too much to do and too tired and too bloody hot to do it.

Too clapped out to bother whether or not the spuds had chits placed up, down, sideways or if they had any at all.

There were many, many more.

One aspect of unwinding an operation, even a small one like ours, was to dispose of all the crap and garbage accumulated over the years. The one and only piece of agricultural equipment that we ever possessed was our "Work Horse". A still very sturdy but totally clapped out and knackered old Howard rotavator. It had been manufactured in nineteen sixty-six the year that the company had achieved the Queen's award to Industry and we had purchased it second hand here. My engineering instincts told me that if a machine or any piece of mechanical equipment worked efficiently, then leave well alone, don't tinker. A view not shared by many other people. Therefore not a lot of attention had been paid to it over the years other than an annual clean up and overall maintenance. The design had not included for the tasks I made it perform and it was continually overworked year in and year out. Three new sets of blades and cutters had been fitted and all had been worn out. The gearbox from the engine to the driving wheels had seized up and needed replacement parts for it to work again and I could not whip any enthusiasm so it was given away.

We both had lumps in our throats and felt very choked when it was loaded onto a truck and driven off up the drive. The couple who now have it purchased some land on the other side of the village, near Cotifo, land that we had looked at and decided not to make an offer for back in nineteen eighty-five. They intend to operate on a similar, but smaller, basis to the one that we had successfully carried out over the years and we have wished them the very best of luck.

All the rest of the rubbish has been disposed of over a period of time, one way or another. On a sentimental note we still have two of the original tea chests that were used to pack our personal effects and they are stored in the pool pump house.

Chapter Twenty

It is now just over twenty-five years since two weary travellers staggered out of the old fart box which had come to a halt in the exact position where the top of the driveway to the Quinta is now. I thought that now it might be a most opportune time to reflect on the events and changes that have occurred since then.

The old dirt track, once the highway for donkeys and carts, runs from the western edge of the village of Bensafrim through zones named, Hortinha, Azoia and Machada. Eventually it links up with the eastern side of Barao St Joao. The zones have remained peacefully rural and continue to be classified as a "Green belt Area". To our great relief all of the area has escaped the ever-expanding urbanisation sprawl which insidiously continues unabated in many of the surrounding localities. Now only one donkey and cart uses it, very infrequently, and a few western type stagecoach drivers cum farmers charge along on their tractors. The main users are the local residents in their modern motorcars.

Up until recently, one part time farmer's herd of cattle regularly ambled backwards and forwards from one grazing ground to another, alas no longer as they have all been sold since he took retirement from his position in the Lagos police force. That herd provided us with the never-ending deliveries of truck loads of fresh manure which we eagerly worked into our land. Along a distance of one and a half kilometres of the tracks length from the Estrada Nacional 120, the main road from Bensafrim to Lisboa there are only eight villas, two deserted old farm cottages and two small agricultural stores to the north side and two Quintas including ours, three villas and another deserted farmhouse to the south.

Some degree of progress has at long last caught up with us. A mains water distribution pipeline has recently been installed. As we have a borehole, which supplies water to the Quinta and a well which provides it for the land and garden irrigation, we remain as yet, unconnected. The track now proudly boasts an asphalted surface although somewhat narrow with only a three and a half metre width. Passing cars coming in the opposite direction at high speed is quite hair-raising and overtaking is certainly not recommended. These long awaited mega improvements have meant that it has now lost its appeal to cross-country safari vehicles heavily laden with tourists and the Sunday morning high-speed dirt track motorbikers. Neither of them has put in an appearance since the works were completed.

The main benefits to us and the other residents are that there are no longer the clouds of choking dust drifting over us with every passing car lorry or donkey cart in the summer months. Also we have lost the awful slimy layers of mud and the ever-recurring deep potholes, which always appeared as if by magic after the onset of the first winter rains. A major bonus for me is that the number of times that I have to vacuum the bottom of the swimming pool has been reduced considerably.

The "Track" has now been reconstructed to run under the viaduct of the newly opened extension to the Algarve East-West motorway, the A22, via Infant de Sagres, about three hundred metres to the east of our Quinta. One could argue that a motorway is the most drastic form of urbanisation, but we are extremely fortunate in that the Quinta was built in a shallow valley and we therefore cannot see the viaduct and track cross over point. On the very few occasions that we are made aware of any traffic noises is when the wind blows in from Spain. The prevailing wind is northwesterly and it helps considerably in minimising this potential nuisance. In the winter and in early spring this wind can be very cold and at those times we refer to it as the lazy wind as it blows right through you and not around you.

Access to the current end of the motorway junction at Bensafrim, someday it may be extended north to Sines with good connections to Lisboa, can be made in a little over two minutes and a journey time to the airport at Faro is only forty-five minutes with the use of a slightly heavy right foot. A day trip to Sevilla is not out of the question now as it is only a two and a half hours drive away.

The village population has more than doubled between the census years nineteen ninety and two thousand. The Junta de Freguesia, Council Office, is centrally situated and has and still is a blessing to us. It is possible to pay all of our utility bills at its hole in the wall, ATM machine and use it as a Poste Restante for our mail, buy postage stamps and it also still retains its public phone booth although we have not used this facility for many years. Of great importance to us was that it has been possible to obtain many of the attested documents that have had to be submitted to the various authorities over the years. These were in connection with resident's permits, driving licences and identity cards.

There is a primary school, now modernised and the facilities greatly extended, and a crèche. The health centre was originally only a small consultancy room and waiting corridor in the Junta de Freguesia. A purpose-designed building was opened in two thousand and three, which is very well appointed. A lady doctor attends three afternoons a week, Monday, Wednesday and Friday for general consultations and on Thursday mornings for pregnant mothers and small children. A qualified nurse also visits on these days and on some occasions I have had my blood pressure taken and wounds; small but in need of medical attention expertly dressed. These were all sustained from accidents or agricultural mishaps that occurred on the horta. To obtain a repeat prescription is simplicity itself. You specify your requirements to the doctor's secretary pay a nominal fee for a consultancy and she will deliver it to the pharmacy later on in the afternoon.

The small pharmacy was originally situated about two hundred metres away from the health centre on the EN 120. We now have a brand new much larger building, which is situated right next door to the health centre so things could not be more convenient.

Also within the village is a small library, the football pitch and sports club with a children's playground and a large area for family BBQ's and games, notably boules. The fresh fish and vegetable market, locally caught and mostly locally grown is always well supported. It boasts two very good restaurants with some bars/cafes, one of which is M's. To this day, although the language would not present me with a problem, I have never had the nerve to tell him what we called his bar that first time we had visited on holiday.

All things considered it's a very nice and engaging part of the Western Algarve to live in. It offers facilities that villages in many other countries still sadly lack and maybe always will. The community spirit is strong but very sensitive and, although residing on the outskirts, we have integrated exceedingly well and find ourselves embraced in the emotional bonding of it. We have never felt that anybody is in our back pockets and a distinct sense of privacy is encouraged and still prevails to this day.

Quite noticeable is that the children of this generation in the village are far taller than their parents and grandparents, some often being some twenty-five centimetres higher. This must be due to a different dietary factor and whether or not their life expectancy can equal their forebears remains to be seen. The average age of the village has reduced considerably, youngsters have married and grandchildren abound and lots of new young families have moved in as the village expands. Also, sad to say, many of the older generation who had lived to the ripe old age of eighty-five odd years or more, have since passed on.

The three popular Saints day celebrations in June, Santo Antonio on the twelfth, Santo Joao on the twenty-third and Santo Pedro on the twenty-eighth, for some unknown reason were not held in the village one year but thankfully have restarted. For as long as we can remember a street representing a particular Saint would endeavour to outdo the other two. All three hung up arches covered with intricate handmade decorative buntings made of brightly coloured paper to which were fixed hundreds of balloons and provided the evening's entertainment and food. There was always snails in abundance and many other titbits, drinks a plenty and live music for dancing. The evening culminated with fireworks and most of the rockets were lit in the hand before being released. There was one traditional game where small sheaves of straw and grass were set alight on the street floor and only males were invited to charge up and jump over them. It represented a miniature bonfire and followed an ancient pagan tradition with the revellers who succeeded believing that they had gained protection, from what I never discovered, for the rest of the year.

It was therefore possible to enjoy these festivities on three different days and was immensely popular with all of the villagers, young and old and was visited by many people from the surrounding districts. Sadly over the years the music has become more modern, loud and intrusive, totally dominating the whole event and as such diluting the old charm and the sense of personal involvement in the occasion. Progress maybe? Another sad example is that the hot dogs on sale at the large annual fair in Lagos are now cooked in microwaves rather than the traditional bread ovens.

The asparagus crowns now twenty-five years old, have been cut for twenty-one years and as anticipated now give a substantially reduced yield and during all that time not one single crown has died off. Having attained this ripe old age other major factors affect their annual production. They do not get the tender loving care lavished on them in the early years, no more watering every two weeks in the summer and the hoeing and hand weeding of the beds, up to three times during the winter months. They have not been irrigated for many years and have had to rely on natural rainfall to survive.

Survive they have, despite one of the hottest summers we can remember and the driest winter since our arrival. There was not a drop of rain one January, the first time that this had occurred in over one hundred years. From the Christmas holiday period until the end of February, over an incredible sixty-two consecutive day period, clear blue sunny skies resulted in higher than normal daytime temperatures followed by cold and heavy frosty nights. Being in a shallow valley the night time temperatures plummeted to three or four degrees Centigrade lower than that on the track. During this extremely cold spell a temperature of minus six degrees was recorded. One day as I drove into Lagos at nine thirty in the morning, with the sun visor folded down against the glare of a very bright sun, the temperature never rose above minus two degrees for the whole journey. The water in the cistern was almost frozen solid and all of the irrigation pipe work was. I threw two large beach balls into the swimming pool to avoid damage from expansion should the water freeze over and switched the re-circulating pump on early in the evenings to prevent any ice formation.

Everything green took a considerable and severe hammering. All of the new growth on the fruit trees was destroyed with even the old wood suffering badly. The leaves were left brittle, curled with a yellowish pallor and looked like very sorry anaemic potato crisps. Only time will tell if a full recovery can be made. Every section of the mature hedging was also badly taken by the frost with lots of the foliage turning brown and looking distinctly sick.

That year the Almond blossom, we never discovered why some of it was pink and the other white, arrived late but was very heavy and the prettiest that we had ever seen. The blossom remained on the branches for a considerable time as there were no blustering winds or torrential downpours to wreck their normal damage and the profusion of wild flowers was conspicuous by their absence. I had never had to water fruit trees and hedges before but it had to be done then in January and February and the ground soaked up the water like blotting paper.

The water level in the well at that a stage was seven and a half metres below the wellhead. This did not compare favourably with the average winter level of around six. Only twice before had it been lower and that was after lengthy periods of irrigation during our peak vegetable production years and the continuous weekly filling up of the pool in the summer. On those occasions the winter rains had been more than sufficient to top up the deficit. But now this was no longer the case, in the December of the year that we had retired the level was as expected, around six metres below the wellhead. Since that time we had drawn out basically no water at all, any small amounts for our kitchen vegetable gardens had been pumped from the borehole. At the last level check I found, much to my surprise and dismay, that it has dropped to its lowest level ever, a staggering eight metres and thirty centimetres below the wellhead and this was after the winter rainfalls that were considered to be well above the average. On that basis I asked myself, why oh why does the expanding urbanisation continue unabated on a hyperbolic curve basis and the proliferation of golf courses allowed to continue on relentlessly?

If these circumstances are as a result of the somewhat argumentative global warming scenario then it bodes terribly ill for the future. It is my strong unwanted belief that mankind, civilisation, call it what you will, is hell-bent on the pathway to self-destruction and obliteration. Our planet Earth will survive, it may well suffer some catastrophic ecological upheaval but it will still be rotating around the sun in the forthcoming millennium. As to the survival prospects for the human race I think that the Portuguese expression "Vamos Ver", let us see, sums it up very succinctly.

I no longer have to carry out the daily red and black asparagus beetle patrol killing them between finger and thumb. It was a messy but effective process when there were only a few of them even though a sharp knife had to be continually used to scrape off the gunge that built up to enable the eradication process to proceed efficiently. As a last resort, when there was a bad infestation I always reverted to the backpack sprayer. Nearly half a litre of the chemical used to kill them off is left but I would hate to hazard a guess at its potency now as the best before date must have expired years ago and I cannot decipher it on the label.

The weekly removal of all the red ripe seed berries was an important exercise but is no longer conducted. Any resulting seedlings discovered are now pulled out during the asparagus-harvesting season. It has turned out to be quite fortunate that despite the large percentage of female plants, and thence a high proportion of berries and potential seedlings, the number of crowns where production of good sturdy spears has been diminished through plants growing on top of them only numbers around twelve.

Neither do I have to play my "Con artist" role any more. In the very early days when clients asked to visit us and see for themselves the asparagus growing and how I cut the spears to make up their bundles I always used, with a flourish, a long bladed asparagus knife with a serrated edge. This type of knife could cut the spears ten centimetres beneath the normal surface of the soil and was essential when cutting from ridged beds. As ours were flat ones, a bog standard sharp kitchen knife cutting only one centimetre below the surface of the soil was more than adequate and was always used when there was not an audience.

My exaggerated performances certainly seemed to meet with enthusiastic grunts and nods of approval and appeared to be very impressive. Good old fashioned bull-shit and waffle was the order of the day and accepted by all. No one ever left disappointed as they had never seen a performance like it in their lives before. The long handled knife was also prominently displayed on the stall in the market to deliberately promote a topic of conversation and also to embellish the hoax. At most of those times it was difficult to keep a wry smile off my face.

Unlike in England, where the asparagus fern is cut down in the autumn, new spears appearing only in the spring, which gave each crown a substantial dormant period, here in the Algarve, new spears quickly turned to fern appeared after the early rains in September as the soil temperature was still very warm. All of this together with the existing fern had to be cut down, removed well away from the main beds and then burnt during late December. Sometimes in late January and certainly by mid February a new crop of spears gradually emerged. These crowns therefore had only a little or non-existent period of rest to build up their strength and reserves. To have survived all of these years must be considered a minor miracle.

The fern was cut down for fourteen years using a pair of heavy-duty hand shears. It was, as one would expect, laborious and very time consuming, also the most intensely physical operation of the whole year. Three beds were the maximum that could be tackled in any one day. How I did not develop the largest ever biceps and associated chest muscles remains a mystery. Other methods were tried including an electric hedge cutter and a bladed motorised strimmer, both proved unsuccessful. One year we even tried to burn the dead fern on the actual beds, a kind of scorched earth policy, but yet again to no avail.

It is only nine years since I became the proud owner of a motorised bike handled brush cutter suitable for a nylon line cutting head or metal cutting tools. We bought this after several discussions with power tool manufacturer's agents and witnessed field tests. This purchase has made my life so much easier as the whole of the asparagus fern can be now be cut down in less than half a day. It's a pleasurable exercise compared to the exhausting hand shearing times. Now after cutting it down, the fern is roughly gathered into several small heaps and then burnt in-situ, on the beds themselves, thus saving the need for a full-scale clearance exercise. Little or no detrimental effects to the dormant crowns has, as yet been detected.

For us the difficult seasons of harvesting and selling the asparagus are over. The next few years yield is already sold, as and when, or even if, it is eventually cut.

Asparaguseurs still telephone us a few weeks before the season actually starts and remain loyal addicts. To this day, when making a booking at one of the restaurants that remained one of our biggest clients over the years, the tabletop reservation card is still hand written for "The Algarve Asparagus Man plus One".

Despite having to stoop and bend over more than three hundred thousand times, and at each one cut an asparagus spear from which the beds have now yielded nearly five thousand kilos, my hips appear to have stood up to the strain remarkably well. AC however suffers somewhat with her neck and shoulders, due to the washing, sorting and cutting all of those spears to an equal length and then making them up by tying them into half-kilo bundles. Up to a couple of years ago all the bundles were tied using raffia, the classical English method, Now with the very small yield we use elastic rubber bands, the same size as we used to use for the spring onions. Her problem was also exacerbated by the number of these that she had bunched, well over fifteen thousand of them. I hate to think of how many twenty-five gramme packets of "elasticos" we purchased, always from the same newsagent along the way.

I find that the rubber bands are much easier to get on with, AC, who still remains head of quality control, prefers the raffia. There were many occasions when some of the asparagus off cuts she threw into the compost bins were in my opinion readily saleable or definitely more than suitable for excellent home made asparagus soup.

Who would believe that from an initial investment in one two hundred gramme packet of asparagus seeds, ignoring the manpower and the time and effort expended, that the income return would be in the order of many thousand per cent!!!!. This was true of all our produce and surprisingly spring onions, overall, gave the best return by far.

With asparagus now being available here all year round, imported from South America in the winter and from Spain in the spring, selling at cheap prices, how much the producer gets paid beggars belief. That is the unfortunate problem facing farmers the world over as competition and demand increases. Since my first sighting in the small vegetable shop in Lagos of asparagus imported from Israel, to this day we have never ever seen any more, not one single bundle. We consider that now is the time to call it a day. Our policy was always to charge all clients the same price, no discount for bulk was ever offered. What the mark up the marketers and supermarkets added was of no concern to us. Only once did we have to resort to selling to a wholesaler who only offered us half price. It was no sweat really as it only involved ten kilos. They telephoned us many times afterwards for a lot more, offering a slightly increased price but we were happy to tell them that we did not have any spare, basically piss off.

My favourite cuts were the ones after the seven or eight week main harvesting period. Then with the fern at armpit level, and from the more robust crowns at my head height, I then walked the beds and cut a selected choice of green gems. From these we were able to enjoy a secondary gastronomic pig out where we devoured, sometimes up to two kilos a day, going through our full range of recipes. At those moments we were able to really appreciate the expressions "Chefs Perks", or in our case "Gardeners Perks" and "living off the fat of the land". The least enjoyable cuts were the two cleansing cuts when all of the beds had to be cleared of the small spears that had been left over from the previous three weeks harvesting.

In the Project, I had put forward all those years ago, I had outlined the possibility of sales to Lisboa and potential exports in a very small way. Despite AC's misgivings at that time, we actually did just that! Many Portuguese who lived and worked in Lisboa had families in this part of the Algarve and often came down on holiday over the Easter weekend. Lots of them were grateful to be able to take a couple of bundles back home. Tourists from all over Europe were also pleased at the opportunity to return from holiday with a special treat. One kilo was actually taken to South Africa and several to Vancouver in western Canada.

Since my retirement over the past few years I have acted as an unpaid consultant to five clients who wished to grow asparagus. Four are growing it not on a commercial basis only for domestic consumption. The other however is a chef, with a plot of land not that far from ours and owns a restaurant in the village, so one day asparagus may well appear on his menu as long as he continues to follow my advice.

How truly thankful we have been during all the past years, that our over ambitious target of growing one acre of asparagus failed dismally. It would have been impossible for us to cope with that size of crop on our own. The production would have been sufficient to flood the whole of the Algarve and shipping up to Lisboa would have been essential. The daily, weekly and annual peaks that we had cut from our few beds would have to have been multiplied by a factor five. I still mentally struggle to grasp the fact that it would have meant cutting up to one hundred kilos, two hundred bundles daily. As soon as I had finished one cut I would have had to immediately begin again, seven days a week for up to eight weeks. A mind-boggling thought! Production on that scale would have probably put us in direct competition with the professional growers in southern Spain and there was not any possibility of us exporting our asparagus there. We knew that outlet was unavailable, as when we had travelled back on the road to Sevilla from Cordoba and Granada, after a short holiday in the November ten years ago, we had seen hectare after hectare of asparagus fern growing on either side of the roadway.

Even if we had grasped the opportunity and had opened a "come and cut your own" business there would not have been a sufficient number of clients and who would want people traipsing over the beds probably ruining more than they cut. Certainly not us! At the back of my mind I recollected that one asparagus farm in Shropshire had done just that in the mid nineteen eighties but had no idea how successful the venture had been.

My father was, however, correct in his statement that an acre of asparagus would produce an extremely healthy annual income. Provided it could be harvested and sold directly to clients it gave a very substantial positive cash flow. We proved the point by simply multiplying our annual asparagus sales figures by five. The price charged for a half-kilo bundle is now five Euros. This is exactly double that of the first bundle I sold. This represents an increase of just below seven per cent per annum.

Our luck was in again, as it turned out, not to have installed an overhead sprinkler irrigation system in the asparagus beds. The optimum height of the sprinkler head to achieve the most effective water coverage would be just over one metre above ground. As the ferns grew a lot higher than this they would prevent efficient water distribution and have to be cut down to the head level or more preferably, even slighter lower. I did not have a cordless hedge cutter in those days and even if I had, the battle to manoeuvre through a dense mass of foliage without causing considerable damage would have been well-nigh impossible. Also the effect of cutting off the tops of the growing fern was probably not worth taking the risk as it would have surely weakened the crowns.

Our old cork oak trees, in the early days we had christened some of them Ents, have now had their second haircut since we owned them. The bark was removed and stockpiled for the drying out period and during this time it's bulk density reduced by about half, as it did after the first cut, prior to being weighed.

The "weigh in" was to be carried out early one Sunday morning, the third week in September. What a performance it turned out to be. The Cork Baron arrived around seven thirty, on his own. He did not knock on the front door or ring the bell so had to wait some ninety minutes before I put in an appearance at the weighing location. He had erected a tripod of three quite slender green saplings and attached a scale balance at its apex. The structure was certainly not as robust as the one that had been knocked up at the last weigh in, some eleven years ago, and I thought that it was quite flimsy and not up to the task. It took us both, with every arm and thigh muscle strained to the limit to lift the very heavy crib/ basket and hook it onto the scale. Measuring two metres long and one wide, of open grilled construction made from wrought iron it had seen many years service.

The saplings sagged as he calibrated the balance to zero and sagged even more noticeably after only a few pieces of cork had been placed on the crib. After only a few minutes it settled on the ground so it was necessary to offload all of the cork and readjust the tripod to give us a bigger ground clearance. The process of loading the cork was then repeated but yet again the crib grounded. After much grunting and cursing the tripod was reset to enable us to make a third attempt. This effort proved calamitous as one of the saplings snapped just below the scale connection and doomed the whole exercise. No metal poles were available so more robust supports were promised for the next day.

As in the previous "weigh in" the price per unit measure, "the arroba" approximately fifteen kilos had been previously agreed. In an attempt to save some time and more aggravation I asked the Baron to estimate how many units there were. He quickly came up with a figure, which was double my guess. I nodded agreement and after a quick handshake a cheque was written out in my favour on the spot. Walking back to the Quinta I felt really pleased with myself at this deal but over a late breakfast of a couple of poached eggs on toast laced with brown sauce and a coffee sat on the upper terrace, a sinking feeling came over me. Surely I could not have been "souked" again, like all those years ago in the Middle East?

There is an old adage that being in the right place at the right time with the right product then success is guaranteed. This was perfectly true in our case. We introduced a new range of vegetables into the Western Algarve specifically targeted at northern Europeans, both residents and tourists. As far as I was concerned when we had transplanted our first asparagus crowns and produced a commercially viable crop grown from seed then the snowball effect had begun. We were certainly the only growers of parsnips and swedes and even to this day no one produces, as we did, the true "white Lisbon" spring onions. Lolla Rossa and Oak leaf coloured lettuce, yellow courgettes, coloured peppers, other than green and red and cherry tomatoes we made available as well as many different types of herbs, sold in pots or bunches. Now it's old hat with imports that are readily available and many local growers now produce an equivalent range. Had we realised in the early days how physical the work was going to be we may well have had second thoughts on vegetable production. In our three way financial strategy, income from the sale of the vegetables was to have been the icing on the cake, however it turned out to be what paid for the margarine on the bread and on the good days the cheese or ham in the sandwich. We would have never survived on the pathetic income from the Poxy PG's.

Those that did holiday with us all raved about the accommodation and the hospitality and the visitors book was crammed full with glowing comments, some almost poetical. Here is one slightly modified example:

"Ode to Quinta da Hortinha"
One fine summer's day, we jetted away,
For a week in the Algarve with sun,
Where a warm and friendly welcome from AC and DC,
Set the scene for a time of great fun!

There was Richard and Joan and Rachel and Jim,
From the midlands in the heart of the U.K.,
We had never before set foot in the door,
Where the sun gets hotter each day.

So out came the cream and the novels of steam,
And the shorts that Richard ne'er wore,
Because up in the north where the sun rarely shines,
Such rarities live in a drawer.

At the start of our time we got used to the clime,
By touring the two nearest towns,
In Bensa and Lagos we found cafés fine,
And delights that blew off our frown.

With Bucks Fizz for breakfast in honour of Jim,
Whose birthday was really our aim,
A BBQ followed with mackerel and pork,
Which DC prepared on the flame.

The breakfast at "Collini" were quite a delight,
And will linger a while in the mind,
"Relax" was the watchword our hosts did advise,
We're not keen to return to the grind.

We leave this epistle for all who stop by,
At the Quinta of Aileen and David,
To say quite sincerely we've had a great time,
And a return is all that we crave.

Here is another one.

We're back for our fourth year

and the sun is shining down.
We love to lie out in the heat
And wander round the lawn.
Some of us we like to weed
And some of us play ball.
Some of us just sit around about
and simply do sod all.
The sun is hot the food is good
the pool is always clear.
We're always welcomed with a smile
that's why we love it here.
Now it's time to go back home
I'm sure we'll come again.
So we can buy another frog
and of course another hen!
It's been a lovely holiday
with happy memories too.
So to our hosts we give our thanks
with love from us to you.

There were many more and all threatened to return next year, a very few did, most did not.

The garden shed, our first project, built at the side of the existing cistern has recently been re-roofed for the third time and is now fully waterproof. It had leaked on and off for many years and had become past a joke. A new door, in black aluminium and the same style as the one in the pool pump house, has been fitted to replace the original framed and braced timber one which was falling to pieces. As well as housing our chest freezer it stores all the usual garden implements, lawn mowers, one, petrol driven and the other electric, the brush cutter, cordless hedge cutter, DIY tools and tackle with numerous half empty paint tins which sooner or later may be of some use. The garden fork, brought over by Don and Sandra from England on their first visit definitely shows signs of its age. With all of the wear and tear the tines are now at least eight centimetres shorter than when new.

Almost all of the many annually prepared lists of projects and other things in my small "Smiley" note book have at long last been completed and crossed off. The two thousand and four year list of them superseded all of the others. No more are planned as I have at long last run out of steam. One or two remain uncompleted and will probably stay that way, such as the rendering of the inside of the garden shed walls, the installation of a power supply to the entrance portals in the drive for lights and the electronically operated front gates. Half-heartedly I had at one time added to it the construction of one multi combination bread and Tandoori oven, a pit and rotating spit for a whole lamb roast but these two still remain in my wildest dreams.

The last major project to be crossed off the list was the East wing carport. The two support columns were halfway built up on "Nine Eleven" and immediately became known as the Quinta's Twin Towers. When I saw on the television the pictures of the mangled wreckage that remained in New York my stomach churned over violently as I dramatically remembered looking down at a similar scene of destruction in a pit at a site near Basingstoke.

On the list every year, was not a project but an essential and not very pleasant task. Since the construction of the Quinta had been completed, despite the addition of a liquid anti-fungus concentration to the paint for the internal walls, we still had problems with outbreaks of mould up on the highest parts of some of them, just below the ceiling level. This was and still is common to most of the older buildings and occurs as a result of the very high humidity during the months of winter. An effective way of removal, although throat choking and eye watering was to treat the contaminated areas with a five to fifteen per cent chlorine solution, bleach. This exercise sometimes had to be carried out on two or even three occasions during the winter.

Modern building methods combined with built in air conditioning units counteracts the problem. Another method is to use portable dehumidifiers. Both systems are quite expensive to operative and rely on a high level of energy consumption. Three years ago I experimented and bought several coloured ornamental glass vases, which I filled to the brim with bog standard dishwasher salt and strategically placed them in all of the rooms, the lounge being an exception. What an unqualified success it has turned out to be. Minimal outbreaks of fungicidal patches have occurred, in some rooms none at all. For us it's a very economical and decorative solution to the problem, only necessitating one change of salt between winter and spring.

Lots of the fruit trees in the small orchard have been allowed to die off, only four lemons, four grapefruit and eight oranges remain. There is one apricot left but it has not fruited for the past two years and will probably be hacked down next year.

My tolerance level to snakes has improved dramatically. I am still a little nervous, but for the first time ever I have been able to walk around in open sandals when watering the various parcels of land and the orchard, as opposed to Wellingtons. Even in green ones that have been available for many years now. At all times I am very careful where I place my feet and my eyes are continuously fixed ahead. I categorised snakes on my sightings, the first time I classed them as just visitors, the second time as holidaymakers and on the third as residents so they then had to be got rid of. It was a totally irrational logic as they could be of the same species but be different snakes. In any event it made me feel a lot better about them.

The area now used for domestic vegetables is approximately the same size as that of the two allotments we tended some twenty years ago and over the years the earthworm population has, from zero, reached very healthy proportions, maybe as a result of the constant addition to the soil of rich farmyard manure. Again any surplus produce is given away, what a turnaround! How pretentious we are, the plot of land where the majority of spring onions were grown, is just strimmed in the winter and ignored in the summer, and referred to as our West Wing paddock. Harvested vegetables are all washed in the water from the cistern, as they have been since the first ones were lifted from the soil. The dirty water from this exercise was always poured over the roots of the Wisteria. The hundreds of bucketfuls all through the long hot summer would explain its phenomenal growth. The top of the cisterns re-built wall, by the garden shed, is the main cleaning and washing zone. We have still never used any of the three washing slab facilities built into the one cistern wall although some of our clothes have been washed in cold water at times, during our caravan days.

We regularly sit on our south facing terrace, overlooking the swimming pool, sipping freshly made orange juice or eating half a grapefruit from our trees, with the escarpment on the horizon basically unchanged since our arrival. At all of these times our contentment knows no bounds. It's matched only by a sense of pride in our achievements. All in all we experience a deep feeling of being distinctly chuffed with everything. During these periods of relaxation we are constantly aware of the fact that we are so privileged, really, really privileged to be able to share moments with the often heard fluty whistle of the male Golden Oriole. We have only ever seen one twice close to, as they normally haunt the upper branches of the trees in the cork oak and eucalyptus wood.

In the springtime we are accompanied by the Bee Eaters with their liquid calls as they swoop in the air above us and glide with outstretched pointed wings. Their brilliant colours are best seen when they are perched on the nearby telephone lines, sometimes ten or more in numbers. Hoopoes, Azure Winged Magpies and Ring Necked Doves all settle within twenty metres of the terrace. One very friendly little chappy obviously a bit thick in the head, with the unmistakeable brilliant colouring and shape of the Kingfisher, visits frequently and cheekily stands motionless, always looking for food that is never there, on the coping stones at one end of the pool giving a trilling whistle. It only flies off if we make a sudden movement or if our cat puts in an appearance. Most days we are able to watch little "Olley" Owl, awake in the day time with its head bobbing up and down as it sits on top of one wall of the old ruin.

Often high above us in a soaring circular flight we are able to see a pair of mating Bonelli's Eagles making their typical whistling kluee calls. We believe, but cannot be sure, that they are the same ones who have returned over many years. When they are not in the air, they can often be sighted on top of adjacent telephone poles below our orange trees, using them as look out posts before flying off with slow wing beats after their prey. One day we were fortunate enough to witness a kill. The male had swooped down to the ground at a terrific speed, below the asparagus beds, and had seized a large rabbit. We were then fascinated and a little unnerved as we watched it, with its talons firmly gripping the carcass tear it apart with its strong beak and proceed to devour most of it.

Many pairs of Red Rumped, Tailed Swallows had attempted to build their nests, with the tube shaped entrance, under the roof of the upper terrace but were always driven away as we had seen the crappy mess they produced on many houses in the village. On many occasions storks with wings motionless, long necks outstretched glided noiselessly past us high in the sky.

I had read in one of my many bird books, in the section on exotic birds that the Bee Eaters nests could be up to three metres deep in a bank. Some years ago in the middle of winter my inquisitiveness got the better of me. I cut a length of bamboo from one of the thickets and inserted it into one of a colony of nest holes in the roadside bank along the track, about three hundred metres from the Quinta. I shone a torch into the hole and saw that it was an unlined tunnelled nest chamber and been excavated horizontally. The bamboo pole was then inserted very carefully and the depth found to be almost two metres.

In the following spring I toyed with the idea of using the same pole with masticated chewing gum attached to its end and try to remove one of the newly laid eggs but decided against it, much to AC's relief.

This would have been the same principle that I had used as a young teenager to extract an egg from a Long Tailed Tits nest with the use of a drinking straw that had moist gum fixed to it. That same year together with a friend, on a visit to a large lake in a park east of Worcester we found an old dilapidated punt stuck in the reed beds. It did not take us long to patch up the small holes in the bottom with leaves and mud to make it, after a fashion, sailable. With the use of bulrushes as makeshift paddles we eventually made it, in tacking style, to the island in the centre There we discovered a birds egg collectors paradise as we circled around it and saw so many different types of nests. They included Little Grebe, Canada Geese, Teal, Mallard, Moorhen and many others. In the shore line on the other side from where we had set off there was a grey Herons nest. Eggs, of all breeds, were put on the floor of the punt except that of the Heron, which was the last nest we visited, as only two had been laid.

We had concentrated so hard on keeping the punt afloat that we had not noticed the gamekeeper who was standing on the lakeside with a twelve bore shotgun cradled in his arms. Looking up he seemed like a giant as he gave us a really stern look and, without any mincing of words, a severe bollocking. We were quite frightened at this verbal outburst and this must have been clearly seen on our faces. He finished off and told us to put all of the eggs back in the nests and bugger off home straight away afterwards and then nothing more would be said about the matter, much to our relief. I knew all the egg sizes and markings but as I felt quite dazed by the incident and in my rush to get away, they were not all put back into their respective nests or even in the correct quantities. Safely back at home I suddenly realised that the parent birds would have mega surprises when the eggs hatched out.

With the beautifully coloured Dragon and Damselle flies hovering over the pool surface, it is still possible to swim with them, their wings beating rhythmically, only a few centimetres above our heads in the latter part of the evenings. They are the present day descendant of one of the most ancient insect larvae. An aerial hunter with great agility as they can speed across the pool at up to fifty kilometres an hour yet hover apparently motionless except for their wing movements.

With all of the Quinta's lights switched off, and with only the limited lighting along the track, it is possible to lie on one's back on a lilo in the pool and gaze in wonderment at the brilliantly clear evening skies. The various constellations and the Milky Way can be seen in all their majestic glories night after night. The clarity of the air here in the Algarve always amazes us.

Another important bonus is that now that the surrounding gardens are mature, if one has the inclination, there are innumerable opportunities to skinny dip in the pool with complete privacy. My preferred and favourite time is just before the Sunday lunchtimes, as I wait for AC to return from church, after having spent most of the morning as the resident pool attendant, cleaning, vacuuming as necessary, checking the water analyses and tidying up the terraces. As I slowly swam my statutory twelve lengths in a very languid breast cum crawl stroke style I could readily soak up the peaceful and tranquil paradise that surrounded me. It really was our Garden of Eden.

There has been an extra bonus for me this last year. My favourite spring wildflower, it grows in abundance all over our land, has at last been identified after searching through almost every book of field guides on the flowers of South West Europe. It is the Linaria Algarvian Toadflax. As it sways gently in the spring breezes on slender stems about twenty centimetres high it shows from one to eight flowers on each stem. The stigma is deeply two lobed, almost Snap Dragon shaped with a colouring of deep violet, spotted with white or yellow on the throat boss and complete with a spur up to twelve millimetres in length.

We have been surprisingly fortunate in our venture and have lost count of the number of times when on many occasions circumstances arose, the outcome from which, more by luck than divine or other judgement, has always turned out to be beneficial to us. The one classical case was when we were sitting outside a café in Lagos having a coffee doing the tourist bit, the first and only visit to that particular one when I eavesdropped on some English residents who were talking about the unavailability of good quality asparagus. The discussions that followed went a long way to ensure our success, as did those with Dolores in the central covered market in Lagos.

Thank goodness my attempts to host asparagus luncheons failed. It seemed like a brilliant idea at the time to offload some of the surplus bundles and make an exceptionally good profit. The starter was not a problem but to cook, with over ten people eagerly awaiting their main course, some five kilos of the stuff on a relatively small gas hob with new potatoes having to be cooked at the same time certainly would have been. The small grill would have also given us a headache in coping with the amount of gammon steaks. We had a small domestic kitchen layout, not a full-scale restaurant one.

During one extremely harsh winter we were rudely reminded of the advice we were given from a German who ran a bar in Lagos. He told us, when we were on a holiday during the early nineteen eighties, that it was essential to install some form of heating when building a Quinta as he had found that the only warm place in his was when he had a soak in the bath. We were lucky to be given this advice and the log-burning stove in the lounge continues to make our lives comfortable. Thank goodness AC suggested relocating its position when we poured over the original plans. It has always performed very well and in one particular extremely cold winter ate up a considerable amount of fuel, nearly seven cubic metres of medium to large logs over a five-month period. This was more than double the normal annual consumption. The logs are still protected from the prevailing northwesterly winds and rains by the yellow tarpaulin sheet.

We still order from the same "log man" and last year was the first time that the price per cubic metre had increased since his initial delivery. I believe however, that the actual annual volume had been gradually reduced to compensate for the fixed price but even so we still had a good deal.

Recently Air-Conditioning units have been installed in the three bedrooms and the lounge. What a difference that has made to our and our visitors comfort. Although it is early days it appears that the cost of the increased energy consumption is compensated by the savings on the quantity of logs that have been used. Only on seriously cold or during very dismal weather conditions was a fire lit in the log-burning stove.

I intend to purchase another chain saw as the eucalyptus trees in the cork oak wood have re-grown to a height of over ten metres and several have died. Rather than repeat the agreement with the "log man" all those years ago, I will convert the dead ones into logs for the fire and attempt to source a buyer for all of the others. From previous experience and now with fewer fires during the winter months I estimate that we should accumulate sufficient logs to last us for around a further six years. As an alternative solution I can fell all of the trees and cut them into logs for the log burning stove. The green ones can be stored under cover to dry out over the initial six-year period and may give us a further ten years supply of fuel. This indicates to me that the price of renewable energy is really well worth consideration on an international level. Oil, Natural gas, Coal and other fuels when exhausted are never available again. Timber however is inexhaustible as for every tree that is felled and one replanted then the cycle will continue. Obviously alternative forms of energy are desperately needed and many wind turbine farms have recently been installed in the surrounding districts. With the latest design of the curved windmill blades AC and I consider them to be far more aesthetically pleasing and much safer than to have a nuclear power station on our back door!

It would be wrong to give the impression that all has gone according to plan and that everything has come up smelling of roses. There were always the downsides and on many occasions, certainly in the early years, the substantial regular monthly salary cheques were desperately missed.

AC has been disappointed at the lack of cultural activities, book fixes, concerts etc. Lagos now has a new centre offering a variety of programmes. Unfortunately these rarely commenced before nine thirty in the evening and finishing well past our normal bedtime hour. She did however thoroughly enjoy being a member of the choir at the Anglican Church services held in Praia da Luz where the local Catholic community allowed the ex-pats to attend and worship in their church. The Friday choir practices were a boon to our vegetable sales as she managed to fit in several deliveries before the sessions started. For a period of four years she held the post of Congregational Warden but has moved on and now attends the services at another church.

As a child and a choirboy I cynically thought that Vicars, Priests and Chaplains only worked on the day that God said that we should rest, how mistaken I was in that assumption.

My greatest singular disappointment was that playing regular rounds of golf never materialised. It was far too expensive relative to our annual income. Saturday's games were out of the question as we were marketing vegetables and those in the middle of the week were also impossible again due to the market gardening operation and the influx of the many golfing holidaymakers who tended to fill up the courses. The mid-summer high temperatures were also far from conducive to plod around pulling a heavy trolley. All in all it was very frustrating. Although I gave up smoking all those years ago I suffer with extreme pain in the calf muscles of my left leg when I am walking and frequently have to stop and rest. This is due to intermittent claudication, the thickening and furring up of the inner coat of the Common iliac artery due to a long period of heavy smoking. Last year I reluctantly admitted to myself that I would never be able to walk around eighteen holes again and took my old golf trolley to the "doggy shop", an organisation which accepts all forms of unwanted articles and then sells them off at ridiculously low prices. The proceeds are then used to assist in the treatment, care and fostering of unwanted animals. It had been stored in the garden shed since the day we had completed the construction and I can count on the fingers of one hand how often it had been temporarily removed for a game.

During our early days it was difficult for me to get my head around the principle of paying quite a substantial annual membership fee and then having to fork out a green fee every time you wanted to play a round.

In a somewhat pathetic attempt to minimise my frustration I have often smacked a couple of buckets of balls on the golf practice ranges. I have also built a tube into

277

the ground next to the last of the apricot trees. A golf ball attached to a long length of strong cord was fitted to a stout pole. This pole was then inserted into the tube and the ball could then be teed up and struck as often as I wished. The beauty of this simple piece of equipment meant that I did not have to walk very far to retrieve it and I could achieve some form of practice although I found the exercise terribly boring.

Frequently to relieve some aggro I have teed a golf ball up on the lawn and given it one hell of a belt. A really good smack would see it still rising as it cleared our land, flying over the track which separated us from Alfonso2, to land amongst the vegetable plot in his orange orchard. I don't know what he must have thought finding a white dimpled foreign body in the midst of the plants and to this day he has never returned one.

Some of our neighbours, and others, have moved on. Whispering death and his wife, Bulldozer Joe's mother, Picasso, our parsnip salesman Stephen, who we were led to believe had a serious alcohol problem, the Alface man and his wife have all gone to see St Peter, as has, sad to say, the last of the "Manchester mob". She had become a very great and true friend over all of the years and often visited with her family and friends. A very kind and generous person she has left us with all sorts of things to remember her by. A lemon tree and her handmade patchwork quilts for our two double and two single beds together with numerous hand embroidered cushions and lots more. Another very sad loss has been that of Simon, the male half of "The dreadeds".

Happy Harry and Nora Batty have not been seen for many months but the Meals on Wheels service visits daily. Alfonso 1, whose land is now up for sale as his health has sadly declined rapidly has been found accommodation in the village and is no longer around. Alfonso 2, now eighty-seven years young, still sprightly walks from his home in the village to his land twice daily. Despite their early misgivings they have seen us, over the years, successfully doing things "our way" and have tended to let us get on with it. Alfonso 3 has sold his land, is now retired and doing very well for himself.

We often see the builder in the village but the question of the retention monies is never raised. Bobbly hat has moved away and is frequently encountered, when we call into the Council offices to collect our post. To see him now it is difficult to visualise the scenario that Margaret described when she called in one frosty November morning to collect pre-ordered parsnips for some friends. She arrived at the bottom of the drive somewhat flushed and agitated so was invited in for a coffee. It transpired that she had seen him standing under the two cork oak trees and a closer look revealed that the fully unbuttoned trouser flies had exposed his glory, which he vigorously wiggled in a strong stroking motion. She said, "I saw him, I saw him," but was unable to finish the sentence but fully knew what he was playing at and immediately calmed down when I said that, "he was only Hand Cranking". It was an expression that she had never heard of before and found it quite amusing and very appropriate.

The prowler's visits have not disturbed us for many years. His appearances can no longer be described as regular although in the winter months when we batten down the hatches early, there is no way we can tell if he is around or not. A neighbour reliably informed us that on his last escapade at their villa his youthful agility had greatly diminished. What a relief say one and all, especially those that suffered his attentions the most, like "The dreadeds" holiday makers in their villa.

He really was a complete pain in the butt, a bloody nuisance and a voyeur, but thankfully not a thief or a burglar.

Two local farmers hanged themselves, one being the "Vaca" man and the other the kind gentleman farmer who towed the old fart box along the track when it broke down. The deaf and dumb man still smiles when our paths cross but any form of communication remains impossible. Two movements of the head, one a yeah the other a nay, a thumb up or down and two fingers pointed rudely up are the only signs that I know. The German who bought the caravan told us when he last collected some asparagus, that it was still being used by his mother-in-law when she comes over on her regular holidays. Ben Hur now has a small Vespa and clutches the steering handles so tightly that his knuckles are white as he slowly wobbles past. He is too frightened to let go and wave but just flashes a grim smile at us with now an almost toothless grin.

The young man on the cruise liners had a long time ago built and now runs the bar and games room next to his mother's villa where he lives. Many hours have been spent trying to re-hone the darts and pool skills we had developed in the pubs back in England with quite encouraging results. Maureen when we occasionally meet up always has a bright smile and time for a chat and Dolores still has her busy stall in the market. There are times nowadays when we buy produce from her, another turn around! Margaret and Bob have moved villas for the second time and now live further away than before.

The permanent residents along the track including ourselves are three Swiss couples, a German and Norwegian pair, a Welshman, a young Portuguese girl with her German husband and three children and four Portuguese families. It's quite an odd mixture of nationalities and is almost as cosmopolitan as Down Town Vancouver.

Cheryl, the female half of "The dreadeds" no longer visits frequently as her holiday villa has been sold to an English couple who intended to and have now become residents here.

Susie "Q" from the Exeter days visits regularly and is far less demanding than in the early years and has remained one of our dearest friends. I don't think that she ever finished her book. Don, Sandra Mark and Alan continue to make their annual pilgrimage and it's difficult to believe that the boys are now teenagers with Mark off to "Uni" next year.

Our mothers still enjoy their holidays here. Well we assume so as they visit twice and occasionally three times a year. Once it was a must on their stay, to visit and to have lunch at the "Chippery". Alas no longer, the original shack was flattened long ago and rebuilt over a period of nearly three years. As such all of the original old world charm and quaintness has been lost. Worse still the chips they now serve are the mass-produced ones that are stored in the deep freeze. Their combined age is one hundred and seventy-five years and they must surely qualify as one of the world's most itinerant and intrepid female couple.

Karen and Norman have never returned although we still communicate sporadically. They eventually sold their time share, which we thought was an extremely risky investment, but the house conversion in France was very successful and has been fully habitable over the past three years. They regularly commute and spend a lot of their time in residence there.

Jack and Jill spend more time with their grandchildren so their holiday periods in Bensafrim have become much less. Jean and Derek eventually got married but have never returned. We received an invitation to the wedding but found that it was impossible to attend. However we were fortunate to be present at the marriage of Peter the surgeon's eldest daughter. She was the one who Quinta and parsnip sat for us on Shelle's big day. We flew into Bristol and in a hire car hurtled down to Jack and Jill's cottage in Devon to spend a few days with them before we met up with Susie "Q" in Totnes and then on to Dorset for the wedding.

Other friends and associates call in or stay with us and we are always glad to see them all. When we return to the U.K. for holidays – we try to slot in at least one visit a year – it is very difficult to accommodate reciprocal visits to all of them. It would mean that so much of our precious time would have to be spent travelling by car or public transport, the many hundreds of miles that separate them.

Five years ago the, by then, knackered old Fiesta had just passed its obligatory inspection when AC somehow accidentally managed to give it a drastic modification to the front end and wrote it off. It occurred on the spur road from the motorway to the west of Lagos as she was driving to a choir practice in the church in Praia da Luz. The reasons for the crash remain a mystery but she luckily suffered no whiplash damage and did not even have a scratch. Three sections of the kerb side crash barrier were severely buckled and as a result had to be replaced. She was very very lucky.

Jack and Jill had driven down from England in her Skoda so we were able to borrow their old Peugeot as we looked around for a replacement motor. The Insurance Company coughed up in full for the total resale value of the car at the time of the crash, the charges for towing away the wreckage and the ambulance fees to take her to Lagos hospital for a thorough check up.

I wanted a car with a bit more umph as the old Ford was as flat as a fart going up hill with four people on board and a boot full of luggage. It needed to have an engine of at least 1.4 cc's and AC's mandate was that it had to have air conditioning. After many weeks of inspecting the, by now numerous open air car stands – there was not a single one around when we had had to replace the Cortina – we had had no success at all and were beginning to give up hope. As a last resort I spoke with the manager of the car hire company, who did not have any when I had approached them before and our luck changed. They had two for sale that fitted exactly in with our requirements

The Fiesta had been a hire car so we had no problems in buying another one. We choose a two-year-old Burgundy coloured Renault Megane, registration number 81.85.TU with only thirty-eight thousand kilometres on the clock. It only needed a short test drive to satisfy me and a shorter one by AC to agree to purchase it. After it had been given a thorough service I proudly drove it away. The documents to transfer the ownership into AC's name were soon completed and a receipt obtained.

A new car tax system came into force here recently and when I went to tax the Megane I was asked if AC also wanted to tax the Cortina as it was on their files still in her name and remained her responsibility. I quickly explained that it had been sent to a scrap yard some thirteen years before and had never been taxed by her since that time. We had handed over the change of ownership documents then and their records should be amended accordingly. The Fiesta was no longer in her name on the computer records as at the scene of the accident the police had confiscated the car documents so her details had then been deleted.

Unfortunately we never got around to our dirty weekend at Caldas de Monchique. I had stopped making New Years resolutions as I always broke them.

Maybe I will make one next year to have the weekend date as there will be every incentive to keep it. We rarely visit the beach of Amado any more. If we are here over Christmas and not back in the UK, we make a point of taking turkey sandwiches there for a picnic on Boxing Day. At least then the Surfing centre, which from the first time we were there I sensed was bound to develop eventually, is closed!

If identifying the spring flower was a bonus then the icing on the cake, a real cream topping, is to be able to appreciate the benefits of having my youngest daughter, Michelle and her daughter, Naomi living almost next to us in the village. They arrived here some six years ago. Michelle took a six-month sabbatical away from her high pressure job in Birmingham. It was always odds on that they would remain here if suitable employment could be found. Luckily for me it was, and they have.

Naomi attends school in Lagos and has integrated extremely well and quickly in all disciplines. Her command of the Portuguese language far exceeded mine in her first two years so it is impossible to provide any assistance with the copious amounts of homework. Now I have the delights and benefits of grandparenthood and lots of time is spent with her. AC is giving her piano lessons, both in practice and theory and she is progressing very well. Her strong aptitude in mathematics is of considerable benefit. Both of us assist her with the English language using the booklets offering practice in literacy skills sent by her grandmother. Her music and some of her schoolbooks are kept in the still temporary homemade bookcases. We have sussed out two local cabinetmakers but I have not yet prepared a sketch of AC's requirements to obtain a quotation.

There have been many golden and magical moments for us all to share at home, on various beaches and at our numerous picnics. One memorable one was when we launched a small four metre long offshore dingy in the swimming pool. Jack, as in Jack and Jill had been given a boat building kit for his birthday and had spent many hours assembling the Jimmy Skiff in the open area at the rear of the ruin. Come the day and it was carried down to the pool, the mast fitted and the sail rigged and then the dingy was lowered carefully into the water. Jack and Naomi jumped in and with some difficulty managed to complete two quick lengths before it was hoisted out, de-rigged and returned to the ruin.

I finally decided to remove the wisteria as its roots had lifted large areas of paving and were threatening to invade the sewage system. It was massive and had spread all over the front car port and some branches had grown up to the two cork oaks and even further and had almost reached the track, Although it flowered profusely and gave a magnificent display in the spring, AC was quietly relieved as her tri-annual period of drudgery would cease. She had had to continually clear up the thousands of fallen blossoms in March and again in June, although thankfully not so many the second time. Then there was the four or five weeks daily sweeping up of the leaves in the autumn. What was left of the old greenhouse collapsed during a fierce storm and all of the timbers were cut into kindling for the stove.

The old car scrapyard has been closed and only a tumbled down shed remains in what is now an empty field. It is the only vacant plot of land, south of the EN 125 road between Espiche and Praia da Luz and is ripe for development. If and when that does occur then the once pretty little village of Praia da Luz will have expanded and expanded until it is only a stone's throw across that road to the village of Espiche.

Our borehole has finally been registered and we now have a license to extract water and have only recently got around to getting it analysed, so many years after the first abortive effort. Although we have always drank the water it is nice to be reassured that it is potable.

We are managing to drag ourselves into the twenty-first century and have scrapped the old video and now possess a DVD recorder. To top that a new LCD slimline HD television set graces the lounge. The first draft of this story was typed up onto Compact floppy Discs, a definition I always thought quite contradictory, using an Amstrad Word processor and Printer with installed software that was twenty-two years old. Thanks to friends we now own a second hand modern day laptop and were also given a computer and monitor to which we have added a wireless keyboard and mouse and a combined photocopier, scanner and printer. In a very short space of time we have, at long last joined and caught up with most modern day families.

There are moments in our privileged sessions on the terrace, that during calmer days when the wind is in the right direction and we listen carefully, it is possible to hear a somewhat vaguely familiar and almost forgotten sound. It's the Black and Decker D.I.Y. tape music once again, but different, slightly different than in the past. The tone is much clearer with a more precisely defined sound. It took us quite a while to realise why the sound had changed. The reason was obvious after we had sussed out the answer. The music has been recorded onto a Compact Disc.

We feel that the time has now come for us to make the biggest decision since we emigrated here. Both of us have never remained for so long in one dwelling and as a result have developed itchy feet. There are lots of advantages and benefits in moving on. There is far too much land to look after properly and we rattle around in the Quinta like two small peas in a large pod. I am tired of having to use the brush cutter up to five times over a normal winter to keep a couple of hundred square metres of grassland under some form of control. It has become a struggle to even mow the lawn and AC has taken over responsibility for its upkeep on top of the boring housework routines to look after the place which seem to take up more and more of her time. Even buying vegetables seems a more attractive proposition than growing our own. Although we still do and secretly enjoy it.

What attracted us to the piece of land in the first place and what we have created here places us in a quandary as we continually blow hot and then extremely cold at the idea of selling up. We would miss all of the benefits of its tranquillity and privacy but not miss, at all, the hard work.

We intend to downsize and our ideal re-location would still be in this area living in a single story villa not actually in the village, but still close by. A swimming pool is no longer necessary as Lagos has opened a covered Municipal one but I would have to comply with the basic rules and buy a lycra bathing costume and a swimming cap. Unfortunately there very few local choices available and prices for what little there is seem to be at the very top end of the market. If no villas come onto the market we have the possibility of buying a plot of land and then renting somewhere whilst our new villa is being built.

Properties are not moving very quickly and some of the asking prices do seem to us to be totally unrealistic, always on the high side. Our plot would not suit buyers that wish to live in an ex-pat English-speaking ghetto. It would only appeal to people with like minds to our own and they could be few and far apart so it is a bit of a moving feast.

Regarding the immediate future, we have not yet fully made up our minds whether to stay put or sell. The thought of us living in an apartment in Lagos, even with a garden terrace, we treat as a very sick joke. New spears have started to appear again and I have cut a sufficient amount for our first asparagus supper of the year. I think it likely that any decisions will now be put on hold, indefinitely, as "The Algarve Asparagus Man plus One" gird their loins to prepare for yet another season. This situation could, or could not, be an annual dilemma. Vamos ver mais uma vez. Let us see once again!!!!